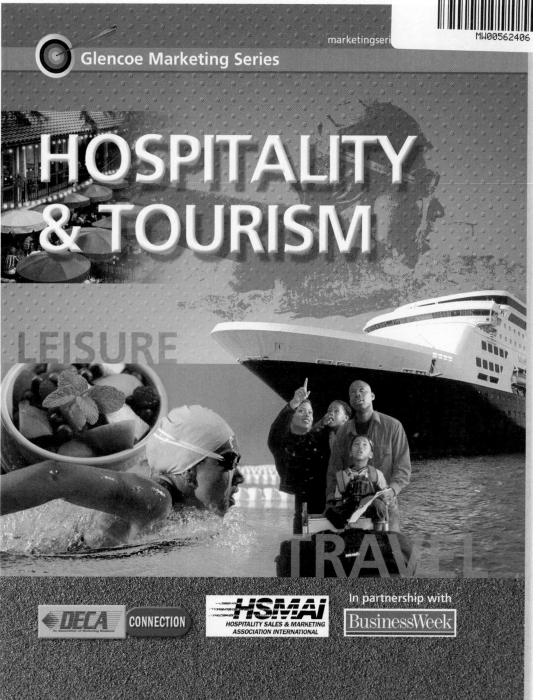

Glencoe Marketing Series

marketingseri

HOSPITALITY & TOURISM

LEISURE

TRAVEL

DECA CONNECTION

HSMAI
HOSPITALITY SALES & MARKETING
ASSOCIATION INTERNATIONAL

In partnership with
BusinessWeek

Karen E. Silva, Ed.D.
Debra M. Howard, M.Ed.

McGraw Hill **Glencoe**

New York, New York   Columbus, Ohio   Chicago, Illinois   Peoria, Illinois   Woodland Hills, California

About the Authors

KAREN E. SILVA As the director of advising and department chair for The Hospitality College at Johnson & Wales University in Providence, Rhode Island, Karen E. Silva has decades of experience as an educator and administrator. She is also an experienced hospitality and tourism professional, serving as curriculum director for the Institute of Certified Travel Agents. In addition, she gained broad-based experience in travel-service operations, meeting planning, and tour pricing for Collette Tours. She has also authored a number of textbook publications in the field of travel and tourism. In 2004, she was recognized by Who's Who Among Executive and Professional Women. She holds a doctorate of education from Boston University and is a certified hospitality educator.

DEBRA M. HOWARD Debra M. Howard is the former director of education of The Travel Institute, a nonprofit educational institute in Wellesley, Massachusetts. With 30 years of experience in teaching, training, and instructional design, Debra's accomplishments include creating interactive multimedia training packages, executive leadership seminars, and industry certification programs. She is the author of several sales, service, and product-knowledge textbooks used in classroom settings and as training tools in the corporate arena. Recognized in Marquis's *Who's Who of American Women in Business,* she holds a master's degree in education. Debra and her husband reside on Cape Cod, Massachusetts, where they own a bed-and-breakfast inn overlooking Cape Cod Bay.

90548000002463

Glencoe

The *McGraw·Hill* Companies

Printed in the United States of America.

Send all inquiries to:
Glencoe/McGraw-Hill
21600 Oxnard Street, Suite 500
Woodland Hills, CA 91367

ISBN 0-07-868296-7 (Student Edition)
ISBN 0-07-868813-2 (Teacher Annotated Edition)

2 3 4 5 6 7 8 9   079   10 09 08 07 06 05

Advisors

To best research and address the needs of today's workplace, Glencoe/McGraw-Hill assembled an advisory board of educators. The board lent its expertise and experience to establish the foundation for this innovative, real-world, marketing education program. Glencoe/McGraw-Hill would like to acknowledge the following individuals for their support and commitment to this project:

THOMAS CRABB
Woodrow Wilson High School
Dallas, Texas

SARAH MARSH
Independence High School
Charlotte, North Carolina

BARBARA DIVENUTI
Manchester School of Technology
Manchester, New Hampshire

HOWARD ZAGER
Culver City High School
Culver City, California

Contributing Writer

PRISCILLA R. McCALLA
Professional and Program Development Director
DECA
Reston, Virginia

Consulting Editor

ATKINS D. "TREY" MICHAEL, III
Marketing Education Consultant
North Carolina Department of Public Instruction
Raleigh, North Carolina

Hospitality Researcher

SANDRA J. LINDBLOM
Hospitality Research Coordinator
Johnson & Wales University
Cranston, Rhode Island

Exploring the World of Hospitality & Tourism

As part of the Glencoe Marketing Series, this first edition of *Hospitality & Tourism* focuses on the real-world business perspective by using examples to illustrate features, concepts, and activities. Information on featured professionals, companies, organizations, their products, and services is included for educational purposes only and does not represent or imply endorsement of the Glencoe marketing programs. The following are a few of the companies that appear in features and throughout the text:

Chapter 1 Defining Hospitality & Tourism

Chapter 2 Economics and the Impact of Tourism

Chapter 3 The Restaurant Business

Chapter 4 The Hotel Business

Chapter 5 The Tourism Business

Chapter 6 Destination Marketing

Chapter 7 Sports, Events, and Entertainment

Chapter 8 The Marketing Environment

Chapter 9 Market Information and Research

Chapter 10 Designing Products

Chapter 11 Pricing Products

Chapter 12 Distribution

Chapter 13 Promoting Hospitality & Tourism

Chapter 14 Customer and Employee Relations

Chapter 15 Finding a Job

Chapter 16 Careers in Hospitality & Tourism

Walt Disney World Resort

Abercrombie & Kent

Red Lobster

Madonna Inn

BELLAGIO

Maritz RESEARCH

COLLETTE VACATIONS

Expedia.com

jetBlue AIRWAYS

Lonely Planet

Table of Contents

To the Student x

UNIT 1 THE HOSPITALITY & TOURISM BUSINESS. 2

Chapter 1 Defining Hospitality & Tourism 4

SECTION **1.1** The World of Hospitality & Tourism 6

SECTION **1.2** Hospitality & Tourism: Past and Present 10

Case Study— Serving Food and Fun
    Part 1 5
    Part 2 15
Profiles in Hospitality—*A Seaworthy Career* 16
Chapter Review and Activities 22

Chapter 2 Economics and the Impact of Tourism 24

SECTION **2.1** The Impact of Hospitality & Tourism 26

SECTION **2.2** Why Do People Travel? 34

Case Study—See the Whales
    Part 1 25
    Part 2 37
Profiles in Hospitality—*Complete Outfitting* 36
Chapter Review and Activities 42

UNIT 1 BusinessWeek News Far From the Cancún Crowd 44

UNIT LAB —The Inn Place Historic Hotel—
                                Plan and Renew a Hotel 45

UNIT 2 HOSPITALITY & TOURISM MARKETS 46

Chapter 3 The Restaurant Business 48

SECTION **3.1** Types of Restaurants 50

SECTION **3.2** Restaurant Operations 59

Case Study—Another Plate of Mind
    Part 1 49
    Part 2 63
Profiles in Hospitality—*Burger Know-How* 64
Chapter Review and Activities 70

Table of Contents

Chapter 4 The Hotel Business 72

SECTION **4.1** Types of Lodging Businesses. 74

SECTION **4.2** Hotel Operations 82

Case Study—Desert Chic
  Part 1. 73
  Part 2. 87
Profiles in Hospitality—*Training for Hospitality* 86
Chapter Review and Activities 92

Chapter 5 The Tourism Business. 94

SECTION **5.1** Travel and Tourism. 96

SECTION **5.2** Transportation Providers. 102

Case Study—Gear on the Go
  Part 1. 95
  Part 2. 109
Profiles in Hospitality—*Northern Exposures*. 100
Chapter Review and Activities 114

Chapter 6 Destination Marketing. 116

SECTION **6.1** Destination Markets. 118

SECTION **6.2** Basics of Destination Marketing 127

Case Study—Star Power
  Part 1. 117
  Part 2. 121
Profiles in Hospitality—*A Unique Peek* 124
Chapter Review and Activities 134

Chapter 7 Sports, Events, and Entertainment. 136

SECTION **7.1** Sports and Recreation. 138

SECTION **7.2** Events and Entertainment. 147

Case Study—He Shoots, He Scores!
  Part 1. 137
  Part 2. 149
Profiles in Hospitality—*Formula for a Festival*. 148
Chapter Review and Activities 158

Table of Contents

UNIT 2 BusinessWeek News   Fine Dining? Just Across the Lobby 160

UNIT LAB —The Inn Place   A Taste of Destinations—
Design a Food Tour 162

UNIT 3   MARKETING HOSPITALITY & TOURISM. 162

Chapter 8   The Marketing Environment 164

SECTION 8.1 The Role of Marketing Basics 166

SECTION 8.2 Planning Marketing 171

Case Study—Eco-Friendly Car Club
Part 1 165
Part 2 177
Profiles in Hospitality—*Festival Planning* 176
Chapter Review and Activities 162

Chapter 9   Market Information and Research 164

SECTION 9.1 Target Markets. 166

SECTION 9.2 Market Research 192

Case Study—Cowboy Up
Part 1 165
Part 2 197
Profiles in Hospitality—*Higher Ratings* 194
Chapter Review and Activities 202

Chapter 10   Designing Products. 204

SECTION 10.1 Hospitality & Tourism Products. 206

SECTION 10.2 Product Planning 211

Case Study—The Next Generation
Part 1 205
Part 2 215
Profiles in Hospitality—*Close-Up on Food* 209
Chapter Review and Activities 220

Table of Contents

Chapter 11 Pricing Products 222

SECTION **11.1** Pricing Strategies. 224

SECTION **11.2** Factors Affecting Price 230

Case Study—True Blue
Part 1 223
Part 2 231
Profiles in Hospitality—*Vineyard Management* 233
Chapter Review and Activities 238

Chapter 12 Distribution 240

SECTION **12.1** Selling Hospitality & Tourism 242

SECTION **12.2** Channels of Distribution 248

Case Study—Superfuture Guide
Part 1 241
Part 2 247
Profiles in Hospitality—*Ranch-Style Getaway* 249
Chapter Review and Activities 256

Chapter 13 Promoting Hospitality & Tourism 258

SECTION **13.1** Promotion and Advertising 260

SECTION **13.2** Public Relations and Sales Promotion 267

Case Study—Marketing New Mexico
Part 1 259
Part 2 271
Profiles in Hospitality—*Promoting Through Product* 270
Chapter Review and Activities 276

UNIT 3 BusinessWeek News Home Sweet Home 278

UNIT LAB —The Inn Place Positive Press—
Create a Resort's Promotional Plan 279

Table of Contents

UNIT 4 EXPLORING CAREERS IN HOSPITALITY & TOURISM . . 280

Chapter 14 Customer and Employee Relations 282

SECTION **14.1** Customer Relations 284

SECTION **14.2** Employee Relations. 290

Case Study—Sea Cruise
Part 1 283
Part 2 295
Profiles in Hospitality—*In the Kitchen* 292
Chapter Review and Activities 300

Chapter 15 Finding a Job. 302

SECTION **15.1** Employment Skills 304

SECTION **15.2** Employment Process 311

Case Study—Foods for "Dudes"
Part 1 303
Part 2 313
Profiles in Hospitality—*Caribbean Flavors* 309
Chapter Review and Activities 320

Chapter 16 Careers in Hospitality & Tourism 322

SECTION **16.1** Career Choices 324

SECTION **16.2** Educational Resources 334

Case Study—Island Riding
Part 1 323
Part 2 327
Profiles in Hospitality—*Executive Search* 332
Chapter Review and Activities 344

UNIT 4 BusinessWeek **News** Start Your Rockets. 346

UNIT LAB—The Inn Place Publishing Tourism—
Advertise Jobs 347

Glossary 348
Index 356

Welcome to
Hospitality & Tourism

Welcome to *Hospitality & Tourism*, part of the Glencoe Marketing Series. Get ready to learn about two of the most diverse and global businesses. Hospitality and tourism are topics that you can relate to and make your own. Everyone goes to restaurants, travels, and stays in lodging facilities. These businesses continue to grow, generating profits and employing a vast number of people interested in exciting careers.

Understanding the Unit

The units introduce you to the scope of the hospitality and tourism businesses, in which marketing plays a vital role. Each unit opens with a preview and concludes with application activities featuring a reading activity from *BusinessWeek* magazine and a hospitality or tourism simulation. The 16 chapters in *Hospitality & Tourism* are divided into four units:

UNIT 1: The Hospitality & Tourism Business

UNIT 2: Hospitality & Tourism Markets

UNIT 3: Marketing Hospitality & Tourism

UNIT 4: Exploring Careers in Hospitality & Tourism

Previewing the Unit

Each unit opener focuses on the content of the upcoming unit.

Unit Opener Photo

The unit opener photo illustrates a concept that is relevant to the upcoming unit. Ask yourself, "How does the photo relate to the content of the unit?"

Unit Overview

The *Unit Overview* provides a brief road map of the unit chapters.

In This Unit...

The titles of the unit chapters are listed on the left-hand side of the unit opener spread. Think about what you can learn in each chapter. A quotation helps you focus on what is to come.

Unit Lab Preview

The *Unit Lab Preview* prepares you for *The Inn Place,* the unit's culminating real-world simulation and hands-on activity.

The Marketing Wheel

This visual representation of the National Marketing Education Standards highlights the two main parts of marketing—the foundations and the functions. The functions of marketing relate to how marketing is applied to hospitality and tourism: Distribution, Financing, Marketing-Information Management, Pricing, Product/Service Management, Promotion, and Selling. The functions or foundations addressed in each unit are listed on this page.

Closing the Unit

UNIT 1 ACTIVITIES

BusinessWeek News

FAR FROM THE CANCÚN CROWD

Remote resorts offer the treasures of the Yucatan without the tourist crush. Drive south along Mexico's Caribbean coast—also known as the Riviera Maya—and you will find a 75-mile stretch of quiet white beaches, turquoise sea, lush jungle, world-class snorkeling and scuba diving, and a region packed with wildlife and Mayan culture.

Secluded Spas

Drive only ten miles south from the airport to escape the hubbub. There you'll find remote resorts tucked a mile or so off the main highway, more often than not down bumpy, potholed roads. One of the best bargains is Ceiba del Mar Spa Resort. There are many other lodging options, starting at $15 a night for a cabana with a hammock and a mosquito net. True spa junkies should check out the 22,000-square-foot spa at Paraiso de la Bonita & Thalasso.

Ancient Mayan Ruins and More

All of these hotels are the perfect base to explore the Yucatán's treasures, including the Mayan ruins. The Maya, who occupied a swath of Central America from Honduras to Mexico from as early as 1500 B.C., were masters of architecture as well as mathematics and astronomy. Their legacy extends inland to the mysterious pyramids of Chichén Itza and Cobá in a postcard-perfect setting on a bluff overlooking the Caribbean.

Tulúm, which means "wall" in Maya, is a walled city, one of the few the Mayans built. They called it *Zama* or "City of Dawn." Tulúm is majestic. It is no wonder hundreds of iguanas sun themselves on the rocks of Tulúm's gray castle.

Within a ten-mile radius inland from Tulúm, you'll find *cenotes*. The Mayans believed these freshwater springs surrounded by limestone walls were windows into the underworld. Take a dip in one, and you might see a manatee. The Yucatán also boasts the world's second-largest barrier reef, which is why it is a popular spot with snorkelers and divers. Nature lovers should also

check out the Sian Ka'an Biosphere Reserve, named a World Heritage Site by the U.N. in 1997. The 300,000-acre park, directly south of Tulúm, is home to more than 360 species of animals, including jaguars and crocodiles. Tulúm, like other Yucatán beach towns, is getting discovered. But for now, nature prevails. As we left for the airport, a spider monkey jumped in front of our van and scurried off into the jungle.

By Lauren Young
Edited by Adam Aston

Excerpted by permission. February 23, 2004. Copyright 2000-2004, by The McGraw-Hill Companies, Inc. All rights reserved.

◼ CREATIVE JOURNAL

In your journal, write your responses.

CRITICAL THINKING
1. What attractions draw travelers to the Yucatán? Why?

APPLICATION
2. If you were organizing a package tour to the Riviera Ma[ya], what accommodations and features mentioned in the [article] would you include? To what type of traveler would yo[u market] this package? Why?

Go to businessweek.com for current *BusinessWeek Onl[ine]*

BusinessWeek NEWS

A reading and writing exercise entitled *BusinessWeek News* concludes each unit. A relevant excerpt from a real *BusinessWeek* article caps the unit content.

◼ UNIT LAB

UNIT 1 ACTIVITIES

The Inn Place

You've just entered the real world of hospitality and travel and tourism. The Inn Place owns and operates a number of hospitality and tourism businesses, offering the finest accommodations and most desirable destinations in the world. Acting as the owner, manager, or employee of this diverse company, you will have the opportunity to work on different projects to promote the business.

Historic Hotel—Plan and Renew a Hotel

SITUATION You have recently purchased a hotel called the Bayside Hotel. The hotel is approximately 60 years old and needs refurbishing and redecorating. The building itself has been well maintained. The hotel is located on the shore of a salt-water bay within a three-hour drive of a metropolitan area. The Bayside Hotel has 30 guestrooms, a restaurant, and lounge. The restaurant is very popular with hotel guests and with the local population. The food selections are basic, with fresh seafood dishes as the main attractions.

You have determined that the hotel will be refurbished to keep its rustic, old-fashioned charm. You need to add services to attract upscale customers. Some of your ideas include adding a boat dock, a swimming pool, tennis courts, an exercise room, and a spa. You need funds to add all of these services.

ASSIGNMENT Complete these tasks:
• Determine the services to your target market and receive the best return for your investment.
• Estimate the cost of each service.
• Prepare a report of your findings.

TOOLS AND RESOURCES To complete the assignment, you will need to:
• Conduct research at the library, on the Internet, or by talking to local hotel owners/managers.
• Ask a banker about financing your services.
• Have word-processing, spreadsheet, and presentation software.

RESEARCH Do your research:
• Research the appeal of each service for your target market.
• Determine the costs of installing a nd maintaining each of the service features.
• Determine which services you will offer.

REPORT Prepare a written report using the following tools:
• *Word-processing program:* Prepare a written report listing the features and benefits of each service under consideration.
• *Spreadsheet program:* Prepare a chart comparing the costs of the services you are considering.
• *Presentation program:* Prepare a ten-slide visual presentation with key points, mockups of each proposed service feature, and a key descriptive text.

PRESENTATION AND EVALUATION You will present your report to the bank that may finance your plan. You will be evaluated on the basis of:
• Your knowledge of each service feature under consideration and which ones would best suit your hotel's needs.
• Continuity of presentation
• Voice quality
• Eye contact

◼ PORTFOLIO
Add this report to your career portfolio.

◼ UNIT LAB

The Inn Place

At the end of each unit, the unit lab simulation *The Inn Place* will take you on an exciting journey through the world of hospitality and tourism.

Understanding the Chapter

Each unit of *Hospitality & Tourism* includes two to four chapters. Each chapter focuses on one specific area of hospitality and tourism, such as the restaurant business or destination marketing.

Previewing the Chapter

The chapter opener resources are designed to capture your interest and set a purpose for reading.

Chapter Opener Photo

The chapter opener photo focuses on the chapter topic. You might ask yourself, "How does this photo relate to the chapter title?"

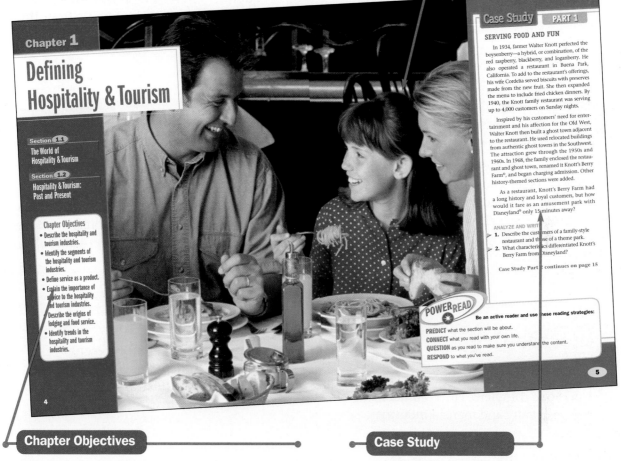

Chapter 1

Defining Hospitality & Tourism

Section 1.1
The World of Hospitality & Tourism

Section 1.2
Hospitality & Tourism: Past and Present

Chapter Objectives
- Describe the hospitality and tourism industries.
- Identify the segments of the hospitality and tourism industries.
- Define service as a product.
- Explain the importance of service to the hospitality and tourism industries.
- Describe the origins of lodging and food service.
- Identify trends in the hospitality and tourism industries.

Case Study   PART 1

SERVING FOOD AND FUN

In 1934, farmer Walter Knott perfected the boysenberry—a hybrid, or combination, of the red raspberry, blackberry, and loganberry. He also operated a restaurant in Buena Park, California. To add to the restaurant's offerings, his wife Cordelia served biscuits with preserves made from the new fruit. She then expanded the menu to include fried chicken dinners. By 1940, the Knott family restaurant was serving up to 4,000 customers on Sunday nights.

Inspired by his customers' need for entertainment and his affection for the Old West, Walter Knott then built a ghost town adjacent to the restaurant. He used relocated buildings from authentic ghost towns in the Southwest. The attraction grew through the 1950s and 1960s. In 1968, the family enclosed the restaurant and ghost town, renamed it Knott's Berry Farm©, and began charging admission. Other history-themed sections were added.

As a restaurant, Knott's Berry Farm had a long history and loyal customers, but how would it fare as an amusement park with Disneyland® only 15 minutes away?

ANALYZE AND WRITE
1. Describe the customers of a family-style restaurant and those of a theme park.
2. What characteristics differentiated Knott's Berry Farm from Disneyland?

Case Study Part 2 continues on page 18

POWER READ

Be an active reader and use these reading strategies:

PREDICT what the section will be about.
CONNECT what you read with your own life.
QUESTION as you read to make sure you understand the content.
RESPOND to what you've read.

Chapter Objectives

The objectives help you identify exactly what you should know upon completion of the chapter.

Using the Sections

Each chapter of *Hospitality & Tourism* is divided into two sections. By using the activities and resources in each section, you can maximize learning.

AS YOU READ ...

You Will Learn lists the knowledge you can expect to learn.

Why It's Important explains how the chapter concepts relate to hospitality and tourism.

Key Terms list major terms presented in each section.

Case Study

Each chapter opens with the Case Study, Part 1, which presents a real-world industry situation. Critical-thinking questions help focus content. Part 2 continues within the chapter.

Photographs and Figures

Photographs, illustrations, charts, and graphs reinforce content. Captions with questions guide you.

Quick Check

The section-ending *Quick Check* helps you to review and respond to what you have read.

Understanding the Features

Special features in each chapter are designed to interest and promote your understanding of the chapter content. Features incorporate activities and critical-thinking questions to help you integrate what you have learned.

World Market presents interesting highlights from the global world of hospitality and tourism.

Hot Property

Hot Property profiles successful or creative hospitality and tourism businesses, both large and small. To close the feature, two critical-thinking questions focus on chapter topics.

Profiles in Hospitality

Profiles in Hospitality provides insight through personal interviews of successful or noteworthy individuals working in industry-related careers. A chapter-related, critical-thinking question follows the feature. The "Career Data" column provides education, skills, outlook, and career-path information for this career.

THE Electronic CHANNEL

The Electronic Channel links chapter content to the expanding world of e-commerce and communication in the hospitality and tourism industries.

Key Point

Key Point presents brief, memorable facts to illustrate fashion industry issues and trends.

ETHICS & ISSUES

Ethics & Issues links chapter content to current ethical issues in hospitality and tourism, as well as legal, community-service, and character-education issues and practices.

Math Check

Math Check provides a math problem related to chapter discussions.

TECH NOTES

Technology is today's number-one marketing trend. *Tech Notes* highlights the wide range of technological applications enhancing the hospitality and tourism industries today. An exercise directs you to the book's Web site at **marketingseries.glencoe.com**.

Worksheets and Portfolio Works

At the end of each chapter's text, before the review section, special write-on worksheet pages provide review and skill-building activities related to chapter content.

Chapter Worksheets

Two one-page worksheets give you the opportunity to complete an activity or exercise and apply the chapter content in a variety of interesting formats.

Portfolio Works

The *Portfolio Works* worksheet at the end of each chapter guides you through the development of an employability portfolio. The portfolio is developed throughout the course. You can assess, reflect on, and plan for your career. Record what you have learned and how you would demonstrate those necessary values, skills, personal qualities, and knowledge. These activities provide the foundation for a career development portfolio. Save these pages for a prospective employer to demonstrate your combination of knowledge and workplace skills needed to succeed in a hospitality and tourism career.

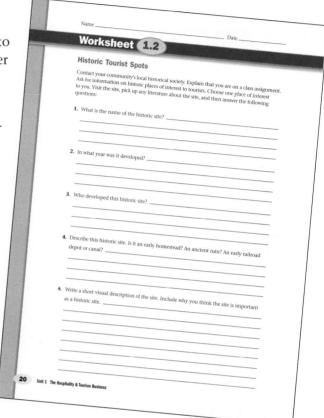

You can also include in your portfolio various documents that demonstrate your marketing competencies, employability skills, career goals, service and leadership activities. Recommendation letters, a résumé, and a job application form are also valuable additions.

Building an employability portfolio helps you relate what you learn in school to the skills you will need for success on the job. When you have completed the project, you will have an expanded résumé to use in your job search.

Understanding Assessments

At the end of each chapter, *Chapter Review and Activities* presents a chapter summary with key terms, recall and critical-thinking questions, and a variety of activities to help develop and apply your academic and workplace skills.

Chapter Summary

The *Chapter Summary* is a bulleted list of the main points developed within each section and related to the chapter objectives. The key terms are listed with page references alongside the summary points.

Cross-Curriculum Skills

These skill-building exercises are divided into two categories: work-based learning and school-based learning. *Work-Based Learning* activities are hands-on projects that help you develop foundation skills and workplace competencies. *School-Based Learning* activities ask you to apply academic skills, such as math, science, and literacy skills, to real-life scenarios related to the world of hospitality and tourism.

Chapter 1   Review and Activities

CHAPTER SUMMARY

Section 1.1 The World of Hospitality & Tourism

hospitality industry (p. 6)
bed-and-breakfasts (p. 6)
tourism industry (p. 6)
service (p. 7)
variables (p. 8)
perishability (p. 8)
intangibility (p. 8)
changeability (p. 9)

- The hospitality industry is a group of businesses composed of establishments related to lodging and food-service management. The tourism industry is a group of businesses that encompass travel/transportation vendors for air, rail, auto, cruise, and motor-coach travel and promote travel and vacations.
- The hospitality and tourism industries are composed of several segments: lodging, food service, travel, tourism, and sports and entertainment events.
- A product can be both goods and services offered to customers. A service is an intangible thing that is a task performed for customers by a business.
- In the hospitality and tourism industries, most products are services. Service is what differentiates these industries from most other industries. However, service can be affected by several variables.

Section 1.2 Hospitality & Tourism: Past and Present

diversity (p. 15)
ecotourism (p. 15)
market segments (p. 15)

- The first hospitality establishments were probably taverns in Greece and Rome. By the end of the 13th century, horse-drawn coaches brought travelers to inns known as *post houses.* Ancient travel required effort for purposes of survival rather than pleasure. The invention of the wheel around 3000 B.C. enabled easier travel.
- Trends in the hospitality and tourism industries are affected by current events as well as trends in safety, diversity, ecology, markets, convenience, and technology.

CHECKING CONCEPTS

1. **Define** the hospitality industry.
2. **Define** the tourism industry.
3. **Describe** the segments of the hospitality industry and those of the tourism industry.
4. **Explain** the meaning of service and provide examples in hospitality and tourism.
5. **Identify** three variables that affect the marketing of service in hospitality and tourism.
6. **Explain** the origin of the word *hospitality.*
7. **Identify** examples of tourism during the Renaissance.

Critical Thinking

8. **Discuss** how technology is used in hospitality and tourism.

Chapter 1   Review and Activities

CROSS-CURRICULUM SKILLS

Work-Based Learning

Basic Skills—Writing
9. Write an advertisement for a hotel that is the "Hotel of the Future." Describe the most important thing this hotel can offer guests.

Thinking Skills—Reasoning
10. Explain in a brief written report why safety is a global concern for the hospitality and tourism industries.

School-Based Learning

History
11. Choose a country that you would like to visit. Then use the library or Internet to learn about a museum where you could explore travel in that country during the 4th to 5th centuries, 1400s to 1600s, or 1800s.

Math
12. Explain in a brief written report why ecotourism might be a good investment.

DECA CONNECTION

Role Play: Management Team Member

EVENT You are to assume the role of management team member for an historic home located in the southern region of the United States. The home was the residence of a Revolutionary War hero who signed the *Declaration of Independence.* It has been a popular tourist attraction. However, recent estimates for some repairs reveal the need for additional revenue. The foundation that manages the home (judge) will review the management plan to convert unused buildings to lodging space for guests. The construction costs would be less than the costs to repair the home.

ACTIVITY You are to explain the reasons for the proposal in terms used by the hospitality and tourism industries. Explain how accepting the proposal is vital to maintaining the site.

EVALUATION You will be evaluated on how well you meet the following performance indicators:
- Describe the nature of the hospitality industry.
- Describe the nature of the travel and tourism industries.
- Explain factors affecting the development and growth of the travel and tourism industries.
- Prepare for the sales presentation.
- Make oral presentations.

INTERNET ACTIVITY

Use the Internet to access the Web site of the Mount Vernon Hotel Museum and answer the following questions:
- In what state is the Mount Vernon Hotel Museum?
- Who built the hotel and why did the builder(s) name it Mount Vernon?
- What time period does the hotel museum represent?
- Why would someone want to visit a historic hotel?

For a link to the Mount Vernon Hotel Museum Web site to do this activity, go to **marketingseries.glencoe.com**.

Checking Concepts

Seven review exercises help you check your understanding of the text by defining terms, describing processes, and explaining concepts. The eighth exercise focuses on your critical-thinking skills.

DECA Connection

In every chapter-review section, the *DECA Connection* offers specially created, DECA-approved role-play activities. These activities provide opportunities to practice for DECA's events that relate to fashion marketing—and they are based on a real DECA role-play situation.

Internet Activity

In every chapter-review section, the *Internet Activity* provides a Web-based research activity. Resources for each exercise can be found through the book's Web site at **marketingseries.glencoe.com**.

The DECA Connection

DECA is an association of marketing students that sponsors skill-building events. It is a co-curricular club with chapters in more than 6,000 high schools. The membership includes representation from all 50 states, four U.S. territories, the District of Columbia, and two Canadian provinces. All DECA activities further student development in one or more of the following areas: leadership development, social intelligence, vocational understanding, and civic consciousness. Through individual and group DECA activities with the marketing education instructional program, students develop skills to become future leaders in the areas of marketing and management.

DECA Builds Leadership Skills

The structure of a DECA chapter encourages leadership development for student members. Each chapter elects officers who, with the membership, choose an annual program of work. Committee chairpersons may organize and execute the activities in the program. Local activities encourage every member to act responsibly as a leader or member of a group. Chapter activities focus on the advantages of participating in a free enterprise system, marketing research, and an individual's civic responsibility.

National DECA provides opportunities for local chapter officers and members to receive additional training. Annual Regional Conferences are held in the fall each year. In the spring, students may attend the Leadership Development Academy at the Career Development Conference (CDC). During the summer, students can attend a State Officer Leadership Institute. The skills and leadership qualities gained are shared with all members of the chapter. The recognition received by individuals and teams within a DECA chapter serve as a showcase of your marketing program to your local school and community.

The following is a listing of the individual DECA competitive event areas:

- Apparel and Accessories Marketing Series
- Business Services Marketing Series
- Food Marketing Series
- Full-Service Restaurant Management Series
- Marketing Management Series
- Quick-Serve Restaurant Management Series
- Retail Merchandising Series
- Vehicles and Petroleum Marketing Series

The *Hospitality & Tourism* Web Site

The *Hospitality & Tourism* Web site draws on the vast resources of the Internet to extend your exploration of career topics.

The student site provides many resources, including the following:

- Chapter Objectives
- Interactive Practice Tests for each chapter with automatic scoring
- *Math Check* solution tips
- E-flashcard games
- Web links for doing feature exercises from *Tech Notes*, *The Electronic Channel*, and *Internet Activities*
- DECA Competitive Events practice
- Disability Support Links

At the *Career Clusters* Web site, you can explore career options with print and .pdf resources as well as links to job-search tips, external career planning sites, and educational resources.

Reading Strategies

How can you get the most from your reading? Effective readers are active readers. Become actively involved with the text. Think of your textbook as a tool to help you learn more about the world around you. It is a form of nonfiction writing—it describes real-life ideas, people, events, and places. Use the reading strategies in the *Power Read* box at the beginning of each chapter, followed by more strategies in the margins throughout the chapter to help you read actively.

PREDICT Make educated guesses about what the section is about by combining clues in the text with what you already know. Predicting helps you anticipate questions and stay alert to new information.

Ask yourself:
- What does this section heading mean?
- What is this section about?
- How does this section tie in with what I have read so far?
- Why is this information important in understanding the subject?

CONNECT Draw parallels between what you are reading and the events and circumstances in your own life.

Ask yourself:
- What do I know about the topic?
- How do my experiences compare to the information in the text?
- How could I apply this information in my own life?
- Why is this information important for understanding the subject?

QUESTION Ask yourself questions to help you clarify meaning as you read.

Ask yourself:
- Do I understand what I have read so far?
- What is this section about?
- What does this mean?
- Why is this information important for understanding the subject?

RESPOND React to what you are reading. Form opinions and make judgments about the section while you are reading—not just after you've finished.

Ask yourself:
- Does this information make sense?
- What can I learn from this section?
- How can I use this information to start planning for my future?
- Why is this information important for understanding the subject?

More Reading Strategies

Use this menu for more reading strategies to get the most from your reading.

BEFORE YOU READ . . .

SET A PURPOSE
- Why are you reading the textbook?
- How does the subject relate to your life?
- How might you be able to use what you learn in your own life?

PREVIEW
- Read the chapter title to preview the topic.
- Read the subtitles to see what you will learn about the topic.
- Skim the photos, charts, graphs, or maps. How do they support the topic?
- Look for key terms that are boldfaced. How are they defined?

DRAW FROM YOUR BACKGROUND
- What have you read or heard concerning new information on the topic?
- How is the new information different from what you already know?
- How will the information that you already know help you understand the new information?

AS YOU READ . . .

PREDICT
- Predict events or outcomes by using clues and information that you already know.
- Change your predictions as you read and gather new information.

CONNECT
- Think about people, places, and events in your own life. Are there any similarities with those in your textbook?
- Can you relate the textbook information to other areas of your life?

QUESTION
- What is the main idea?
- How do the photos, charts, graphs, and maps support the main idea?

VISUALIZE
- Pay careful attention to details and descriptions.
- Create graphic organizers to show relationships that you find in the information.

NOTICE COMPARE AND CONTRAST SENTENCES
- Look for clue words and phrases that signal comparison, such as *similarly, just as, both, in common, also,* and *too.*
- Look for clue words and phrases that signal contrast, such as *on the other hand, in contrast to, however, different, instead of, rather than, but,* and *unlike.*

NOTICE CAUSE-AND-EFFECT SENTENCES
- Look for clue words and phrases, such as *because, as a result, therefore, that is why, since, so, for this reason,* and *consequently.*

NOTICE CHRONOLOGICAL SENTENCES
- Look for clue words and phrases, such as *after, before, first, next, last, during, finally, earlier, later, since,* and *then.*

AFTER YOU READ . . .

SUMMARIZE
- Describe the main idea and how the details support it.
- Use your own words to explain what you have read.

ASSESS
- What was the main idea?
- Did the text clearly support the main idea?

- Did you learn anything new from the material?
- Can you use this new information in other school subjects or at home?
- What other sources could you use to find more information about the topic?

UNIT 1

THE HOSPITALITY & TOURISM BUSINESS

In This Unit . . .

Chapter 1
Defining Hospitality & Tourism

Chapter 2
Economics and the Impact of Tourism

"Though we travel the world over to find the beautiful, we must carry it with us or we find it not."
—Ralph Waldo Emerson
Writer and poet

UNIT OVERVIEW

3

Welcome to the truly exciting worlds of hospitality and tourism. In Chapter 1, you will learn that hospitality and tourism are two of the fastest-growing industries today. They encompass several segments, including lodging, food service, travel, tourism, and sports and entertainment events. The future is bright and promises new opportunities and challenges for students interested in hospitality and tourism careers. Chapter 2 explores how travel, tourism, and hospitality affect the world. The effects are not just economic; the social and cultural impact of tourism is significant around the world. The chapter also discusses how most people travel for business, family, or leisure reasons. Different types of people travel for different reasons as they seek new sights, sounds, and cultures.

UNIT LAB | Preview

The Inn Place

Think about all the hotels and resorts you have seen advertised. How do hotel owners and managers determine which services their hotels will offer? Does it matter which services a particular hotel offers?

Functions of Marketing

Marketing-Information Management · Financing · Pricing · Promotion · Product/Service Management · Distribution · Selling

Foundations: Professional Development · Economics · Business, Management, Entrepreneurship · Communication, Interpersonal Skills

Business Concepts · Technology · Academic Concepts

These functions are highlighted in this unit:
- Products/Service Management
- Financing
- Distribution
- Pricing

3

Chapter 1

Defining Hospitality & Tourism

Section 1.1

The World of
Hospitality & Tourism

Section 1.2

Hospitality & Tourism:
Past and Present

Chapter Objectives

- Describe the hospitality and tourism industries.
- Identify the segments of the hospitality and tourism industries.
- Define service as a product.
- Explain the importance of service to the hospitality and tourism industries.
- Describe the origins of lodging and food service.
- Identify trends in the hospitality and tourism industries.

Case Study — PART 1

SERVING FOOD AND FUN

In 1934, farmer Walter Knott perfected the boysenberry—a hybrid, or combination, of the red raspberry, blackberry, and loganberry. He also operated a restaurant in Buena Park, California. To add to the restaurant's offerings, his wife Cordelia served biscuits with preserves made from the new fruit. She then expanded the menu to include fried chicken dinners. By 1940, the Knott family restaurant was serving up to 4,000 customers on Sunday nights.

Inspired by his customers' need for entertainment and his affection for the Old West, Walter Knott then built a ghost town adjacent to the restaurant. He used relocated buildings from authentic ghost towns in the Southwest. The attraction, renamed Knott's Berry Farm©, grew through the 1950s and 1960s. In 1968, the family enclosed the restaurant and ghost town, and began charging admission. Other history-themed sections were added.

As a restaurant, Knott's Berry Farm had a long history and loyal customers, but how would it fare as an amusement park with Disneyland® only 15 minutes away?

ANALYZE AND WRITE

1. Describe the customers of a family-style restaurant and those of a theme park.
2. What characteristics differentiated Knott's Berry Farm from Disneyland?

Case Study Part 2 continues on page 15

POWER READ

Be an active reader and use these reading strategies:

PREDICT what the section will be about.
CONNECT what you read with your own life.
QUESTION as you read to make sure you understand the content.
RESPOND to what you've read.

The World of Hospitality & Tourism

AS YOU READ ...

YOU WILL LEARN

- To describe the hospitality and tourism industries.
- To identify the segments of the hospitality and tourism industries.
- To define service as a product.
- To explain the importance of service to the hospitality and tourism industries.

WHY IT'S IMPORTANT

By identifying and understanding the nature and variety of these industries, businesses and marketers function more effectively.

KEY TERMS

- hospitality industry
- bed-and-breakfasts (B&Bs)
- tourism industry
- service
- variables
- perishability
- intangibility
- changeability

PREDICT

What might the hospitality industry have in common with the tourism industry?

hospitality industry a group of businesses composed of establishments related to lodging and food-service management

The Importance of Hospitality & Tourism

Hospitality and tourism are two of the fastest-growing and most exciting industries in the world today. They encompass more than 15 related businesses, including lodging, food service, transportation vendors, and tour operators. These industries employ more than 8 million people who earn more than $165 billion in wages and salaries. Annually, hospitality and tourism generate in excess of $525 billion in sales. In the United States, the tourism industry is the third-largest retail industry behind automotive and food stores, and it is our nation's largest service-export industry. One out of every seven Americans is employed either directly or indirectly because of visitors traveling to and within the United States. Opportunities are endless for well-prepared and motivated individuals who want a challenging, fast-paced future in hospitality and tourism.

Industry Segments

Few industries in the world are as complex, diverse, and interrelated as hospitality and tourism with many segments—lodging, food service, travel, tourism, and sports and entertainment events. (See **Figure 1.1**.)

Hospitality Industry

Traditionally, the **hospitality industry** is a group of businesses composed of establishments related to lodging and food-service management. These businesses include hotels, motels, inns, and **bed-and-breakfasts (B&Bs)**, or small unique inns that offer a full breakfast with a night's stay, as well as casinos, restaurants, catering companies, hospitals, schools, and many other facilities.

Tourism Industry

The **tourism industry** is a group of businesses that encompass travel/transportation vendors for air, rail, auto, cruise, and motor-coach travel, and promote travel and vacations. Destination marketing firms, such as tourism offices, convention and visitors' bureaus, and chambers of commerce, distribute information to travelers.

Other Providers

In addition, providers of recreational facilities and meeting-planning services are included under the umbrella of the important and rapidly growing industries of hospitality and tourism. The sports and entertainment industries rely on consumers who spend their money and free time watching or participating in their favorite pastimes and activities.

Product as Service

A product is not only a tangible item, or good, it can also be a **service**, or an intangible thing that is a task performed for customers by a business. It is simple to think that hotels sell rooms, and restaurants provide food. However, no guest will return to a facility—hotel or restaurant—unless the service provided with the room or the food is quality service. For example, hotel guests will not be satisfied if the sleeping room is pretty, but the front-desk clerk is rude. Similarly, no customer will enjoy a dining experience if he or she has to wait more than an hour to receive food after placing an order—even if the food is excellent.

The Service Factor

Products can be goods or services. In the hospitality and tourism industries, most products are services. This service factor in all segments—lodging, food service, travel, tourism, and sports and entertainment events—is what differentiates these industries from most other industries. Therefore, it is necessary to take both a goods and a service approach to hospitality and tourism products.

GOODS VS. SERVICES Physical products, or goods, are easy to identify. For example, hotels have sleeping rooms, meeting rooms, recreational facilities, and restaurants. Food-service establishments may offer products such as food and beverages, which are types of goods. A restaurant may also offer service in the form of entertainment. It is easy to determine whether a room is clean and whether food is tasty. However, it is more difficult to determine if quality service is being provided.

bed-and-breakfasts (B&Bs) small unique inns that offer a full breakfast with a night's stay

tourism industry a group of businesses that encompass travel/transportation vendors for air, rail, auto, cruise, and motor-coach travel, and promote travel and vacations

service an intangible thing that is a task performed for customers by a business

CONNECT
What factor makes hospitality and tourism different from other industries?

Figure 1.1

Hospitality & Tourism Industry Segments

HOSPITALITY & TOURISM VARIETY All of these industry segments share a common characteristic: All rely on providing a quality service experience to the guest. *Can any of these businesses be listed under more than one segment? Why or why not?*

Lodging	Food Service	Travel	Tourism	Sports & Entertainment Events
Hotels	QSR restaurants	Cruise lines	DMOs	Arenas
Motels	Catering companies	Rail service	CVBs	Arts centers
B&Bs	Banquet facilities	Car rentals	Tour operators	Theaters
Resorts	Fine-dining restaurants	Motor coach	Visitor centers	Parks

What is the meaning of *intangibility?* How does it relate to hospitality and tourism?

variables factors that can cause something to change or vary

perishability the probability of a product ceasing to exist or becoming unusable within a limited amount of time

intangibility a state of being abstract, as are things that cannot be touched

Product Variables

When marketing the service side of the hospitality and tourism industries, you need to consider these **variables**, which are factors that can cause something to change or vary:

1. **Perishability**—In hospitality and tourism, **perishability** is the probability of a product ceasing to exist or becoming unusable within a limited amount of time. For example, the owner of a 100-room hotel needs to sell as many rooms each night as possible. Any rooms that remain vacant on a particular date cause lost revenue that can never be recovered. On the food-service side, if a restaurant orders 100 pounds of fish, and customers do not order fish from the menu, the owner will lose money. From a travel/tourism perspective, a cruise ship can service 2,100 passengers. If the ship sails with only 1,100 guests, the lost income will never be returned.

2. **Intangibility**—In general, **intangibility** is a state of being abstract, as are things that cannot be touched. Hospitality goods and services relate to memories and experiences. They are impossible for people to sample or touch prior to arrival. Brochures, Web pages, maps, graphics, and menus may provide a basic idea before a guest makes a purchase, but the actual experience is *intangible* in nature. After the experience the guest may have only photos, ticket stubs, and receipts to remind him or her of the trip.

Hot Property

More Than an Amusement Park

Walt Disney World Resort After the success of Disneyland® Park, Walt Disney wanted to create a family destination grander than the Anaheim landmark. He bought acres and acres of land in Florida and started sketching out plans. His dream would be more than an amusement park—it would be an "Experimental Prototype Community of Tomorrow," or EPCOT.

Walt Disney died before his Florida project became a reality, but Walt Disney World Resort lives on as the materialization of his dream. In addition to the Magic Kingdom theme park, Walt Disney World Resort houses three other theme parks, two water parks, hundreds of dining areas, and thousands of hotel rooms. It's a massive complex on 47 square miles of land. Millions of tourists visit every year.

FAMILY MATTERS

Walt Disney World Resort works hard to ensure that millions do keep coming. Disney's marketers look for tourism trends in their target demographic group and then market to those potential customers. For example, Walt Disney World created their Magical Gatherings Program in 2003 to tap into the "togethering" trend. Disney executives first saw the trend developing on their cruise ships, where extended-family and friend groups traveled together. Today Disney provides a Magical Gatherings Planner on its Web site. Walt Disney World Resort is a good example of how hospitality and tourism can blend.

1. What products does Walt Disney World Resort offer?
2. How has Walt Disney World Resort tried to attract new tourists?

AT YOUR SERVICE Good or bad service determines whether customers return to any hotel or restaurant. *Would you complain if the service was unsatisfactory in a restaurant—or would you simply not return? Explain your answer.*

3. **Changeability**—In hospitality and tourism, the service provider and guest both play important roles in the success of the service encounter. Thus, service transactions differ from other types of sales transactions. They are subject to **changeability**, a condition of being subject to change or alteration. For example, if a guest checks into a hotel and is disturbed by someone in the next room, his or her impression of the hotel will change. Similarly, if a guest is greeted by a rude dining-staff attendant, his or her perception of the restaurant will not be favorable. Service training for front-line personnel is essential to eliminate changeability in guest service.

changeability a condition of being subject to change or alteration

Hospitality & Tourism Today

Tourism was not common until the late 1800s. However, today's tourism is truly a global industry, catering to every type of traveler. Hospitality is also a global industry that includes a number of important and unique segments. Throughout history, all segments have relied on the importance of service. Future success depends on understanding consumers' needs and preparing for them.

MARKETING SERIES *Online*

Remember to check out this book's Web site for information on hospitality and tourism products as well as more great resources at **marketingseries.glencoe.com**.

Quick Check ✓

RESPOND to what you've read by answering these questions.

1. What are the segments of the hospitality and tourism industries? _____

_____

2. What is the difference between goods and services? _____

_____

3. Identify three variables of hospitality and tourism products. _____

_____

 marketingseries.glencoe.com

Chapter 1 Defining Hospitality & Tourism **9**

Hospitality & Tourism: Past and Present

History of Hospitality

The word *hospitality* is derived from the Latin word *hospes*, meaning "guest, visitor, or one who provides lodging for a guest or visitor." Today the spirit of hospitality refers to the welcoming of guests to any type of facility that offers food and shelter.

Early Hospitality

Historically, taverns were perhaps the first establishments to offer hospitality. These properties were first found in Greece and Rome. The first fixed-price menus for food appeared in a type of tavern called an *ordinary*. Privately owned inns became popular for providing overnight accommodations as well as plentiful food and drink.

By the end of the 13th century, the horse-drawn coach, carrying travelers on main roads, led to the development of wayside inns known as *post houses*. Such establishments offered the most basic of accommodations: a mattress on the floor and some bread, beer, and perhaps meat. Despite the lack of amenities, such properties also became gathering places for social functions.

Signs of Hospitality

Some early inns were named and identified by easily recognized symbols. These symbols were later replaced with coats of arms to signify the territories of noble families. Examples of some names of inns were:

- White Swan
- Black Bear
- Green Dragon

THE PINEAPPLE SYMBOL The image of the pineapple is another sign of hospitality. It has a rich and romantic heritage as a symbol of welcome, friendship, and hospitality. Early explorers brought pineapples back from their expeditions to the West Indies. Grown and cultivated in Europe during the 17th century, the pineapple became the favorite fruit of royalty. A colonial sea captain, returning from travels, would display a pineapple sign at his door to give notice to friends that he had returned and was welcoming guests. Today the pineapple is the international symbol of hospitality.

Hospitality in the 1700s

The word *restaurant* comes from the Latin word *restaurare*, which means "to restore." The concept of a formal restaurant began in Europe. By the French Revolution in the late 1700s, many chefs of the French nobility were settling throughout Europe. Some ventured as far as America, taking with them their tradition of fine cuisine.

Hospitality in the 1800s

By the 1800s, numerous fine eating-and-drinking establishments were operating globally. However, the development of civilized sleeping accommodations was just beginning. Pioneers such as César Ritz and Conrad Hilton rushed to create the luxury accommodations that are associated with their names today.

History of Tourism

The word *travel* is related to the French word *travail,* which means "work." Ancient travel history suggests that a great deal of work was required in terms of time and effort to make a journey, usually for purposes of survival rather than pleasure. Earliest travelers may have been migrating nomads seeking shelter from predators, or they may have been searching for food. Throughout history, the growth of tourism has relied upon the development of transportation systems to reduce the work involved with traveling.

Ancient Travel

Around 3000 B.C. travel was revolutionized by the invention of the wheel. People could cover greater distances in less time. In addition, animals assisted travelers by pulling wagon-like devices to transport goods and passengers. About 1,000 years later, the Egyptians further advanced travel by building water vessels. Throughout the Mediterranean, many cultures used water power to facilitate travel for purposes of commerce and trade.

THE Electronic CHANNEL

Take a Tour Online

The best pictures of exotic travel destinations used to be found on the cardboard-cutout displays in travel agency windows. But these days you can see and find out about exciting travel locations online. For example, most cities, states, and countries have official travel and tourism sections on their official Web sites. Many of these sites are easy to find because they have addresses that are as simple as **www.nameoftheplace.com.**

➡ Go online and type in various country or city names in between the letters *www.* and *.com.* Make a list of your favorites and then see a list of examples through **marketingseries.glencoe.com.**

A GOOD SIGN The pineapple symbol is displayed in homes and businesses as a sign of welcome, warmth, friendliness, and graciousness. *What is the origin of the use of the pineapple as a symbol of hospitality?*

➤ **ON THE ANCIENT ROAD**
Travelers in the 14th century often made journeys on horseback over main highways, as depicted in Geoffrey Chaucer's *The Canterbury Tales.* *At this time, what type of exploration took place?*

Tourism in the 5th Century

Tourism really began as an outgrowth of travel during the Greek and Roman Empires, beginning in the 5th century B.C. Local residents of an area would offer their services as guides to wealthy travelers. Government officials also traveled on state business. Many enterprising Romans built second homes and inns to service these travelers. In addition, Greek citizens traveled every four years to celebrate the god Zeus—a practice honored as the Olympics.

The fall of the Roman Empire in the 5th century A.D. resulted in political instability. Travel by missionaries and priests for religious purposes increased. Pilgrimages to the Holy Land and religious shrines were popular. Monasteries were built along improved roads to house the traveling pilgrims.

Tourism in the Renaissance

During the Renaissance period of the 14th, 15th, and 16th centuries, innovative ocean exploration took place. Individuals, who were financed by royal courts, sought a new world and new adventures. The names Marco Polo, Columbus, Magellan, and Cook became synonymous with global exploration by sailing ships on the high seas.

On land the *grand tour* became popular for the aristocracy. This was a two- to five-year travel experience for the sons of the wealthy to study language, culture, and history to complete their formal education.

Tourism in the 1800s–1900s

During the 1800s in the United States and Europe, the Industrial Revolution of the 1700s had changed the face of travel forever. Rail service enabled tourists to journey by train across countries and continents. In the 1900s, mass production of the automobile and the construction of superhighways made more destinations accessible to more travelers. Visionaries in hospitality and tourism, such as Hilton, Escoffier, and Cook, pioneered innovations that have continued to influence hospitality and tourism into the 21st century. (See **Figure 1.2**.)

➤ **DESTINATION WORLD**
The top-ten overseas destinations for Americans are the United Kingdom, Germany, France, Italy, Netherlands, Spain, Ireland, Switzerland, Sweden, and Belgium.

Modern Tourism

The Wright brothers' experiment with the first airplane, a winged bicycle at Kitty Hawk, North Carolina, launched today's modern air-travel system. Giant ocean liners, used primarily for transatlantic crossings by the wealthy, were replaced by cruise ships, or floating resorts for the masses. Current trends, discussed in the next segment, and coming innovations in travel and tourism will continue to change the nature of travel in future years.

CONNECT

What form of transportation do you think is the most used? What form have you used most often?

Figure 1.2

Hospitality & Tourism Hall of Fame

Conrad Hilton	Auguste Escoffier	Thomas Cook
Hotelier and philanthropist	**Master chef, "The Chef of Kings"**	**Travel agent and tour operator**
Born: December 25, 1887, San Antonio, New Mexico, USA	Born: October 28, 1846, Villeneuve-Loubet, France	Born: November 22, 1808, Melbourne, England
• Founded Hilton Hotels Corp., the international chain of hotels, including the prestigious Waldorf-Astoria of New York City, Sir Francis Drake of San Francisco, and Palmer House of Chicago • In 1919, bought first hotel, the Mobley Hotel in Cisco, Texas; in 1925, opened first Hilton Hotel in Dallas, Texas • Founded the Conrad N. Hilton College of Hotel and Restaurant Management at the University of Houston • Believed in promoting world peace through international trade and travel	• Established standards of haute cuisine; the first great chef who worked for the public, serving kings, heads of states, and celebrities in collaboration with Cesar Ritz at the Ritz Hotel of Paris, France • In 1858, began apprenticeship in uncle's restaurant in Nice, France • Dedicated to improving skills and knowledge through education; wrote articles and books, including *A Guide to Modern Cookery* • As the father of modern cuisine, innovated the simplified art of cooking, established sanitation standards, and developed methods of food preservation	• Founded Thomas Cook and Son, a worldwide travel agency, and innovated the conducted tour • In 1841, organized the first publicly advertised excursion by train in England, carrying 570 passengers from Leicester to Loughborough and back; in 1856, set up the Circular Tour of Europe and later arranged tours of the United States • Introduced traveler's checks (then called *circular notes*) in the early 1870s • Laid the foundations for the tourist and travel-agent industry of the 20th century

INNOVATORS OF THE PAST
The roots of today's hospitality and tourism industries are international and centuries old. Innovators such as Hilton, Escoffier, and Cook still influence these industries. *List at least three ways these individuals have influenced modern-day hospitality and tourism.*

Trends in Hospitality & Tourism

We can consider current events and trends in safety, diversity, ecology, markets, convenience, and technology to clearly forecast future scenarios in hospitality and tourism. However, unforeseen circumstances and innovations may cloud predictions. No matter how the industries change, one factor will remain constant—the need for dedication to personal service.

Safety

Safety and security will continue to be of primary concern to the hospitality industry. Food-service regulations, particularly in the area of sanitation, are stringent to protect the safety of both guests and servers. Similarly, alcohol awareness and beverage-service programs ensure the safety of patrons and bartenders alike. Lodging facilities have added increased security in the forms of keyless electronic locks and "women only" floors. Cruise lines carefully restrict entry at each port of call through passport control and photo identification cards. Aware of their vulnerability after the terrorist events of September 11, 2001, airlines have adopted tighter controls for all passengers, both domestic and international. Stadiums that host major sporting or entertainment events have stricter entrance procedures. Most guests understand the necessity of these inconveniences and added expenses of increased security.

World Market

The Queen's Ship

Until recently, history's golden era of the ocean liner had almost been forgotten in the age of jet planes and cruise ships. In January 2004, the Queen Mary 2 set sail on her maiden voyage from her homeport of Southampton, England. Newspapers celebrated the run—and the world's largest, longest (almost four football fields in length), and tallest (21 stories high) passenger ship.

As the first "real" ocean liner built in more than 30 years, the QM2 accommodates 2,620 passengers in deluxe-duplex suites to small staterooms. Onboard facilities offer something

for everyone. Athletes can play basketball on a full-size court. Couples can dance the night away in the largest ballroom at sea. Studious passengers can attend lectures, count stars in the planetarium, or browse through the library. There are also fashionable shops, ten restaurants, five swimming pools, and several English nannies to care for children. Prices vary for those seeking the grandeur of the past aboard the Queen Mary 2.

Why would travelers not take a plane to save time and money?

Diversity

Due to its global nature, the tourism industry has fostered a climate of increasing **diversity**, which is ethnic variety as well as socioeconomic and gender variety in a group or society. Women and minorities will continue to be drawn to the opportunities offered. The managers of tomorrow will need the skill sets to effectively relate to all cultures.

Ecology

The need to guard our environment for enjoyment by future generations is not merely common sense, but also makes financial sense for planners and developers. Awareness of ecology and respect for and protection of our planet will continue to be a global concern and trend. **Ecotourism** is a branch of tourism encompassing adventure tourism and sustainable development of regions for future generations. This focus has grown as a result of awareness. For example, hotel properties have increased recycling efforts and the use of environmentally friendly products.

Markets

As the hospitality and tourism industries have grown, so have their market segments. **Market segments** are groups of consumers categorized by specific characteristics to create a target market.

For example, spas will continue to grow in popularity as the market segment of the baby boomer generation (born 1946–1964) becomes older and seeks to increase wellness and decrease stress.

Another example of the response to increasing markets relates to gaming. As more states legalize gambling, the numbers and variety of casino properties will also continue to increase with the market segment of people who seek this type of recreation.

Worldwide vacation ownership, or time sharing, is one of the fastest-growing market trends due to the global-exchange opportunities involved.

Convenience

Consumers in the future will place continued emphasis on the value of time and money. Products and services must be convenient and easily accessible. Restaurants will reflect this in their extensive take-out offerings, food courts, 24-hour locations, and casual atmospheres. Lodging facilities will allow convenient express check-in and check-out with special programs for preferred guests. Travelers will continue to use the Internet to make arrangements for all sorts of travel and hospitality products.

Case Study — PART 2

SERVING FOOD AND FUN

Continued from Part 1 on page 5

Recognizing that Knott's Berry Farm did not have to compete directly with Disneyland, the Knott family presented the park as a secondary southern California attraction—not as an alternative to the Magic Kingdom.

To answer Disney's Mickey Mouse, the Knott family licensed characters from the comic strip *Peanuts* to provide a theme for Camp Snoopy. This attraction was the very first theme-park area to be made especially for children. Knott's Berry Farm also constructed roller coasters and thrill rides, which were not part of Disneyland. In the 1970s, Knott's Berry Farm opened the first double-corkscrew roller coaster and log-flume ride. Other innovations included seasonal events, such as the Halloween-themed Knott's Scary Farm and Christmas-related Knott's Merry Farm. Sold to the amusement park company Cedar Fair LP in 1997, Knott's Berry Farm remains a popular and profitable attraction to this day.

ANALYZE AND WRITE

1. What innovations did Knott's Berry Farm introduce that allowed it to compete with Disneyland?
2. What market segment did Knott's target?

---

diversity ethnic variety as well as socioeconomic and gender variety in a group or society

ecotourism a branch of tourism encompassing adventure tourism and sustainable development of regions for future generations

market segments groups of consumers categorized by specific characteristics to create a target market

A SEAWORTHY CAREER

Captain John Rigney
President
Blue Water Excursions

What is your job?

"I own and operate the Huron Lady II, a 73-foot, two-deck sight-seeing cruise and charter boat."

What do you do in your job?

"In the off season, I prepare marketing materials, answer the phone giving information, and take orders for the upcoming season. I go to industry conferences and research ways to improve the business. During the season I supervise a staff of about seven full-timers, including office and vessel staff. I shop for supplies, arrange marketing, pilot the boat, clean the boat, maintain the engines, and make decisions."

What kind of training did you have?

"I had marine experience before starting the business. I could drive a boat. But that is only a small part of the operation. Most of my time is spent actually piloting the business. I took business classes at our community college, but most of my education was on-the-job training."

What advice would you give students?

"I would recommend working for someone in the business you choose. Learn all you can about running a business and about running an office. Then write a business plan. Make sure there is a demand for what you want to do and that you can earn enough money to make a profit. Be prepared to work long hours while starting out."

What is your key to success?

"Long hours of hard work—and earning income from other jobs while I was getting started. That's how I could afford those years until I could pay myself."

What uses of technology could benefit a boat tour business?

Career Data: Tour Operator

Education and Training On-the-job training and associate degree or bachelor's degree in business

Skills and Abilities Office-management skills, patience, willingness to put in long hours

Career Outlook Average growth through 2012

Career Path Many tour operators launch their careers from a personal hobby, such as boating

---

QUESTION

In what areas of hospitality and tourism is technology most visible?

Technology

As a factor in everyday life, technology has changed the world of work forever. For hospitality and tourism, technology is especially visible in the areas of marketing and communication. Specific applications include Web sites, Internet access in hotels and other locations, information-management systems, and guest services.

Web Sites

Many hotels, restaurants, facilities, vendors, and destinations host creative Web sites to entice customers to purchase products and services. Booking reservations for these products and services via the Internet is commonplace. Often, properties offer discounts for Internet patrons, because the Internet saves the businesses money by eliminating in-house sales staff who would perform the booking arrangements.

Internet Access

The Internet's presence in the hospitality industry is growing. Formerly used only as a support tool, it is rapidly becoming a necessity. Internet access in hotel rooms and lobbies has become a valued sales feature. Many properties offer high-speed Internet connections in guest rooms in addition to standard telephone service. Wireless hotspots, where guests can connect to the Internet without using a dial-up system, are in many upscale hotels, restaurants, and airports. Some airlines also offer Internet access on airplanes. In fact, wireless companies compete to offer these services to the hospitality industry.

Information Management

Through computerized reservation networks, properties are able to obtain guest information and create profiles to better serve repeat guests. Management of this data, using computers and software to create information-management systems, aids in predicting future sales, planning promotions, and developing better guest communications. Similarly, restaurants can maintain information to assist in menu planning. Transportation vendors can use systems to determine the most effective specials and deals to attract customers.

TECH NOTES

Airline Amenities

While some airlines have cut costs by eliminating meals and in-flight movies, others can afford to provide passengers with new high-tech amenities. Those who fly Lufthansa in the northern hemisphere have broadband Internet access and free use of its FlyNet® portal. JetBlue passengers can watch DIRECTV® digital television on a small seat-back screen. AirTran offers music, news, and other digital audio programming through XM Satellite Radio.

➡ Do these airlines want to attract business travelers, leisure travelers, or both by offering technological amenities? Answer this question after reviewing the information at **marketingseries.glencoe.com**.

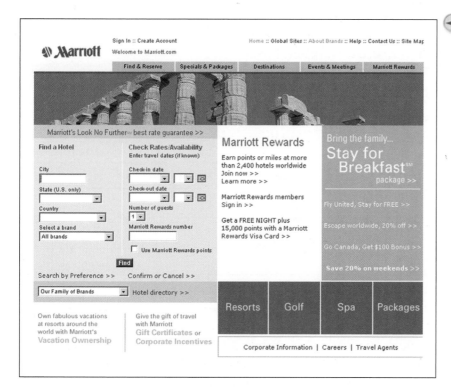

ONLINE SERVICE **With do-it-yourself systems on the Internet, booking reservations is quick and accessible from anywhere in the world.** *What other uses of the Internet have hotels adopted?*

Guest Services

Technology systems have been used to replace routine tasks relating to guests. At hotels, wake-up calls can be automatically programmed to ensure that many guests are serviced efficiently and accurately. Video check-in and check-out help speed up service for time-conscious guests. Such services allow front-desk staff to focus on guests with problems or those who may need more individual attention.

Other Computerized Systems

Computerized systems can regulate heating/cooling and lighting systems in case of emergencies. They can also indicate when and where repairs are necessary. A variety of computerized systems have been used on airplanes and cruise ships:

- **Airplanes**—Since 2001, airlines have increased their reliance on computerized security systems to scan passengers and their luggage.

- **Cruise Ships**—On cruise ships, computer-generated photo IDs are scanned and compared to images stored in central computer memory banks. Keyless entry systems ensure guest-room privacy for passengers.

Looking Forward

The hospitality and tourism industries of today, including lodging, food service, travel/tourism, recreation, and sports, have progressed from their beginnings. The future of these industries looks bright and promises new opportunities and challenges to anyone who is interested in these fields and is anxious to meet the challenge of service excellence.

Quick Check ✓

RESPOND to what you've read by answering these questions.

1. What is the tourism industry? _____

_____

_____

2. What is the origin of the term *hospitality*? _____

_____

_____

3. What are three future trends in hospitality and tourism? _____

_____

_____

Worksheet 1.1

Hospitality for Tourists

Contact the local convention and visitors' bureau, tourists' office, or chamber of commerce in your community. Explain that you are on a school assignment. Ask for information for travelers visiting your community. Make a chart that includes lodging, food service, travel/transportation, and any sites, attractions, art centers, and arenas. Add two or more facts about each listing.

_____

_____

_____

_____

_____

_____

_____

_____

_____

_____

_____

_____

_____

_____

_____

_____

_____

_____

_____

_____

_____

_____

_____

_____

_____

_____

_____

Worksheet 1.2

Historic Tourist Spots

Contact your community's local historical society. Explain that you are on a class assignment. Ask for information on historic places of interest to tourists. Choose one place of interest to you. Visit the site, pick up any literature about the site, and then answer the following questions:

1. What is the name of the historic site? _____

_____

_____

_____

2. In what year was it developed? _____

_____

_____

_____

3. Who developed this historic site? _____

_____

_____

_____

4. Describe this historic site. Is it an early homestead? An ancient ruin? An early railroad depot or canal? _____

_____

_____

_____

5. Write a short visual description of the site. Include why you think the site is important as a historic site. _____

_____

_____

_____

_____

_____

_____

Portfolio Works

ASSESSING SERVICE

Complete a checklist of important factors for good service. Go to two local restaurants and have meals in each one. Score each restaurant and decide which one would get your recommendation if you were a restaurant critic for a local newspaper. On a separate sheet of paper, write a paragraph as a restaurant review of the best or the worst restaurant.

Scoring:
1 – Needs improvement
2 – Good
3 – Excellent

Restaurant #1: _____
Service Factor

	Needs Improvement	Good	Excellent
1. Service with a smile			
2. Seated without much waiting			
3. Table set properly with clean dishes and utensils			
4. Order taken when customer ready to order			
5. Food prepared and served in reasonable amount of time			
6. Servers and attendants checked customers for needs			
7. Dishes removed promptly when customers finished			
8. Other: _____			

Subtotals =
Total Score =

Restaurant #2: _____
Service Factor

	Needs Improvement	Good	Excellent
1. Service with a smile			
2. Seated without much waiting			
3. Table set properly with clean dishes and utensils			
4. Order taken when customer ready to order			
5. Food prepared and served in reasonable amount of time			
6. Servers and attendants checked customers for needs			
7. Dishes removed promptly when customers finished			
8. Other: _____			

Subtotals =
Total Score =

Add these pages to your career portfolio.

CHAPTER SUMMARY

Section 1.1 The World of Hospitality & Tourism

hospitality industry
(p. 6)
bed–and–breakfasts
(p. 6)
tourism industry (p. 6)
service (p. 7)
variables (p. 8)
perishability (p. 8)
intangibility (p. 8)
changeability (p. 9)

- The hospitality industry is a group of businesses composed of establishments related to lodging and food-service management. The tourism industry is a group of businesses that encompass travel/transportation vendors for air, rail, auto, cruise, and motor-coach travel and promote travel and vacations.

- The hospitality and tourism industries are composed of several segments: lodging, food service, travel, tourism, and sports and entertainment events.

- A product can be both goods and services offered to customers. A service is an intangible thing that is a task performed for customers by a business.

- In the hospitality and tourism industries, most products are services. Service is what differentiates these industries from most other industries. However, service can be affected by several variables.

Section 1.2 Hospitality & Tourism: Past and Present

diversity (p. 15)
ecotourism (p. 15)
market segments (p. 15)

- The first hospitality establishments were probably taverns in Greece and Rome. By the end of the 13th century, horse-drawn coaches brought travelers to inns known as *post houses*. Ancient travel required effort for purposes of survival rather than pleasure. The invention of the wheel around 3000 B.C. enabled easier travel.

- Trends in the hospitality and tourism industries are affected by current events as well as trends in safety, diversity, ecology, markets, convenience, and technology.

CHECKING CONCEPTS

1. **Define** the hospitality industry.
2. **Define** the tourism industry.
3. **Describe** the segments of the hospitality industry and those of the tourism industry.
4. **Explain** the meaning of service and provide examples in hospitality and tourism.
5. **Identify** three variables that affect the marketing of service in hospitality and tourism.
6. **Explain** the origin of the word *hospitality*.
7. **Identify** examples of tourism during the Renaissance.

Critical Thinking

8. **Discuss** how technology is used in hospitality and tourism.

CROSS-CURRICULUM SKILLS

Work-Based Learning

Basic Skills—Writing

9. Write an advertisement for a hotel that is the "Hotel of the Future." Describe the most important thing this hotel can offer guests.

Thinking Skills—Reasoning

10. Explain in a brief written report why safety is a global concern for the hospitality and tourism industries.

School-Based Learning

History

11. Choose a country that you would like to visit. Then use the library or Internet to learn about a museum where you could explore travel in that country during the 4th to 5th centuries, 1400s to 1600s, or 1800s.

Math

12. Explain in a brief written report why ecotourism might be a good investment.

Role Play: Management Team Member

EVENT You are to assume the role of management team member for a historic home located in the southern region of the United States. The home was the residence of a Revolutionary War hero who signed the *Declaration of Independence*. It has been a popular tourist attraction. However, recent estimates for some repairs reveal the need for additional revenue. The foundation that manages the home (judge) will review the management plan to convert unused buildings to lodging space for guests. The construction costs would be less than the costs to repair the home.

ACTIVITY You are to explain the reasons for the proposal in terms used by the hospitality and tourism industries. Explain how accepting the proposal is vital to maintaining the site.

EVALUATION You will be evaluated on how well you meet the following performance indicators:

- Describe the nature of the hospitality industry.
- Describe the nature of the travel and tourism industries.
- Explain factors affecting the development and growth of the travel and tourism industries.
- Prepare for the sales presentation.
- Make oral presentations.

Use the Internet to access the Web site of the Mount Vernon Hotel Museum and answer the following questions:

- In what state is the Mount Vernon Hotel Museum?
- Who built the hotel and why did the builder(s) name it Mount Vernon?
- What time period does the hotel museum represent?
- Why would someone want to visit a historic hotel?

➡For a link to the Mount Vernon Hotel Museum Web site to do this activity, go to **marketingseries.glencoe.com**.

Chapter 2

Economics and the Impact of Tourism

Section **2.1**

The Impact of Hospitality & Tourism

Section **2.2**

Why Do People Travel?

Chapter Objectives

- Explain the economic multiplier.
- Define sustainable tourism.
- Identify the different areas impacted by tourism.
- Explain the cyclical nature of travel.
- Describe business and pleasure travel.
- Explain different motives for travel.

SEE THE WHALES

In the 1600s, the first Pilgrims landed in America on Cape Cod near Provincetown, Massachusetts. They learned to hunt and use whales for meat, oil, and bone. By 1760, a dozen whaling ships were based in Provincetown's harbor. By 1846, over 50 docks serviced those vessels. The whaling industry did not end until 1921, when whales were becoming extinct and petroleum was being used for fuel.

In 1975, Al Avellar began operating a charter fishing-boat service in Provincetown. Fifty years had passed since whale hunting had discontinued, and the whale population was stable. Avellar noticed how his clients enjoyed spotting whales while out fishing. So he decided to offer cruises for whale watching. Customers were excited to observe the fin, minke, right, and humpback whales roaming the local waters, which are full of plankton food for whales. Partnering with scientist Stormy Mayo of the Provincetown Center for Coastal Studies, Avellar's Dolphin Fleet was the first whale-watching business on the East Coast. However, with increasing competition and fewer whales, the Dolphin Fleet faced challenges. How would the business survive?

ANALYZE AND WRITE

1. List some environmental effects of a whale-watching business.
2. Write a paragraph discussing economic benefits of a tour-boat business.

Case Study Part 2 on page 37

POWER READ

Be an active reader and use these reading strategies:

PREDICT what the section will be about.

CONNECT what you read with your own life.

QUESTION as you read to make sure you understand the content.

RESPOND to what you've read.

The Impact of Hospitality & Tourism

PREDICT

Describe sustainable tourism in your own words.

infrastructure the physical components of a destination, such as hotels, restaurants, roadways, and transportation, that support tourism

Effects of Hospitality & Tourism

Travel, tourism, and hospitality have numerous effects on the world. The economic effects reach many levels of society, and profits from tourism can support regions visited by tourists. The effects of hospitality and tourism are not just financial. The social and cultural impact of tourism is significant around the world. In addition, a vital issue today is the environmental effect of hospitality and tourism on destinations that are ecologically fragile. The continuing life cycle of destinations and the success of the travel industry depend on careful planning that considers these impacts of hospitality and tourism.

Economic Impact

People's desire to travel and explore the world stimulates the economies of destinations. The development of infrastructure that supports the needs of travelers helps to create jobs. **Infrastructure** is the physical components of a destination, such as hotels, restaurants, roadways, and transportation, that support tourism.

Ongoing Economic Impact

New hotels and restaurants require employees to staff them. Food and beverage suppliers enjoy increased business. Newspapers and other media outlets benefit from advertising dollars spent on promoting businesses. Local and federal governments receive tax revenue, which may help fund other local, regional, and statewide programs. As tourism increases, the local economy continues to benefit as tourist dollars are recycled. (See **Figure 2.1**.)

Economic Multiplier

New tourists spend money on hotels, restaurants, attractions, airline tickets, or cruises. The money earned by those businesses goes toward paying employee wages, covering operating expenses such as rent and utilities, and purchasing food and beverages to be sold or served. These activities contribute to the **economic multiplier**, which is the process of how money filters through a local economy and is spent and re-spent, creating income for other businesses. The amount of the multiplier depends on how much money tourists spend per year and how much those tourist dollars "leak" offshore. **Leakage** is tourist dollars spent on imported goods so that revenue ends up in foreign economies.

PATH OF TOURIST DOLLARS Here is an example of the economic multiplier principle and leakage when an American tourist in Brazil spends $100 on a hotel room.

The hotel owner spends the $100:
- $40 employee wages
- $20 produce from local farmer
- *$20 imported food for hotel restaurant*
- $20 profit

The employee spends the $40:
- *$20 imported shoes*
- $10 groceries
- $10 savings

The local farmer spends the $20:
- *$10 imported fertilizer*
- $10 savings

Leakage in this case—through spending on imported, or foreign, goods—totals $50.

Employment

In 2002, U.S. residents and international travelers spent more than $545 billion dollars on travel. The income generated from travel produced nearly 7.2 million jobs for Americans. Because of travel spending, approximately one out of 18 U.S. residents was employed in hospitality and tourism-related positions during 2002.

EMPLOYMENT SECTOR Next to federal governments, the hospitality and tourism industries are the largest employers in the world. For service-oriented individuals, these fields can be exciting and rewarding—and demand for motivated workers is growing. Over the next several years, experts predict that job opportunities in hospitality and tourism are going to multiply.

---

economic multiplier the process of how money filters through a local economy and is spent and re-spent, creating income for other businesses

leakage tourist dollars spent on imported goods so that revenue ends up in foreign economies

Math Check

NET WORTH
Hotelier Armand Marmah has assets of $186,412 and liabilities of $176,549. Lodge owner Alan Berry has assets of $25,500 and liabilities of $2,600. What is each person's net worth?

➡️For tips on finding the solution, go to **marketingseries.glencoe.com**.

CONNECT
Think of five different jobs that could be related to hospitality and tourism.

Figure 2.1

Economic Impact of Travel in the United States

BOOSTING THE ECONOMY
For business or pleasure, the travel industry helps keep the U.S. economy healthy. *How much money is generated for state and federal governments as a result of travel within the U.S.?*

Travel expenditures	$545.5 billion
Travel-generated payroll	$157.0 billion
Travel-generated tax revenue	$93.2 billion
Travel surplus	$5.5 billion
Travel-generated employment	7.2 million jobs

SOURCE: Travel Industry Association of America and Bureau of Economic Analysis/U.S. Department of Commerce, 2002

Globalization and Tourism

globalization the increasing integration of the world economy

In the past 50 years, the world has experienced more globalization. **Globalization** is the increasing integration of the world economy. This trend has helped generate unprecedented prosperity globally. The economic importance of hospitality and tourism is undeniable. However, continued growth in these industries around the world depends on responsibly protecting and maintaining the human and natural resources that make tourism possible.

Sustainable Tourism

sustainable tourism tourism that allows a destination to support both local residents and tourists without compromising future generations

With globalization, the world faces enormous challenges. Poverty in many areas, mismanaged economic development, damage to environments, disappearing cultural heritage, and social inequalities all threaten progress. Today businesses and governments must create **sustainable tourism**, which is tourism that allows a destination to support both local residents and tourists without compromising future generations.

Social and Cultural Impact

In the business of hospitality and tourism, the products are the places people visit and the resources available to them. Unique cultures and established social customs and traditions can be affected by tourism. Failure to protect these aspects can destroy the appeal of a destination.

World Market

Paradise Island

Many people have dreamed of trading their busy lives for the tranquility of a faraway island. For vacationers on Bora Bora, the most famous of the volcanic islands of French Polynesia, the dream lives. One traveler described Bora Bora as "a tiny emerald in a setting of turquoise, encircled by a sheltering necklace of sparkling pearls." Bora Bora is surrounded by smaller palm-fringed islands, or *motus,* and a coral reef that forms a crystal-clear lagoon. Travelers to the island can enjoy deluxe accommodations, paddle a canoe at sunset, watch a shark feeding, hike lush island trails, or parasail over the South Pacific Ocean.

SUSTAINING TOURISM

Most destinations where tourism is the main source of income have environmental concerns. Fragile coral reefs that support marine and land life can all be affected by unmanaged tourism. But several hotels on Bora Bora have made progress in recycling waste and water purification to preserve what some believe is paradise on earth.

What type of traveler would choose Bora Bora as a destination?

FRENCH POLYNESIA

WORLD IMPACT Travelers to locations around the globe, no matter how remote and untouched, can impact environments. *What are some steps that tourists on vacation might take to avoid damaging a natural environment?*

Trading Cultural Influences

Tourists traveling to new places—with their cameras, luggage, and traveler's checks—also bring with them personal beliefs and behaviors. The way they dress, what they eat, and how they interact with others are all products of the customs and traditions of their home countries or towns. This is also true of the inhabitants of the destinations. Besides seeking sites and attractions, tourists wish to see and experience cultural diversity during their travels—the ways in which other people dress, celebrate, live, eat, and work. All of these factors contribute to the travel experience. Thus, cultures can influence each other.

Cultural Revival

The traveler's desire to see traditional costumes of people, to hear their music, taste their food, visit their historic sites, and experience folkloric traditions has created a renewed sense of pride among some cultures. Interest in a region's culture and traditions has led to the revival of native arts and crafts. Creating and producing arts and crafts can provide a means for residents of many countries to earn income. Also, many ancient monuments and artifacts have been restored and are tourist attractions. Local festivals and cultural events receive support to preserve ancient customs and celebrations, which provide a channel to pass on traditions from generation to generation.

Negative Cultural Influences

Tourists can also negatively impact local cultures. In poor and undeveloped areas, sudden economic growth among residents can lead to unrealistic expectations. As a surge of wealthy travelers parade through a community of simple means, locals may react with a desire for more luxury items. Sometimes, this leads to negative effects such as an increase in crime within the community.

Environmental Impact

The environmental impact of tourism has become a critical issue for the travel industry and the international community. The use of energy, raw materials, and water to build hotels, tourist attractions, new highways, and transportation centers can drain the availability of the natural resources of a destination. Negative impacts from tourism occur when visitors' use of a resource is greater than the destination's ability to handle that usage. Overuse can lead to increased pollution, harmful wastewater in water resources, erosion, and the loss of natural habitats for plants and animals. Tourism can have an impact on various aspects of a destination, including water resources, land and air resources, waste disposal, noise levels, and visual appearance.

Water Resources

Think about the increased demand for water resources when a new resort is built. In an area of open land that once supported native birds and animal life, a grand resort with 200 luxury suites sprawls across the landscape. The rooms feature dual-headed showers and whirlpool bathtubs. On the grounds there are two outdoor and one indoor swimming pool, a manicured golf course, and water features that accent the landscaped gardens. The increased personal water use combined with the water needed to maintain the pools, golf course, and gardens can lead to water shortages.

Land and Air Resources

Growth in tourism can negatively impact land resources, such as fertile soil and forests. Tourism can also invade wetlands and natural habitats of endangered species. Air pollution may increase, due to increased energy production necessary to support tourism, as well as more air, road, and rail traffic to the area. In addition, air pollution is linked to acid rain, global warming, and photochemical pollution, all of which affect land resources.

Waste Disposal

The disposal of solid waste and trash poses a serious problem for many destinations, including locations with fragile ecosystems. Each year in the Caribbean, cruise ships generate more than 82,000 tons of garbage. Wastewater can pollute seas and lakes surrounding tourist attractions. Sewage runoff can seriously threaten eco-sensitive coral reefs because it stimulates the growth of algae, which chokes the reefs.

THREATENED LOCATIONS Every year thousands of tourists leave behind garbage, oxygen tanks, camping equipment, and human waste on Mount Everest and other peaks in the Himalayan mountains of India. They trample vegetation and take firewood from forests. But the Himalayas are not the only environment to suffer as a result of tourism. Other equally threatened environments include the alpine regions, rain forests, wetlands, mangroves, and sea-grass beds.

Noise Pollution

Noise pollution from recreational vehicles, such as Jet Skis® and snow-mobiles, is another negative byproduct of tourism. Such loud noises can lead to hearing loss in humans and can cause significant stress to wildlife.

Visual Pollution

Tourism development can also damage the beauty of a natural region. Examples of this type of pollution include bright neon lights and bill-boards. Large stylized buildings can be eyesores that look out of place in a natural setting or may block a view of the ocean or mountain. The result is **aesthetic pollution**, which is the the spoiling or contami-nation of the natural beauty and features of an environment, due to poor planning and design of tourism projects.

Positive Environmental Impact

On a more positive note, there is much that tourism can do to ensure the health of an environment. Revenues generated from park entrance fees and similar sources can help pay for the protection and manage-ment of sensitive environments. User fees, taxes on recreation equip-ment, and license fees for hunting or fishing licenses can provide funds for conservation programs and park ranger salaries.

MARKETING SERIES *Online*

Remember to check out this book's Web site for information about the impact of tourism and more great resources at **marketingseries.glencoe.com**.

aesthetic pollution the spoiling or contamination of the natural beauty and features of an environment, due to poor planning and design of tourism projects

QUESTION

What are five negative environmental effects of tourism?

Hot Property

At Home in Africa

Abercrombie & Kent If you see a tour bus ripping through the African jungle, you can be sure it is not an Abercrombie & Kent (A&K) group. Tour operators at A&K believe in respecting the land, the wildlife, and the people who call Africa home.

Colonel John Kent, his wife Valerie, and their son Geoffrey started Abercrombie & Kent in 1962 by offering tours through East and Central Africa. The British family had adopted Kenya as their new home and based their company in the city of Nairobi. In 1967, Geoffrey took over as managing director. With his wife Jorie, he worked to bring Abercrombie & Kent's unique brand of luxury travel to destinations around the world.

COMFORT AND CONSERVATION

An Abercrombie & Kent tour is not complete without a comfortable night's rest. Even on adventure tours, A&K makes sure vacationers have gourmet meals, soft beds, and showers.

In addition to luxury, A&K delivers vacations with low-environmental impact. This tour business uses its status as a successful tour operator to promote conservation and cooperation among travel companies, local governments, and native inhabitants. For example, the Olonana resort in the Masai-Mara region of Kenya donates a share of its revenues to the local community and provides a shop where artisans can sell their arts and crafts. A&K also sponsors a wetlands project and a forestry project to help protect the ecosystem, and runs a global foundation for conservation. Abercrombie & Kent can do all that and still give tourists a great vacation.

1. How does A&K impact its tour locations?
2. What can tour operators do to protect the environment?

ENVIRONMENTAL MANAGEMENT Thoughtful tourism planning and controlled development can lead to effective environmental management of tourism facilities and natural areas. "Living green" campaigns in hotels and other lodging facilities can greatly reduce water use and sewage. Campaigns to raise the level of awareness among travelers and tourism providers influence their appreciation of the environment. Such campaigns can educate tourism consumers about the consequences of their actions upon the environment.

MANAGEMENT BY GOVERNMENTS State and local governments can also protect the environment on a local level. For example, the state government of West Virginia collects a whitewater-rafting tax from everyone who participates in a commercial rafting trip. The fee goes toward studying the environmental impacts of rafting. In addition, the rafting companies participate in several river-cleanup days each year. Conscious environmental management is part of creating sustainable tourism, which can prolong the life cycles of destinations globally.

Cyclical Nature of Travel

Every destination has a life cycle, which includes phases such as introduction, growth, maturation, decline, and sometimes renewal.

Introduction and Growth Phases

During the introduction stage, tourists begin to discover a new destination, and word quickly spreads among the venturers of the world. **Venturers** are travelers who tend to be the first to discover a new, unspoiled destination. As more and more travelers discover the destination, it experiences a period of growth. During the growth phase, more tourist dollars enter the region, and more and better facilities are built to continue to attract new business.

venturers travelers who tend to be the first to discover a new, unspoiled destination

Maturation and Decline Phases

After several years of steady growth, most destinations enter the maturation phase. Business is strong and steady but not continuing to grow. At this point, the venturers have moved on to new and more unique destinations. The mature destination is then visited by **dependables**, or travelers who prefer familiarity and creature comforts and seldom try anything new or different. Then the destination may experience a period of decline—unless it can be reinvented by adding or improving attractions to draw new tourists.

dependables travelers who prefer familiarity and creature comforts and seldom try anything new or different

Renewal Phase

Competition among destinations is fierce to attract new and repeat business in a constantly changing tourist market. Destinations that fail to manage growth, due to poorly planned or inappropriate infrastructures, may experience a decrease in visitors. The same is true for destinations that have been marred by violence, political instability, natural disasters, or overcrowding. If tourism starts to fall off in a particular region, destinations may enter a renewal phase by reinvesting or reinventing. Otherwise the business will decline and close.

RENEWAL CASE STUDY The greater Orlando, Florida, area is a perfect example of a destination that has experienced renewal. It continues to add new attractions to draw new and repeat business to the area. First there were The Magic Kingdom and Epcot Center at Walt Disney World. Later Disney diversified by adding the Disney-MGM Studios and Disney's Animal Kingdom. The variety of hotels and restaurants within each park was expanded to appeal to all budgets and tastes. Well-planned transportation near and between the Disney theme parks simplified traffic congestion. Disney also built water parks and evening entertainment centers, including the Downtown Disney area and Disney's Boardwalk. The Disney cruise line was added to the mix, offering family cruises that could be combined with land packages that include any of Disney's land-based products. Disney has successfully invested in its destinations and reinvented itself to keep tourists coming back.

Continuing Hospitality & Tourism Influences

Renewal and reinvestment can help prolong and continue the positive or negative effects of travel, tourism, and hospitality on destinations. People continue to travel and enjoy hospitality services for a variety of reasons as these industries significantly affect economic, social, and environmental conditions around the world.

TECH NOTES

Protecting Travelers
In 2004, Transportation Security Administration officials tested a new explosive-detection system on rail passengers at a train station in Maryland. Made by General Electric, the EntryScan[3] machine can "sniff out" traces of explosive material on people's hair, skin, or clothing. As passengers walk through a security gate, the machine sucks in a small amount of the air, and then tests the sample for explosive residue. Some passengers worry that the device will cause delays.

➡ Write a paragraph stating your opinion of using this equipment after reading reference material through **marketingseries.glencoe.com**.

Quick Check ✓

RESPOND to what you've read by answering these questions.

1. What is the economic multiplier? _____

_____

_____

_____

2. Why is sustainable tourism important? _____

_____

_____

_____

3. What is one positive and one negative impact of tourism? _____

_____

_____

_____

Why Do People Travel?

AS YOU READ . . .

YOU WILL LEARN
- To describe business and pleasure travel.
- To explain different motives for travel.

WHY IT'S IMPORTANT

Being aware of the motives, or reasons, that people travel will help you understand how to market hospitality and tourism products.

KEY TERMS
- business travel
- meeting and incentive travel
- meeting planner
- VFR travel
- leisure travel
- Maslow's hierarchy of needs

PREDICT

What type of traveler are you? Explain.

business travel travel for the sole purpose of conducting an individual's or company's business

The Reasons for Travel

In every country, different people travel for different reasons. Some people are born adventurers who simply enjoy new sights, sounds, and cultures. However, most people have business commitments, family occasions, or leisure time that cause them to book a plane flight or take a bus to a new town or even a foreign country. Hospitality and tourism professionals study these reasons in order to adapt products and services to their customers' needs.

Business Travel

Business travel is travel for the sole purpose of conducting an individual's or company's business. Business travelers conduct company business. They may attend training sessions or sales meetings or make individual sales calls on new or existing clients. Business travelers are not traveling for pure enjoyment but to pursue the mission of the organization for which they work.

Business Traveler Needs

A business traveler's needs can be very different from the needs of the leisure traveler. Business travel usually occurs during the week, not on the weekend, and can involve multiple destinations and methods of travel. Business travelers want to travel efficiently and economically.

Business Travel Challenges

Business travel can be stressful for an individual, usually keeping him or her away from home for several days or weeks. The traveler may cross several time zones and arrive at unfamiliar destinations. There may be language or cultural barriers to overcome and social customs to understand. The business traveler looks for efficient service, comfort, flexibility, and support. Special amenities, or conveniences, that make business travel easier can include data ports and high-speed Internet access.

Business Travel Incentives

Many travel businesses, such as airlines, will offer several perks, or benefits, to go along with business travel. Benefits may include frequent-flyer miles, travel in business or first class on airlines, and favored treatment at car rental companies and hotels.

Business With Pleasure

A business traveler can also travel for pleasure if he or she extends a stay into the weekend. He or she might have a nonworking traveling companion. A branch of business travel is **meeting and incentive travel**, which is business travel by employees to attend a business meeting or as a reward for having met or exceeded company goals.

Planning Meetings and Conferences

A **meeting planner** is a person who organizes and plans a meeting. He or she may organize a conference or convention that will be attended by hundreds or thousands of business travelers. Meeting planners have a variety of responsibilities:

- Find a site for the meeting.

- Arrange for travel to, from, and around the meeting site.

- Coordinate meeting space, hotel rooms, and meals.

- Schedule speakers and multimedia services.

- Handle registration.

INCENTIVE TRAVEL A meeting planner may also be called on to plan travel for individuals or groups as a reward for having achieved or exceeded goals. This kind of travel is granted in recognition of job performance. The destination as well as all the elements of the travel package (hotel accommodations, meals, activities, etc.) are perceived as something special. There may be a separate program for spouses or partners, if the company offering the travel reward has included a business and a pleasure component to the trip.

THE Electronic CHANNEL

Travel Online

The Internet has changed the way people fly, rent, make reservations, and relax. In 2002, researchers found that 59 million people in the United States made online travel purchases. With so many online travel options, user friendliness and low rates keep travel Web sites competitive.

➤Choose two online travel sites and price a round-trip flight from New York to Los Angeles for an upcoming holiday weekend. Choose the best site. Find links through **marketingseries.glencoe.com**.

meeting and incentive travel business travel by employees to attend a business meeting or as a reward for having met or exceeded company goals

meeting planner a person who organizes and plans a meeting

TRAVEL FOR ALL REASONS People travel for business, pleasure, and related reasons, such as education and family events. *What kind of accommodations might students have when visiting colleges?*

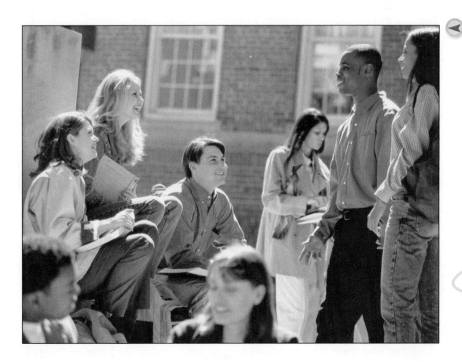

CONNECT

What was the reason for the majority of your trips in the last ten years?

Profiles in Hospitality

SPECIALIZED TOURISM

Judy Heller
President
Access Aloha Travel

What is your job?

"I am the owner and supervisor of a small, high-volume travel agency that specializes in the needs of travelers with disabilities, but the agency also assists all travelers. We are one of only 14 such agencies in the United States that specialize in the disabled and the only one in Hawaii."

What do you do in your job?

"Our services include booking air travel, hotels, cruises, and tours. I also do a lot of *pro bono* (free) work with the disabled community. As the owner, I oversee employees and all aspects of the general office. We also do inbound groups, the last of which was 63 blind/deaf clients, a very challenging but wonderful and humbling experience."

What kind of training did you have?

"I have been in the industry for over 30 years and have taken many classes and courses related to travel. I travel all over the world, which I find is the best education of all."

What advice would you give students?

"You have to love what you do."

What is your key to success?

"The same for any other business—lots of hard work, dedication, and service, service, service! We pride ourselves on very good personal service, and therefore, our repeat business is very high. Also, to be successful in any business, I think it is absolutely mandatory to work with integrity."

What needs and services might travel agents need to consider for tourists with disabilities?

Career Data: Travel Agent

Education and Training
High school diploma, associate degree, or bachelor's degree in business, communications, or travel

Skills and Abilities
Interpersonal, organizational, and task-management skills

Career Outlook Average growth through 2012

Career Path Entry-level agent at established agencies to freelance to part- or full-time positions to agency owner

Pleasure Travel

When traveling for pleasure, some people engage in **VFR travel**, or travel for the purpose of visiting friends and relatives. They may be attending a niece's graduation, a friend's wedding, or a family reunion. They may require lodging, transportation, or planning assistance. The purpose of their travel is straightforward and limited by their budgets and available free time. The needs of people who engage in **leisure travel**, or travel for the sole purpose of enjoyment, can be more complex.

VFR travel travel for the purpose of visiting friends or relatives

leisure travel travel for the sole purpose of enjoyment

Travel Motive Theories

Business and pleasure are two basic motives for travel. But what motivates one person to want to travel to the beach, another to the mountains, and another to a foreign country? Why do some people strike off on their own, exploring unique destinations with only a backpack, while others require the comfort of an all-inclusive resort or escorted tour? Two theories, developed by researchers Maslow and Plog, can help explain traveler behavior.

Maslow's Hierarchy of Needs

Noted sociologist Abraham Maslow developed a theory of human motivation. **Maslow's hierarchy of needs** is a theory that explains what motivates people to act in certain ways or make certain decisions. He proposed that human behavior and choice are driven by a desire to satisfy a variety of needs. These needs are arranged in pyramid form. (See **Figure 2.2** on page 38.) The most basic needs are represented at the bottom of the pyramid, and the more self-fulfilling needs are at the top. This hierarchy means that needs such as esteem and self-actualization motivate people only if other more basic needs for food, safety, and love have been satisfied.

According to Maslow, there are five types of needs that motivate people:

1. **Physiological needs**—food, water, and sleep
2. **Safety needs**— personal security and a source of income
3. **Recognition needs**—love and affection
4. **Esteem needs**— self-respect and respect for others
5. **Self-actualization needs**—developing one's full potential

Plog's Psychographic Analysis

Stanley Plog, a researcher of travel behavior, believed that psychological characteristics, such as values, beliefs, and lifestyle, could predict a person's vacation preferences. He developed Plog's psychographic analysis to describe two types of travelers—venturers and dependables.

TRAVEL FOR VENTURERS Types of travelers can be represented by a continuum, or scaled line, beginning with venturers. Venturers are the first to discover unspoiled destinations and explore without using tourist services.

TRAVEL FOR DEPENDABLES At the other end of Plog's continuum are dependables. They tend to value familiarity and comfort. They prefer creature comforts and seldom try anything new or foreign.

Case Study PART 2

SEE THE WHALES

Continued from Part 1 on page 25

The Dolphin Fleet in Massachusetts offers high-quality whale-watching tours. The company also promotes the preservation of whales through its relationship with the Center for Coastal Studies (CCS). On each of the 1,000 whale-watching cruises during the April-to-October season, a CCS spokesperson talks about the region's history, ecology, or related topics. The CCS naturalists observe and record information for the center's collection of scientific data. The CCS also benefits from sales of Dolphin Fleet T-shirts—profits that help the whales and the Dolphin Fleet.

The Dolphin Fleet has also formed bonds with other organizations, such as the Audubon Society, Cetacean Society International, Greenpeace, and the Oceanic Society. These groups and others support the tour business and sail on Dolphin Fleet tours. These beneficial relationships have not only contributed to the success of Dolphin Fleet, but they have also raised public awareness of the need to protect a natural wonder for the world.

ANALYZE AND WRITE

1. The Dolphin Fleet's season runs from April through October. List possible activities for the business during the other months of the year.
2. Discuss in a paragraph the motives for taking a Dolphin Fleet tour.

Maslow's hierarchy of needs a theory that explains what motivates people to act in certain ways or make certain decisions

Figure 2.2

Hierarchy of Needs

BASICS FIRST Maslow's hierarchy of needs theory states that people must satisfy basic needs before satisfying higher-level needs, such as self-actualization. *What human needs would travel or hospitality satisfy? Explain your answer.*

SOURCE: "Hierarchy of Needs" from *Motivation and Personality*, 3rd ed., by Abraham H. Maslow. Revised by Robert Frager, James Fadiman, Cynthia McReynolds, and Ruth Cox. Copyright 1954, 1987 by Harper & Row, Publishers, Inc. Copyright 1970 by Abraham H. Maslow. Reprinted by permission of HarperCollins, Inc.

QUESTION

According to Plog, what characteristics can predict vacation preferences?

Applying Theory to Marketing

The theories of Maslow, Plog, and others are interesting and can be helpful for understanding the motives for travel, but each theory must be applied to individual situations. When asked by a team of Plog researchers why they traveled, most Americans gave the following answers:

- To get rid of stress

- To enrich perspective on life

- To bring family closer together

- To do what they wanted, when they wanted

- To feel alive and energetic

    Everyone has reasons for travel and preferences for destinations. The tourism marketer's job is to understand these reasons and preferences to create a product and marketing strategy that addresses them.

Quick Check

RESPOND to what you've read by answering these questions.

1. What are three needs of the business traveler? _____

_____

2. What are a venturer and a dependable? _____

_____

3. What are some of the motivations for travel? _____

_____

Worksheet 2.1

Impact of Tourists

Choose a country as a destination. Find out information about the impact of tourism on that country. Contact the country's embassy by phone or Internet. Explain that you are doing a class assignment and ask the following questions. Then write the answers on the lines.

1. What is name of the country? _____

_____

_____

2. What percentage of the country's income is generated from tourism? _____

_____

_____

3. What is the economic impact of tourism on this country? Include information about the economic multiplier. _____

_____

_____

4. What percentage of the population is employed in hospitality and tourism? _____

_____

_____

5. From what countries do tourists originate? _____

_____

_____

6. What social or cultural impact has tourism had on this country? _____

_____

_____

_____

_____

7. What environmental impact has tourism had on this country? _____

_____

_____

_____

_____

Name _____ Date _____

Worksheet 2.2

Business and Leisure Travelers

Contact a travel agent in your community who works with business travelers and leisure travelers. Explain that you are doing a class assignment and would like to ask a few questions by phone or in person. Set an appointment to interview the travel agent. Ask the travel agent the following two questions. Then create a chart that compares the two types of travelers.

1. What are the main needs and requirements of a business traveler? Efficient service? Data ports? Meeting rooms? _____

   _____

   _____

   _____

2. What are the main needs and requirements of a person traveling for leisure? Luxury accommodations? Personal security? Other needs? _____

   _____

   _____

   _____

Portfolio Works

BUSINESS PLANS

Make a list of elements that might be necessary for a two-day business conference for ten people at a hotel. Choose the type of business and the conference event. Consider the attendees' needs and wants over the 48-hour period.

Type of Business: _____

Event: _____

Elements: _____

_____

_____

_____

_____

_____

_____

_____

_____

_____

_____

_____

_____

_____

_____

_____

_____

_____

_____

_____

_____

Add this page to your career portfolio.

CHAPTER SUMMARY

Section 2.1 — The Impact of Hospitality & Tourism

infrastructure (p. 26)
economic multiplier
   (p. 26)
leakage (p. 26)
globalization (p. 28)
sustainable tourism
   (p. 28)
aesthetic pollution
   (p. 31)
venturers (p. 32)
dependables (p. 32)

- In relation to hospitality and tourism, the economic multiplier is the process of how tourist spending filters through a local economy and is spent and re-spent, creating income for other businesses.

- Sustainable tourism is tourism that allows a destination to support both local residents and tourism without compromising future generations.

- Tourism impacts many areas, including economic, social and cultural, and environmental conditions.

- Every tourist destination has a life cycle of existence and goes through different phases, which include introduction, growth, maturation, decline, and sometimes renewal.

Section 2.2 — Why Do People Travel?

business travel (p. 34)
meeting and incentive
   travel (p. 35)
meeting planner (p. 35)
VFR travel (p. 36)
leisure travel (p. 36)
Maslow's hierarchy of
   needs (p. 37)

- Business travel is travel for the sole purpose of conducting an individual's or company's business. Travel for pleasure can include VFR travel, which is travel for the purpose of visiting friends or relatives as well as leisure travel, which is travel for the sole purpose of enjoyment.

- There are two reasons for travel—for business or pleasure. There are two theories that help explain the motives for travel—Maslow's hierarchy of needs and Plog's psychographic analysis.

CHECKING CONCEPTS

1. **Explain** two factors that determine the amount of the economic multiplier.
2. **Define** globalization.
3. **Explain** the importance of sustainable tourism.
4. **Identify** aspects impacted by tourism.
5. **Describe** the first two phases of a destination's life cycle.
6. **Explain** the difference between travel for business and for pleasure.
7. **Define** Plog's psychographic analysis.

Critical Thinking

8. **Explain** at least three reasons for travel provided by Plog researchers.

CROSS-CURRICULUM SKILLS

Work-Based Learning

Basic Skills—Math

9. Describe the economic multiplier by using the following people: tourist, hotel owner, food importer, farmer, hotel employee, grocery store owner, and banker. Begin with: A tourist spent $100 at a local hotel.

Interpersonal Skills—Teaching Others

10. Using the key words from this chapter, create your own crossword puzzle. Trade puzzles with another student and solve.

School-Based Learning

History

11. Name three different countries that may be in the decline stage of tourist travel, due to political unrest.

Art

12. Create a colorful poster that depicts and explains aesthetic pollution. Display poster in your classroom.

Role Play: Management Team Member

SITUATION You are to assume the role of a management team member for a midsize mountain resort. The resort has been in business for 60 years and is the major employer in the small local community. The resort was purchased by a group of investors. The facility has fallen into a state of disrepair. Your investors plan to spend over $3 million to refurbish the facility. A group of citizens (judge) is unaware of the plans to restore the resort and is concerned about the economic and social impact if the resort is shut down or not restored.

ACTIVITY You are to address the group of local citizens (judge) about the plans and the importance of the resort to the local economy.

EVALUATION You will be evaluated on how well you meet the following performance indicators:

- Explain the role of business in society.
- Explain the concept of private enterprise.
- Describe the nature of the hospitality industry.
- Describe current business trends.
- Foster positive working relationships.

INTERNET ACTIVITY

Use the Internet to access the Web site of the travel company Abercrombie & Kent.

- Find information about its global foundation.
- Write a summary of the information.
- Present your findings to the class.

➡ For a link to the Abercrombie & Kent Web site to do this activity, go to **marketingseries.glencoe.com**.

BusinessWeek News

FAR FROM THE CANCÚN CROWD

Remote resorts offer the treasures of the Yucatán without the tourist crush. Drive south along Mexico's Caribbean coast—also known as the Riviera Maya—and you will find a 75-mile stretch of quiet white beaches, turquoise sea, lush jungle, world-class snorkeling and scuba diving, and a region packed with wildlife and Mayan culture.

Secluded Spas

Drive only ten miles south from the airport to escape the hubbub. There you'll find remote resorts tucked a mile or so off the main highway, more often than not down bumpy, potholed roads. One of the best bargains is Ceiba del Mar Spa Resort. There are many other lodging options, starting at $15 a night for a cabana with a hammock and a mosquito net. True spa junkies should check out the 22,000-square-foot spa at Paraiso de la Bonita & Thalasso.

Ancient Mayan Ruins and More

All of these hotels are the perfect base to explore the Yucatán's treasures, including the Mayan ruins. The Maya, who occupied a swath of Central America from Honduras to Mexico from as early as 1500 B.C., were masters of architecture as well as mathematics and astronomy. Their legacy extends inland to the mysterious pyramids of Chichén Itza and Cobá in a postcard-perfect setting on a bluff overlooking the Caribbean.

Tulúm, which means "wall" in Maya, is a walled city, one of the few the Mayans built. They called it *Zama* or "City of Dawn." Tulúm is majestic. It is no wonder hundreds of iguanas sun themselves on the rocks of Tulúm's gray castle.

Within a ten-mile radius inland from Tulúm, you'll find *cenotes*. The Mayans believed these freshwater springs surrounded by limestone walls were windows into the underworld. Take a dip in one, and you might see a manatee. The Yucatán also boasts the world's second-largest barrier reef, which is why it is a popular spot with snorkelers and divers. Nature lovers should also check out the Sian Ka'an Biosphere Reserve, named a World Heritage Site by the U.N. in 1997. The 300,000-acre park, directly south of Tulúm, is home to more than 360 species of animals, including jaguars and crocodiles.

Tulúm, like other Yucatán beach towns, is getting discovered. But for now, nature prevails. As we left for the airport, a spider monkey jumped in front of our van and scurried off into the jungle.

By Lauren Young
Edited by Adam Aston

CREATIVE JOURNAL

In your journal, write your responses.

CRITICAL THINKING

1. What attractions draw travelers to the Yucatán? Why?

APPLICATION

2. If you were organizing a package tour to the Riviera Maya, what accommodations and features mentioned in the article would you include? To what type of traveler would you offer this package? Why?

 Go to **businessweek.com** for current *BusinessWeek* Online articles.

UNIT LAB

The Inn Place

You've just entered the real world of hospitality and travel and tourism. The Inn Place owns and operates a number of hospitality and tourism businesses, offering the finest accommodations and most desirable destinations in the world. Acting as the owner, manager, or employee of this diverse company, you will have the opportunity to work on different projects to promote the business.

Historic Hotel—Plan and Renew a Hotel

SITUATION You have recently purchased a hotel called the Bayside Hotel. The hotel is approximately 60 years old and needs refurbishing and redecorating. The building itself has been well maintained. The hotel is located on the shore of a salt-water bay within a three-hour drive of a metropolitan area. The Bayside Hotel has 30 guestrooms, a restaurant, and a lounge. The restaurant is very popular with hotel guests and with the local population. The food selections are basic, with fresh seafood dishes as the main attractions.

You have determined that the hotel will be refurbished to keep its rustic, old-fashioned charm. You need to add services to attract upscale customers. Some of your ideas include adding a boat dock, a swimming pool, tennis courts, an exercise room, and a spa. You need funds to add all of these services.

ASSIGNMENT Complete these tasks:
- Determine the services to offer to your target market and receive the best return for your investment.
- Estimate the cost of each service.
- Prepare a report of your findings.

TOOLS AND RESOURCES To complete the assignment, you will need to:
- Conduct research at the library, on the Internet, or by talking to local hotel owners/managers.
- Ask a banker about financing your services.
- Have word-processing, spreadsheet, and presentation software.

RESEARCH Do your research:
- Research the appeal of each service for your target market.
- Determine the costs of installing and maintaining each of the service features.
- Determine which services you will offer.

REPORT Prepare a written report using the following tools:
- *Word-processing program:* Prepare a written report listing the features and benefits of each service under consideration.
- *Spreadsheet program:* Prepare a chart comparing the costs of the services you are considering.
- *Presentation program:* Prepare a ten-slide visual presentation with key points, mock-ups of each proposed service feature, and key descriptive text.

PRESENTATION AND EVALUATION You will present your report to the bank that may finance your plan. You will be evaluated on the basis of:
- Your knowledge of each service feature under consideration and which features would best suit your hotel's needs.
- Continuity of presentation
- Voice quality
- Eye contact

PORTFOLIO
Add this report to your career portfolio.

UNIT 2

HOSPITALITY & TOURISM MARKETS

In This Unit ...

Chapter 3
The Restaurant Business

Chapter 4
The Hotel Business

Chapter 5
The Tourism Business

Chapter 6
Destination Marketing

Chapter 7
Sports, Events, and Entertainment

" Certainly, travel is more than the seeing of sights; it is a change that goes on, deep and permanent, in the ideas of living. "

—Miriam Beard
Author

46

UNIT OVERVIEW

Unit 2 explores the diversity of hospitality and tourism markets, which provide many opportunities for those interested in related careers. Chapter 3 focuses on the food-service business and the different types of restaurants and their operations. In Chapter 4, you will learn about the variety of lodging businesses, including hotels and inns for all types of guests. Chapter 5 examines travel and tourism businesses, focusing on tour operations and transportation. The exciting world of destinations is the highlight of Chapter 6, with a discussion of market segmentation. Chapter 7 concludes Unit 2 by exploring new hospitality and tourism markets in sports, entertainment, and event destinations and activities.

UNIT LAB Preview

The Inn Place

Think about all the tours and tourist destinations you have visited. How do the tour operators select the sites? How do they determine prices?

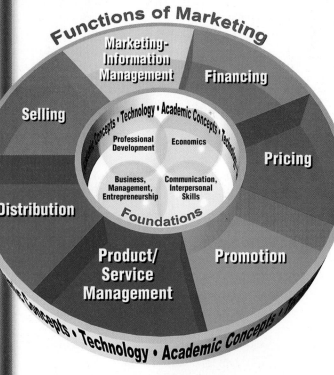

These functions are highlighted in this unit:
- Marketing-Information Management
- Products/Service Management
- Distribution
- Financing
- Promotion

Chapter 3

The Restaurant Business

Section 3.1

Types of Restaurants

Section 3.2

Restaurant Operations

Chapter Objectives

- Explain the difference between commercial and on-site food-service facilities.
- Identify the various categories of the commercial food-service industry.
- Describe types of restaurant businesses.
- Explain front- and back-of-the-house operations.
- Identify ways restaurants can increase and measure profits.

ANOTHER PLATE OF MIND

Many diners associate Korean cuisine with barbecued ribs. However, New York's Hangawi restaurant challenges that notion by serving Korean dishes that use no animal products.

Under the leadership of manager Terri Choi and chefs Peter Woo and Madeline Lee, the award-winning restaurant offers these foods as a dining alternative in Manhattan. To complement the simple and purifying aspects of the food, diners are asked to remove their shoes at the entrance. Guests then sit on pillows placed around low tables. Food is served in traditional wooden and ceramic bowls and dishes by waiters dressed in monk-like fashion.

Hangawi has gained a following, not only from Korean food fans and adventurous diners, but also from those who appreciate fine dining. The hearty soups, tasty breads, and fresh vegetables satisfy the hungriest guests. But would this restaurant's specialized concept limit the possibilities for expansion?

ANALYZE AND WRITE

1. What type of restaurant is Hangawi? Write a short description for a print advertisement.
2. List the staff members you think are needed to operate this type of restaurant.

Case Study Part 2 on page 63

POWER READ

Be an active reader and use these reading strategies:

PREDICT what the section will be about.

CONNECT what you read with your own life.

QUESTION as you read to make sure you understand the content.

RESPOND to what you've read.

Types of Restaurants

AS YOU READ ...

AS YOU READ ...

YOU WILL LEARN

- To explain the difference between commercial and on-site food-service facilities.
- To identify the various categories of the commercial food-service industry.
- To describe types of restaurant businesses.

WHY IT'S IMPORTANT

Most people enjoy dining out, and the food-service sector is one of the largest employers in the hospitality industry.

KEY TERMS

- commercial site
- on-site facility
- full-service restaurant
- quick-service restaurant (QSR)
- chain
- franchise

commercial site an establishment, such as a restaurant, where a food-and-beverage business competes for customers

PREDICT

What might be the main difference between a full-service and quick-service restaurant?

Introduction to Food Service

The production and enjoyment of food plays a significant role in every culture and society. Not only does food satisfy a basic need, it can also provide comfort. Food accompanies celebrations or simple conversations with friends and family. It is one of the few sensory activities that allows people to taste flavor, smell aroma, see a visual presentation, touch texture, and perhaps hear the sounds of cooking. It is no wonder that the food-service segment (also known as *foodservice* segment) of the hospitality industry continues to grow.

Impact of Food Service

The National Restaurant Association estimated that the 878,000 locations of food-and-beverage outlets served more than 70 billion meals and snacks in 2004. Sales generated from food service totaled more than $440 billion. Moreover, 12 million employees work in some segment of the United States food-service industry.

Food-Service Locations

A variety of facilities offer food service away from home. Traditionally, food-and-beverage operations are divided into two general categories—commercial sites and on-site facilities. A **commercial site** is an establishment, such as a restaurant, where a food-and-beverage business competes for customers. An **on-site facility** is an institutional or noncommercial establishment, such as a hospital or corporation, that provides meals for people involved with the property.

However, to be successful at any location, all food-service establishments must consider these factors: market, location, atmosphere, concept, and menu. These factors are equally important and interdependent and make each food venue unique. For example, a desirable location may attract a particular market, or group of customers, but if the menu selection does not reflect the guests' expectations, business may suffer.

Commercial Sites

The commercial for-profit segment of the food-service industry is broad. It includes full-service sites, such as fine-dining, casual-dining, limited-service, and specialty restaurants. Commercial sites can be chains, franchises, or independent facilities. They also include stand-alone facilities, in-house restaurants, or off-premise take-out and catering companies. Some properties may exist in more than one category. Only marketplace needs and consumer preferences limit the variety.

Full-Service Restaurants

Full-service restaurants are destinations for customers. A **full-service restaurant** is a restaurant where a customer sits at a table, gives an order to a server, and is served food at the table. These establishments offer a variety of menu styles with items usually cooked to order. Restaurant atmospheres for full-service restaurants can range from formal to casual. In addition, style can vary according to price and menu items. The types of full-service restaurants include fine dining, casual dining, and limited service.

FINE DINING Fine-dining, or "white tablecloth," establishments distinguish themselves by price, service, ambiance, location, and menu offerings. Each course is carefully prepared with attention to detail. They offer wines from extensive wine lists, other alcoholic beverages, and imaginative food/wine pairings. Tableside cooking and spectacular pastry creations by celebrity chefs are typical. Restaurants plan ambiance, or atmosphere, before opening an establishment by choosing the right location and an appropriate interior and exterior design.

CASUAL DINING As part of the fastest-growing segment of the hospitality industry, casual-dining restaurants have adapted to suit the needs of middle-class, baby-boomer, and family markets. These kinds of facilities attract diners who seek a relaxed atmosphere and reasonable prices. At casual-dining restaurants, speed of service and efficiency is more important than a three-hour gourmet dining experience at a fine-dining establishment.

on-site facility an institutional or noncommercial establishment, such as a hospital or corporation, that provides meals for people involved with the property

full-service restaurant a restaurant where a customer sits at a table, gives an order to a server, and is served food at the table

Good Taste in Spain

A small restaurant overlooking a picturesque ocean bay on Spain's northeastern coast, El Bulli (Spanish for "The Bulldog") attracts "foodies" and gourmets from around the world. Patrons with a taste for the offbeat make reservations as much as a year in advance.

UNIQUE DISHES

Those lucky enough to get a reservation experience the meal of a lifetime. People from all over the world reserve tables at El Bulli months in advance. El Bulli promises a menu famous for pushing the limits. Dishes such as colorful blocks of vegetable jellies, liquid ravioli, raspberry foam, and carrot "air" are only a few of the epicurean creations. El Bulli's celebrated chef explains, "The most important thing is to make people happy—but give them something to think about."

Do you think customers wait for reservations for an unusual experience or for good food?

Limited-Service Facilities

Limited-service facilities focus on combining speed of service at convenient locations with limited menu offerings. These restaurants are designed for corporate clients who are in a hurry as well as working moms and families juggling activities. A limited-service facility is not the destination itself. It is a stop on the way to another destination or activity.

quick-service restaurant (QSR) a restaurant offering speedy basic services, convenience, and consistent quality at low prices

QUICK-SERVICE RESTAURANTS Quick service, previously known as fast food, has long been considered the standard and most profitable category of restaurant in the limited-service sector. A **quick-service restaurant (QSR)** is a restaurant offering speedy basic services, convenience, and consistent quality at low prices. (See **Figure 3.1** for a list of the top QSR chains.) Off-premise dining options have increased because consumers are comfortable with QSR take-out services. In response, many casual-dining restaurants have joined the ranks of QSRs by offering the convenience of "home meal replacements." Some restaurants provide separate product lines that are available by delivery only. All of these limited-service offerings help meet the changing needs of the marketplace.

Figure 3.1

Top Quick-Service Chains

QUICK-SERVE SUCCESS Billions of dollars of revenue are generated by quick and easy food service in the United States. *Which segment of the QSR industry dominates the top-ten restaurants?*

Chain	Segment	2002 Systemwide Sales ($Mil)	Number of Franchised Units	Number of Company Units
1 McDonald's	Burger	$20,305.7	11,389	2,102
2 Burger King	Burger	$8,582.0	7,568	578
3 Wendy's	Burger	$7,100.0	4,366	1,183
4 Taco Bell	Mexican	$5,200.0	4,881	1,284
5 Subway	Sandwich	$5,200.0	14,548	1
6 Pizza Hut	Pizza/Pasta	$5,100.0	5,839	1,760
7 KFC	Chicken	$4,800.0	4,188	1,284
8 Domino's Pizza	Pizza/Pasta	$2,910.0	4,271	577
9 Starbucks*	Snack	$2,830.7	1,078	3,496
10 Dunkin' Donuts	Snack	$2,769.9	3,833	3

*North America
SOURCE: "2003 QSR 50," GE Capital Franchise Finance (GECFF) and *QSR* magazine ©2004

Specialty Restaurants

Specialty restaurants offer something for every taste. Restaurant specializations include theme, ethnic (for example, Mexican and Chinese), family-style, and breakfast restaurants as well as sandwich shops. Some of the more popular types of specialty meal offerings include pizza, chicken, steak, seafood, and hamburgers.

THEME Theme restaurants are the best example of creating a concept and tailoring the menu, ambiance, and decor to a particular market. Many theme properties feature specialized entertainment or celebrity involvement.

ETHNIC The increasingly diverse offering of ethnic restaurants reflects the growing diversity of the population in the United States. While Asian and Italian favorites still dominate the market, new competition is coming from south-of-the-border-style food, most notably Mexican.

PIZZA The convenience of delivery has made pizza restaurants a favorite with busy people, families, and late-night diners. Chains recognized the lucrative possibilities of this product and offer combination platters and specials to capitalize on it.

CHICKEN Since Colonel Sanders and KFC (formerly Kentucky Fried Chicken) revolutionized the marketing of chicken meals, other chains have competed for a share of this high-profit product line. Sometimes considered a healthy alternative to the standard burger, chicken meals offer diversity at moderate prices.

STEAK Once considered a risky investment due to health-conscious consumer warnings, steak houses have experienced a rebirth. The Atkins-diet focus on protein versus carbohydrate intake contributed to this expansion. Mid-priced, casual, and upscale steakhouse chains have also benefited from renewed demand for steak.

SEAFOOD The seafood segment is a small portion of the overall industry. The largest seafood chain in the United States is Long John Silver's. As a healthful alternative to meat and chicken, seafood is a popular choice.

HAMBURGER No discussion of specialties would be complete without mention of the QSR favorite, the hamburger. As long-standing leaders in QSRs, hamburger chains represent a substantial portion of the limited-service market. Restaurants such as McDonald's, Burger King, Wendy's, and smaller chains compete in this market.

Types of Restaurant Businesses

With the increase in business consolidation and mergers, some business analysts believe that independent restaurants cannot compete with a corporate chain's brand or a franchise's flexibility. However, each type of business—chain, franchise, or independent—has strengths that are difficult to match or duplicate.

ETHICS & ISSUES

Reality Restaurant

In 2003, NBC first broadcast the series *The Restaurant*. The show promised viewers an inside look at the running of a chic New York City bistro. In reality, many of the waiters were actors; many events were staged; and the entire show featured obvious product placement by its sponsors—American Express, Coors, and Mitsubishi. According to a restaurant review in the *New York Post*, the food was not very good. For most restaurateurs, building a reputable establishment with a satisfied, loyal clientele takes years of hard work, a dedicated and professional staff, and excellent food. *Should corporate sponsors present a staged presentation of how a restaurant operates as if it is reality?*

CONNECT

What is your favorite type of specialty restaurant?

The Lobster Tale

Red Lobster In the 1960s, America was ready for a new kind of restaurant—one that would bring the best elements of fast food and fine dining together. Bill Darden found the perfect balance when he opened Red Lobster in 1968. He worked to deliver great customer service, good food, and fast turnaround times at low prices. The casual seafood restaurant was an immediate hit in Lakewood, Florida. At that time, casual-dining restaurants began to fill a developing niche.

REVISITING RED LOBSTER

Decades later, Darden Restaurants became the largest casual-dining company in the United States. The business expanded its lineup to include Olive Garden, Bahama Breeze, and Smokey Bones BBQ Sports Bar.

However, by late 2003, Red Lobster faced sinking sales and declining numbers of customers. Red Lobster added pricy new items to the menu and offered all-you-can eat promotions. Some analysts thought these items alienated longtime customers and reduced profits. Red Lobster needed a comeback strategy. In 2004, executives revamped the menu for moderate $10 to $15 entrees and cut down on costly giveaways. They also brought back an old catch phrase: "For the seafood lover in you." Initial results have been positive as this lobster tale continues.

1. In what type of restaurant category does Red Lobster belong?
2. How do you think Red Lobster can attract more customers?

Chains

chain a type of business that has more than one location with the same name under the same ownership

A **chain** is a type of business that has more than one location with the same name under the same ownership. Chain restaurants promise customers consistency of product and experience. Examples of this type of restaurant include Outback Steakhouse® and Olive Garden. Chain restaurants rely on the strength of the brand to promote their services and the volume of their business. Chains are less risky investments than traditional restaurants.

Franchises

franchise a type of business that is set up through a franchise agreement, which is a contract between a franchisor and franchisee to sell a company's goods or services at a designated location

A **franchise** is a type of business that is set up through a franchise agreement, which is a contract between a franchisor and franchisee to sell a company's goods or services at a designated location. Franchising in the hospitality industry is the system of expanding or operating a business under a recognized brand name. Franchisees consider themselves independent businesspersons who report to the franchisor. Franchises include restaurants such as Subway™ and McDonald's®.

Independents

Most successful independent restaurants have owners who are well known and respected in the community. An independent restaurant can create its own image with its menu, ambiance, and style of service. The personal service by an independent restaurant is difficult to match.

Restaurants Within Other Properties

Free-standing facilities as well as other types of properties house commercial restaurants. These properties include private clubs, sports and theme parks, retail establishments, and lodging establishments.

Private Clubs

Private clubs offer a variety of dining options for members and their guests. A typical country club has a snack bar, lounge area, banquet space, and formal dining room. After golfing, a game of tennis, swimming, or yachting, club members can relax in the restaurant and enjoy favorite recipes and exquisite service. For less-formal occasions, guests can use the snack bar or lounge. Primarily for business clientele, city clubs offer private dining in a downtown setting. City clubs also cater to social organizations, athletic interests, professional groups, and fraternal societies.

Sports and Theme Parks

Previously known for serving only snacks or fast food, stadiums, arenas, theme parks, and recreational areas now provide a variety of dining establishments. For traditionalists, hot dogs and peanuts are available, along with more elaborate food service. Private dining rooms with VIP or club seating, modern microbrew pubs, chain restaurants, food courts, and concession stands provide food service.

Retail Establishments

Shopping is a favorite pastime of travelers and residents. As a result, malls have become destinations. Many chains and QSRs profit from providing convenient locations for shoppers and mall employees. Some restaurants are located in mall locations, such as food courts, while others are owned and operated independently by retailers within malls.

Lodging Establishments

Since most travelers prefer to experiment with local restaurants outside of a hotel, full-service properties offer in-house restaurants as a courtesy to overnight guests. Venues can range from coffee shops to lounges or pubs to traditional restaurants in the midprice range. As a result of this trend, many lodging businesses have leased their dining spaces to well-known chain or franchise restaurants. Thus, guests experience the convenience of in-house dining with the prestige of a name-brand eatery.

LARGE ESTABLISHMENTS Large lodging businesses offer banquet or catering departments to service a number of daily on-site and off-premise functions. Catering functions, such as weddings, corporate banquets, and sales meetings, can produce a great deal of food-service revenue. Room service, or in-room dining, provides an alternative for guests who seek a quick, relaxed, and private quality dining experience.

MARKETING SERIES *Online*

Remember to check out this book's Web site for information on the restaurant business and more great resources at **marketingseries.glencoe.com**.

Tipping, though voluntary, is a common practice for full-service and delivery-style food service in the United States. Tips can amount to over 50 percent of a service provider's annual income.

QUESTION

Why do primary and secondary schools operate food-service programs?

On-Site Facilities

On-site facilities provide meal options primarily for customers directly involved with a property, such as employees of a corporate building or hospital. Food is not the primary service the particular facility provides, but it serves as a convenience or source of revenue for the facility. The primary businesses or organizations manage or operate some of these venues, called *self-ops*. Third parties manage other food-service facilities called managed services.

Some types of on-site facilities include:

- Primary/secondary schools

- Colleges and universities

- Health-care facilities

- Business and industry

- Military

- Airlines and airports

- Correctional facilities

- Convenience stores

Primary and Secondary Schools

To address circumstances, such as more underprivileged students and women in the workforce, schools have offered food-service programs since the 1940s. Most schools with government funding provide nutritious lunches. Since 1998, many school cafeterias also serve breakfast.

SCHOOL MEAL OPTIONS School kitchens have a variety of options for providing nutritious food:

- Schools may prepare and serve their own meals.

- Larger districts may operate central commissaries, or cafeterias.

- Schools may purchase ready-to-serve meals.

- Schools may allow popular QSR chains to provide on-site meals.

NUTRITION AWARENESS The menu-planning process for school food service changed due to consumer demand. Smaller portions and lighter, healthier foods are offered to combat childhood obesity. In addition, most students receive nutrition education in schools.

Colleges and Universities

Colleges and universities have changed traditional meal plans to accommodate the demands of a more sophisticated college-student market. Flexible meal plans, extended dining hours, take-out service, kiosks, and college supermarkets have replaced the college cafeteria. Most campuses offer dining options in the form of faculty clubs, student unions, catering services, convenience stores, and vending machines.

◄ COOL SCHOOL FOOD
Hungry students have more options today for on-site food services. *What chain restaurant might be successful if placed on a college campus?*

Health-Care Facilities

Health-care facilities include hospitals and extended-stay residences, such as nursing home-care centers. The challenge for these facilities is to provide specialized nutrition services to a variety of patients on budgets set by federal guidelines. These facilities provide extended-hour food service for patients, their visitors, and health-care employees. They also provide food service for special events such as barbecues and birthday celebrations for patients. Many health-care facilities prepare home-meal replacements for ambulatory residents in the local community. Lobby kiosks, vending services, coffee shops, and in-house bakeries are all classified under health-care food service.

Business and Industry

Business and industry facilities provide in-house offerings to employees, guests, and prospective clients. Their emphasis is on menu variety and speed of service. Some companies provide operations ranging from executive dining rooms to coffee shops with limited service. Some business facilities also house specialty restaurants.

Military

Military food service focuses on troops and officers stationed abroad and at home in all branches of the military. Recent increases in personnel from the National Guard reserves have caused a growth in the military food-service sector. The traditional "mess hall," officers' clubs, military hospitals, and facilities in the field of operations all provide dining service. Many limited-service chains operate at military outposts to provide options to troops that are stationed on and off military bases.

Airlines and Airports

In-flight food-service providers must serve appealing and tasty food at the right temperature for 200 or more passengers at a time. However, with the exception of first-class service, most airlines today provide only basic options for travelers. Some low-cost airlines offer only beverage service with a snack. Airport restaurants, including recognized chains and franchises, continue to expand options, providing "food on the fly" for passengers on their way to the next destination.

Correctional Facilities

Budget limitations, basic nutrition, and safety determine the quality of food service at penitentiaries. Many inmates at minimum-security prisons train for food-service careers in areas such as baking and pastry arts.

Convenience Stores

Convenience stores receive 30 percent of their gross profits from food service. Some convenience-store formats include kiosks, mini-marts, limited-service, and hyper stores. Food offerings may include confections, beverages, snacks, baked goods, and fast food.

Range of Food Service

The food-service segment of the hospitality industry includes restaurants for every taste and price range. Whether you feel like dining out or taking out, the variety is endless. Talented and eager individuals are in high demand in food service to satisfy the ever-changing needs of customers. Opportunities exist on all levels of this growing industry for front- and back-of-the-house positions, as discussed in Section 3.2.

Quick Check ✓

RESPOND to what you've read by answering these questions.

1. What is a full-service restaurant? _____

_____

_____

2. What are three examples of specialty restaurants? _____

_____

_____

3. What are on-site dining facilities? _____

_____

_____

Restaurant Operations

Restaurant Organization

The success of any food-service establishment depends on many factors, including the quality of its operations. Most restaurants are divided into two areas: front of the house and back of the house. The **front of the house** is the area in a hospitality establishment that guests view, such as the entrance and dining room. The **back of the house** is the area in a hospitality establishment that guests usually do not view, including all areas responsible for food quality and production, such as the kitchen and receiving, office, and storage areas. Understanding the operations in these areas is essential for any hospitality professional.

General Manager

The general manager (GM) is responsible for the overall management of front- and back-of-the-house operations. (See **Figure 3.2** on page 60.) General managers create weekly, monthly, and annual budgets based on predicted sales. They forecast the number of guests, or covers, to be served and the amount of the average guest check. Based on these calculations, the general manager determines the number of staff members needed for each shift at each station in the restaurant.

Front of the House

Front-of-the-house operations focus on professionally servicing and satisfying the guest in a QSR or a fine-dining establishment.

Front-of-the-House Service

The tasks at the front of the house depend on the facility. Front-of-the-house service generally includes the following functions:

1. **Initial impression**—exterior appeal, cleanliness, parking, and valet
2. **Greeting**—welcome greeting and fulfilling seating preference
3. **Taking and transmitting orders**—introduction and presentation of specials, upselling, and confirmation of customer orders
4. **Serving food**—delivering meals, refilling beverages, and presenting dessert specials
5. **Presenting bill**—accepting payment, thanking the guest, and inviting the guest to return
6. **Preparing for next guest**—clearing table, resetting, and restocking

Positions

Front-of-the-house hospitality employees are public figures who provide individual attention to each guest's unique needs. Each member of the front-of-the house staff contributes to the guests' dining experience.

ASSISTANT MANAGER Many GMs have assistant managers to supervise day-to-day operations. These assistants may also be responsible for opening or closing the facility.

OPENING MANAGER The opening manager unlocks the facility including all storage or walk-in areas. This person also checks cleanliness and overall sanitation. These managers ensure that all systems—electrical, refrigeration, and plumbing—are working properly. They make sure the proper staff is available for each shift.

CLOSING MANAGER The closing manager is the last to leave the restaurant and checks security, sanitation, and preparations for the next day's service.

Figure 3.2

Positions at Front and Back of the House

FOOD-SERVICE ORGANIZATION The legendary French chef Escoffier was the innovator of organized kitchen "brigades." *Which area of a restaurant requires more service from its staff?*

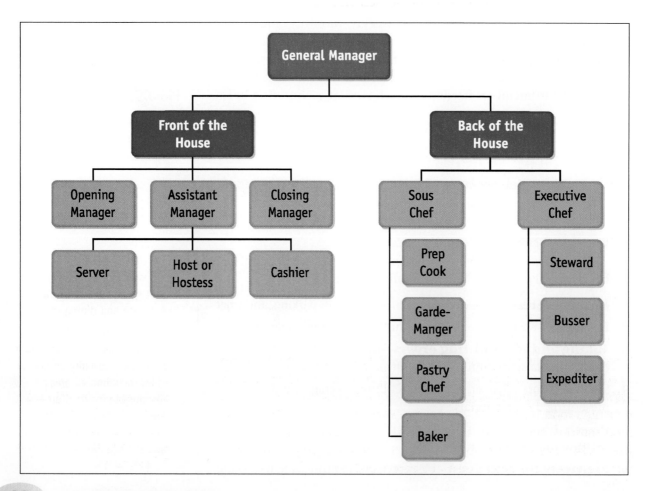

CASHIER A cashier's main responsibility is handling money and returning change to guests. The cashier reports the receipts and may prepare bank deposits.

HOST AND/OR HOSTESS The host or hostess stands near the entrance at a table or stand. He or she provides the initial greeting to guests, seats guests, and takes reservations by phone.

SERVER Servers have the most direct contact with guests. They discuss the menu, offer suggestions, deliver the orders, clear the table, and present the check. Servers may work as part of a team with bussers.

BUSSER In larger or moderately sized restaurants, bussers, or buspersons, assist servers and clear tables, pour water, and deliver food.

BARTENDER In restaurants that have full-service bars, the bartender has multiple functions in the restaurant. This is the only staff member who might take the guest's order, prepare it, and deliver it to the guest. This person also assists the servers with all drink orders.

Back of the House

Although not seen by the guest, operations in the back of the house are vital to the dining experience. The staff in this area of the restaurant is responsible not only for food preparation, or production, but also for safety, sanitation, cost control, purchasing, storage, receiving, and control for the restaurant. Back-of-the-house staff performs these tasks:

- Plan menu.

- Prepare food and beverages.

- Determine product specifications.

- Develop purchase orders.

- Obtain bids or quotes.

- Select and contact vendors.

- Place orders or award contracts.

- Receive and inspect deliveries or shipments.

- Store and issue products.

- Evaluate service and products.

Production and Kitchen Positions

Depending on the size of the property, production is handled by a chef, head cook, or food-production manager. In larger facilities, a team assists with meal production. **Production** is an assembly-line process by which food is prepared, plated, and expedited by teams at various food stations, such as salad, cooking line, prep, and dessert. Some of the kitchen positions are executive chef, sous chef, prep cook, garde-manger, pastry chef, baker, steward, and expediter.

TECH NOTES

Restaurants Go Wireless

Wireless technology can streamline the processes of seating customers and placing orders in restaurants. When a staff member notices that a customer is leaving, he or she can use a handheld wireless device to communicate the location of the table directly to the hostess station. Computer software signals a waiting customer's pager to announce the available table. Servers can also use handheld wireless devices to send orders to the kitchen instantly.

➡ List three ways that wireless technology can improve restaurant operations after reading information through **marketingseries.glencoe.com**.

production an assembly-line process by which food is prepared, plated, and expedited by teams at various food stations

► **BEHIND THE SCENES**
Guests rarely know how much time and effort go into their meals that take only minutes to consume.
Which staff member(s) would be responsible for good sanitation in the kitchen?

CONNECT

Have you ever been in a restaurant kitchen during operating hours? If so, how busy was it?

EXECUTIVE CHEF The executive chef reports to the GM and oversees the daily operations of the back of the house. This chef is a trained professional cook who must also be a good manager. The executive chef performs duties such as hiring, training, and supervising employees and planning meals at the right price.

SOUS CHEF The sous chef (or "sauce chef") assists the executive chef in the daily operations. This chef is the second in command in the kitchen. He or she is involved in the daily food production, overseeing quality, consistency, and presentation of all items produced.

PREP COOK The prep cook assists in a specific area of the kitchen. This staff member performs *mis en place*, which is the French term used for preparing the workstation for the shift. *Mis en place* includes chopping vegetables; restocking oils, butter, spices and wine; and organizing the workstation to allow the chefs to work efficiently.

GARDE-MANGER This staff member makes all garnishes that are used in preparation of food. The garde-manger also makes platters and display items for buffets and other special presentations.

PASTRY CHEF The pastry chef prepares sweets and cakes. This person works closely with the baker. If there is no baker, the pastry chef performs those duties as well.

BAKER The baker makes all breads and cakes. This person works in the same area of the kitchen as does the pastry chef.

STEWARD Stewards oversee china, silverware, glassware, linen, and small items, such as salt and pepper shakers, vases, and candle holders.

EXPEDITER This staff member is the link between the front of the house and the back of the house. The expediter communicates an order to the kitchen staff. When the order has been prepared, the expediter makes sure it leaves the kitchen promptly.

Production and Other Operations

Production is critical to the success of any restaurant's concept and menu. Efficient production helps control portions, waste, and therefore, costs. Managers and the executive chef calculate production sheets to ensure that enough products are on hand for each meal and station. Standardized recipes are then created, following particular specifications, to provide consistent quality in terms of portion control, cook and/or prep time, seasoning, and delivery.

Purchasing

Purchasing includes not only paying for a product or service, but also the selection and obtaining of that item. When purchasing, buyers may choose from a variety of different brands to select the best alternatives. They also need to compare suppliers' services relating to timeliness, quality, and company specifications. Regardless of the size of the operation, some common purchasing activities include maintaining an adequate supply of products, establishing and maintaining quality standards, negotiating the best price, and maintaining a competitive advantage.

Inventory

Maintaining and tracking inventory is vital for any successful business. The most commonly used inventory system for restaurants in the United States is FIFO, or first-in-first-out. This method requires older items to be used before more recently delivered items. New items are stocked behind older ones to ensure that the system is followed properly.

PAR The PAR is the amount of each item that the restaurant wants to keep in stock. Having this amount on hand can offset missed deliveries, deliveries of defective items or spoiled goods, and any unforeseen circumstance in which an order did not arrive on time. The PAR ensures that the establishment does not run out of an item before the next delivery, even when a scheduled delivery is cancelled.

Case Study | PART 2

ANOTHER PLATE OF MIND
Continued from Part 1 on page 49

The restaurant was a success, but sales had not increased at Hangawi. So, recognizing its diners' appreciation of a restaurant's ambiance and visual appeal, the Hangawi management began selling tea sets, candles, and other specialty items. When ancillary sales proved to be successful, plans were made to open a teahouse called Franchia.

The atmosphere at Franchia teahouse is designed to be more casual than at Hangawi. Visitors keep their shoes on. The three-story teahouse offers lighter fare, such as fresh salads, silken noodles, and vegetable dumplings. However, tea is the main event. Several grades of tea are on the menu—each with its own medicinal or spiritual benefits. Guests can also take classes to learn how to present a traditional tea service. Like the restaurant that inspired it, Franchia's combination of flavor, health, and atmosphere has proven to be a success.

ANALYZE AND WRITE
1. Who would be the main kitchen staff members at a restaurant such as Hangawi? Make a list.
2. Do you think keeping fresh produce in stock for a vegetarian restaurant would be more challenging than for a restaurant serving all types of food? Write a short paragraph in response.

BURGER KNOW-HOW

Larry Harnick
President
Blue Moon Burgers

What is your job?
"I operate a hamburger chain called Blue Moon Burgers."

What do you do in your job?
"I open new locations and train managers to run restaurants according to our requirements. Since most restaurants have very poor success records, you must identify the reasons why they fail. Some of the reasons are lack of knowledge as to what the market desires, lack of consistency in product preparation, poor management skills, poor location, and understaffing."

What kind of training did you have?
"I haven't received any formal training, but I have worked in the industry for a number of years."

What advice would you give students?
"It is very important to completely understand all aspects of the business. Anyone wishing to enter the industry should first work in the field for a few years. You must understand all the employee duties within your business to properly appreciate the value of the team components. When offering your product, make it the best it can be. A customer must find value in what you serve them. If they do not, then they will not come back. Know your competition."

What is your key to success?
"Giving the people what they want at an affordable price—and never compromising quality for increased profits."

Why is it important for management to understand the duties of each employee? What might be the duties of employees at Blue Moon Burgers? Give three examples.

Career Data: Restaurant Manager

Education and Training High school diploma, bachelor's degree in business and management, and/or real-world experience

Skills and Abilities Interpersonal, time-management, organizational skills

Career Outlook As fast as average growth through 2012

Career Path Any entry-level position to high-level opportunities

Return on Investment

In the food-service industry, an operator can either increase sales or reduce costs to generate more profits, or receive a return on investment. **Return on investment (ROI)** is a calculation used to determine the ability of a product to generate profits.

return on investment (ROI) a calculation used to determine the ability of a product to generate profits

Increasing Profits

One way to increase sales is to increase the average check amount. Amounts can increase by raising prices or by selling more items, such as dessert, wine, bottled water, or appetizers. A second strategy to boost sales is to increase the number of customers, or covers, through better marketing and advertising campaigns. Each strategy has costs associated with it.

Costs

Cost of sales measures the cost of products consumed by the guest. The most common costs are: 1) food cost, or the cost of food prepared for and served to customers, and 2) beverage/bar costs, or the cost of ingredients used for beverages served to customers. Managers and executive chefs have formulas for calculating such costs:

Calculating Food-Cost Percentage

Food sales for the period	$6,000
− Starting inventory	($2,000)
− Purchases	($1,000)
=	$3,000
− Spoiled items	($200)
− Employee meals	($300)
− Complimentary meals	($500)
= Cost of Goods Sold	$2,000

Formula: $\dfrac{\text{Cost of goods sold}}{\text{Sales}} \times 100 = \text{Food-Cost Percentage}$

Example: $\dfrac{\$2,000}{\$6,000} \times 100 = 33.3\%$

KEEPING TABS
Technological tools help restaurants keep accurate records of check amounts and food costs. *What other technology equipment is useful for restaurant operations?*

Math Check

MARKETING COSTS

Sari signed a $1 million contract for a marketing program for her restaurant chain. The contract calls for five equal payments. How much is each payment?

➡️ For tips on finding the solution, go to **marketingseries.glencoe.com.**

QUESTION

What are the most common costs of products consumed by customers?

Cost Reduction

Restaurants can also increase profits by reducing costs and increasing efficiency through applying portion control, monitoring usage, and controlling breakage of dishes and other equipment. Many restaurants use point-of-sale systems (POS) to create efficiency. These handheld devices allow the staff to send orders to the kitchen or bar quickly.

Budget Tools

To control costs, restaurants create annual budgets. Budgets measure fixed costs, which are items that are constant regardless of volume of business. Budgets also measure variable costs, which are expenses that fluctuate, based on volume such as payroll benefits and marketing. To measure profit, the restaurant industry uses the Uniform System of Accounts (USAR). This standard allows comparison between restaurants by measuring expenses.

BALANCE SHEET A balance sheet compares what an operator owns (assets) to what he or she owes (liabilities). This demonstrates the financial reliability of the business.

INCOME STATEMENT An income statement visually displays the income received, the cost of sales, and expenses on a monthly or annual basis.

Working Together

Despite advances in restaurant concepts and operations, food quality and guest satisfaction remain the critical factors for every type of commercial or on-site, food-service facility. Both the front- and back-of-the-house staffs must work as a team to ensure that a restaurant maintains the standards necessary to compete in the fast-paced and challenging industry of hospitality.

Quick Check

RESPOND to what you've read by answering these questions.

1. How would you define the term *front of the house*? _____

_____

_____

2. How would you define the term *back of the house*? _____

_____

_____

3. What are three purchasing activities? _____

_____

_____

 marketingseries.glencoe.com

Name _____   Date _____

Worksheet 3.1

Your Favorite Restaurant

Visit your favorite restaurant. Take this worksheet and answer the following questions:

1. What is the name of the restaurant? _____
_____

2. What type of restaurant is this? Full service? Fine dining? Casual dining? _____
_____
_____

3. What types of food does this restaurant serve? _____
_____
_____
_____

4. Is this restaurant located within another property? If so, what type of property? _____
_____
_____
_____

5. What appeals to you about this restaurant? The food? Decor? Atmosphere? _____
_____
_____
_____

6. Describe your favorite experience at this restaurant. Then use this information to write a script for a 30-second radio ad for the restaurant. _____
_____
_____
_____

   Radio Ad _____
_____
_____
_____
_____

Name _____ Date _____

Worksheet 3.2

Compare and Contrast Restaurants

Compare and contrast a favorite restaurant with one that you may dislike.

Restaurant I Like: _____

    Initial impression _____

    Ordering _____

    Presenting food _____

    Presenting the food _____

    Preparing for the next guest _____

Restaurant I Dislike: _____

    Initial impression _____

    Ordering _____

    Presenting food _____

    Presenting the food _____

    Preparing for the next guest _____

Ways to Improve: _____

_____

_____

_____

_____

_____

_____

_____

Portfolio Works

NEW RESTAURANT

Create a concept for a restaurant and describe the following elements:

Name of Restaurant: _____

_____

_____

Type of Restaurant: _____

_____

_____

Market: _____

_____

_____

Location: _____

_____

_____

Atmosphere: _____

_____

_____

Concept: _____

_____

_____

Menu (items for one dinner): _____

_____

_____

Add this page to your career portfolio.

CHAPTER SUMMARY

Section 3.1 **Types of Restaurants**

commercial site (p. 50)
on-site facility (p. 50)
full-service restaurant
   (p. 51)
quick-service restaurant
   (QSR) (p. 52)
chain (p. 54)
franchise (p. 54)

• A commercial site is an establishment such as a restaurant where a food-and-beverage business competes for customers. An on-site facility is an institutional or noncommercial establishment where meals are provided for people directly involved with the property.

• The commercial food-service industry has many categories, such as full-service, fine-dining, casual-dining, limited-service, quick-service, and specialty establishments.

• Different types of restaurant businesses include a chain, a type of business that has more than one location with the same name under the same ownership; a franchise, a type of business set up through a franchise agreement; and an independent, which is independently owned and is distinguished by service and flexibility.

Section 3.2 **Restaurant Operations**

front of the house
   (p. 59)
back of the house (p. 59)
production (p. 61)
return on investment
   (ROI) (p. 64)

• Front-of-the-house operations occur in the area that guests view, such as the entrance and dining room. Back-of-the-house operations take place in the area that guests usually do not view, including the kitchen and receiving, office, and storage areas.

• Restaurants can increase profits in two ways: 1) by increasing check amount by raising prices or selling more and 2) by increasing the number of customers through marketing.

CHECKING CONCEPTS

1. **Identify** the primary difference between commercial and on-site facilities.
2. **Cite** the factors all food-service establishments must consider.
3. **Name** three examples of on-site facilities.
4. **Describe** examples of food-service options available at colleges and universities.
5. **Define** a chain restaurant business.
6. **Define** a franchise restaurant business.
7. **Identify** the staff members who work in both the front and back of the house.

Critical Thinking

8. **Discuss** some strategies that might increase business in a failing restaurant.

CROSS-CURRICULUM SKILLS

Work-Based Learning

Interpersonal Skills—Teaching Others

9. With a partner, create a poster-size graphic organizer that charts and describes both the front- and back-of-the-house restaurant positions.

Thinking Skills—Seeing Things in the Mind's Eye

10. Imagine a restaurant that you would like to operate. Describe in detail your restaurant to a peer. Include the food you want to serve, the décor, and the atmosphere with as much detail as you can imagine.

School-Based Learning

Language Arts

11. Think of experiences with family or friends in two restaurants. Write an essay that compares and contrasts the restaurants.

Social Studies

12. Use the Internet or library to research a restaurant in a different country. What type of restaurant did you find? What food is served? Prepare a short report of your findings.

 **CONNECTION**

Role Play: Restaurant Manager

SITUATION You are to assume the role of manager of a highly successful, fine-dining restaurant located in a popular downtown hotel. The restaurant is known for its high-quality meals and creative presentations. You have received requests to provide catering for private parties and meals in customers' homes. The hotel does not currently offer catering. You have considered the idea and researched the costs and other factors before offering catering service from your restaurant.

You are to present your ideas to the hotel's general manager (judge) during a meeting to be held in one-half hour.

EVALUATION You will be evaluated on how well you meet the following performance indicators:

- Develop a project plan.
- Arrange special services for customers.
- Forecast sales.
- Develop the program's budget.
- Explain types of business risk.

 **INTERNET ACTIVITY**

Use the Internet to locate a restaurant in your community or a nearby community.

- Click on any restaurant.
- Write down the address of the restaurant.
- Go to MapQuest for a map of the community.
- Type in the address of the restaurant.
- Find the restaurant on the map and print the map.
- Circle the restaurant's location on the map.

➡ For a link to MapQuest to do this activity, go to **marketingseries.glencoe.com**.

Chapter 4

The Hotel Business

Section 4.1
Types of Lodging Businesses

Section 4.2
Hotel Operations

Chapter Objectives

- Identify the types of hotel classifications.
- Differentiate between business and leisure guests.
- Explain the importance of yield management.
- Identify the front-office positions in the rooms division of a hotel.
- Describe guest services in the hotel industry.
- Identify the support-staff positions in the back of the house of a hotel.

DESERT CHIC

In 1999, Fraser Robertson and his wife Sarah Robarts moved from London to Palm Springs, California, and proceeded to renovate the local lodging business. The couple purchased the neglected Mira Loma hotel, built in 1938 and popular through the 1950s. They restored the hotel with an emphasis on the styles that were popular during its heyday and renamed it Ballantines Original. The rooms are decorated with celebrity themes, such as Marilyn Monroe, James Dean, and Audrey Hepburn. Vintage chrome toasters and shocking-orange rugs are mixed and matched with modern designer furnishings by Ray and Charles Eames and Herman Miller.

The stylish but affordable hotel was an instant hit, gaining exposure in magazine articles and as a set for fashion photo shoots. *Condé Nast Traveler* magazine described the hotel as "kitschy glam meets modernist chic." The unique hotel also appealed to trendy travelers. However, with only 14 rooms and rising competition, how could Robertson and Robarts keep their stylish lodging business growing?

ANALYZE AND WRITE

1. What type of hotel is Ballantines Original? Write a paragraph explaining your answer.
2. In a few sentences, describe the customer group that Ballantines Original Hotel targets.

Case Study Part 2 on page 87

CASE STUDY See the Teacher Manual for answers.

LESSON PLAN See the Teacher Manual for the Chapter 4 planning guide and lesson plan.

POWER READ

Be an active reader and use these reading strategies:

PREDICT what the section will be about.

CONNECT what you read with your own life.

QUESTION as you read to make sure you understand the content.

RESPOND to what you've read.

Types of Lodging Businesses

AS YOU READ ...

YOU WILL LEARN

- To identify the types of hotel classifications.
- To differentiate between business and leisure guests.
- To explain the importance of yield management.

WHY IT'S IMPORTANT

Every type of lodging facility focuses on generating revenue. Understanding the characteristics of lodging facilities allows marketers to target specific customers.

KEY TERMS

- transient guest
- meal plan
- yield management
- average daily rate (ADR)
- occupancy percentage (OCC%)
- revenue per available room (revPAR)

PREDICT

What are some categories of guests who use hotels?

Lodging Businesses

According to the American Hotel and Lodging Association, the United States has more than 47,040 properties, generating 2 million jobs and $102.6 billion in sales. These properties come in all shapes and sizes. While early lodging businesses became popular due to their easy accessibility via rail or highway, today's facilities may be destinations.

Classification of Facility

In the past, all lodging properties built near highways were called motels. The guest rooms in these facilities could be accessed through exterior doors or public courtyards. Hotels, on the other hand, were most often located in city centers. Hotel guest-room access was limited to doors in central interior corridors. Today, however, many different types of lodging facilities are available. Lodging classification is based on four factors:

- Guest type
- Price
- Location
- Style and function

Guest Type

Guests can be classified into two major categories—business guests or leisure guests. Subcategories of guests are identified by type of travel or stay. Four subcategories include walk-in, transient, corporate, and group guests. Most lodging businesses may choose one or two types of guests and focus on that market segment when designing products and promotional campaigns.

BUSINESS GUESTS Business guests are traveling for business purposes and include convention attendees, association professionals, or corporate managers. Most business travel is short term in nature and is necessary for the success of the business.

LEISURE GUESTS Leisure or vacation guests can range from single individuals to groups of family and friends. Leisure travel is discretionary in nature, or done by personal choice, and so leisure guests may stay at lodging facilities for longer time periods.

TYPE OF STAY Guests are classified by type of travel or stay. The four categories are:

- **Walk-in**—A walk-in is a guest without a reservation.

- **Transient**—A **transient guest** is an individual traveler with a reservation, staying in a hospitality property for a maximum of 30 consecutive days.

- **Corporate**—A corporate guest is an individual or group traveler with a reservation made with a corporate rate negotiated between the hotel and the guest's company.

- **Group**—A group guest is a traveler who receives a special rate negotiated between the group and the hotel. Group travelers can be corporate or SMERF, which means social, military, educational, religious, or fraternal.

Price

Lodging properties typically have price categories—budget, midprice, and upscale.

BUDGET Budget, or economy, properties are inexpensive hotels with limited services. They offer a standard sleeping room and bath. Food service is limited.

MIDPRICE Midprice, or midscale, properties provide standard sleeping rooms and baths. However, unlike budget properties, these facilities have more rooms, amenities, and food-and-beverage options.

UPSCALE Upscale, or luxury, properties combine desirable location with a full array of features and services, such as full-service dining, recreation, and meeting space.

ROOM PRICE The price of a room within a property is based on a number of factors:

- **Location of Property**—The location of the property can be the single most important factor determining the rate of the room. A desirable location carries a higher price.

- **Location of Room**—The location of the room in the property can also affect a rate. An upper-floor, oceanfront room, for example, will be more expensive than a room near a parking lot.

- **Amenities**—The amenities and the size of the room impact its price.

- **Length of Stay**—The length of stay may also affect a guest's rate. A loyal frequent guest will be afforded a better discount than a walk-in. A guest staying for two weeks will receive a better rate than an overnight transient guest.

- **Season**—"High season" is the most expensive season and the most desirable period because of holidays, vacations, or weather.

- **Type of Guest**—Discounts are available for senior citizens, business travelers, travel agents, members of AAA, or student groups.

transient guest an individual traveler with a reservation, staying in a hospitality property for a maximum of 30 consecutive days

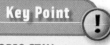

Key Point

HISTORIC STAY
The oldest hotel operating in the United States is Mills House in Charleston, North Carolina, built in 1853.

meal plan a room rate that includes meals; some choices of meal plans are: European Plan, Continental Plan, Bermuda Plan, Modified American Plan, and American Plan

CONNECT
What type of meal plan do you think is most popular? Why?

yield management a system of maximizing revenue through adjusting room rates according to demand

average daily rate (ADR) a rate based on total sales for the day divided by the total number of sold rooms

occupancy percentage (OCC%) a percentage calculated daily and based on the number of rooms sold as a percentage of the total number of available rooms

revenue per available room (revPAR) a rate that reflects a hotel's revenue per available room

■ **Meals**—Room rates, particularly in the United States, do not traditionally include meals. However, some all-inclusive resorts do include meals in their prices. A **meal plan** is a room rate that includes meals; some choices of meal plans are:

■ **European Plan (EP):** no meals included, room only.

■ **Continental Plan (CP):** continental breakfast included. Breakfast most often includes coffee/tea, rolls/toast, and jams.

■ **Bermuda Plan (BP):** full breakfast, coffee/tea, juice, toast, eggs, and sometimes breakfast meats.

■ **Modified American Plan (MAP):** full breakfast and lunch or dinner.

■ **American Plan (AP):** also called full pension/full board, includes three meals per day.

YIELD MANAGEMENT The goal of any hotel is to maintain a high occupancy rate. Occupancy is based on the supply (number of rooms available) and the demand (the number of guests needing sleeping rooms). Guests want to get the best value for the dollar. Hotels balance this against their goal of achieving a high daily rate. Most properties do this through yield management. **Yield management** is a system of maximizing revenue through adjusting room rates according to demand. Hotels use various formulas to calculate their rates. (See **Figure 4.1**.)

■ **Average Daily Rate (ADR)**—The ADR is a rate based on total sales for the day divided by the total number of rooms sold.

■ **Occupancy Percentage (OCC%)**—The OCC is a percentage calculated daily. It is based on the number of rooms sold as a percentage of the total number of available rooms.

■ **Revenue Per Available Room (RevPAR)**—RevPAR is a rate that reflects a hotel's revenue per available room. Room revenue is a good indicator of a hotel's performance.

Figure 4.1

Hospitality Yield Management

MAXIMIZING REVENUE
Hotels keep track of various rates, including occupancy rates and revenue collected, to know what rates should be charged. *What is the definition of yield management?*

Total Available Rooms:	500
Rooms Sold:	450
Revenue:	$56,250

ADR: revenue ÷ rooms sold = ADR
$56,250 ÷ 450 = $125

OCC%: rooms sold ÷ total available rooms = OCC%
50 ÷ 500 = .90 or 90%

RevPAR: revenue ÷ total available rooms = RevPAR
$56,250 ÷ 500 = $112.50

Location

It is said that you can change anything about a lodging property except its location. Therefore, location is a critical factor affecting the room rate that a property can charge its guests.

RESORTS Resort facilities are usually located in private or secluded areas. They provide a variety of recreational offerings to their guests, ranging from multiple pools, tennis courts, and golf courses to less-structured offerings, such as walking trails, beaches, and bike paths. Ski resorts specialize in winter sports, including snowshoeing, tobogganing, snowmobiling, and cross-country and downhill skiing. All resorts combine luxurious amenities, well-appointed guest rooms, dining options, and meeting or convention space with top-notch service. Resorts are destinations where guests may choose to remain for weekends or for more extended vacations.

AIRPORT Leisure travelers may use airport hotels the night before taking an early flight for an extended vacation. Business clients prefer airport properties as a central and convenient place for meetings and conventions. Airlines contract with airport properties for accommodations for their crews. Passengers, who may be stranded due to weather and other unforeseen circumstances, also use airport hotels.

HIGHWAY Roadside properties attract transient guests traveling to a final destination. These travelers, who are often families, seek accessible locations, convenient food-and-beverage offerings, and limited recreational facilities, such as pools, game rooms, and vending-machine services. The typical length of stay for guests at a highway property is one night.

DOWNTOWN City properties located in downtown areas cater to business, convention, and leisure travelers. Most of these lodging facilities are in desirable locations near theater, office, shopping, and fine-dining sites. Services range from food-and-beverage, business, meeting, and concierge services.

- **Business Services**—Business centers or in-room facilities, such as faxes, modems, computers, and printers

- **Meeting Services**—Audiovisual (A/V) equipment rentals, modems, and special decor

- **Concierge Services**—Arrangements for transportation, restaurant reservations, event reservations, entertainment tickets, and activities in the area

CONFERENCE CENTERS Conference or convention-center properties cater to guests attending large meetings or trade shows. Many of these accommodations are attached to a conference or civic center. These facilities specialize in handling groups of 500 or more persons. They provide assistance with audiovisual equipment and technical support, a range of meeting-room space, and numerous food-service outlets and recreational facilities.

Hot Property

Fantasy Inn

Madonna Inn The Madonna Inn of San Luis Obispo, California, has been inspiring journalists for years. In 1982, a *New York Times* writer called it "a dizzying blend of a Swiss Alpine village, an ice cream pie and Disneyland." In 2004, a writer for *The Telegraph* of London playfully described it as "too grotesque for words."

Alex Madonna opened the Madonna Inn on Christmas Eve in 1958. Dissatisfied with the professional architects he interviewed, Madonna designed the inn with his own larger-than-life style. Common areas, such as the restaurant, were decked out in the brightest shades of pink. Golden cherubs and an eight-foot-tall waterfall in the men's room made it the talk of the town. Even after the original 12 rooms burned down, Madonna was undaunted. He rebuilt, creating 109 guest rooms, each designed with a different theme. His wife Phyllis helped outfit rooms such as a caveman's lair, a Swiss chalet, a jungle-rock room, and a safari room.

MUST SEE

Perched beside Highway 101, the Madonna Inn is just one of many colorful roadside motels appealing to passing drivers. Its ability to provoke makes it unique. Countless articles have been written celebrating and mocking the caveman room and the pink decor. Madonna himself fought many battles with civic leaders over his development plans and the enormous pink billboard advertising the inn. Clearly, he wanted to give weary travelers a good reason to pull off the road.

1. What makes the Madonna Inn unique?
2. If you designed a hotel, what would it look like?

Style and Function

The style and function of a property are based on its usage. Style and function affect the services provided, the type of guest attracted to the facility, and guests' length of stay. Prices will vary based on style and function for different types of hotels, such as all-suite facilities, extended-stay facilities, bed-and-breakfasts, spas, boutique hotels, vacation properties, and retreat centers.

ALL SUITE All-suite facilities provide large guest rooms, complete with separate living-room areas. Most all-suite facilities provide business centers, laundry services, on-site food service, recreational opportunities, and concierge service. The goal of an all-suite property is to offer more amenities to travelers such as businesspeople or families needing additional space.

EXTENDED STAY Similar in nature to all-suite properties, extended-stay facilities provide additional space as well as more extensive kitchen areas. In addition to traditional business services, many also offer grocery shopping because on-site food is not always included. As the name implies, extended-stay properties are ideal for guests relocating to a new area or working on long-term work-related projects.

BED-AND-BREAKFASTS (B&BS) The concept of the bed-and-breakfast inn began in Europe when guests would stay in an owner's private home. Today most B&Bs offer 3 to 12 sleeping rooms with baths and outstanding personal service. Breakfast is included in the price; however, no traditional on-site restaurant is available. Whether seaside, in the mountains, or in the heart of a city, each property is unique.

SPAS Spas used to refer to resorts with natural hot-water springs. Today, however, spas include properties offering a variety of health-related services, such as yoga, massage, fitness, and stress-reduction techniques. Professional staff is on hand to provide pampering. On-site food service can range from gourmet cuisine to low-fat diet food.

BOUTIQUE HOTELS Boutique hotels offer guests a variety of interior styles, atmosphere, and image. Price ranges of rooms vary for these unique properties.

VACATION PROPERTIES Vacation properties, also known as *time shares*, allow guests the opportunity to purchase a fully furnished accommodation for a specific time period. Most owners pay an initial fee for use of the facility, and then a yearly maintenance fee. Condominiums with fully equipped kitchens, available parking, and laundry facilities are popular time-share offerings. Many upscale properties also include recreational amenities, such as pools, tennis courts, and exercise rooms.

Math Check

WHOLESALE TO RETAIL
Shore's Bed-and-Breakfast bought 15 lamps from a wholesaler. Each lamp wholesales for $5 with a 10 percent discount. What did the lamps cost?

➡For tips on finding the solution, go to **marketingseries.glencoe.com.**

QUESTION

What type of lodging facility offers kitchens in its rooms?

◄ **OUTSIDE OF THE BOX**
Boutique hotels are unique properties that specialize in providing a trendy image and artistic atmospheres to worldly, experienced travelers who desire something extra. *What characteristic distinguishes boutique hotels from B&Bs?*

World Market

Tree House in Africa

In a poem about trees, Robert Frost writes that he'd "like to get away from earth awhile." He might have been talking about Treetops in Kenya. Treetops was built just inside Kenya's Aberdare National Park in 1932. It was the first of Africa's treetop lodges. Dedicated to game watching, Treetops was originally two rooms nestled among the limbs of a wild fig tree. Today it overlooks a salt lick and watering holes for local wildlife. Its four-deck structure rests on stilts. The complex boasts glass-front lounges, a rooftop platform, open decks, and photographic "hides." The lodge also has installed bedside, animal-alert buzzers to wake sleepers. The 50 guest rooms are called "nests," and dining arrangements are communal. Although simple, Treetops offers a close-up look at lions, rhinos, giant forest hogs, water buffalo, and elephants. It also has been a retreat for the rich and famous. In 1952, one of its guests was Princess Elizabeth who learned she was about to be Queen of England while at Treetops.

Why do you think Treetops has enjoyed success for almost a century?

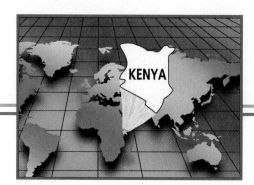

RETREAT CENTERS Retreat centers are designed for the executive business market. Offering secluded, private locations, many retreats are rustic in nature and lack modern conveniences such as televisions and in-room telephones. Food service is available.

For All Types of Travelers

Lodging accommodations come in all types and sizes to suit the needs of many kinds of guests. Travelers consider price, location, and style of a property when making reservations. Every lodging facility strives to provide guest service geared for its particular guests.

Quick Check

RESPOND to what you've read by answering these questions.

1. What are three different types of hotel properties? _____

_____

2. What are the two categories of hotel guests? _____

3. What are three factors that can determine the price of a room? _____

_____

Hotel Operations

Hotel Organization

All lodging accommodations, regardless of size, maintain a delicate balance between generating profit and servicing the public. Both of these functions are critical. A property that makes a great deal of money but provides few comforts of home for its guests will not be a long-term success.

Hotels have many revenue centers, all overseen by a general manager (GM). Similar to the general manager of a restaurant, the GM of a hotel is responsible for both front- and back-of-the-house operations. **Front of the house** is the area in a lodging facility that guests view, such as the lobby. **Back of the house** is the area in a lodging facility where support services take place, which guests usually do not view. The hotel operating staff consists of three segments: food-and-beverage (see Chapter 3), front-office, and support staff. (See **Figure 4.2** on page 83 for a complete staffing chart.)

The Rooms Division

The largest revenue center of a lodging facility is the rooms division. This center would include the front office, reservations, housekeeping, guest or uniformed services, and communications.

The Front Office

From a guest's perspective, the front office is considered the heart and soul of any property. This is the first and last contact area for a guest. As part of the front office, it is critical for front-desk personnel to provide prompt, efficient, and friendly service to every guest. The primary functions of the front-desk staff are to sell rooms, maintain accounts, and provide guest services.

Selling Rooms

Depending on the size of the property, the sales division or the reservations staff sells rooms during the day. In the evening, the front-desk staff assumes this responsibility.

Maintaining Accounts

Many lodging facilities have property management systems (PMS). These automated systems help the front-desk staff to store and access information about guest reservations, special requests, and billing instructions. Sophisticated information technology allows the front desk to provide better service while also reducing costs for the property.

THE Electronic CHANNEL

Hotels Online

Hotels.com books rooms at over 4,500 hotels throughout the world. Similar hotel booking services have made it easier and cheaper for travelers to find accommodations. These Web sites feature photos and descriptions of rooms and amenities. Rating systems help guests know the level of quality they can expect in a particular destination. Online reservation services also save travelers the hassle of calling and booking overseas rooms in different languages and time zones.

➡Visit an online hotel booking service and look at three different hotel options in the same city. Make a list of the information through **marketingseries.glencoe.com**.

night auditor the hotel staff member who does the night audit and balances the guests' accounts each evening

guest service agent (GSA) a hotel staff member who performs all of the functions of a desk clerk/agent, concierge, and valet

CONNECT

What work shift would you prefer if you were a front-desk clerk? Why?

Guest Services

Perhaps the most important task of the front-desk staff is providing exemplary guest service. Particularly during check-in, guests contact the front desk with questions, requests, and special needs. Clerks, or agents, and managers need to be familiar with the lodging property itself, the local attractions of the destination, and other services available for guests.

Positions

The front desk is staffed by a front-desk manager who oversees daily operations. Larger properties may also have an assistant front-desk manager to assist with these responsibilities, which include checking reports, reviewing occupancy and ADR, preparing for daily arrivals and departures, and checking staffing and scheduling requirements.

DAY-SHIFT POSITIONS Most properties have an A.M. and P.M. shift for front-desk staff. The day shift is responsible for handling guests during check-out. This includes notifying the housekeeping staff that guests have departed and designating which rooms are vacant. Clerks, or agents, on the day shift also monitor special requests for arriving guests such as VIPs.

EVENING-SHIFT POSITIONS The evening-shift staff is responsible for checking in guests as they arrive.

- **Clerks, or agents**—Like clerks working the day shift, these staff members answer questions from walk-in guests relating to the sale of rooms.

- **Night auditor**—The **night auditor** is the hotel staff member who does the night audit and balances the guests' accounts each evening. Night auditors post all charges, run reports, balance guest accounts, and create a daily report for the front-desk manager. Typically, the night auditor is part of the accounting department, but the position is the only front-of-the-house accounting position.

GUEST SERVICE AGENT Some properties may also employ a **guest service agent (GSA)**, a hotel staff member who performs all of the functions of a desk clerk/agent, concierge, and valet. A GSA greets the guest upon arrival, assigns a room, and escorts the guest to a room.

Reservations

Depending on the size of the property and its possible chain affiliation, guests can make room reservations directly with the property or through a centralized reservation system (CRS). For example, guests may telephone the property's reservation department or make arrangements for special events, such as conventions, through travel agents, meeting planners, or tour operators using a CRS.

Figure 4.2

Hotel Staffing

HOSPITALITY ORGANIZATION **From resorts to B&Bs, lodging establishments must have staff to perform all the necessary tasks expected by guests.** *How many employees might be needed for the front office of a beach resort hotel?*

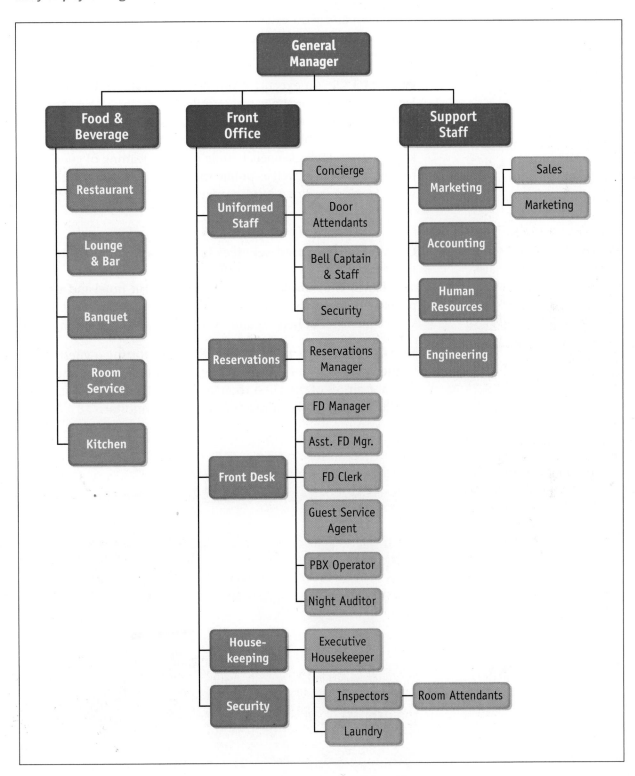

POSITIONS The reservation manager monitors room availability and pricing of rooms. The reservations department has a staff of agents with telephone and technical skills. It may be open from 8 A.M. to 6 P.M. Central reservation systems, accessed through 800 numbers or Web sites, operate 24 hours per day, seven days per week.

Housekeeping

The largest and most essential department in a hotel is the housekeeping department. This department directly affects a guest's perception of cleanliness, safety, and security at a property.

POSITIONS An executive housekeeper is the head of the housekeeping staff. He or she is responsible for leading a large and diverse staff. Larger properties may also employ an assistant housekeeper as well as a variety of supervisors, or inspectors, to oversee the housekeeping staff. Housekeepers handle routine cleaning of guest sleeping rooms and baths as well as public spaces, such as lobby areas and hallways. Laundry or linen services may be provided by this department.

Guest or Uniformed Services

guest or uniformed services staff members in uniforms, including the bell staff, valets, security officers, concierge, and door or garage attendants

Guest or uniformed services include staff members in uniforms: the bell staff, valets, security officers, concierge, and door and garage attendants. They wear the official uniform of the hotel and are the first people whom guests approach upon arrival at the property. The guest service manager or bell captain oversees these staff positions.

BELL STAFF The bell staff handles transporting a guest's luggage to the guest's room from the lobby area. A bell person also explains special features of the guest room and provides other services, such as refilling the ice bucket and adjusting the thermostat.

➤ **FRONT-DESK SERVICE One of the most important staff members at a hotel is the clerk because clerks deal directly with guests.** *What can clerks do to make a guest's stay an enjoyable experience?*

VALET STAFF The valet staff works closely with bell staff to ensure that a guest's automobile and luggage are safely transported to and from guestrooms. Door attendants are responsible for greeting the guest, assisting valet or bell staff, hailing taxis, and providing general information to the guest.

CONCIERGE The concierge position is found at larger properties, often in city or resort locations. The word *concierge* comes from the French term for "caretaker." The **concierge** is a hotel staff member who helps guests make arrangements for transportation, restaurant reservations, event reservations, and entertainment tickets, and advises guests about activities in the area. Most individuals in this position are extremely familiar with the local area and vendors. They may also speak more than one language.

SECURITY STAFF Security is a critical consideration in every hotel. Protecting the guest, the property, and guest valuables can mean dealing with a variety of situations. Most common security issues involve guest-room and key security, safety-deposit boxes, loss prevention, and emergency procedures. Technology assists in maintaining security in this area of the front office, but a uniformed staff member still serves as reassurance to the guests.

Communications

The communications department of a hotel is another revenue center. In-house communications can include voice mail, fax service, e-mail, message centers, and pagers. Often a responsibility of the front desk, PBX services are provided 24 hours daily. PBX, or Private Branch Exchange, is the generic name for the type of private telephone network systems used by many hospitality properties. These systems link individual room telephones with a central operator system. A PBX system has special features, such as multiple outside lines, faxing capabilities, wake-up calls, voice mail, intercom for calling within the property, 911, and many other features.

Systemwide Departments

Larger hotels, particularly chain properties, maintain centralized systems for groups of units. These departments would include sales and marketing functions, human resource or personnel planning, engineering and maintenance, and centralized accounting. Employees are classified as line employees and staff employees.

Line Employees

Line employees are in daily contact with the guests. They are considered front-of-the-house employees.

Staff Employees

Staff employees support the front of the house. They do not interact much with the guests. Examples of staff departments are human resources, accounting, and marketing.

marketingseries.glencoe.com

TECH NOTES

Hotels Check Out Kiosks
Several major hotel chains have installed computerized kiosks in their lobbies so that guests can register themselves. Business travelers are warming up to the new check-in procedures because they are already familiar with using kiosks at airports. Though many guests still seem to prefer the personal touch, a major benefit of having kiosks is the possibility of cutting costs by reducing customer-service staff. In the future, kiosks may allow hotel guests to do more tasks independently, such as printing airline boarding passes.

➡ Discuss the pros and cons of putting kiosks in hotel lobbies after reading information through **marketingseries.glencoe.com**.

concierge a hotel staff member who helps guests make arrangements for transportation, restaurant reservations, event reservations, and entertainment tickets, and advises guests about activities in the area

QUESTION
What issues might hotel security personnel handle?

TRAINING FOR HOSPITALITY

Carol Verret
Consultant and Trainer
Carol Verret & Associates

What do you do?

"I am a consultant and trainer for hospitality companies." Located in Colorado, Carol Verret & Associates helps train employees at hotels and other hospitality providers.

What do you do in your job?

"I serve clients in the hospitality industry who need help in the areas of sales, marketing, and customer service. It has been my experience that, in the hospitality industry, we do not train our sales associates as well as we could. Part of my mission in conducting sales training is to provide tools to sales associates that might not be available to them otherwise."

What kind of training did you have?

"After having served as vice president of marketing for Sunstone Hotels, I decided to embark on a consulting and training business. Part of my ability to advance rapidly in the hotel industry was due to the excellent sales training that I received on the job in another industry."

What advice would you give students?

"The hospitality industry is very contagious: Once you have been bitten by the bug, you will always want to work in it. Find an area that you love, and then seek training. If I had it to do over again, I would have focused my education on hospitality management. Though a degree is not necessary for success, it is a great foundation."

What is your key to success?

"I love the hospitality industry and the opportunities that it has given me. With a good grounding in the basics of an area that you love, it is possible to travel anywhere in the world and work in hospitality."

Why might sales training be important for a hospitality consultant?

Career Data: Hospitality Consultant

Education and Training
Bachelor's degree or master's degree in hospitality management or general business

Skills and Abilities
Administrative and interpersonal skills

Career Outlook Faster than average growth through 2012

Career Path Entry-level sales positions to higher-level sales-related positions

Support Staff

Behind the scenes of every lodging establishment, various departments and staff contribute to operations and maintenance. Support staff in the back of the house includes engineers, groundskeepers, attendants, sales and marketing staff, and human resources staff.

Engineers

Engineering is critical to the safe and secure image of a property. Often referred to as facilities maintenance, this department oversees the hotel's physical plant, buildings, and grounds. If a hotel is large, it may employ a chief engineer to oversee operations and supervise staff. The staff attends to the daily operations and maintenance of heating and air conditioning systems, refrigeration units, lighting, elevator systems, and other utilities.

Groundskeepers and Attendants

The groundskeepers maintain and upgrade the exterior of the facility by landscaping the property. At resort properties, other attendants will oversee recreational facilities such as pools, tennis courts, and golf courses. Hotels with internal recreational facilities, such as health clubs or spas, will contract out these services or employ additional staff for maintenance purposes. Maintenance staff is also needed for on-site, audiovisual equipment and arcade games, if these features are offered by the property. Smaller lodging properties may employ one or two individuals to handle all routine maintenance and repairs.

Sales and Marketing Staff

Sales and marketing departments persuade guests to stay at a particular property or chain. At smaller properties, the general manager is responsible for this function. In chain facilities, a centralized system is used to measure marketing results. Chapter 16 discusses these functions.

SALES STAFF The sales force of a lodging business may include different types of sales personnel:

- Sales representatives
- Sales assistants
- Technical-support staff
- Telemarketers

RESERVATIONS DEPARTMENT Though not always categorized with the sales staff, reservation specialists speak with a majority of a facility's guests. Training reservation staff in sales techniques results in higher occupancy rates.

Case Study PART 2

DESERT CHIC

Continued from Part 1 on page 73

Following the success of the Ballantines Original Hotel, Fraser Robertson and Sarah Robarts purchased and renovated a second hotel. Ballantines Movie Colony is a short walk from Ballantines Original. The new hotel has 19 rooms with themes similar to the first location. There are three Marilyn Monroe rooms, a splattered Jackson Pollack room in honor of the artist, and a surf room with hula-girl decorations and a longboard surfboard. Vintage gear and furnishings range from melmac plates to Bertoia chairs. Visitors who are smitten by the appointments can buy them. Everything is for sale. The hotel owners haven't let their profits go to their heads, though—the rates are still moderate, and during the off-season, prices are half off.

ANALYZE AND WRITE

1. List the staff needed for a hotel such as Ballantines Original Hotel.
2. In a paragraph, describe uniforms you would design for service staff of a hotel such as Ballantines Original.

Human Resources Staff

The human resources department is responsible for recruiting, selecting, training, and compensating a hotel's employees. Depending on the size of a property, a human resources director or a personnel director is in charge of this important department. In smaller properties, this function is controlled by the general manager or managers of the various departments.

Servicing Guests

Hotels have numerous revenue centers ranging from the food-and-beverage division to the front office to the support staff in the back of the house. Every property balances servicing guests with making a profit from each revenue center. It is the responsibility of each employee to project a professional image of the property, regardless of his or her position, so that guests will return.

Quick Check ✓

RESPOND to what you've read by answering these questions.

1. What are three functions of the front office? _____
_____
_____
_____
_____
_____

2. What are examples of three uniformed-services positions? _____
_____
_____
_____
_____

3. What is the difference between line and staff employees? _____
_____
_____
_____
_____
_____

Worksheet 4.1

Hotel Amenities

Visit three places of lodging in your community. Make a chart on a separate sheet of paper that provides the following information about each establishment.

1. Name of the establishment: _____

   _____

   _____

2. Classification of the establishment: _____

   _____

3. Primary guest type: _____

   _____

4. Price range: _____

   _____

5. Pricing plans or discounts available: _____

   _____

6. Location: _____

   _____

7. Number of rooms: _____

   _____

8. Guest amenities: _____

   _____

Question:

If you were from out of town, would you stay in any of these establishments? Why or why not?

_____

_____

_____

_____

_____

_____

Worksheet 4.2

Guest Services

Use the Internet or library to research five different places of lodging in your community to rate their level of guest service on a scale of 1–10, with 1 being the least favorable rating and 10 being the best. Then justify the rating you gave each establishment.

Name of place of lodging:	Rating
1. _____	1 2 3 4 5 6 7 8 9 10
2. _____	1 2 3 4 5 6 7 8 9 10
3. _____	1 2 3 4 5 6 7 8 9 10
4. _____	1 2 3 4 5 6 7 8 9 10
5. _____	1 2 3 4 5 6 7 8 9 10

Establishment 1: _____

_____

_____

_____

Establishment 2: _____

_____

_____

_____

Establishment 3: _____

_____

_____

_____

Establishment 4: _____

_____

_____

_____

Establishment 5: _____

_____

_____

_____

Portfolio Works

YOUR HOTEL

Your ambition is to be owner or manager of a place of lodging. Answer the following questions:

1. What type of lodging facility do you want to own or run? _____

_____

2. What type of guest do you want to attract? _____

_____

_____

3. In what price range is your place of lodging? _____

_____

4. What plan do you offer your guests? Describe the plan. _____

_____

_____

_____

_____

5. What is the location of your place of lodging? Why is this a good location? _____

_____

_____

_____

6. Describe any features your place of lodging offers to your guests that will make people want to choose it over your competition. _____

_____

_____

_____

_____

_____

_____

Add this page to your career portfolio.

CHAPTER SUMMARY

Section 4.1 Types of Lodging Businesses

transient guest (p. 75)
meal plan (p. 76)
yield management
(p. 76)
average daily rate (ADR)
(p. 76)
occupancy percentage
(OCC%) (p. 76)
revenue per available
room (revPAR) (p. 76)

- Lodging classification is based on: guest type, price, location, and style of service and function.

- Guests are categorized as two types—business and leisure guests. Business clients are those traveling for business purposes, such as convention attendees, association professionals, or corporate managers. Leisure guests range from single individuals to groups of family and friends who have longer stays.

- The goal of any hotel is to maintain a high occupancy rate. Yield management is a system that lodging establishments use to maximize revenue through adjusting room rates according to demand.

Section 4.2 Hotel Operations

front of the house
(lodging) (p. 81)
back of the house
(lodging) (p. 81)
night auditor (p. 82)
guest service agent (GSA)
(p. 82)
guest or uniformed
services (p. 84)
concierge (p. 85)

- The various positions in the rooms division of a hotel include front-office jobs at the front desk, in reservations, housekeeping, guest or uniformed services, and communications.

- Guest services are provided by the front-desk staff. Front-desk managers, assistant managers, clerks, or agents, as well as auditors, provide these services. Guest services include checking in guests, responding to guest questions, requests, and special needs.

- Support staff positions in the back of the house of a lodging facility include engineers, groundskeepers, attendants, sales and marketing staff, and human resources staff.

CHECKING CONCEPTS

1. **Name** the factors used to classify lodging facilities.
2. **List** the categories used to describe types of guests by type of stay.
3. **Describe** a business guest.
4. **Identify** three rates hotels use for yield management.
5. **Identify** properties by type of style and function.
6. **List** three positions in the rooms division.
7. **Name** the staff in uniformed services.

Critical Thinking

8. **Discuss** the importance of the sales and marketing staff in back-of-the-house lodging operations.

CROSS-CURRICULUM SKILLS

Work-Based Learning

Interpersonal Skills—Participating as a Team Member

9. You and two other students are the marketing team for a hotel chain that is competing for business from the local business community. Create a presentation to draw customers to your hotel.

Basic Skills—Listening and Writing Skills

10. Interview a marketing department employee at a major hotel. Ask what the hotel offers guests. Write a report based on what you learn.

School-Based Learning

History

11. Contact the local historic society or use the Internet to learn about a historic hotel in your area. Give an oral presentation to the class.

Math

12. Choose two national hotel chains, such as Marriott and Hyatt. Contact the hotels to get a list of their room rates. Compare rates and then report findings to the class.

Role Play: Management Team

SITUATION You are to assume the role of a management team member for a 1,600-room hotel located in walking distance of the convention center of a very popular tourist destination. The hotel's bookings have fallen recently, even when there are major conventions at the convention center. The hotel offers basic guest services, and the facility has not been renovated in several years. Your major competition offers full guest services in a facility that is only three years old.

ACTIVITY You are to review the hotel's guest services and offer suggestions to add to the selection.

EVALUATION You will be evaluated on how well you meet the following performance indicators:

- Monitor guest satisfaction with services/facilities.
- Determine customer/client needs.
- Recommend specific products.
- Determine services to provide customers.
- Select guest service options for establishment.

Use the Internet to access the Web site of the Lenox in Boston.

- Click on Awards and News.
- Make a list of the awards the Lenox has received.
- Tell a classmate why you think the Lenox has won so many awards and why you think the awards are important to the Lenox.

➡ For a link to the Lenox Web site to do this activity, go to **marketingseries.glencoe.com**.

Chapter 5

The Tourism Business

Section **5.1**

Travel and Tourism

Section **5.2**

Transportation Providers

Chapter Objectives

- Identify factors that contribute to the growth of tourism.
- Discuss the reasons that people travel.
- Describe the different types of tours.
- Explain the importance of transportation providers.
- Identify the different types of transportation.
- Discuss the impact of the cruise industry.

GEAR ON THE GO

In 1938, Lloyd and Mary Anderson, along with 23 other mountain climbers, founded Recreational Equipment, Inc. (REI), to get a better deal on ice axes from Europe. It was difficult for outdoor enthusiasts in North America to acquire climbing gear at the time. Since then the sporting goods retailer has become America's largest commercial co-op. Based in the state of Washington, REI sells gear to cyclists, hikers, campers, paddlers, skiers, and snowboarders. In 2003, more than two million co-op members of REI (who paid a one-time fee of $15) divided up an annual refund of $41 million. The company is regularly included in *Fortune* magazine's "100 Best Places to Work," and its products have won "Gear of the Year" awards from *Outside* magazine.

REI Adventures was introduced in 1987 when the co-op discovered that its customers wanted the best equipment—and the best experiences. Adventure vacations include hiking the Swiss Alps, cycling from Vienna to Prague, and paddling the islands around Vancouver. How would REI handle the transition to being a travel agency?

ANALYZE AND WRITE

1. What circumstances led REI to create REI Adventures?
2. What advantages did REI have for starting a tourism business?

Case Study Part 2 on page 109

POWER READ

Be an active reader and use these reading strategies:

PREDICT what the section will be about.

CONNECT what you read with your own life.

QUESTION as you read to make sure you understand the content.

RESPOND to what you've read.

Travel and Tourism

AS YOU READ ...

YOU WILL LEARN

- To identify factors that contribute to the growth of tourism.
- To discuss the reasons that people travel.
- To describe the different types of tours.

WHY IT'S IMPORTANT

The travel and tourism industry is a broad and ever-changing industry with great growth potential. Understanding the scope of the industry helps professionals serve their customers.

KEY TERMS

- disposable income
- niche market
- package tour
- charter tour
- customized tour

PREDICT

Why might the travel and tourism industry continue to grow?

disposable income the money left from a person's gross income after taking out taxes

Introduction to Travel and Tourism

The travel and tourism industry includes businesses and government agencies that service travelers. For most countries, travel and tourism can represent a large percentage of total revenue. For example, in the United States, nearly one-third of all households took at least one trip away from home each month during 2003. In 2004, overall spending by domestic and international visitors in the United States increased more than 4 percent to $568 billion.

The Growth of Tourism

The growth of travel and tourism, despite instability in different parts of the world, is due to many factors that affect travel trends. Today some of these factors include trends toward dual family incomes, baby boomers who enjoy travel, health consciousness, available leisure time, new transportation options, increased Internet use, niche travel markets, and the growth of adventure travel.

Dual Family Income

In many two-parent families, both parents work outside of the home. Their income may provide additional **disposable income**, which is the money left from a person's gross income after taking out taxes. Disposable income may be spent on items such as cars, appliances, travel, and other recreation. Because leisure time is scarce, Americans treasure the quality time they are able to spend on vacations with their families.

Baby Boomers

Because of its size and spending power, the baby-boomer market makes up a large percentage of the traveling public. Over the next decade, this group will continue to travel. However, for older adults (55 years and above), expectations and needs regarding travel and accommodations may be different.

Health

Due to advanced health-care options, many senior citizens are traveling more frequently. Health-care options contribute to the increase of available tour programs, such as tour packages for people with disabilities, to a variety of destinations. Cruise lines offer specially designed packages for these groups.

Leisure Time

Many employers indirectly support the growth of the travel and tourism industry by providing their workers with more liberal vacation time and flexible-time benefits. To take advantage of long holiday weekends and additional holidays thoughout the year, many travelers take mini-vacations in addition to traditional one-week or two-week vacations.

New Transportation Options

New low-cost airline carriers have increased the options for travelers considering long-distance trips. Low-cost airlines serve destinations previously available only to passengers who paid higher fares or who were willing to make many connections. This ease of access through new airlines has increased the number of travelers—especially travelers who visit family and friends.

The Internet

The convenience of booking a trip online has also contributed to the increased number of travelers. Previously used only for gathering information, the Internet is now a source of transportation, lodging, and sightseeing bargains. Many travel and tourism businesses operate full-service Web sites that provide information and booking capabilities. Travelers are taking a do-it-yourself approach to finding and booking travel and tourism options on the Internet.

Niche Markets

The emergence of niche markets has increased tourism. These markets draw more travelers. A **niche market** is a new market in tourism that bases travel on specific interests:

- Travel for the disabled

- Adventure travel

- Geotourism

- Agritourism

TRAVEL FOR THE DISABLED One large niche market includes over 22 million people with disabilities, or 71 percent of adults with disabilities. Each of these people traveled at least once during 2003. The majority of people with disabilities travel for pleasure. Specialty tours, especially on cruise ships, have attracted a number of travelers who seek special services.

ADVENTURE TRAVEL As a niche market, adventure travel offers a broad spectrum of outdoor tourist activities, such as hiking, boating, mountain-climbing, exploring rainforests, or walking on glaciers. These activities may involve interaction with the natural environment away from the participant's home area. With adventure travel, there may be various risks, which must be overcome by the participant.

ETHICS & ISSUES

Getting Everyone There

Many travel and tourism professionals realize that making travel possible for *everyone* is good business. For example, over 194,000 travel-related jobs are generated by travelers with disabilities. In 2002 alone, this market segment spent $13.6 billion on travel and tourism. According to the Open Door Organization, cruises are the most popular form of travel for people with disabilities, because cruise lines provide special services to meet their needs. If other segments of the travel and tourism industry improved accessibility, revenue from this market could double. *Do you think travel and tourism businesses should be required to accommodate travelers with disabilities? Why or why not?*

niche market a new market in tourism that bases travel on specific interests, such as ecotourism

GEOTOURISM/ECOTOURISM Another niche-market trend is geotourism, or ecotourism, which is tourism in exotic or threatened ecosystems for the purposes of observing wildlife or to help preserve nature. A study done by the Travel Industry Association of America (TIA) reported that about 75 percent of all Americans feel that their tour visits should not damage the destination's environment. Geotourism sustains or enhances the geographical location's character, which includes its environment, community, culture, heritage, and aesthetics.

AGRITOURISM Agritourism involves visiting a working farm or any agricultural, horticultural, or agribusiness operation. Tourists go to these sites for the purpose of enjoyment, education, or active involvement in the activities of the farm or operation.

Reasons to Travel

People travel for a variety of reasons. Basically, there are two main reasons for travel—business and leisure. Business travel could be motivated by meetings, conventions, or other general business reasons. Leisure travel involves travel for pleasure. Some reasons for leisure travel are listed in **Figure 5.1**.

Tourism's Economic Impact

All types of travel and tourism offer positive economic benefits. In the United States, one out of every eight people is either directly or indirectly employed in the travel and tourism industry. Travel employers include transportation providers and tour providers. In addition, the travel and tourism industry is one of America's largest retail industries, ranking third, according to the TIA. It is one of the largest employers in 29 U.S. states. Travelers in the United States spend approximately $17,000 per second, $1 million per minute, $60 million per hour, and $1.4 billion per day.

Figure 5.1

Reasons for Leisure Travel

TOURIST ATTRACTIONS Many people enjoy traveling for a variety of reasons. *What do you think is the number-one reason for leisure travel? Why?*

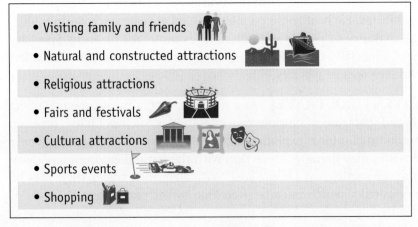

- Visiting family and friends
- Natural and constructed attractions
- Religious attractions
- Fairs and festivals
- Cultural attractions
- Sports events
- Shopping

◄ THE GRAND TOUR
A hosted tour allows travelers to be independent while having the convenience of guided tours in unfamiliar places. *Could a customized tour include a guided sightseeing tour?*

Types of Tours

Many travelers pay for some type of tour. A tour incorporates a wide variety of components. These components can include accommodations, transportation, food service, and entertainment. Tours that include these services for one price are called *all-inclusive tours*. Other tours combine only transportation options, such as fly/drive packages. The basic types of tours are package tours and customized tours.

Package Tours

A **package tour** is a prearranged tour that offers value, guaranteed sightseeing, and a quality product. A tour operator or company may develop a package tour as a **charter tour**, which is a tour in which a tour operator buys all the seats on an airplane, train, or bus and resells them to travelers. Package tours can be planned as independent tours, hosted tours, or escorted tours. The difference between these tours is the amount of structure offered to the traveler.

INDEPENDENT TOURS These tours are arranged so guests can choose from a variety of dates, accommodations, meal plans, and sightseeing options. Guests get volume discounts without sacrificing their independence.

HOSTED TOURS Hosted tours are similar to independent tours. However, they position a host at each destination to assist with a less-structured tour.

ESCORTED OR GUIDED TOURS The most structured tours are escorted or guided tours. Guests travel together as a group with a tour director to assist them. This type of tour offers relaxation and efficiency.

Customized Tours

A **customized tour** is a tour that is more expensive than a package tour and is designed specifically for an individual tourist. This type of tour may include accommodations, transportation, and sightseeing.

package tour a prearranged tour that offers value, guaranteed sightseeing, and a quality product

charter tour a tour in which a tour operator buys all the seats on an airplane, train, or bus and resells them to travelers

CONNECT
What type of tour package would you prefer for visiting a foreign country? Why?

customized tour a tour that is more expensive than a package tour and is designed specifically for an individual tourist

NORTHERN EXPOSURES

Cynthia Billette, CTP
President
Columbia Crossroads

What is your job?

"I operate Columbia Crossroads, a tour agency."

What do you do in your job?

"I plan tours throughout the Pacific Northwest for small groups, corporate events, and conventions. I plan all tours and oversee the events. I negotiate with all types of suppliers, such as hotels and transportation providers. I also oversee general management and accounting departments."

What kind of training did you have?

"I was a tour manager for over 20 years and traveled in about 60 countries. Then I was hired as a consultant to create a tour operation for two different companies before starting my own company in 1995. I received a college degree through the National Tour Association where I earned a Certified Tour Professional (CTP) degree. There are only about 550 certified tour professionals in the world. It takes five years of experience and two years of study to qualify for certification."

What advice would you give students?

"Go to college. I have a general studies degree that keeps me well-rounded, but tourism degrees are also available. Business and accounting courses are useful as well. People skills are most important. Be an intern or get a summer job in the travel industry as a tour operator, hotelier, or transportation-and-attractions supplier to see and learn about the business."

What is your key to success?

"I work hard and try to be available when needed. Also, I've traveled the world as a tour manager to learn about different cultures and people in many destinations. Establishing a business does not happen overnight, so having a stick-to-it attitude helps."

What type of tour does Cynthia Billette plan?

Career Data: Tour Planner

Education and Training
Bachelor's degree or master's degree in travel and tourism, general business, or management

Skills and Abilities
Communication, interpersonal, business, accounting, and time-management skills; flexibility and love of travel

Career Outlook Faster than average growth through 2012

Career Path Internship to agency employee to independent or upper-level tour planner

Tour Benefits

All types of tours offer benefits to travelers. Tourists can receive volume discounts, guaranteed sightseeing entrances, prepayment options, and stress-free travel. Tour packages provide retailers and distributors ease of booking and maximum earning potential.

Tour Positions

The growing travel and tourism industry offers a variety of career options for tour operations, including tour escort, tour guide, tour host, and positions working for the tour operator.

Tour Escort

The most common entry-level position is tour escort. This individual is also referred to as a tour director or tour conductor. The tour escort accompanies a group on tour. As the operator's representative, he or she is responsible for the efficient operation of the entire tour.

Tour Guides

Tour guides are individuals hired at specific destinations to provide detailed commentary on particular sights or destinations. Many tour guides are licensed by the particular destination.

Tour Hosts

Tour hosts provide assistance when guests arrive at a destination. They answer questions, recommend dining options, and offer transportation alternatives. Tour hosts also arrange additional sightseeing for travelers.

QUESTION
What are some tasks performed by tour hosts?

Other Tour Positions

Tour operators also employ reservationists, sales staff, accounting personnel, and product managers. The general manager of the tour company oversees the entire personnel team, from managers and assistant managers to administrative assistants.

Growth of Tourism

Travel and tourism is one of the largest and fastest-growing industries in the world. Many factors contribute to this growth. Tours are just one segment of the travel and tourism industry. Other vital segments of the tourism business include the transportation providers, as discussed in Section 5.2.

Quick Check

RESPOND to what you've read by answering these questions.

1. What three factors may contribute to the growth of tourism? _____

_____

2. What are two reasons that people travel? _____

_____

3. What are three types of package tours? _____

_____

Transportation Providers

AS YOU READ ...

YOU WILL LEARN

- To explain the importance of transportation providers.
- To identify the different types of transportation.
- To discuss the impact of the cruise industry.

WHY IT'S IMPORTANT

Without support from transportation providers, the travel and tourism industry would not function. Opportunities in the travel and tourism industry exist within all types of transportation businesses.

KEY TERMS

- hub-and-spoke system
- frequent-flyer program
- Amtrak
- windjammer

PREDICT

What might be three different types of transportation?

Modes of Transportation

Passenger transportation is *intermodal*, which means that it relies on air and ground as well as land and water transportation methods. Travel within a state or country and around the world would not be possible without efficient transit programs and state-of-the-art transportation systems. The different modes of transportation include:

- Air transportation

- Ground transportation (rail, car, or motor coach)

- Water transportation (passenger and cruise vessels)

History of Air Transportation

Since the Wright brothers' first successful airplane flight in 1903, air travel has evolved into a multibillion-dollar industry. Passenger service on airplanes traveling short distances began in 1919. Then in 1927, Charles Lindbergh crossed the Atlantic Ocean, making long-distance air travel a reality. However, jet service was not available until 1952. Many events during the 20th century affected the air-travel industry.

Air Travel, 1945

The International Air Transport Association (IATA) reorganized to promote cooperative agreements for passengers traveling across international borders. Today this major trade association consults on financial, legal, and technical issues relating to international travel.

Air Travel, 1958

By the late 1950s, the skies over the United States were becoming crowded as air travel increased. After an aircraft collision over the Grand Canyon, Congress enacted the Federal Aviation Act in 1958, which created the air safety agency the Federal Aviation Administration.

Air Travel, 1978

In the United States, the Airline Deregulation Act of 1978 allowed new competitors to offer services in new markets to create a more efficient national airline system. Price competition in the form of discount fares became common for the first time in history. However, as a result of deregulation, many airlines were unable to compete and filed for bankruptcy or merged with larger airlines.

Air Travel, 1980s

To compete in the competitive market of the 1980s, larger carriers changed their routing systems and adopted the **hub-and-spoke system**, which is an effective network for an airline formed by a hub, or a large airport, connected to other smaller airports called *spokes*. (See **Figure 5.2** on page 104 for more airline terms.) This system allows passengers from smaller cities (spokes) to fly to a larger, more central city (hub) to connect on a flight to the final destination. Passengers can fly to and from a greater number of cities and choose from a variety of airlines. This provides the airlines with greater cost savings.

TRAVELER BENEFITS To increase passenger loyalty, airlines also created frequent-flyer programs. A **frequent-flyer program** is a program in which an airline offers free travel, upgrades, and discounts to program members. Under this system, passengers accumulate miles in the form of points with the airline or the airline's partner. Passengers can exchange these mileage points for valuable benefits, such as upgrades to first class, reduced-price tickets, or future travel.

Air Travel, 1990s

Point-to-point service by regional, or short-haul, low-cost airlines has offered an alternative to the hub-and-spoke system. Regional airlines are smaller and offer direct service, without connections, between less-populated, regional cities. Most of these carriers provide only basic amenities, such as luggage handling and onboard beverage service. These airlines offer lower fares and more frequent flights on their schedules.

Air Travel, 2000

Many airlines formed partnerships with other carriers for non-competing or international routes. This has allowed airlines to provide direct service through another carrier to a variety of destinations. Passengers get convenience in making reservations, lower fares, and additional frequent-flyer benefits.

Imagine going to Mars for spring break. Some people believe that space tourism will become a reality in the near future. In June 2003, Mike Melvill became the first civilian astronaut to fly a privately funded spacecraft. Melvill piloted *SpaceShipOne* more than 62 miles above the earth. Richard Branson of Virgin Atlantic Airways plans to buy five similar spaceships from designer Burt Rutan for his new Virgin Galactic space-tourism business.

➡ Describe your ideal space vacation after learning more about space tourism through **marketingseries.glencoe.com**.

hub-and-spoke system an effective network for an airline formed by a hub, or a large airport, connected to other smaller airports called *spokes*

frequent-flyer program a program in which an airline offers free travel, upgrades, and discounts to program members

AFFORDABLE TRAVEL
Because of developments in air travel over the last few decades, airfares are less expensive, making travel affordable for many people. *How did developments in air travel during the year 2000 affect air travel?*

Figure 5.2

Air Travel Glossary

AIRLINE-SPEAK Travel and tourism agents need to know the lingo of the air-travel industry in order to plan and book trips for their customers.

What is the difference between a direct flight and a nonstop flight?

Air Travel Glossary	
ARTCC	Air Route Traffic Control Center is a facility established to provide air-traffic-control service to aircraft operating on authorized flight plans within controlled airspace—and during the en route phase of flight. There are 20 ARTCCs in the continental United States.
ATC	Air Traffic Control is a service operated by the appropriate authority to promote the safe, orderly, and expeditious flow of air traffic.
Bumping	A passenger with a ticket gets moved to another flight without consent. Bumping is also used when a passenger is moved from one class to another.
Charters	Flight for which a tour operator buys all seats and resells them to travelers. Some tour operators own their own charter aircrafts. Charter fares are less expensive than regular airfares because the tour operator negotiates a discount rate with the airline.
Connection	The airplane makes one or more stops en route to the destination. The passenger must physically leave the aircraft and board another flight. Generally, if there are more connections to a destination, the price of the ticket is lower.
Denied boarding	A passenger is not allowed to board the aircraft under certain circumstances: The passenger cannot provide personal documentation; the passenger is considered dangerous due to his or her behavior; or the passenger is too intoxicated to be considered reliable.
Direct flight	The flight has no connections, but the aircraft may stop. Passengers may or may not deplane, depending on the flight.
Hub-and-spoke network	This effective network for an airline is formed by a hub, or a large airport, connected to other smaller airports called *spokes*. Most large airlines in the United States have more than one hub.
Leg	Each part of a flight that has several connections.
Nonstop flight	The flight does not stop during the trip but goes directly to the destination. This flight is the most expensive type.
One-way trip	A trip (ticket) that takes a passenger to a destination with no return ticket. In many cases, one-way tickets are permitted only on domestic flights.
Round trip	A trip (ticket) takes a passenger from city A to city B, with a return ticket back to the point of origin (city A).
Waitlisting	When a flight is full, travelers who do not get booked may be put on a waiting list. Passengers who have long layovers may request this service so they can get an earlier flight should there be any free seats. This system is also used for first-class upgrades.

Airline Careers

Numerous opportunities exist in the airline industry. Careers range from direct customer-contact positions, such as flight attendants, to support or service positions, such as sales or ground crew.

Onboard Positions

When onboard, the pilot and his or her copilot and navigator, or flight engineer, are in charge of the safety of the plane and its passengers. All of these individuals have years of specialized training and education. The purser is in charge of the entire cabin crew and all passengers' safety and comfort. Flight attendants handle special duties, such as announcements, meal and/or beverage service, and boarding procedures. Their most important assignments, however, are ensuring passenger safety and overall passenger service.

Ground Positions

At the airport, the ground personnel or crew handles the daily responsibilities of passenger check-in and luggage. With concerns for passenger and employee safety, security for all airport personnel has been elevated. Gate agents reconfirm scheduled departures, check carry-on baggage, and provide flight information. Reservation agents may be at the airport to assist with flight arrangements. These agents may be part of a complete sales force at the airline's centralized headquarters.

Ground Transportation

The oldest mode of transportation takes place on the ground. Some travelers prefer ground transportation by rail, automobile (car rentals), or motor coach. This mode of travel may take more time. However, ground transportation is usually available and can cost less than other forms of transportation.

Rail Transportation in Europe

Internationally, rail service is extremely popular as a primary means of ground transportation. Particularly in Europe, rail travel is commonplace. It is an ideal way to see sights comfortably and meet new people. One of the fastest trains in the world, the TGV (Train à Grande Vitesse), travels throughout France and is more popular than the expensive air-travel alternatives. Trains in Europe offer different classes of service, sleeping accommodations, and dining cars. Rail passes provide the convenience of traveling within and between many countries in Europe for one discount fare.

Rail Transportation in the United States

In the United States, rail service has not been as popular as it was in the first half of the 20th century. This is due to the introduction of the automobile as the primary method of transportation. Shortly after the automobile's introduction to the public, new highways were constructed, and rail service and rail destinations declined in popularity.

CONNECT

Do you think flying non-stop justifies a higher-priced airfare? Why or why not?

Key Point

FASTER THAN A SPEEDING...

According to the Guinness World Records, the highest speed recorded on any national railroad is 320 miles per hour. The record was set by the French high-speed train, the TGV Atlantique (Train à Grande Vitesse) on May 18, 1990. Today you can recognize this train in France by the blue ribbon painted across its nose.

Amtrak a company that operates a railroad system with combined passenger and rail service throughout the continental United States

AMTRAK In the 1970s, the National Railroad Passenger Corporation was founded. Known today as **Amtrak**, it is a company that operates a railroad system with combined passenger and rail service throughout the continental United States. The most popular railway routes are the scenic California coastal route and the northeast corridor route between Boston and Washington, D.C., which is serviced by the high-speed Acela train. Amtrak has remained competitive by offering rail-tour packages that include overnight accommodations, sightseeing options, and additional onboard amenities.

Automobile Transportation

Automobile rentals represent an alternative for travelers who do not want to use public ground transportation, such as taxis or buses. Car-rental agencies primarily serve airline passengers upon arrival at a final destination. Car rentals provide relatively inexpensive transportation with convenience, personal comfort, and control. Rental agencies also offer flexible rental plans by the day, week, or month. Car rental is especially beneficial for family or group travel when plans may change and extra baggage space is needed.

Other automotive modes of transportation are available:

- **Limousines**—Limousines can also be rented for all-day sightseeing trips, airport shuttle service, or an evening's entertainment.

- **Vans and Shuttles**—In larger cities, local van service is available for airport and hotel shuttle transportation.

World Market

Riding the Orient Express

Today tourists who seek a unique experience can travel in classic style on the American Orient Express. They can see the United States from the height of a glass-domed observation car or from the comfort of their own private compartments. The American Orient Express is a collection of sixteen royal-blue-and-gold passenger cars elegantly renovated from the 1940s and 1950s.

The railway service offers a variety of tours. Follow the epic journey of Lewis and Clark in the Pacific Northwest. Travel to the historic plantations of the South. Visit the national parks of the West. Glide through New England in autumn. All of this comes with first-rate meals, live music in the lounge, and chocolates at bedtime. The journey is half the fun.

Select an American historical event and plan a railway tour with that theme.

UNITED STATES OF AMERICA

Motor-Coach Transportation

Motor-coach transportation can be categorized as charter-tour transportation. Scheduled intercity passenger service is provided by bus lines such as Greyhound. Formerly regulated by the Interstate Commerce Commission (ICC), the motor-coach industry was deregulated in 1982. As a result, many intercity and interstate motor-coach companies consolidated their services and routes. Today scheduled motor-coach travel is popular in major cities as an alternative to rail service, car rental, or taxis. As a less-expensive travel option, intercity and interstate motor coaches go to numerous locations.

CHARTER MOTOR COACHES Charter motor coaches are popular with tour groups, particularly the mature-traveler market whose primary considerations are safety, comfort, and quality service. Tour motor coaches include amenities such as stereo and video systems, small galleys for food service, bathrooms, and wide reclining seats.

Careers in Ground Transportation

Many people enter the transportation side of the travel and tourism industry through entry-level, customer-service positions such as car-rental agents.

GROUND TRANSPORTATION STAFF Most providers of ground transportation have sales and reservations staff as well as upfront agents. Safe and capable drivers, dispatchers, and chauffeurs are all needed for all forms of ground transportation.

RAILWAY STAFF Amtrak has a full staff of union employees. Lead service agents who work for rail transportation providers are similar to flight attendants, providing guest services on the train. Other onboard railway staff includes conductors who check tickets, schedules, and passengers, and engineers who are concerned with safety and routing.

Water Transportation

Many people think that luxury cruise ships are the main form of water transportation. However, there are other types of water-surface providers. Different types of water transportation include ferry boats, freighters, riverboats, yachts, and windjammers as well as cruise ships.

Ferry Boats

Ferry boats, or ferries, offer a practical and vital link for island travelers and resident commuters. Most vessels provide food service, retail shopping, and room for passengers and automobiles. For long trips, many ferries provide overnight sleeping accommodations and additional amenities.

Freighters

Freighters carry goods, cargo, or supplies, but many also offer cabins for rent. They often travel to international ports.

QUESTION
What are the different types of ground transportation?

Riverboats

Riverboats travel famous rivers, such as the Mississippi River in the United States and the Danube River in Europe. Schedules are often flexible, and accommodations are basic.

Yachts

Typically, yachts are chartered privately by small groups for special voyages. In most cases, a group will choose the route or itinerary, and the professional crew aboard the boat will provide food and other services.

Windjammers

windjammer a sailing ship that offers passengers the opportunity to sail privately and work with a crew

A **windjammer** is a sailing ship that offers passengers the opportunity to sail privately and work with a crew. Such trips are less structured and are usually offered at warm-weather destinations.

Cruise Ships

Cruise ships offer all of the amenities of a resort. Most people choose to travel by cruise ships because of the luxury appointments, accommodations, and amenities. The cruise-ship segment is one of the fastest-growing segments of the industry. Cruise ships are travel bargains that offer lodging, food service, travel, sports, and entertainment.

Hot Property

The Fun Ship

Carnival.
Just more fun...

Business did not look promising when the *Mardi Gras* ran aground. The ship was Carnival's only vessel, and it was stuck on a Miami sandbar. That was in 1972. By 2004, however, Carnival became a multibillion-dollar corporation, operating 12 different cruise lines, representing virtually every market segment.

Ted Arison founded Carnival with just one ship and good marketing sense. The vessel was a few years old and did not have many amenities. So Arison charged less than his competitors charged customers. He targeted young travelers looking for fun, instead of older, wealthier travelers.

THE DIVERSE SHIP

Then Arison brought his son aboard. Under Micky Arison's management, the company continued to market itself as the low-cost "fun" alternative.

However, it grew beyond the single ship and demographic. Carnival commissioned new ships to be built and kept costs down by holding builders to tight budgets. It ran upbeat TV commercials. Carnival Cruise Lines appealed to families with its kid-friendly activities. Marketers created special programs to satisfy different kinds of travelers, from golf fans to spa lovers to dieters.

Despite these special features, Carnival had to make an extra effort to maintain its strong profit margins when security and illness fears slowed the industry. So the cruise line cut prices and offered cruises departing from additional ports, and more passengers came aboard. Fun is a powerful marketing tool when the price is right.

1. How did Carnival Cruise Lines broaden its appeal?
2. What kind of activities would you want on a cruise ship?

ACCOMMODATIONS Cruise ships offer a wide range of onboard sleeping accommodations, from luxurious suites to basic cabins. Every size and style of cabin includes a sleeping area, closet, private bath, and basic amenities. Suite amenities can include hairdryers, wet bars, refrigerators, bathtubs, and living-room areas.

FOOD SERVICE Food service is offered 24 hours daily on cruise ships. Breakfast, lunch, and dinner are offered in the dining rooms at scheduled times, at poolside buffets and snackbars, or in private rooms. Specialty services such as afternoon tea or midnight buffets are also available.

ENTERTAINMENT Entertainment is included throughout each day on a cruise, with activities ranging from guided tours to poolside games to port talks. Onboard features, such as spas and fitness salons, casinos, lounges, movie theaters, duty-free shops, and activity centers, rival those of any luxury hotel property.

CRUISE-SHIP PRICING No two ships or cruises are exactly alike. In this way, the cruise industry is able to appeal to a variety of families, couples, and singles of all ages with different budgets. Trips aboard cruise ships are priced according to five basic factors: the ship, the season of sailing, the length of stay, the cabin location, and the itinerary.

1. **The ship**—"Mega ships" can charge higher prices because they offer grand amenities such as climbing walls and ice rinks, which are not found on older, smaller ships.

2. **The season of sailing**—The season of sailing affects the price of the cruise. Just as hotels and airlines have peak seasons, so do cruise lines. For example, the more popular holiday seasons are the most expensive times to sail.

3. **The length of stay**—The length of stay also determines price. Longer trips are more expensive than three- or four-day trips, due to the amount of time spent on board by passengers.

4. **The cabin location**—In addition, the location and style of cabins affect the cruise price. For example, spacious suites on upper decks with balconies are more expensive than smaller inside cabins on lower decks.

5. **The itinerary**—Finally, the itinerary, or routing, may affect the price of a cruise. Cruises to popular destinations, such as the Caribbean, are less expensive due to greater competition in the industry. Other popular cruise destinations include Alaska, Hawaii, the Panama Canal, Bermuda, Europe, and the Mediterranean.

Case Study — PART 2

GEAR ON THE GO

Continued from Part 1 on page 95

With its loyal membership, consumer base, and strong identification with the outdoors, REI was able to successfully introduce REI Adventures. Since the first trips were organized, the travel and tourism company has added options and accommodations to appeal to first-time trekkers as well as experienced mountaineers. Whether it is a rafting trip or a cycling tour, excursions are led by experts for all skill levels. Accommodations can be economical or deluxe. REI Adventures takes care of everything except the airfare. Travel arrangements are available for singles, families, and private groups. With the growth of adventure tourism, over 70 trips are organized annually in North America and around the world.

ANALYZE AND WRITE

1. Describe how REI might appeal to beginning adventurers.
2. Why would REI arrange trips for families and private groups? Write a paragraph explaining your answer.

Cruise-Ship Positions

Positions on ships for citizens of the United States are limited because most ships sail under foreign flags. These ships are registered in other countries to save on labor and construction costs. However, Americans do find numerous positions working in sales and reservations. Onboard opportunities are available in areas such as the front desk, known as the purser's office, the tour or shore excursion desk, recreational activities, and entertainment. All shipboard workers sign contracts to work for six to eight months. Many assignments are performed six days per week. Payment is agreed upon in a contract, but some positions provide employees the opportunity to receive tips or other forms of gratuities.

Integrated Tourism Systems

Air, ground, and water transportation services and providers are significant contributors to the travel and tourism industry. The cruise-ship segment, in particular, is one of the fastest-growing segments of the industry. Without a reliable system of transportation, the travel and tourism industry could not be successful.

Quick Check ✓

RESPOND to what you've read by answering these questions.

1. What are three significant events that affected the airline industry? _____
_____
_____
_____
_____
_____

2. What are three forms of ground transportation? _____
_____
_____
_____

3. What five factors affect the price of a ship cruise? _____
_____
_____
_____
_____
_____
_____

Worksheet 5.1

Reasons to Travel

Survey eight adults to learn about their travel habits. Ask the following questions. On a separate sheet of paper, make a chart that organizes the answers.

Why do you travel? Is it to visit family or friends, to see attractions, for religious purposes, to attend a sporting event, or to shop?

1. _____
2. _____
3. _____
4. _____
5. _____
6. _____
7. _____
8. _____

Do you ever take a tour? Why or why not?

1. _____
2. _____
3. _____
4. _____
5. _____
6. _____
7. _____
8. _____

How do you arrange for travel? Do you arrange it yourself or use a travel agent?

1. _____
2. _____
3. _____
4. _____
5. _____
6. _____
7. _____
8. _____

Worksheet 5.2

Tourism Growth

Use the space below to make a graphic organizer that illustrates the factors that contribute to the expected growth of tourism. Include information on dual family income, baby boomers, health, leisure time, transportation options, the Internet, and niche markets.

Portfolio Works

AIRPORT EMPLOYMENT

Visit a commercial airport near your community or visit the Web site of a commercial airport in the United States. Make a list of the airlines, ground transportation, car-rental agencies, motor coaches, and taxi services available at the airport. Use the space below to make a graphic organizer of the transportation services that provide employment at the airport.

Add this page to your career portfolio.

CHAPTER SUMMARY

Section 5.1 **Travel and Tourism**

disposable income
(p. 96)
niche market (p. 97)
package tour (p. 99)
charter tour (p. 99)
customized tour (p. 99)

- Tourism has grown as an industry due to various factors, including trends toward dual family incomes, baby boomers who enjoy travel, health consciousness, available leisure time, new transportation options, increased Internet use, niche travel markets, and the growth of adventure travel.

- People travel for a variety of reasons: to see family and friends, natural and constructed attractions, religious attractions, fairs and festivals, cultural attractions, and sports events—and to shop.

- Types of tours include tour packages, such as independent, hosted, and escorted or guided tours, and customized tours, which are tours that are more expensive than package tours and are designed for individual tourists.

Section 5.2 **Transportation Providers**

hub-and-spoke system
(p. 103)
frequent-flyer program
(p. 103)
Amtrak (p. 106)
windjammer (p. 108)

- Travel would not be possible without efficient transit programs and state-of-the-art transportation systems.

- The modes of transportation in the passenger transportation category include: air transportation, ground transportation (rail, car, and motor coach), and water transportation (passenger and cruise vessels).

- Most people choose to travel by cruise ships because of the luxury appointments, accommodations, and amenities. The cruise-ship segment is one of the fastest-growing segments of the industry. Cruise ships combine all areas of the hospitality and tourism industries—lodging, food service, travel, sports, and entertainment.

CHECKING CONCEPTS

1. **List** the factors affecting the growth of travel and tourism.
2. **Identify** the niche markets in tourism.
3. **Describe** the reasons for leisure travel.
4. **Explain** the impact of tourism in the United States.
5. **List** the types of tours and tour packages.
6. **Discuss** the importance of transportation for the travel and tourism business.
7. **Identify** the three modes of transportation, giving examples of each.

Critical Thinking

8. **Explain** why cruise-ship tourism has become popular.

CROSS-CURRICULUM SKILLS

Work-Based Learning

Thinking Skills—Reasoning

9. Consider how the events of September 11, 2001, affected the airline industry. Have a discussion with three other students about the impact. Write down your conclusions and present them to the class.

Basic Skills—Speaking

10. Give a brief speech to the class about a trip you took with your family or friends. Describe your reasons for traveling.

School-Based Learning

Social Studies

11. Write a description of a geotour or ecotour that you would like to take. Describe the place and include information on the location's environment, community, culture, heritage, and aesthetics.

Artwork

12. With a partner, design a poster that celebrates airline travel. Use airline terminology in your poster. Display the poster in class.

Role Play: Tourism Manager

SITUATION You are to assume the role of tourism manager for a convention and visitor's bureau of a city located in the Pacific Northwest. The city is headquarters for major industries, sports teams, and cultural venues. Features also include shopping, mountain and forest scenery, and a busy harbor. The city is a popular tourist destination for visitors from Asia, but few tourists from other parts of the world visit.

ACTIVITY The president of the convention bureau (judge) has asked you to prepare some ideas to increase tourism from countries around the world.

EVALUATION You will be evaluated on how well you meet the following performance indicators:

- Describe the nature of the travel and tourism industry.
- Explain the nature of travel and tourism marketing.
- Discuss the interdependence of travel and tourism industry segments.
- Describe the cyclical/seasonal nature of tourism.
- Describe geographic factors that foster travel and tourism.

Use the Internet to access the Web site of the National Park Service to learn about aviation history related to the Wright brothers in Dayton, Ohio. Then answer the following questions:

- What did the Wright brothers invent?
- What three historic places related to aviation and the Wright brothers can you visit while in Dayton?

➡️For a link to the National Park Service, Dayton Aviation Heritage Web site to do this activity, go to **marketingseries.glencoe.com**.

Chapter 6

Destination Marketing

Section 6.1
Destination Markets

Section 6.2
Basics of Destination Marketing

Chapter Objectives
- Define the term *destination*.
- Discuss the concept of seasonality.
- Identify the classifications of destinations.
- Describe a destination resort.
- Identify the various businesses that promote and provide destination tourism.
- Explain the concept of perishability.
- Discuss how tourism is distributed.

STAR POWER

The Tribeca Film Festival of New York City was launched by Robert DeNiro, Jane Rosenthal, and Craig Hatkoff in an effort to help spur "the economic and spiritual revitalization of lower Manhattan." Backed by the Tribeca Film Institute, the inaugural festival was arranged in just 120 days, following the events of September 11, 2001. With more than 1,300 volunteers and 150,000 attendees from around the world, the event generated over $10.4 million for the local economy in 2002.

The festival takes place each May in the area known as *Tribeca*, or the "Triangle Below Canal Street." Highlights include premiere screenings of domestic and foreign films, panel discussions with filmmakers and actors, and documentary and short-film programming. Moviegoers, the media, and stars create a week-long buzz, with films screening from morning to midnight. During the festival's second year, attendance grew and helped local businesses rake in $50 million from local residents and destination tourists. How could the festival continue its growth and establish an identity as a destination?

ANALYZE AND WRITE

1. List two reasons why the Tribeca Film Festival is able to draw volunteers.
2. List some challenges the film festival might face as a tourist destination.

Case Study Part 2 on page 121

POWER READ

Be an active reader and use these reading strategies:

PREDICT what the section will be about.

CONNECT what you read with your own life.

QUESTION as you read to make sure you understand the content.

RESPOND to what you've read.

Destination Markets

YOU WILL LEARN

- To define the term *destination*.
- To discuss the concept of seasonality.
- To identify the classifications of destinations.
- To describe a destination resort.

WHY IT'S IMPORTANT

Being aware of the types of destinations and why they appeal to travelers is critical to understanding how to market tourism products.

KEY TERMS

- destination
- destination marketing
- seasonality
- resort
- destination resort

PREDICT

Define seasonality.

destination the final stop of a journey, or the goal for travelers

destination marketing the process of developing, promoting, and distributing specific locations to travelers and maintaining appeal as long as possible

What Are Destinations?

By strict definition, a **destination** is the final stop of a journey, or the goal for travelers. However, in the context of tourism, it has a much broader definition. The destinations people explore already exist or have been developed to fill the needs of travelers. Destinations can be towns and cities with historic value, such as colonial Williamsburg in Virginia or Plymouth in Massachusetts. Cities such as Paris, Rome, or Athens combine historic value with art, culture, restaurants, and unique scenery. Destinations can also be regions that have specific tourist appeal, such as the Great Barrier Reef in Australia, Napa and Sonoma wine regions in California, or the scenic Adirondack Mountains in the northeastern portion of the United States.

Destination Geography

A basic understanding of geography is important for understanding the world's destinations. Beyond knowing where a destination is located, you must also know how to get to the destination. Other important considerations include the physical landscape, the climate, the seasons, and the cultural attributes of a destination. What languages are spoken there? What religions are practiced by the residents? What is the political atmosphere of the region? These are a few of the factors that make a destination unique and appealing to tourists.

Marketing a Destination

Any place can be a destination—a town, a region, a country, or a continent. Each place can offer its own tourist products and hospitality services, natural and constructed resources, attractions, climate, and culture. **Destination marketing** is the process of developing, promoting, and distributing specific locations to satisfy travelers and maintain appeal as long as possible.

Seasonality

Consider how or why a destination is popular in relation to the seasons. **Seasonality** is the concept that certain destinations appeal to travelers at certain times of the year, based on climate and geography.

COLD-WEATHER DESTINATIONS Ski resorts in Colorado, Vermont, New Hampshire, and Maine developed out of a need for winter sports such as skiing, snowshoeing, ice skating, and snowmobiling. Because of their favorable climates for natural and machine-made snow, these areas became winter destinations.

WARM-WEATHER DESTINATIONS Warm-weather destinations, such as Florida, the Caribbean, and Hawaii, are known for scenic beaches and water-related activities. People who enjoy surfing, snorkeling, skin diving, and jet skiing are drawn to these areas because of climate, geography, and recreational options. Travelers seeking to sunbathe or escape the cold are drawn to these destinations primarily in the winter months. However, warm-weather destinations appeal to visitors year-round. Summer destinations include all geographic regions, including national parks, foreign countries, the mountains, and beach resorts.

COMPETITIVE MARKET Most destinations cannot afford to be one-season operations. In a highly competitive market, successful destinations offer something for everyone. Tour planners seek to expand market appeal beyond seasonality. Seasonality can be a prime factor for choice of destination, but it can also limit year-round revenue.

Classifying Destinations

In Chapter 2, you learned the various reasons why people travel. Understanding where people go to satisfy their travel needs is equally important. To classify destinations, we must look at the characteristics shared by destinations in a category. This will help us create a framework for understanding the similarities and differences among types of destinations. Several types of destinations attract travelers: resorts and destination resorts, amusement parks, gaming facilities, shopping sites, museums and historical sites, and national parks. Cruise ships as well as sports, recreation, and entertainment facilities are also considered destinations in the context of destination marketing.

TECH
NOTES

Online Promotion
Located off the coast of Australia, Papua New Guinea (PNG) has an estimated population of 4.1 million. The country's Tourism Promotion Authority created an official Web site in an effort to increase the number of tourists who visit PNG. The Web site features detailed information about the country's landscape, people, and products.

➡ If you wanted to visit Papua New Guinea, would you find this Web site useful? Why or why not? Write a review after visiting the Web site through **marketingseries.glencoe.com**.

seasonality the concept that certain destinations appeal to travelers at certain times of the year, based on climate and geography

Ⓐ JOURNEY TO PARADISE **Many people travel to resorts because they include all the amenities and activities that travelers might enjoy in one place.** *How would the season and geographical location of a resort affect business?*

resort a destination that provides entertainment, recreation, leisure activities, accommodations, and food for guests

Resorts and Destination Resorts

Pictures of a resort might depict a large expanse of manicured grounds, perhaps a beach or golf course, multiple pools, restaurants, lavish accommodations, and spa facilities. However, the early resorts in Europe and the United States were built around natural mineral springs and focused on physical and mental-health benefits for guests. Today a **resort** is more than a health spa; it is a destination that provides entertainment, recreation, leisure activities, accommodations, and food for guests.

Localized Facilities

Resorts can be in geographic destinations, such as the desert resorts of Palm Springs, the beach resorts of Palm Beach, or the ski resorts of Aspen. But a resort can also be a destination in itself. A **destination resort** is a resort property in a specific location with a concentration of resources or facilities. For example, The Walt Disney World Resort is a destination resort. The complex nature of its offerings—theme parks, a wide variety of accommodations, meeting and convention facilities, and diverse attractions—makes Disney World appealing to a variety of markets.

Cruise Ships

Cruise ships with their many features for all types of travelers are among the fastest-growing vacation destinations. More ships are added to lines every year, each with a new set of amenities and value-added extras. Some ships offer five-star luxury, while others focus on family features. The new class of megaships carries large numbers of passengers and staff. They offer everything from onboard skating rinks and mini golf courses to multiplex theaters and world-class dining. Many cruise vacations offer onboard as well as onshore activities.

Figure 6.1

Theme Park Traits

THE RIGHT COMBINATION
The success of a theme park depends on a variety of traits that attract guests. *What trait do you think is the most important for a theme park to succeed? The least important? Why?*

1. A workable theme, hook, or gimmick around which to develop the park's image
2. Sufficient natural and human resources to develop and maintain the park
3. Space to grow and expand
4. A favorable climate to ensure maximum attendance
5. Sufficient transportation and other tourist infrastructure to support travel
6. An easy driving distance from metropolitan areas

Itineraries

Cruise itineraries are expanding and changing as fast as the industry grows. Some small ships specialize in ports of call that the larger ships cannot access. New ecotour cruises take place in environmentally fragile areas.

No Seasonality

Unlike land-based resorts, cruise ships are not subject to the seasonality factor. As the weather changes, so do the ports of call. Summer cruise ships in the Mediterranean head to the Caribbean during the winter. Cruises to South America and the Panama Canal are popular during winter months, while Alaska's inland waterway cruises get under way during the summer. Cruise itineraries vary in length from three days to two weeks. Trans-Atlantic voyages last from 18 to 80 days or more, as do around-the-world cruises.

Shoulder Season

The shoulder season is the period between the peak seasons of summer or winter. It is a time when cruise lines reposition and schedule ships for the upcoming season's destination.

Theme Cruises

Theme cruises capture large and diverse markets. Designed for passengers with special hobbies or interests, cruise themes range from big-band music to cooking to sports. Theme-related activities give passengers opportunities to pursue their special interests or learn something new.

Sports, Recreation, and Entertainment Destinations

Destinations with special events such as the Olympic Games, the Super Bowl, Wimbledon tennis championships, NASCAR racing, and the World Series of baseball have global interest. These events attract national and international attention and draw millions of travelers to destinations around the world annually.

Something for Everyone

Sports and recreation destinations also include ski and golf resorts and hunting and fishing lodges. These places range from modest destinations for people who enjoy nature to elegant resort destinations that cater to affluent travelers who can afford luxury in remote locations. Some resort properties specialize in retreats for corporate team building and family reunions. Dude ranches offer guests an opportunity to live like cowboys and participate in the activities of a horse or cattle ranch.

Case Study PART 2

STAR POWER

Continued from Part 1 on page 117

The founders and planners of the Tribeca Film Festival developed ways to draw visitors, involve the community, and create an inviting, energetic experience. Festival programming includes critically acclaimed movies from around the world, many of which are followed by question-and-answer sessions with the cast and crew. There are also discussions on subjects from humor to superheroes. Free outdoor screenings take place in local parks. The festival's awards are presented at the Stuyvesant High School Auditorium. The addition of a Family Film Festival also helps to maintain the festival's broad appeal. Executive Director Peter Scarlet explains, "It's not just lay down your ten bucks, buy the popcorn, and be ejected from the multiplex. You feel a part of a community."

ANALYZE AND WRITE

1. Would a film festival be subject to seasonality? Why or why not? Write a paragraph explaining your answer.
2. Why would a film festival be classified as a destination? Write a paragraph explaining your answer.

destination resort a resort property in a specific location with a concentration of resources or facilities in a localized area

Key Point

Snowboard Bound
Ski resorts generate about $4.1 billion. These winter playgrounds are popular among extreme athletes who account for almost a third of all ski-resort visitors.

Hot Property

A Villa on the Lake

BELLAGIO At the foot of an 8.5-acre lake sits a sprawling villa. Surrounded by gardens, the villa would seem at home in the Italian countryside. Instead, it sits at 3600 Las Vegas Boulevard South. In 1998, Bellagio joined a growing number of theme-based Las Vegas mega-resorts competing for billions of tourist dollars.

Pioneering developer and Mirage Resorts CEO Steve Wynn conceived of Bellagio as a new kind of Las Vegas destination. He wanted to push beyond the fantasy flair of Mirage and the family fun of Treasure Island to create an upscale oasis for discriminating travelers. Wynn assembled an extensive art collection, world-renowned chefs, and design professionals who created a uniquely beautiful atmosphere. He designed a shopping mall that featured luxury brands, a championship golf course, and a world-class spa.

BUILT TO LAST?

Wynn's dream came to life, but Mirage Resorts stock was falling, nevertheless. MGM purchased the company in the year 2000, and with it, the upscale resort and casino. To maximize profits, MGM sold off much of the expensive art collection and opted to use Bellagio's gallery as an exhibition space.

Despite those changes, Bellagio remains a top-level destination. It is the only hotel with two restaurants rated five stars by AAA. In addition, it consistently wins recognition from magazines such as *Condé Nast Traveler* and *Travel + Leisure*. Such praise should make the Bellagio a guaranteed winner, but in the competitive Las Vegas tourism sector, every hotel is a gamble.

1. In what ways does Bellagio appeal to luxury travelers?
2. What theme would you choose for a new Las Vegas destination resort?

CONNECT

What would be your favorite sports or entertainment destination?

MARKETING SERIES *Online*

Remember to check out this book's Web site for destination marketing information and more great resources at **marketingseries.glencoe.com**.

Live Entertainment

In addition to sporting events and recreation, travelers seek live entertainment by attending concerts, theater, and ballet. New York City's famed Broadway theater district attracts tourists from around the world. In Washington, D.C., performances at the Kennedy Center for the Performing Arts are a big draw, as are shows at the Sydney Opera House in Australia. London's theater district is a must-see for most travelers to the United Kingdom. Towns such as Branson, Missouri, and Nashville, Tennessee, have built much of their tourist appeal around the music industry. Branson, for example, provides family-style entertainment and all types of accommodations in the Ozark Mountains and is the number-two driving destination in the United States.

Amusement Parks

Considered destinations in themselves, modern amusement parks began with Disneyland in the 1950s. Advances in technology have contributed to the realism of thrill rides and simulated environments at the parks. A common trait of most amusement and theme parks is the opportunity for guests to escape the real world and be transported to a land of imagination. (See **Figure 6.1** on page 120 for other traits.)

All in One

On-site hotels, restaurants, shopping centers, entertainment venues, transportation, and medical facilities make it unnecessary to leave a park. Amusement and theme-park marketers promote all-in-one convenience, offering family vacations, romantic honeymoons, or corporate meeting sites.

Gaming Facilities

Gaming is no longer restricted to Las Vegas or Atlantic City. Tourists choose from a number of gaming sites across the United States and out of the country. Full-scale casinos operate on American-Indian reservations from rural Connecticut to California. Riverboats are also gaming destinations along the Mississippi River and the Gulf Coast of Louisiana. Small mining towns, such as Deadwood, South Dakota, have taken advantage of historic points of interest from the gold rush era to create theme-based casinos. More than half the states in the United States offer some type of legal gaming.

Gaming Market

Gaming is considered a form of entertainment for a variety of people, especially retirees. Gaming marketers focus on this market. In addition, tours are packaged specifically for people on limited budgets. Many travel agents and tour operators offer day-trip packages. Many Las Vegas hotels and resorts have also added theme-park attractions and a broad range of entertainment for all age groups.

Math Check

INTEREST COST

For her travel agency, Kari borrowed $25,000 at 6 percent interest for four years. Calculate the amount of interest that she will pay.

➡ For tips on finding the solution, go to **marketingseries.glencoe.com**.

Holiday Shopping

The sights and smells of city streets during November in Germany remind passersby that the holidays are around the corner. Shopkeepers open their "luminous world" of holiday markets to locals and visitors alike. This is a century-old tradition.

Almost anything can be found in the markets, including handcrafted toys, aromatic candles, delicate lace, colorful glass, and tree ornaments of every kind. World-famous, doll-sized nutcrackers are favorites. Just as tempting are good things to eat. Children gobble down warm gingerbread cookies and candied fruits. Adults savor grilled sausages and hot spicy drinks. Many cannot resist the traditional *stollen,* a sugar-dusted sweetbread

filled with fruits and nuts. In Dresden, Germany, the town bakers make a stollen that weighs three tons. With fresh snow, twinkling lights, and the sound of carolers, the holiday markets of Germany are a favorite destination for many travelers on a shopping holiday.

Of the special markets that you patronize, what are some characteristics that might make them destinations?

GERMANY

A UNIQUE PEEK

Anne Block
Take My Mother, Please
Custom-Made Tours

What is your job?

"I am the founder and tour planner of Custom-Made Tours."

What do you do in your job?

"I create and lead tailor-made tours of both well-known and unusual sites and attractions in Los Angeles and select cities in Europe, such as Paris, Venice, Rome, Barcelona, to name a few. My trips take people beyond the conventional and deeper into the heart of each destination we visit." Anne develops unique tours throughout the world—such as a "chocolate-lover's tour" through France and Spain.

What kind of training did you have?

"I am self-taught, having been a traveler all over America since the 1960s—and in Europe since 1984. I began by offering tours to visitors of friends when I was living in San Francisco, and then expanded the service to Europe in the early 1990s. My first paying client was actress Lily Tomlin. When she encouraged me to share my knack for showing off places, a company was born."

What advice would you give students?

"Look around and imagine showing the things you enjoy to a newcomer. These things can be a place with a beautiful view, a good spot to eat, an odd or unusual event or building, a tree, or a legend about someone in your town."

What is your key to success?

"Perseverance. I have been in business since 1992. I started small and grew little by little—and never gave up. Knowing I can make someone's day special keeps me going."

Would you classify Anne Block's tours as "destination" tours? Why or why not?

Career Data: Tour Guide

Education and Training
Associate degree or bachelor's degree and real-world travel experience

Skills and Abilities
Communication, interpersonal, and planning skills; a creative eye for interesting attractions

Career Outlook Better-than-average growth through 2012

Career Path Tour planner at a tour company to freelance tour planner to owner of tour to own business

Shopping

Outlet shopping malls, megamalls, and malls featuring entertainment and amusement park rides have contributed to the popular pastime of recreational shopping. As a typical activity for most vacationers, shopping has become one of the principal reasons for travel among many travelers on vacations.

A Major Shopping Destination

The West Edmonton Mall in Edmonton, Alberta, Canada, is the biggest shopping mall in the world. With its on-site hotel, water park, miniature golf course, ice rink, casino, multiplex cinema, amusement park, bowling alley, and underwater adventure park, the mall attracts more than 20 million visitors from all over the world each year. The West Edmonton Mall is a major destination as well as a significant source of tax revenue and a key employer in the region.

Museums and Historical Sites

People are fascinated by history, art, science, and nature. From zoos and aquariums to monuments and memorials, the range of opportunities to experience history and consider the future is vast. These sites are among the world's most popular and most-visited destinations. For example, the Smithsonian Institution in Washington, D.C., is a collection of museums featuring art, natural science, and air and space exhibits. It draws millions of visitors to the U.S. capital. While there, tourists can visit the other monuments and attractions. By driving a few hours, tourists can experience history at colonial Williamsburg in Virginia, the Civil War battlefields of Gettysburg, Pennsylvania, and Arlington National Cemetery in Arlington, Virginia.

NATIONAL TREASURES The Smithsonian Institution in Washington, D.C., houses artifacts of American history, science, and transportation in several museums. One of its museums, the National Museum of Natural History, is a popular destination for citizens of the United States and the world. *Do you think this museum would have fewer visitors if it were located in another American city? Why or why not?*

National Parks and Gardens

The natural wonders of Yellowstone, Yosemite, and Grand Canyon national parks have inspired tourists since the late 1800s. Traffic to these national treasures can become so heavy at times that travel must be restricted. The national park concept extends beyond our borders to other countries that protect and preserve the natural beauty and unique features of the land.

Gardens and Estates

Botanical gardens, both public and private, are another type of destination. Grand estates such as the Biltmore Estate in Asheville, North Carolina, and Butchart Gardens in Victoria, British Columbia, are well-known attractions.

Promoting a Destination

As locations go in and out of fashion, marketing destination plays a key role. When seasons change or social trends shift, the focus of a marketing campaign must also change. Marketing to special-interest groups is different from marketing to people who are looking for a spa vacation or a destination resort.

Quick Check ✔

RESPOND to what you've read by answering these questions.

1. What are destinations? Describe several types of destinations. _____
_____
_____
_____
_____

2. What is a destination resort? _____
_____
_____
_____
_____

3. What is meant by the term *shoulder season?* _____
_____
_____
_____
_____

Basics of Destination Marketing

Tourism Providers and Promoters

Many travel businesses and organizations provide and promote destination tourism. Providers of travel and tourism products include airline companies, cruise lines, car rental agencies, hotels, restaurants, and tourist attractions. Tourism products are marketed to travelers through television, radio, print, and Internet media as well as brochure distribution at travel agencies and tourist information centers. (See **Figure 6.2** on page 128 for examples of destination activities.) Thousands of people are employed by a variety of businesses and organizations that market and promote destination tourism, including:

- Travel agencies
- Tour operators
- Convention and visitors bureaus (CVBs)
- Trade and government organizations

Travel Agencies

Though the number of travel agencies worldwide has decreased in recent years, travel agents still provide valuable services to the public. Travel agents know about travel products and have access to information that may be unavailable through other sources. They also act as intermediaries for airlines, hotels, cruise lines, and other hospitality providers.

Commission

An **intermediary** is an agent who does not work directly for a travel provider but sells his or her products for a fee. The intermediary is paid by **commission**, which is a fee or payment for services based on a percentage of products sold. Airlines were once the staple of the travel agent's product providers. However, airlines have been steadily decreasing the amount of commission they pay to agents. In some cases, they may impose a cap, or limit, on the amount paid.

Responsibilities

Agents are responsible for knowing current fares and pricing structures, package promotions, rules and regulations, travel warnings, and emerging destinations. The travel agent is an important link between suppliers of travel products and people who buy them.

AS YOU READ . . .

YOU WILL LEARN
- To identify the various businesses that provide and promote destination tourism.
- To explain the concept of perishability.
- To discuss how tourism is distributed.

WHY IT'S IMPORTANT

Understanding who provides and promotes travel products and services for travelers is key to being able to create a successful marketing strategy.

KEY TERMS
- intermediary
- commission
- channel of distribution
- convention and visitors bureau (CVB)

PREDICT

Name some providers of destinations.

intermediary an agent who does not work directly for a travel provider but sells his or her products for a fee

commission a fee or payment for services based on a percentage of products sold

CONNECT

What advantages are
offered by travel agents?

Tour Operators

A tour operator, or tour wholesaler, assembles and markets many travel products as a travel package that is promoted to the public for one all-inclusive price. Usually, a travel package consists of transportation to and around the destination, accommodations, some meals, entertainment or attractions, and an escort or host.

Preferred Tour Rates

Because tour operators can negotiate preferred or discounted rates with the suppliers of travel products, they can pass on the savings to the client. Tour operators must market their packages to the appropriate audience due to perishability, or the tendency of a product to be unusable after a certain amount of time. A tour that leaves with unsold space, much like an unsold airline seat or hotel room, is a missed opportunity to generate income from that package.

Distribution Channels

channel of distribution the path a travel product takes from the producer to the consumer, or traveler

Tour operators are an important link in the channel of distribution for travel products and services. A **channel of distribution** is the path a travel product takes from the producer to the consumer, or traveler. For example, if a couple wants to go to an exotic destination for their honeymoon, the travel agent may provide them with a brochure from the "Too Good To Be True" tour operator. The tour operator uses the travel agent as a *channel of distribution* to distribute the brochure.

Figure 6.2

Destination Activities for U.S. Travelers

DESTINATIONS FOR TOURISM All of these activities are also destinations for travelers in the United States. Each activity provides employment for many people. *What would be your favorite activity while on vacation?*

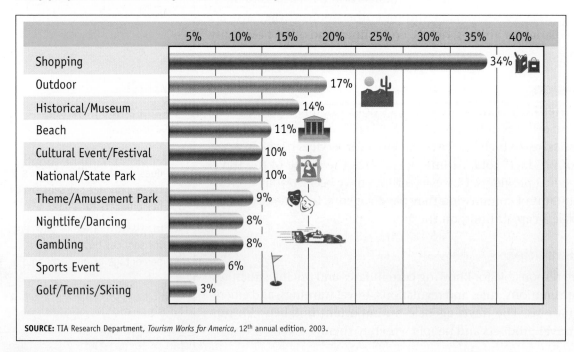

Activity	Percentage
Shopping	34%
Outdoor	17%
Historical/Museum	14%
Beach	11%
Cultural Event/Festival	10%
National/State Park	10%
Theme/Amusement Park	9%
Nightlife/Dancing	8%
Gambling	8%
Sports Event	6%
Golf/Tennis/Skiing	3%

SOURCE: TIA Research Department, *Tourism Works for America*, 12th annual edition, 2003.

Convention and Visitors Bureaus

Most small towns and cities have local chambers of commerce that serve as marketers for travel and tourism in the community. However, in large metropolitan areas that have the infrastructure to support large business meetings and conventions, marketing is provided by CVBs. A **convention and visitors bureau (CVB)** is an organization that works with meeting planners to provide tourist information services to business and leisure travelers.

Trade and Government Organizations

Trade associations are membership organizations that sponsor marketing campaigns, promote destination tourism, and offer education and training to their members. Examples of such organizations include:

- American Hotel and Lodging Association (AH&LA)

- National Restaurant Association (NRA)

- National Tour Association (NTA)

- Cruise Line International Association (CLIA)

These trade associations also lobby governments for the advancement of causes that have a direct impact on their individual industries.

QUESTION

What organization in large cities markets travel?

convention and visitors bureau (CVB) an organization that works with meeting planners to provide tourist information services to business and leisure travelers

▼ ENCHANTING DESTINATIONS
A state tourism agency markets its state as a destination by using attractive print ads in travel magazines. *How does a state benefit from spending tax dollars for tourism campaigns?*

7:42 AM:
NEW MEXICO, USA

MONDAY MORNING
TRAFFIC JAM.

NEW MEXICO
LAND OF ENCHANTMENT
TOURISM DEPARTMENT

FOR MORE INFORMATION
CALL 505-827-7400, FAX 505-827-7402,
E-MAIL SHARON.MALOOF@STATE.NM.US
OR VISIT WWW.NEWMEXICO.ORG

Hondo, New Mexico

Government Tourism Agencies

Most states in the United States, Canadian provinces, and many countries have government agencies that promote tourism to their locales. At the national level, this type of agency is known as a *national tourism office*, or NTO. Funded primarily through tax dollars, these organizations collect information about visitors to the area. They study the data to identify travel trends and consumer behavior. This information can be very helpful to tourist businesses for planning marketing strategies that generate growth and income.

Promoting States as Destinations

A state or provincial organization is responsible for promoting the entire state or province as a destination. Such organizations have budgets to advertise nationally and internationally to increase travel to their regions. For example, when the Democratic National Convention was held in Boston in 2004, the Massachusetts Office of Travel and Tourism (MOTT) funded a direct-mail campaign to thousands of delegates, encouraging them to extend their stays and travel to other parts of the state. This type of promotion can generate revenue from hotel room-and-meals tax. The tax income goes back into the state economy and employment sector and continues to fund tourism promotion.

Sharing Marketing Duties

Travel agencies, tour operators, regional visitors bureaus, trade associations, and government agencies all share in marketing destinations and resorts for tourism and travel. Each business or organization uses different strategies to attract visitors to a region to promote and maintain destination tourism as a source of revenue.

Quick Check

RESPOND to what you've read by answering these questions.

1. What does an intermediary do? _____

_____

_____

2. What is the definition of *perishability?* _____

_____

_____

3. What is the purpose of government tourism agencies? _____

_____

_____

Worksheet 6.1

Destination: Your Hometown

You have been assigned to promote your community as a tourist attraction. Spend time in various places in your community. Write a descriptive advertisement to attract tourists to your community. Include at least two attractions or features of the region in your advertisement.

_____

_____

_____

_____

_____

_____

_____

_____

_____

_____

_____

_____

_____

_____

_____

_____

_____

_____

_____

_____

_____

_____

_____

_____

_____

_____

_____

Worksheet 6.2

Cruise Lines

Choose one of the cruise lines from the following list. Then answer the questions that follow.

- American Cruise Lines
- Bergen Line Services
- Bora Bora Cruises
- Carnival Cruise Lines
- Celebrity Cruises
- Costa Cruise Lines
- Crystal Cruises
- Cunard Line
- Disney Cruise Line
- First European Cruises
- Fred Olsen Cruise Lines
- Holland America Line

- MSC Italian Cruises
- Norwegian Coastal Voyages, Inc.
- Norwegian Cruise Line
- Orient Lines
- Princess Cruises
- Radisson Seven Seas Cruises
- Regal Cruises
- Royal Caribbean International
- Royal Olympic Cruises
- Seabourn Cruise Line
- Silversea Cruises
- Windstar Cruises

1. What is the name of the cruise line? _____

_____

2. Go to the Internet or library and research the cruise line. How did this company get started? _____

_____

_____

_____

3. Has this company ever changed the way it operates? If so, how? Why? _____

_____

_____

4. What other cruise lines on the list are significant competitors? _____

_____

_____

5. If you were going on a cruise, which cruise line would you choose? Why? _____

_____

_____

_____

Portfolio Works

DESIGN A THEME PARK

Use the space below to sketch the layout of your own theme park that includes adjacent land. Include hotels, restaurants, shopping, entertainment, and emergency facilities that you think are necessary.

Add this page to your career portfolio.

CHAPTER SUMMARY

Section 6.1 **Destination Markets**

destination (p. 118)
destination marketing
(p. 118)
seasonality (p. 118)
resort (p. 120)
destination resort
(p. 120)

- A destination is the final stop of a journey, which is the purpose of travel by travelers.

- Seasonality may influence a traveler's choice of destination of a cold or warm environment.

- There are many classifications of destinations: resorts and destination resorts, cruise ships, sports/recreation and entertainment destinations, amusement and theme parks, gaming facilities, shopping sites, historical sites/museums, and national parks.

Section 6.2 **Basics of Destination Marketing**

intermediary (p. 127)
commission (p. 127)
channel of distribution
(p. 128)
convention and visitors
bureau (CVB) (p. 129)

- A variety of businesses promote and provide destination tourism: travel agencies, tour operators, convention and visitors bureaus, trade associations, and government organizations.

- Perishability in tourism means that the travel product must be sold to the right market at the right time, or there will be a missed opportunity and lost revenue.

- Tourism is distributed through tour operators, travel agencies, and hotels.

CHECKING CONCEPTS

1. **Define** the term *destination marketing*.
2. **Name** three summer destinations.
3. **List** three types of destinations.
4. **Describe** a resort.
5. **Name** one travel/tourism organization that may be sponsored by a government.
6. **Describe** a situation to illustrate the perishability of tourism.
7. **Identify** the channel of distribution for a travel brochure.

Critical Thinking

8. **Explain** why you think theme cruises are popular as destinations.

CROSS-CURRICULUM SKILLS

Work-Based Learning

Interpersonal Skills—Serving Clients/Customers

9. Write the script for a TV ad that promotes your favorite amusement park. Include reasons that people should come to this park.

Basic Skills—Listening and Writing Skills

10. You are a tour operator in your community. Prepare a tour brochure that includes highlights in the community, such as a particular site, historic homes, gardens, or art.

School-Based Learning

Social Studies/Computer Technology

11. Use the Internet to contact a national or international tourism office of a favorite state or country. Write a fact sheet with at least six facts about the state or country. Write a brief paragraph that predicts travel trends based on the information you obtained.

Art

12. Use poster board to create and sketch the main attraction of a theme park. Display your poster in class.

 **CONNECTION**

Role Play: Travel Agent

SITUATION You are to assume the role of travel agent for a family-owned agency located in a small town. A new customer has phoned to arrange a trip. He or she would like to go on a vacation to celebrate a special occasion. The customer does not have a preference about where to go or what he or she would like to do.

ACTIVITY You are to explain to the customer the many types of leisure-vacation options available. Your explanation should help him or her decide upon a destination.

EVALUATION You will be evaluated on how well you meet the following performance indicators:

- Describe services offered by the travel and tourism industry.
- Plan tourist destinations.
- Plan a variety of guest/client activities.
- Plan tours.
- Monitor guest satisfaction with service/facility.

 **INTERNET ACTIVITY**

Use the Internet to access the Web site of the American Hotel and Lodging Association.

- Click Join AH&LA.
- Click "click here" to learn about the benefits of membership.
- Make a list of the seven categories of benefits.
- Write two benefits under each benefit category.

➡️For a link to the American Hotel and Lodging Association Web site to do this activity, go to **marketingseries.glencoe.com**.

Chapter 7

Sports, Events, and Entertainment

Section 7.1

Sports and Recreation

Section 7.2

Events and Entertainment

Chapter Objectives

- Describe the types of amateur sports.
- Describe the types of professional sports.
- Identify career opportunities in sports event management.
- Explain the types of recreation.
- Differentiate between public and private events.
- Identify the categories of the entertainment industry.

Case Study   PART 1

HE SHOOTS, HE SCORES!

Colorado-based entrepreneur Philip Anshutz began to amass his fortune in the late 1970s when he discovered an oil field in Utah. After selling a portion of his land to Mobil Oil in the 1980s for $500 million, he bought the Southern Pacific railroad. Profits came when he laid fiber-optic wiring alongside the railroad tracks and arranged a merger with Union Pacific.

Then the Anshutz Entertainment Group (AEG) planned to purchase the NBA's Denver Nuggets. But when those plans failed, Anshutz bought the NHL's Los Angeles Kings. His vision was to build a state-of-the-art sports arena with luxury boxes and sellable naming rights. Thus, the Staples Center was born. Hosting the NBA's Lakers and Clippers, a WNBA team, the Kings hockey club, an arena football team, concerts, and events, the $375 million arena was profitable the day it opened its doors in 1999. AEG's next move was to pick up the soccer team called the Los Angeles Galaxy. But would Anshutz's magic touch soccer, a sport without a major fan base in the United States?

ANALYZE AND WRITE

1. List some reasons why the Staples Center was profitable in its first year.
2. Write a paragraph about the challenges of promoting and hosting soccer.

Case Study Part 2 on page 149

POWER READ

Be an active reader and use these reading strategies:

PREDICT what the section will be about.
CONNECT what you read with your own life.
QUESTION as you read to make sure you understand the content.
RESPOND to what you've read.

Sports and Recreation

YOU WILL LEARN

- To describe the types of amateur sports.
- To describe the types of professional sports.
- To identify career opportunities in sports event management.
- To explain the types of recreation.

WHY IT'S IMPORTANT

Sports are part of today's society. Most Americans are involved in the sports industry as participants or spectators. Sports and recreation events involve hospitality and tourism businesses.

KEY TERMS

- amateur sports
- Paralympics
- commercial recreation
- public recreation
- therapeutic recreation

PREDICT

How might sports relate to tourism?

Sports and Recreation

For generations, people have enjoyed sports and recreational activities during their leisure time. Yet the actual management of the sports and recreation events that draw tourists and other spectators is a relatively new pursuit. The industry has grown in recent years and offers a variety of opportunities, challenges, and career choices for interested individuals.

Ancient History

Greece was one of the first nations to organize sports-related activities and build the necessary sports facilities to house them. That was centuries ago in 776 B.C. when the first Olympic Games took place in the city of Athens. It was a concept that transformed a recreational celebration into a mega sports and entertainment event.

Later History

In past centuries, the wealthy upper class enjoyed organized sports and recreation. This group had the time and extra income to be spectators or participants. During the 1700s, the English aristocracy created private sports clubs with limited membership. The sports of thoroughbred racing, cricket, rugby, and soccer were some of the earliest examples of athletic activities with club management. During the 1800s in the United States, professional sports leagues formed. The first baseball league was established in the 1870s. The first U.S. golf and tennis tournaments took place during the 1930s.

Types of Leisure Activities

With more leisure activities available today, many Americans participate in sports and entertainment events. These recreational opportunities are active or participatory, such as team sports. Leisure activities, such as reading, going to the movies, or playing computer games, are passive and require less action. The different types of leisure activities can be divided into these major categories:

- Sports
- Recreation
- Events
- Entertainment

Categories of Sports

An organized sporting event is a competition that is controlled by an authority, such as a league or association. Organized sports fall into two categories—amateur sports and professional sports.

Amateur Sports

Amateur sports are athletic activities and competitions for athletes who do not get paid. Youth sports, high school sports, and collegiate sports are examples of amateur sports.

YOUTH SPORTS Youth sports programs emphasize participation rather than competition. The Little League and Peewee League give children and teenagers the opportunity to play with friends and develop teamwork. Many other youth sports programs are sponsored by local organizations such as the YMCA, YWCA, and Boys and Girls Clubs of America. Recreational programs may include team play or skills classes, such as swimming lessons.

HIGH SCHOOL SPORTS High school sports focus on team spirit. Local communities are often big supporters of high school teams. Players, coaches, parents, and teachers encourage students to balance the benefits of athletic achievements with academic success. The National Federation of State High School Associations (NFHS) is the national coordinator for high school sports programs. It sets guidelines to ensure everyone enjoys the games without sacrificing academic education.

COLLEGE SPORTS Colleges and universities offer a variety of sports to appeal to a wide range of students. Large universities usually offer more sports options. Competitive divisions of college sports are ranked and governed by the National Collegiate Athletic Association (NCAA). This organization creates guidelines and enforces rules to encourage fair competition. Regulation of college sports is very important because college sports have become a major force in the sports event industry, with careers, funding, and students' futures at stake.

Professional Sports

Professional sports are athletic activities, including local, regional, national, or international events that attract spectators and tourists and generate revenue. Examples of events can include championship tournaments for basketball (NBA Championships), baseball (World Series), football (Super Bowl), soccer (World Cup), and golf championships (PGA Championship), tennis (Wimbledon), and auto racing (NASCAR Nextel Cup).

INCOME AND REGULATION Modern professional sports events produce billions of dollars. Income is generated from the millions of fans who attend games and tournaments as well as from advertisers on radio, TV, the Internet, and in print. Athletes are compensated by the team, or franchise, sponsors, and other corporate endorsement opportunities. Because money and reputations are at stake, leagues and associations also regulate professional sports.

THE Electronic CHANNEL

Sports Travel

The sports industry has teamed up with tourism for a winning combination—sports travel. Several travel agencies are aware of the sports fan's need to "be there." So they have put together tour packages for most major sporting events, from the Super Bowl and NBA All Star games to the World Series and Kentucky Derby. Sports enthusiasts can book a variety of tours online that include transportation, accommodations, tickets, luxury stadium boxes, restaurants, and souvenirs of the sports event of a lifetime. Book tours with known agencies to avoid getting stranded without a ticket. Sports tours can be expensive, but there are tours for every group size, budget, and level of accommodation.

➡ List the features and price of your dream sports tour after viewing a tour Web site through **marketingseries.glencoe.com**.

amateur sports athletic activities and competitions for athletes who do not get paid

COMPETITIVE EVENTS
All types of athletes
participate in competitions
that attract spectators.
*Would you classify this
athlete as amateur or
professional? Why?*

ETHICS & ISSUES

Olympic Bidding
Salt Lake City hosted the
Winter Olympics in 2002.
Unfortunately, 13 Olympic
officials were accused of
accepting bribes in
exchange for voting in favor
of Salt Lake City's Olympic
bid. The officials were
accused of accepting gifts,
including cash, college
scholarships, and tickets to
top sporting events and
holiday destinations. These
accusations affected the
entire Olympic bidding
process. Now cities with
little chance of winning an
Olympic bid are ruled out in
order to save them the cost
of campaigning. *Is this
policy fair to Olympic city
hopefuls, and will it prevent
bribery in the future?*

Other Sports

Sports are not limited to amateur sports, such as youth, high school, college, and professional sports. The world of sports also includes international sports, extreme sports, and sports for athletes with disabilities,
all of which draw large target markets.

INTERNATIONAL SPORTS The popularity of a team varies from
country to country. International sports are sports that are played in
more than one nation. Through sports, different cultures enjoy a common interest. The Olympics played a major role in the development
of international sports. Increasingly, sports teams seek global exposure.
International federations (IFs) govern and regulate international sports.
Each federation establishes its own eligibility rules and manages international competitive events.

EXTREME SPORTS Extreme sports are nontraditional sports. They
feature daring athletes competing in sports such as skateboarding, snowboarding, surfing, and BMX bike riding.

SPORTS AND DISABLITIES Athletes with disabilities have been
participating in organized sports competitions since 1948 when Sir Lud-
wig Guttman organized a contest for World War II veterans with spinal
cord injuries in England, which became the Paralympic Games.

- **Paralympics**—The Paralympic Games are competitions in
  which the world's best athletes with physical disabilities showcase their talents. Games are held during the same year the
  Olympic Games take place.

- **Special Olympics**—The Special Olympics began in 1968 to
  offer a competitive venue for children and adults with develop-
  mental disabilities.

Olympic Games

The first Olympic competition probably took place in 776 B.C. in Olympia, Greece. The tradition of the Olympic Truce, or *Ekecheiria* (Greek for *"truce"*), was established in ancient Greece during the 9th century B.C. by a treaty between three kings. During the Truce period, athletes, artists, and their families as well as ordinary pilgrims could travel in safety to participate in or attend the Olympic Games and then return safely to their respective countries. As the Games approached, the sacred Truce was proclaimed and announced by citizens of Elis, who traveled on foot throughout Greece to pass on the message.

Relevance for Today

The International Olympic Committee (IOC) revived the ancient concept of the Olympic Truce. The IOC's goal is to protect the interests of athletes and sports and to promote peaceful and diplomatic solutions to conflicts around the world. Through this concept, the IOC aims to:

- Raise awareness and encourage leaders to act in favor of peace.

- Mobilize youth for the promotion of the Olympic ideals.

- Establish contacts between communities in conflict.

- Offer humanitarian support in countries at war.

Paralympics competitions in which the world's best athletes with physical disabilities showcase their talents

CONNECT

Do you think the Olympic Truce is relevant today? Why?

World Market

Tee Time: Ice Golf

Although red paint outlines the "green," which is actually white, playing ice golf in Norway is tricky. Just ask the 36 international competitors invited to play in the 2004 World Ice Golf Championships in Svalbard, a group of islands in Norway's northernmost territory. Outfitted in layers of clothing, mittens, goggles, and spiked shoes, the athletes face subzero temperatures. They also face a 36-hole course sculpted out of frozen terrain. Competitors play with orange balls, shoot for large golf cups, and use scrapers to clean snow off the putt line. Tips for playing ice golf include: Dogsleds have the right of way; watch out for seal-breathing holes; and heed rifle shots, which warn of approaching polar bears. Though the challenges may outweigh the fun and sport of the game, ice golf is "the thrill of a lifetime," sums up one competitor.

Why do you think nontraditional sports appeal to players and spectators?

NORWAY

Math Check

COST OF A VENUE

A teen center found a concert hall to rent for $450 per month. To secure that space for their annual music show, the teen center must pay the first and last month's rent with a $250 security deposit. What amount is due?

➡ For tips on finding the solution, go to **marketingseries.glencoe.com**.

Careers

Many people who are not athletes work in the sports industry. The career opportunities are diverse in sports-related businesses and organizations, from sports agencies, facilities, broadcasting, and retailing to teams and associations.

Agencies

Most sports agencies employ sports agents who represent athletes and coaches. The agent is a personal manager who is responsible for promoting his or her client. Functions of an agent include negotiating, marketing, and providing financial assistance and legal advice. Promotional opportunities by the media further boost players' salaries and their opportunities for endorsements. The competitive sports market and growth of free agents (athletes who are free to sign contracts with any team) help fuel the need for sports agents. In addition, there are many other support staff members who work at agencies.

Facilities

Public-assembly facilities, or venues, offer numerous management and marketing-related careers. Venues can include arenas, stadiums, convention/exposition centers, racetracks, casinos, and theaters. Within these facilities is a broad range of career opportunities:

- **Marketing Director**—Sports facilities employ marketing directors who are involved with designing various marketing materials, coordinating promotions, and buying advertising.

- **PR Facility Director**—This staff member is responsible for showcasing the facility and its offerings. The PR facility director creates positive relationships with the community and media.

- **Event Director**—The event director manages planning and implementation of shows and events. Responsibilities also include crowd control, security issues, and personnel supervision.

- **Booking Director**—The booking director works in large facilities with a general manager to rent the facility to teams, entertainers, or organizations.

- **Operations Director**—Responsibilities of the operations director include coordinating and supervising shows and events. This person controls labor, scheduling, repairs, and maintenance.

- **Box Office Director**—The box office director handles the sale of all tickets and final revenues, and provides guest service.

- **Concession Manager**—The concession manager is responsible for providing food at snack stands and other outlets.

All facility managers and directors need to understand marketing, purchasing, inventory control, business law, and insurance issues. Entry-level positions are also available in security, maintenance, parking, vending, and concessions.

Key Point !

➤ **THE SPORTS DOLLAR**

In 2004, the sports industry generated over $213 billion in revenue, making it one of the fastest-growing industries.

Hot Property

Behind the Scenes

During events, thousands of visitors come through the doors of arenas, stadiums, and convention halls. It takes hundreds of employees to operate these facilities. Venue owners can hire consultants, contractors, and concessionaires to get the job done, or they can save time and money by hiring a private firm such as SMG.

Hyatt Hotels created SMG to manage the Louisiana Superdome in 1977. In 1988, the company went solo, with Hyatt retaining partial ownership. Hyatt and Aramark Corp., a service management company, split ownership of SMG. Since 1997, the SMG roster of venues has grown to 49 convention centers, 69 arenas, and 7 stadiums including its Soldier Field in Chicago. At the same time, the company runs 33 performing arts centers and ten recreational facilities.

GROWTH AND GOALS

In 2000, SMG acquired a competitor's company and gained accounts through Aramark. According to SMG president Wes Westley, these acquisitions nearly doubled the size of the company. Westley talked with *Amusement Business* magazine about his four major goals for the company: The goals were to achieve record earnings every year, to integrate the new acquisitions into the SMG fold, to add more accounts to the roster, and to help employees advance within the company. Through acquisitions, investing in employees, and seeking new partners, SMG plans to achieve those goals.

1. What are Wes Westley's goals for SMG?
2. How can you tell when a venue is well managed?

Broadcasting

Television viewers can choose from hundreds of program options, but sports events are a large segment of media entertainment. Sports TV networks, channels, radio stations, and Web sites offer many career opportunities for sports enthusiasts. In many outlets, on-air broadcasters are responsible for broadcasting sporting events. Writers and sales personnel at all levels assist with information gathering and distribution.

ATHLETIC DIRECTORS Colleges employ individuals to serve as liaisons between their sports teams and local broadcasters. Known as *athletic directors,* these individuals work in sales, marketing, and public relations for a particular team.

MEDIA DIRECTORS College and professional sports teams also employ *media directors* and groups of *media specialists* to communicate with the media and to promote the team. A group creates print materials, such as news releases, fact sheets, pregame information sheets, hometown or local news stories, media guides, and programs. The group also arranges press conferences, promotes athletes, and prepares coaches and athletes for on-camera interviews. Some sports organizations or teams produce their games and have control over their image.

Figure 7.1

Professional Sports Associations

MAJOR SPORTS These professional organizations employ many people to promote and regulate sporting events and athletes. *How do sports associations and leagues promote fair competition?*

• MLB	Major League Baseball
• NBA	National Basketball Association
• NFL	National Football League
• NHL	National Hockey League
• MLS	Major League Soccer
• PGA	Professional Golf Association
• NASCAR	National Association for Stock Car Auto Racing
• USPTA	United States Professional Tennis Association

Retail

Sports retailing encompasses the sporting goods industry and the licensing of sports products. The sporting goods industry manufactures equipment, apparel, footwear, and accessories for the sports and fitness market. To license sports products, companies pay a fee to manufacture products identified by official logos and trademarks of a team or player. Opportunities exist in sales, marketing, and manufacturing at wholesale businesses and retail stores.

Teams, Leagues, and Associations

Experience with amateur sports, particularly at the high school level, is useful for working with minor league franchises, college teams, and professional sports leagues. College athletic departments, especially at the Division I or II levels, offer positions in marketing, sales, public relations, and coaching. In addition, all sports have associations or organizations to oversee the rules and regulations of each league, team, or group. Career opportunities in this area can include membership and sponsorship service positions as well as marketing or management jobs. **Figure 7.1** lists some major professional sports associations.

Sports and Lifestyle

Not all Americans participate in organized sports teams or leagues. However, many enjoy healthful recreational and leisure activities. Health-and-fitness industries provide many career opportunities.

Health and Fitness

Years ago health-and-fitness clubs were small facilities or gyms specializing only in weightlifting or boxing. Today commercial health-and-fitness centers offer features such as cardiovascular equipment, strength-training equipment, and aerobic programs. Opportunities exist for counselors, trainers, childcare specialists, instructors, and managers.

QUESTION

How do sports associations and organizations protect the best interests of sports leagues?

Recreation

People seek recreational activities for the same reasons they enjoy sports events: Recreational activities provide fun, relaxation, excitement, social interaction, and/or challenges. There are two types of recreation—commercial recreation and public recreation.

Commercial Recreation

Tourism provides numerous possibilities for recreation. **Commercial recreation** is any recreational activity for which a guest pays a fee. Amusement parks, theme parks, water parks, zoos, aquariums, museums, private clubs, and family entertainment centers offer recreational activities. Theme parks can be resort destinations, combining recreation, food, entertainment, and accommodations.

commercial recreation any recreational activity for which a guest pays a fee

Public Recreation

Public recreation is either free or paid recreation that takes place on state and federal lands and in city, state, or national parks. Monuments, seashores, historic sites, and national parks and preserves are all included in this category. The government protects and preserves these regions for the enjoyment of future generations.

public recreation free or paid recreation that takes place on state and federal lands and in city, state, or national parks

NATURAL RECREATION Yellowstone National Park is one of this country's most popular recreational destinations. *Why do you think public recreational activities are classified with hospitality and tourism?*

High-Tech Treasure Hunt

Geocaching (pronounced *geo-cashing*) is an outdoor activity that has spread to all 50 states and more than 100 countries around the world. Anyone with a Global Positioning System (GPS) receiver may become a geocacher. After entering coordinates into the GPS unit, players receive signals from satellites that tell them where to locate a cache. The cache is a watertight container that is well hidden and contains small, inexpensive treasures. Geocachers leave another treasure behind to replace one they have taken. Then they note the date of their find in a logbook.

➡ How do the states of Nevada and Arkansas deal with geocaching? Answer this question after reading information through **marketingseries.glencoe.com.**

therapeutic recreation any recreation that includes activities to help a person's emotional, mental, or physical health

Other Types of Recreation

Recreation encompasses more than commercial activities and sporting events. Other noncommercial recreation includes therapeutic, outdoor, military, community, and campus programs.

- **Therapeutic recreation**—**Therapeutic recreation** is any recreation that includes activities to help a person's emotional, mental, or physical health. Medical care centers and community social-service agencies offer programs such as outdoor camping, counseling, social work, and elderly adult services.

- **Outdoor recreation**—Outdoor recreation is diverse. Not-for-profit agencies as well as for-profit companies offer whitewater rafting, kayaking, canoeing, camping and hiking, and skiing and snowboarding.

- **Military recreation**—The purpose of this type of recreation is to improve morale and increase the overall physical and mental readiness of military personnel. Social programs develop a sense of community. Service clubs, movies, crafts, hobbies, and youth and family activities are military recreational activities.

- **Community programs**—Recreation through community programs is voluntary and often membership based. Organizations such as the YMCA, YWCA, Boys and Girls Clubs of America, Boy Scouts, and Girl Scouts provide youth and family activities.

- **Campus programs**—Recreational activities at colleges and universities include intramural sports and other campus activities. Clubs offer skiing, hiking, swimming, drama, dance, music, and film activities.

Hospitality & Tourism and Sports

The sports and recreation industries are integral parts of the hospitality and tourism industries. All of these industries produce a vast range of career opportunities for amateurs and professionals.

Quick Check

RESPOND to what you've read by answering these questions.

1. What are the two types of organized sports? _____

2. What are three types of amateur sports. _____

3. What are two types of recreation. _____

Events and Entertainment

The Importance of Events

People have always enjoyed gathering to celebrate important events in their lives. The earliest events centered on myths, legends, or rituals unique to a particular culture. These traditions evolved into community occasions, celebrated on an annual or seasonal basis. Personal milestones such as birthdays or marriages are also marked by celebrations. Today public and private events are sources of revenue for the hospitality and tourism industries. Both types of events bring individuals together to share a common group experience.

Public Events

Public events can be categorized many different ways. The most common categories of public events are:

- Size

- Purpose

Size of Public Events

The size of an event refers to the number of attendees, the amount of media coverage, the venue, or facility, and the destination itself. Some events that are classified by size include mega-events, hallmark events, major events, and local events.

MEGA-EVENTS A **mega-event** is the largest type of event, which is a unique, "must-see" happening that has international appeal. Large in scope, mega-events involve extensive media coverage, high levels of attendance, and high revenues for the host region. The Olympic Games are an example of a mega-event.

HALLMARK EVENTS A **hallmark event** is a local or regional event with national or possible international appeal that occurs once or annually. In most cases, these events showcase an area's appeal to tourists. The Mardi Gras festival held every March in New Orleans, Louisiana, is an example of a hallmark event.

MAJOR EVENTS Smaller in scale than mega- or hallmark events, major events attract a significant number of attendees. An example of a major event is the weeklong Newport, Rhode Island, International Film Festival, which premieres new movies and attracts celebrities and producers.

AS YOU READ . . .

YOU WILL LEARN

- To differentiate between public and private events.
- To identify the categories of the entertainment industry.

WHY IT'S IMPORTANT

Events and entertainment touch our lives on a daily basis and provide a variety of exciting career opportunities in tour planning and management fields.

KEY TERMS

- mega-event
- hallmark event
- consumer show
- performing arts

mega-event the largest type of event, which is a unique, "must-see" happening that has international appeal

hallmark event a local or regional event with national or possible international appeal that occurs once or annually

PREDICT

What is your definition of a mega-event?

Profiles in Hospitality

FORMULA FOR A FESTIVAL

Dave Fooks
Executive Director
Kutztown Folklife Festival

What is your job?
"I am the executive director of the Kutztown Folklife Festival. The Kutztown Festival is an annual, weeklong event celebrating Pennsylvania Dutch folklife and traditions."

What do you do in your job?
"My job entails planning, operation, and oversight of the festival as well as year-round community relations and promotion. I oversee all aspects of the festival, including soliciting for sponsorship or partnering."

What kind of training did you have?
"When I began, there were no formal programs for training in this field. I started out as a craftsman selling at festivals and got involved as a volunteer working within a craft organization. After being hired in a paid position, I joined industry associations and took whatever educational seminars and workshops were offered. Today several universities have programs for festival and event management."

What advice would you give students?
"Get as much experience as possible, starting as a volunteer. I still work as a volunteer for numerous events, because I can always learn something new. I read everything there is to read about the industry. I also write articles and teach seminars."

What is your key to success?
"You must be able to keep everyone focused on the business management of the festival. This is not always easy because the primary purpose of a festival, after all, is to have fun."

In what size category would this event be placed?

Career Data: Festival Director

Education and Training
Associate degree or bachelor's degree in festival and event management, business, or marketing

Skills and Abilities
Organizational, multitasking, and communication skills

Career Outlook Better-than-average growth through 2012

Career Path Volunteer or internship to assistant planner to manager to director

LOCAL EVENTS Local events appeal to local or regional markets. These events tend to attract local residents and local media coverage. Events such as country fairs or chili cook-offs might run one day or several days—and may be held seasonally or annually. Revenue is generated from ticket sales or concession sales. Local events have little impact on overnight accommodations or tourism.

Purpose of Public Events

Public events serve different purposes. The most common purposes are to raise funds and to increase awareness of a particular group, cause, or destination. Different types of events that are classified by purpose include political events, cultural events, military events, tourist attractions, college and university events, nonprofit organizational events, and consumer shows.

POLITICAL EVENTS Political groups stage events and rallies. For example, the national conventions for both the Republican and Democratic parties take place every four years prior to a presidential election. The events generate income for hotels, transportation businesses, and restaurants.

CULTURAL EVENTS Fairs, festivals, and other cultural events can be large or small. They can also have local or national appeal. For example, religious groups hold many events, ranging from the *Passion Play* in the Bavarian town of Oberamergau in Germany to religious retreats and sponsored trips to sacred cities. Art communities and groups create and host a variety of cultural events. Concerts, theater events, museum collections, and movie premieres are all types of cultural events.

MILITARY EVENTS The military branches often participate in parades and flag-raising celebrations. All military events follow strict rules of protocol. Other examples of such events include graduations at Annapolis, West Point, or the United States Air Force Academy.

TOURIST ATTRACTIONS Tourist attractions can also promote events. The SpectroMagic Parade at Walt Disney World in Florida, the National Rodeo in Texas, and Fourth of July fireworks shows are examples of special events at destinations.

COLLEGES AND UNIVERSITIES Many departments in colleges and universities are involved with events. Annual events include orientation, registration, career day, and graduation. Most schools offer a variety, from concerts and guest speakers to awards receptions and trips.

NONPROFIT ORGANIZATIONS Civic and charitable organizations such as Big Sisters or Big Brothers hold events such as golf tournaments, wine receptions, auctions, and pancake breakfasts.

CONSUMER SHOWS A **consumer show** is a single- or multi-day exhibition held at convention or civic center arena. It may present an auto show, boat show, flower show, or recreational vehicle (RV) show.

consumer show a single- or multi-day exhibition held at convention or civic center arena

---

Case Study — PART 2

HE SHOOTS, HE SCORES!

Continued from Part 1 on page 137

Following the strategy of moving the Kings to the Staples Center, Anshutz took the Galaxy soccer team away from the Rose Bowl and moved the team to the Home Depot Center in Carson, California. Built by AEG, the $150 million complex includes soccer training grounds, a velodrome, and a track-and-field facility. There is also a world-class tennis stadium with 18 courts, where local tennis pro Pete Sampras runs an academy. World-class dining facilities are also on site.

As a principal promoter of soccer in America, AEG now operates half of the Major League Soccer (MLS) teams. The group plans to open soccer-specific arenas in metropolitan New York and Washington, D.C. But will MLS draw more fans? Current fans include soccer moms in the suburbs and urban-ethnic groups, such as the Polish in Chicago and Hispanics in Los Angeles. Success will depend on the league's appeal to its target market—and AEG's marketing and management.

ANALYZE AND WRITE

1. How does AEG's business relate to hospitality and tourism? Explain your answer in two sentences.
2. List the kinds of jobs that might be available at AEG.

Private Events

Private events are special events limited to a select group of individuals. A variety of events include social functions as well as business functions. Admission or entrance into a private event is by membership or invitation. Examples of types of private events include:

- Social events
- Meetings
- Corporate events

Social Events

Social events make up a large portion of the private events industry. Weddings, bar mitzvahs, anniversaries, birthdays, and other family celebrations generate a significant amount of banquet and entertainment revenue. Amateur sporting events also are a large component of the social events market. Recitals, dance and community theater productions, and family-focused events are also types of social events.

Meetings

Corporations and associations support the meetings segment of the private events industry. Each of these groups produces special events for their members. For example, the National Restaurant Association holds its annual national convention in Chicago. This event includes a trade-show area, seminars, food tastings, a gala dinner, and local tours. Attendance at these functions is limited to trade members and their guests.

Corporate Events

Corporations sponsor events to introduce new products, reward outstanding performance, increase sales motivation, or simply to provide information. Security is a priority at corporate events, and attendance is strictly monitored. Incentive travel is a lucrative segment of the corporate market. Company employees with outstanding performance may receive unique travel experiences to a desirable destination. Insurance companies, corporate marketing and sales divisions, and the medical community are important contributors to the incentive travel-and-meetings markets.

CONNECT
What types of private events have you attended?

Event Positions

A successful event brings together a wide range of people, services, facilities, and venues. Individuals working in the events industry are experts in time, crisis, and risk management. They also need to have organizational, interpersonal, and communication skills. Event planners should have technology skills and should have experience dealing with labor issues and negotiations. Career opportunities are available in event planning, event marketing, event sponsorship, and event management. Corporations, associations, convention and tourist centers, hotels, banquet facilities, sporting venues, and other special-purpose facilities in the public and private sectors hire experienced as well as entry-level meeting planners.

Entertainment

Today's entertainment industry caters to a wide variety of cultures, ages, interests, and income levels. In fact, it is estimated that 20,000 entertainment companies provide gross revenues of $45 billion to the economy of the United States. The entertainment industry in the United States includes the segments of music, television, movies, radio, and performing arts. A few major companies and businesses represent each segment.

Music

The music industry provides live performances and recordings by artists. Live performances generate revenue from concert tickets, concessions, parking, on-site retail sales, and sponsorship opportunities. Styles of music range from classical, rock, hip-hop, country, and new age to many other styles for all tastes.

21st CENTURY MUSIC FESTS **Live performances at organized music festivals draw many people from out of town for the purpose of entertainment.** *What would be some sources of revenue for a music festival?*

MUSIC TOURS Touring allows artists to connect with fans and increase exposure. Concerts can be held in many types of venues: outdoor arenas, performing arts centers, concert halls, auditoriums, and amphitheaters. Jobs that relate to live-performance events include promoters, agents, writers, and technical crew positions, such as electricians, lighting and sound engineers, and stage technicians.

RECORDINGS Recorded music generates revenue for a musical act or performer. Sales of CDs, DVDs, and other types of recordings earn income for record companies and performers. Music is also used in radio jingles, movies, advertising campaigns, and videos. The music industry has been affected financially by illegal downloading of music from the Internet. This practice breaks copyright laws and prevents musicians, songwriters, and record labels from receiving royalty fees owed to them. However, since 2003, various legal music downloading services, such as iTunes have become popular because of convenience and low cost to customers.

Television

On average, Americans watch at least one television program each day. Whether watching a news broadcast, a movie on cable, a soap opera, a reality show, or a drama, viewers make television the number-one entertainment option. Networks plan programming for specific target markets. TV ratings determine the longevity of shows, particularly during prime time, because advertisers want to sponsor the most viewed programs. The money from advertising supports most of the major networks. In fact, commercials may account for approximately one-third of the time of a traditional network programming schedule.

The growth of the video and computer game industry has also affected television. Interactive in nature, the electronic entertainment segment continues to be a popular at-home alternative.

JOBS IN TELEVISION Television positions may include jobs such as producers, directors, writers, promoters, agents, and the performers or talent.

Movies

A film can generate revenue from first-run release to the public in theaters, from the later release of videos and DVDs, and from the film's sale to a television network for home viewing. Eight major theater chains control about 65 percent of the movie theaters in the United States. Significant film revenue is generated from tourists as well as other moviegoers during certain seasons, on opening weekends, at premieres, and after Academy Awards presentations. (See **Figure 7.2**.) Some previously released films may also attract entirely new audiences at little or no expense to the studios.

JOBS IN FILM The film industry and theaters employ a variety of personnel in production, distribution, marketing, and theater operations. Management opportunities also are available in movie theaters.

QUESTION

What other electronic media compete with TV for entertainment and recreation revenue?

Figure 7.2

Theater Attendance

FILM SEASONS Tourists and all types of travelers go to see movies for recreation. *During what season did the most domestic visitors attend theaters?*

	New York City	Suburbs	Domestic Visitors	International Visitors
Summer 2001	21%	27%	43%	9%
Fall 2001	23%	27%	46%	5%
Winter 2002	36%	29%	33%	3%
Spring 2002	27%	21%	50%	3%
TOTAL	22%	27%	46%	5%

SOURCE: The League of American Theatres and Producers, Inc., *Tourism Works for America*, 12th Annual Edition, 2003

Radio

Before television, radio was the primary medium for at-home entertainment. Avid fans listened to radio show classics in the 1930s, such as the *Shadow* or the *Green Hornet*. Advertisers purchased time and even sponsored entire programs to promote their products on air. Today many Americans listen to radio on their drives to and from work. Stations specialize in particular genres of music, such as alternative rock, country, easy listening, rock, and oldies. News and talk shows are also popular. Specific programming for certain listeners is critical in the radio industry to ensure consistent ratings. Therefore, the mix of music, commercials, talk, and news is vital to the broadcast program.

JOBS IN RADIO Career opportunities are available in the fields of radio production and sales of broadcast airtime. Different opportunities are also available in station management.

Performing Arts

performing arts a segment of the entertainment industry that includes the exhibition of live presentations by artists, such as actors in theaters or performance artists in other venues

Performing arts is a segment of the entertainment industry that includes the exhibition of live presentations by artists, such as actors in theaters or performance artists in other venues. Live theater is a popular entertainment provider to local, regional, national, and international audiences. A Broadway play is a celebrated event in New York City, but it is also recognized on a national basis when the Tony Awards are announced. Touring companies bring the magic of Broadway to local venues.

Special shows also attract target audiences. Ice-skating shows, Olympic trials, circuses, opera, the ballet, and family shows, such as Sesame Street, are all live performances geared toward particular groups.

JOBS IN PERFORMING ARTS Some career opportunities in performing arts can include box-office management, stage technicians, ticket sales agents, and public relations agents.

Making an Impact

The events and entertainment industries affect our lives every day. Sports events as well as recreational opportunities, for which hospitality and tourism play integral roles, generate huge profits. Many career opportunities exist in these exciting and growing industries.

Quick Check ✓

RESPOND to what you've read by answering these questions.

1. What are four types of events? _____

_____

_____

_____

2. What three groups sponsor events? _____

_____

_____

3. What are the categories of the entertainment industry? _____

_____

_____

_____

_____

Worksheet 7.1

Sports Around the World

1. Use the Internet, library, or other resource to learn about various sports around the world. Look up 12 different countries and research the sports played in those countries. Write the name of the country, the name of a sport played in the country, and two facts about the sport.

   Example:

Country	**Sport**	**Fact 1**	**Fact 2**
United States	Basketball	Began in 1891	Began in Springfield, Massachusetts

   _____
   _____
   _____
   _____
   _____
   _____
   _____
   _____
   _____
   _____
   _____
   _____
   _____
   _____
   _____
   _____
   _____
   _____

2. In what country would you want to work, and for which sport? Why?

   _____
   _____
   _____

Worksheet 7.2

Events

Attend two different events. Answer the following questions about each event:

Event 1:

1. What type of event did you attend? *(Circle one.)*

   Mega-event   Hallmark Event   Major Event   Local Event

2. What was the name and purpose of the event? _____
   _____
   _____

3. Was this a private or public event? Explain your answer. _____
   _____

4. Describe what took place at the event. _____
   _____
   _____
   _____
   _____

Event 2:

5. What type of event did you attend? *(Circle one.)*

   Mega-event   Hallmark Event   Major Event   Local Event

6. What was the name and purpose of the event? _____
   _____
   _____

7. Was this a private or public event? Explain your answer. _____
   _____

8. Describe what took place at the event. _____
   _____
   _____
   _____
   _____

Portfolio Works

YOUR PERFECT JOB

If you could create a dream job in the sports or entertainment events management field, what would that be? Use the space below to describe your job.

1. My dream job is:

_____

_____

_____

_____

_____

_____

2. What education or training would you need for this job?

_____

_____

3. What qualities do you have that would make you good at this job?

_____

_____

_____

_____

_____

_____

4. What is one step you could take today toward working in this job?

_____

_____

_____

_____

_____

Add this page to your career portfolio.

CHAPTER SUMMARY

Section 7.1 Sports and Recreation

amateur sports (p. 139)
Paralympics (p. 140)
commercial recreation
    (p. 145)
public recreation (p. 145)
therapeutic recreation
    (p. 146)

- Amateur sports are athletic activities and competitions for athletes who do not get paid. Examples include youth sports, high school sports, and collegiate sports.

- Professional sports are athletic activities, including local, regional, national, or international events, that attract spectators and generate revenue. Examples include basketball, baseball, football, soccer, auto racing, tennis, and other sports.

- The career opportunities in sports and sports event management are found in sports agencies, facilities, broadcasting, retailing, and teams and associations.

- There are two types of recreation—commercial recreation, which is any recreational activity for which a guest pays a fee, and public recreation, which is either free or paid-for recreation that takes place on state and federal lands and in city, state, or national parks.

Section 7.2 Events and Entertainment

mega-event (p. 147)
hallmark event (p. 147)
consumer show (p. 149)
performing arts (p. 154)

- Public events are categorized by size and purpose. Examples include mega-events, hallmark events, and major events as well as political events, cultural events, military events, tourist attractions, college and university events, nonprofit organization events, and consumer shows. Private events are special events that are limited to a select group of individuals. Examples include social events, meetings, and corporate events.

- Categories of the entertainment industry include music, television, movies, radio, and performing arts.

CHECKING CONCEPTS

1. **Define** amateur sports.
2. **Describe** the sources of income from professional sports.
3. **List** at least three careers in facility management.
4. **Identify** types of commercial recreation.
5. **Identify** types of recreation besides commercial and public recreation.
6. **Define** a hallmark event.
7. **Identify** examples of private events.

Critical Thinking

8. **Explain** how sports and entertainment events relate to hospitality and tourism.

CROSS-CURRICULUM SKILLS

Work-Based Learning

Resources—Allocating Money

9. Write a one-page essay that defends or criticizes providing federal dollars for public recreation lands.

Thinking Skills—Creative Thinking

10. Work with three other students to create a teen event. Describe the purpose of the event, the venue, if it will be private or public, and if there will be music or performing arts.

School-Based Learning

History/Language Arts

11. Use the Internet or library to research the history of a favorite sport. Write a two-page essay about your findings.

Social Studies

12. Use the Internet or library to research one of your favorite athletes in another country. Research that country and learn about its political situation. Give a brief oral report to the class.

Role Play: Stadium Catering Manager

SITUATION You are to assume the role of catering manager for a new professional football stadium. Your department caters food and beverages for the luxury skyboxes. The owners of the skyboxes may entertain clients during games. There have been several complaints about the limited menu and the quality of the food. Customers have specifically complained about wilted salads and hot foods served cold.

ACTIVITY You are to meet with the general manager of all the catering functions to make suggestions for improving the menu and the quality of the prepared food.

EVALUATION You will be evaluated on how well you meet the following performance indicators:

• Maintain restaurant quality-control standards.
• Explain the concept of product mix.
• Select menu items.
• Monitor and maintain food-holding temperatures.
• Inspect food deliveries.

INTERNET ACTIVITY

Use the Internet to access the Web site of the International Paralympic Committee.

• Read two or three of the top stories.
• Write a summary of one of the stories.
• Exchange summaries with a classmate and read each other's summaries.
• Give feedback to each other.

➡ For a link to the International Paralympic Committee Web site to do this activity, go to **marketingseries.glencoe.com**.

BusinessWeek News

FINE DINING? JUST ACROSS THE LOBBY

At Trio in the Chicago suburb of Evanston, Illinois, the food is eclectic, to say the least. On any particular night, chef Grant Achatz's menu might include surprises such as Chinese "bubble tea" made with cucumber, crème fraîche, and salmon roe; or Pacific sea urchin with frozen banana, puffed rice, and parsnip milk. Another surprise: The restaurant is in the Homestead, a 90-room hotel.

Today some of the toughest tables to get are located in hotels. Unlike the stuffy, overpriced hotel restaurants of yesteryear, the new dining options can stand up to the best epicurean eateries. Hoteliers from Las Vegas to New York have lured brand-name chefs and up-and-coming talent to create "destination restaurants." Says Tim Zagat, co-founder of the Zagat Survey: "Having a hot restaurant downstairs makes the rooms upstairs more valuable." He cites Jean Georges, the gastronomic temple of Jean-Georges Vongerichten in New York's Trump International Hotel, as an example.

Fresh From the Farm

Whether French, New American, or California Eclectic, the fare being served up at hotels these days is fresh—often bought at local farmer's markets—and prepared in innovative ways. Just don't call it hotel food. "That says to me chicken cordon bleu, veal Oscar...what used to be called Continental cuisine," says chef Todd English, whose company,

Olive Group, has opened seven hotel restaurants since 1998, including Olives at the W in New York and the Bellagio in Las Vegas.

The changes reflect the demands of a more food-savvy clientele. "They want something unique," says Peter Koehler, general manager of the Hotel Palomar in San Francisco. They certainly get that at the Palomar's restaurant, the Fifth Floor. With zebra-striped decor, this purveyor of "modern French" food is among the Bay Area's top-rated restaurants; its chef, Laurent Gras, graced the October cover of *Gourmet* magazine.

The boom in boutique hotels during the past decade has also fueled the trend. Hip boutiques, such as Starwood's W chain, have set a new standard with creative menus and artful decor. Now, big hotels are spending millions to hire celebrity chefs and make over their dining spaces. Most of these establishments have a street entrance as well as lobby access. When diners are coming in through both doors, the food must be good.

By Amy Cortese

CREATIVE JOURNAL

In your journal, write your responses.

CRITICAL THINKING

1. How do hospitality and tourism combine in these new restaurants?

APPLICATION

2. Describe your ideal new hotel and its restaurant in one paragraph. Include information on the names, the style, the design, the staff, the target market, and the promotion for these businesses.

 Go to **businessweek.com** for current *BusinessWeek* Online articles.

UNIT LAB

The Inn Place

You've just entered the real world of hospitality and travel and tourism. The Inn Place owns and operates a number of hospitality and tourism businesses, offering the finest accommodations and most desirable destinations in the world. Acting as the owner, manager, or employee of this diverse company, you will have the opportunity to work on different projects to promote the business.

A Taste of Destinations—Design a Food Tour

SITUATION You are co-owner of a tour company. Your company Foodie Tours specializes in offering scenic tours in rural and urban locations. The unique aspect of your tour business is that you offer food with your tours. You do not simply provide a boxed lunch. Foodie Tours offers food samplings that are tied to the site being toured. For example, when touring the site of a state fair, the tour-group participants receive a sampling of the prize-winning food entries, from chili to freshly baked pies.

You would like to offer a slightly different type of food tour. You would like to offer tours in which a restaurant meal would be part of the package. You plan to approach some well-known fine-dining restaurants in large cities to become part of your offerings. The tour groups would tour the kitchens of the participating restaurants and be given a talk by the chef.

ASSIGNMENT Complete these tasks:
- Determine the best city for the first tour.
- Estimate the approximate cost for the proposed meals, the honorarium to be paid to the speaker, and any other costs associated with the new tours.
- Make a report to your partner.

TOOLS AND RESOURCES To complete the assignment, you will need to:
- Conduct research at the library, on the Internet, or by talking to tour operators.
- Ask a restaurant chef about typical costs.
- Have word-processing, spreadsheet, and presentation software.

RESEARCH Do your research:
- Research the demographics and psychographics of the tour participants.
- Determine local costs of meals, bus rentals, and other tour costs.
- Determine the city and restaurant for the first tour.

REPORT Prepare a written report using the following tools:
- *Word-processing program:* Prepare a written report listing the demographic and psychographic characteristics of participants.
- *Spreadsheet program:* Prepare a chart comparing the costs of starting up the tours.
- *Presentation program:* Prepare a ten-slide visual presentation with key points, photos, and key descriptive text.

PRESENTATION AND EVALUATION
You will present your report to your partner. You will be evaluated on the basis of:
- Your knowledge of the tour participants and the restaurants to be included
- Continuity of presentation
- Voice quality
- Eye contact

PORTFOLIO
Add this report to your career portfolio.

UNIT 3
MARKETING HOSPITALITY & TOURISM

In This Unit . . .

Chapter 8
The Marketing Environment

Chapter 9
Market Information and Research

Chapter 10
Designing Products

Chapter 11
Pricing Products

Chapter 12
Distribution

Chapter 13
Promoting Hospitality & Tourism

" People forget how fast you did a job—but they remember how well you did it. "

—Howard W. Newton
Writer

162

UNIT OVERVIEW

U nit 3 explores the many aspects of marketing hospitality and tourism. Chapter 8 begins the unit by focusing on basics, such as the marketing plan and marketing mix as well as market research. In Chapter 9, you will learn about collecting and managing market-research information and the application of segmentation. Chapter 10 examines hospitality and tourism products and how businesses plan for current and new products. Pricing products is the focus of Chapter 11 with discussions about pricing strategies. Chapter 12 explores how hospitality and tourism products are distributed through sales associates, selling, and channels of distribution. Chapter 13 concludes the unit by focusing on the promotion of hospitality and tourism.

■ UNIT LAB Preview
The Inn Place

Think about all the hotels and resorts. How do resorts overcome negative publicity? How do you create a promotional plan for a resort property?

These functions are highlighted in this unit:
- Marketing-Information Management
- Products/Service Management
- Financing
- Promotion
- Distribution

Chapter 8

The Marketing Environment

Section 8.1

The Role of Marketing Basics

Section 8.2

Planning Marketing

Chapter Objectives

- Describe the marketing process.
- Explain the elements of the basic marketing mix.
- Identify the components of product utility.
- Explain the purpose of a marketing plan.
- Discuss the importance of a mission.
- Identify the internal and external influences of the marketing environment.

ECO-FRIENDLY CAR CLUB

Todd Silberman and Mitch Rofsky were members of the same Ohio Cub Scout troop before they cofounded the alternative auto club, Better World Club (BWC), and the nation's third-largest travel agency, Journeys Travel.

Their adventures began after Rofsky worked on clean-air and mass-transit initiatives. He contacted his friend Silberman about starting an eco-friendly alternative to automobile clubs. The partners' first step was to form the travel agency Journeys Travel, which provides environmentally friendly travel alternatives and "green" lodging options. Then in 2002, the Portland, Oregon, business began offering roadside-assistance services as the Better World Club. The BWC boasted discounts for renting electric and hybrid cars as well as special benefits for cyclists. A percentage of profits was donated for offsetting pollution generated by travel. But could a newcomer survive while challenging established auto clubs with large memberships?

ANALYZE AND WRITE

1. List marketing strategies that Rofsky and Silberman used to promote the businesses.
2. How might the BWC appeal to drivers who are already members of an established auto club? Write a paragraph explaining your response.

Case Study Part 2 on page 177

POWER READ

Be an active reader and use these reading strategies:

PREDICT what the section will be about.

CONNECT what you read with your own life.

QUESTION as you read to make sure you understand the content.

RESPOND to what you've read.

The Role of Marketing Basics

AS YOU READ...

YOU WILL LEARN

- To describe the marketing process.
- To explain the elements of the basic marketing mix.
- To identify the components of product utility.

WHY IT'S IMPORTANT

Understanding the marketing process and the elements of the marketing mix provides a foundation for successful hospitality and tourism businesses.

KEY TERMS

- marketing
- distribution
- marketing concept
- target market
- marketing mix
- utility

PREDICT

Describe in your own words what is involved in the marketing process.

marketing the process of developing, promoting, and distributing products, or goods and services, to satisfy customers' needs and wants

distribution the process of getting the product to the consumer

What Is Marketing?

Marketing is the process of developing, promoting, and distributing products, or goods and services, to satisfy customers' needs and wants. Consumers have thousands of choices when it comes to choosing one product over another. Why go to one restaurant or hotel instead of another one? Convincing people to buy and use a product is the goal of marketing.

The Marketing Process

Developing new products and services involves studying consumer behavior and looking at trends as well as gaps in the market to be filled by a new product. Therefore, the marketing process begins with understanding what product consumers need or want through market research, making consumers aware of it through promotion, and then making it available through distribution.

Market Research

Using tools designed to discover buyers' needs, product developers conduct extensive market research before, during, and after the product-development phase. If you have ever completed a product survey or answered questions asked by a telemarketer, you have participated in market research.

Promoting Products

Before a product exists, there is a need for the product felt by enough people to cause it to be developed. When the product is created and becomes available, marketers must promote it. This involves making people aware of the product and demonstrating the value of the product so they will buy it. Product promotion activities can involve simple advertising in newspapers, on radio, and on television. Other promotional activities can be more complex, such as launching a product with celebrity endorsers and elaborate giveaways.

Distributing Products

Getting a product or service to the market involves retail outlets, such as travel agencies, restaurants, or the Internet. People order a hospitality or tourism product online or over the phone. These products are often pictured in magazines or featured on a Web site. These "places" are considered as channels of distribution. **Distribution** is the process of getting the product to the consumer.

The Marketing Concept

The driving force behind the marketing concept is the customer. The **marketing concept** is the idea that an organization needs to satisfy its customers while also trying to reach its organization's goals. In recent years, most successful businesses have embraced the concept that meeting the needs of their clients is the most important business activity for meeting business goals. Delivering products, or goods and services, that consumers want and need and doing it effectively lead to success and consumer loyalty.

The Market

Any group of potential buyers is a market. Senior citizens are a market, as are teenagers, honeymooners, travelers with disabilities, single parents, adults, grandparents, and almost any other group you can imagine. The common denominator in any group, or market, is sharing a common need. Businesses trying to sell their products and services must identify the specific groups, or target markets, that are likely to buy them. A **target market** is a specific group of consumers that an organization selects as the focus of its marketing plan.

The Marketing Mix

At the heart of marketing and the marketing concept is the **marketing mix**, which is a combination of four basic marketing strategies, known as the four Ps:

- Product

- Price

- Place

- Promotion

This marketing mix is used when businesses make plans for marketing products. (See **Figure 8.1** on page 168.) Businesses must make decisions about what product to sell, where to sell it, what price to charge for it, and how the product information will be communicated to the public.

Product Decisions

Product decisions can include choosing a name for a product, such as choosing a name for a restaurant, and how to package or design the product. But that is not all. Due to the intangible nature of some products, such as travel, marketers must first ask what they are marketing. Are they selling dreams of exotic destinations and wild adventures? Is the product an extravagant cruise to the islands of the South Pacific or a whitewater rafting trip down the Snake River? Will guests be pampered with luxury or go bargain shopping at local craft markets? Is the package considered quality or affordable—or both? Is the product a specialty item or can it be mass produced? The answers to these questions will determine the strategies used in the marketing plan, discussed in Section 8.2.

Key Point ❗

CULTURAL TOURISM
As part of product development, marketers research and watch trends. A 2003 study by the Travel Industry Association of America (TIA) and the *Smithsonian* magazine shows a growing trend toward tourism focused on cultural, arts, historic, and heritage activities. In fact, 81 percent of adult tourists in the United States are historic/cultural travelers.

marketing concept the idea that an organization needs to satisfy its customers while also trying to reach its organization's goals

target market a specific group of consumers that an organization selects as the focus of its marketing plan

marketing mix a combination of four basic marketing strategies, known as the four Ps—product, price, place, and promotion

CONNECT
What restaurant do you think has offered a new product wanted by consumers?

THE Electronic CHANNEL

Listing Last Minute

Lastminute.com is a resource for saving on flights, hotels, and cars for travelers booking just before they travel. Vendors, airlines, and hotels often have space available at the last minute. To sell these rooms and seats, the site offers them at discounted prices to people booking online—at the last minute. Eurostar, the train operating in the English Channel tunnel between continental Europe and England, is included in the Web site's packaging strategy. Customers searching for flights between London, Paris, or Brussels will automatically be given prices for the Eurostar train.

➡ Find and list other examples of packaging through **marketingseries.glencoe.com**.

Price Decisions

What the consumer is able and willing to pay is often the first consideration when determining price. To determine price, marketers focus on prices for similar products, marketing costs, costs to produce the product, and value to the consumer. These are just a few of the factors for determining a price for a product.

Place Decisions

The next component of the marketing mix is distribution, or place. Marketers consider where consumers shop for similar products. Will the target market use the Internet to make travel plans? Will the target market go to a restaurant that has high prices or low-fat menu items? Understanding the target market and where those consumers shop help shape the decisions about distribution. If the product requires personalized service and customization, then the product should be placed where trained sales associates are available to answer questions and influence buying decisions.

Promotion Decisions

Selecting the message and the type of media outlet to use to get the product message out are promotion decisions. What is the best medium to communicate a business's image? Product promotion can include any mix of advertising, sales promotion, personal sales pitches, and publicity. Promotion must also take into consideration who will use that product. What does the customer need or want from the product? Marketers choose the best method to communicate to the consumer how and why the product meets those needs.

Figure 8.1

The Marketing Mix

PURPOSE TO SELL Any combination of one or all of the four marketing components can create a marketing mix. *Which component of the marketing mix is basic to the marketing concept?*

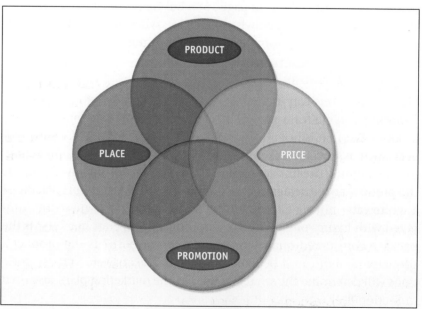

 marketingseries.glencoe.com

PROMOTING TRAVEL **Print advertisements are just one method of promoting hospitality and tourism.** *What are some other methods of promotion that might be effective for promoting travel to tropical destinations?*

"IN REVERENCE I LISTEN TO THE CONCERT OF THE FOREST. THE WIND BLOWING ITS SONG, THE BIRDS SINGING THEIR TUNE."

The people of Hawai'i would like to share their islands with you. HAWAI'I
Plan your trip now at gohawaii.com or call 1-800-Go Hawaii. THE ISLANDS OF ALOHA

Concept of Utility

Marketing provides a service to both businesses and consumers. Through marketing, consumers become aware of new and improved products or services that may add value to their lifestyle. When demand for products increases, prices may decrease and benefit the consumer. Businesses whose products are being sold in greater numbers benefit from higher sales and profits. Adding value to a product is one of the functions of marketing. In economic terms, adding value to a product is called *utility*. **Utility** is the concept of conveying the value of products through appropriate and convenient placement, adequate information, and easy exchange. Utility increases the product or service's ability to meet the needs and wants of consumers. When planning marketing strategies, marketers consider four types of utility—place, time, possession, and information.

utility the concept of conveying the value of products through appropriate and convenient placement, adequate information, and easy exchange

Place Utility

Impulse buying is one example of place utility. Have you ever noticed magazines and candy bars prominently displayed at the checkout counter in a grocery or discount store? Even if customers had no intention of purchasing candy or magazines when they entered the store, they may pick them up on impulse while waiting in line. Placing products where customers can easily purchase them is the idea behind place utility.

Time Utility

Making products available to customers when they need them is time utility. Back-to-school sales in late July and August and displays around the holiday seasons are good examples of how marketers make their products available for the customer.

Possession Utility

Cash, credit cards, travelers checks, personal checks, and gift certificates are the means consumers use to possess a desired item. The exchange of product for money or money equivalent results in the customer possessing the item.

Information Utility

Communicating the message to the consumer is what information utility is all about. Product displays, packaging, product literature, and informed sales people are all examples of information utility. This type of utility as well as the other marketing strategies, including the marketing mix, allow hospitality and tourism businesses to develop, promote, and distribute the best products.

QUESTION

What is adding value to a product called?

Quick Check ✓

RESPOND to what you've read by answering these questions.

1. Why do businesses focus on the marketing concept? _____

_____

_____

2. What are the four Ps of the marketing mix? _____

_____

_____

3. What is the concept of utility? _____

_____

_____

_____

Planning Marketing

The Importance of Planning

Planning involves predicting the future, setting goals and objectives, and taking action to obtain those goals and objectives. As one philosopher said, "If you don't know where you are going, any road will take you there." The same is true for putting together your marketing plan. If you do not know what you hope to achieve (your goals), then you cannot plan how to reach those goals.

The Marketing Plan

A **marketing plan** is a written document that provides direction for the marketing activities of a company for a specific period of time. It serves as a road map, ensuring that all activities of the organization are directed at achieving the same outcome. Sharing the marketing plan with employees assures that everyone is aware of the goals and objectives of the organization and that they are in agreement with them. Having a plan allows an organization to designate resources to accomplish the marketing strategies. A marketing plan creates a way to track and measure success.

The basic elements of a marketing plan include:

- Executive summary

- Situation analysis

- Marketing goals/objectives

- Marketing strategies

- Implementation

- Evaluation and control

Defining the Mission

Before a marketing plan is created, a company must define and share its mission. The **mission** is a business's purpose or goal. It reflects how that business operates both internally (within the organization itself) and externally (with customers, competitors, and the community). A mission usually communicates a statement. For example, a new resort's mission statement might be: "To create an environment of comfort, quality, and relaxation for our guests; and to do so in such a way that it has a positive impact on the environment and the community in which we live."

AS YOU READ...

YOU WILL LEARN

- To explain the purpose of a marketing plan.
- To discuss the importance of a mission.
- To identify the internal and external influences of the marketing environment.

WHY IT'S IMPORTANT

Any business or product in hospitality and tourism needs a marketing plan to succeed.

KEY TERMS

- marketing plan
- mission
- marketing environment
- demographics
- goal
- objectives

PREDICT

What is the purpose of a marketing plan?

marketing plan a written document that provides direction for the marketing activities of a company for a specific period of time

mission a business's purpose or goal

Hot Property

Spirit to Grow

Marriott

An empire can be born in the unlikeliest places. In 1927, J. Willard Marriott and his wife Alice opened an A&W Root Beer stand with nine seats. By 2004, Marriott's company had over 500,000 rooms for hotel guests, conference attendees, and time-share owners. That's quite a leap—even if took 77 years.

How does a root-beer stand grow into a hotel giant? By serving more people. Over the years, Marriott has expanded its customer base in a variety of ways. It built hotels in the United States and overseas. It purchased existing hotels and acquired brands that catered to different kinds of travelers. Today Marriott owns hotels that serve a variety of guests—from executives to families, long term to short term, and modest to upscale.

SPIRIT TO SERVE

Though Marriott looks different than it did in 1927, company leaders hope its heart has stayed the same. For 40 years J.W. Marriott has run the company that his parents created. He supports his father's mission that reflects the "spirit to serve." This "spirit" begins with positive relationships with employees and customers and extends to a relationship with the community. In 2004, Marriott International enjoyed recognition for this approach when it was named as one of the "100 Best Companies to Work For" by *Fortune* magazine—for the seventh year in a row.

1. How has Marriott expanded its business?
2. What does the slogan "spirit to serve" mean to you?

Group Mission

A company should not create its mission in a vacuum—that is, without feedback from management and employees. The entire group involved in the organization should contribute thoughts and ideas regarding the purpose of the business and how employees will interact with each other and with those outside the organization. This helps to create an environment that will support the business's mission. Once created, the company should share its mission with all employees and reinforce it regularly.

Environmental Analysis

marketing environment the internal and external factors that influence marketing decisions and the ability of the marketing plan to reach its goal

Businesses operate within a marketing environment. The **marketing environment** is the internal and external factors that influence marketing decisions and the ability of the marketing plan to reach its goal. The environmental or situation analysis is a study of the internal and external factors that affect a marketing plan. (See **Figure 8.2**.) This analysis, or SWOT analysis, focuses on four factors:

- **S**trengths
- **W**eaknesses
- **O**pportunities
- **T**hreats

Internal Factors

Internal factors of the marketing environment include operations, such as departments interacting within the organization, as well as accounting and public relations. For example, if cleaning materials are harmful to the environment or a health risk to employees or guests, internal adjustments must be made. In addition, if the hotel's labor union strikes and costs increase, the marketing department faces internal problems.

External Factors

External factors are broad and include factors such as external suppliers of resources, product distribution, competition, size of company, demographics, economics, politics, and technology. For example, in order for hotels to provide clean, comfortable rooms to their guests, they must rely on outside sources. Clean bed linens and bath towels are sometimes supplied by such sources. There are other suppliers for cleaning products, carpeting, window and wall treatments, toiletries, and paper products. If the cost of paper goes up or the supply goes down, those external factors can impact the marketing environment. Competitors are an external factor. The marketing concept states that businesses are successful if they can meet the needs of their customers. This means that they must understand the needs of their own customers and understand their competitors' marketing strategies as well.

Math Check

MARKETING COSTS
Priscilla's Coffee Break spends 21 percent of its gross profit on marketing. Gross profit is $157,000. What is the marketing cost?

➡ For tips on finding the solution, go to **marketingseries.glencoe.com.**

Figure 8.2

SWOT Analysis

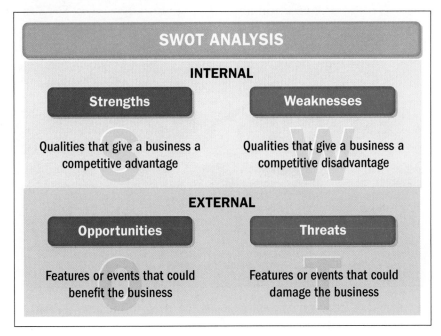

THE MARKETING ENVIRONMENT
Understanding the strengths and weaknesses of a hospitality and tourism product can make the difference in successful marketing. *What might be the internal and external factors when considering the marketing environment of a fast-food restaurant?*

ETHICS & ISSUES

Ecotourism: Pros and Cons

The United Nations declared 2002 the year of ecotourism. Ecotourism includes travel to places that have significant natural or ecological areas that are under the strict supervision of native guides or naturalists. The purpose of ecotourism is to give tourists access to natural wonders, while promoting conservation and bringing revenue to local people. However, according to many nongovernmental organizations, the full impact of ecotourism on ecosystems and indigenous people is yet to be seen. Deborah McLaren of the Rethinking Tourism Project says, "Much of what passes as ecotourism is designed to benefit investors, empower managerial specialists, and delight tourists—not to enhance the economic, social, and ecological health of the host communities."

Do you think ecotourism is an ethical way to bring revenue to indigenous people or an exploitation of fragile natural wonders? Explain your answer.

CONNECT

Think of an airline that you would choose to use. Explain why.

COMPETITION Think for a minute about airlines. Airlines are in the transportation business, carrying passengers from one destination to another. There are literally hundreds of airlines worldwide. Some airlines specialize in international travel, and others provide regional or national transportation. If you travel from point A to point B, you will have several airlines from which to choose. To stand out among the competition, some airlines offer personal entertainment options in every seat. Others strive to provide the best on-time performance. Still others may provide more comfortable seats and optional in-flight food-and-beverage service. No one strategy is best for all airlines.

SIZE OF COMPANY The size of a company is a consideration when dealing with external factors. Large national and international companies can afford marketing strategies that smaller, regional companies might not be able to afford. However, smaller companies can react more quickly to changes in the local marketing environment, giving them a competitive advantage in some markets.

IN-FLIGHT COMPETITION Many airlines are struggling to offer special features to attract passengers. *What services could an airline offer to economy-class travelers?*

Other External Marketing Factors

Other external factors in the marketing environment can affect consumer behavior and shape marketing strategies. These factors and influences include:

- Demographics
- Politics
- Economics
- Technology

DEMOGRAPHICS By studying demographics, marketers can look for patterns of behavior among certain groups of people. **Demographics** are statistics that describe a population in terms of personal characteristics, such as age, gender, income, ethnicity, or education. Marketers then create marketing strategies that target a group. For example, "baby boomers" (people born between 1946 and 1964) make up one of the largest and most powerful demographic groups influencing the marketing environment. Typically, this demographic group looks for action and adventure, resists the effects of aging, and seeks opportunities for continuing education and self-improvement. A marketer would tailor the four Ps of marketing mix—product, price, place, and promotion—to match these characteristics in order to sell a tour package or a new restaurant to baby boomers.

ECONOMICS Personal income, taxes, and real estate value are economic factors that affect most of the population. Consumer confidence is tied to the economy. It determines whether people are willing to spend money on luxury items and other nonessential products. Understanding the factors that influence consumer confidence, such as the unemployment rate, interest rates, and cost-of-living adjustments, is important to marketers. Economic forecasters predict changes in the economy based on trends. Businesses can use that information to adjust to changes in consumer spending.

POLITICS Political situations can strongly affect marketing decisions. After the events of September 11, 2001, the world experienced a shift in national and international policies. Terrorism became an issue, and national security procedures changed how people live, work, and travel. However, politics have always affected consumers on many levels. Laws and regulations have been put in place to protect consumers, regulate fair trade, and prevent unfair practices. Governments pass laws to protect natural resources and workers around the world. Marketers take note of changes in the political environment to design effective marketing strategies.

TECHNOLOGY Advancements in technology have changed society and business quickly and dramatically. E-Commerce, wireless Internet access, and ticketless travel have opened up a world of opportunity for business in the hospitality and tourism industries. Advances in communication technology make the world a global economy. As technology evolves, new distribution channels and competitors emerge. Marketers must embrace new technology as a marketing tool that will help address the needs of their target markets.

TECH NOTES

Cell Phones vs. Hotel Phones

Studies show that the use of telephones in American hotel rooms decreased by 20 percent in 2003. Guests are using their cell phones instead. To reduce the impact of lost telephone revenue, some hotels are offering flat rates and package deals. Marriott's "Wired for Business" program offers 24 hours of high-speed Internet access plus local and long-distance calls for a flat fee of $9.95.

➡ Write a paragraph about hotels marketing high-speed Internet access and in-room phone service after reading information through **marketingseries.glencoe.com**.

demographics statistics that describe a population in terms of personal characteristics, such as age, gender, income, ethnicity, or education

QUESTION

What are three advances in technology that have affected the travel business?

FESTIVAL PLANNING

Gail Sarni
Event Planner
Boston Blues Festival

What is your job?

"I am a planner for events."

What do you do in your job?

"I plan and organize all the logistical details for an event. In hotels, that means getting to know the client, the client's personality and needs, and then communicating this to operations, culinary, and banquets in a manner that makes everybody happy. For the Blues Festival, that means considering every possible detail and ensuring that these details are executed."

What kind of training did you have?

"I had on-the-job experience and learned from some great people over the years. I was the director of catering at the hotel at MIT, a Hilton hotel in Massachusetts. I was there for five years. I was director of catering at various properties for nine years."

What advice would you give students?

"Be prepared to work hard for long hours—but have a lot of fun. If you are not enjoying it, it is not worth doing. Also, find a mentor and emulate that person. Be patient. Do your best to understand what motivates people so that you can better serve them."

What is your key to success?

"Organization. Write everything down. That way you'll never forget the secret to your success on past events, and you can easily repeat it—and more importantly, improve it."

What might be the basic marketing plan for a music festival? List an example for each of the six marketing plan elements.

**Career Data:
Event Planner**

Education and Training
Associate degree or bachelor's degree in business or related area; on-the-job training

Skills and Abilities
Interpersonal, time-management, organizational, and office skills

Career Outlook As-fast-as-average growth through 2012

Career Path Internship to self-employment or position at agency to owning company

Setting Goals and Objectives

goal the eventual desired outcome

objectives the steps that will lead to the goal

A **goal** is the eventual desired outcome, such as achieving a certain profit. Management and employees should understand and be aware of the company's goals and objectives. **Objectives** are the steps that lead to the goal. To be effective, objectives must be clear, specific, realistic, and measurable.

Clear Objectives

If objectives are not clear, the people involved in achieving the objective may not understand the expectations. For example, if an airline company's objective for its product is "to be better than other similar products in the marketplace," what is the meaning of the objective? The company expects to offer a better-looking, better-priced product. However, the word *better* is not clear. Different people's interpretations of the word *better* may vary. Another way to phrase the objective might be "to offer more flights to more cities than other airlines offer in the marketplace."

Specific Objectives

Objectives must be specific. If the objective is to increase market share, meaning to expand the market for the product, the objective should state by how much and in what time frame—one week, one month, or one year. For example, the specific objective might be "to achieve a 50 percent increase in market share within six months."

Reasonable Objectives

To be realistic, an objective must be reasonable, or be attainable under current conditions. If the company's objective is "to achieve a 50 percent increase in market share," the objective would be unreasonable if no plans have been made to increase public awareness through advertising and publicity. In addition, to achieve this objective, the company would need to increase the marketing budget and add staff to increase exposure. If the objective is not achieved, the marketing plan could fail.

Measurable Objectives

Objectives should be measurable. In other words, there must be a way to measure success. For example, if the objective is to "increase bookings by 10 percent in the northeast region by year-end," the objective is measurable, or quantifiable, in numbers by percentage. If sales have grown in the northeast within the time frame by at least 10 percent, that growth is measured as successful. By contrast, marketers can also measure failure.

Every successful marketing plan includes methods to evaluate results. The company should collect data to measure the success or failure of the plan while the plan is being executed. By measuring the results of marketing efforts, a company can adjust or maintain the marketing strategies as needed.

Case Study — PART 2

ECO-FRIENDLY CAR CLUB
Continued from Part 1 on page 165

Continued from Part 1 on page 165

With Rofsky and Silberman's new ecotour travel agency, Journeys Travel, bringing in $10 million annually, their Better World Club (BWC) auto club could gain customers slowly, and the partners could implement a marketing plan. As part of the marketing strategy, the Better World Club developed a Web site where it supports fuel-efficient vehicles and mass transit. The Web site also notes where other auto clubs have fallen short. With competitive membership fees and roadside benefits, the eco-friendly auto club hopes that green-minded motorists will join the ranks.

BWC also created a green campaign: Each time a traveler books a flight through Better World Travel, the company donates money toward restoring Earth's atmosphere when toxic gases are released by airplanes. In addition, 1 percent of all BWC's revenue goes to cleaning up general pollution and waste created by travel. By providing a good product with a conscience, BWC believes it will succeed with its target market and beyond.

ANALYZE AND WRITE

1. Do you think criticizing other auto clubs could backfire as a marketing strategy? Write a short paragraph in response.
2. List some other hospitality and tourism businesses that might incorporate environmental issues in their marketing plans.

Journey to the Bottom of the Earth

Why would anyone visit Antarctica? This southernmost continent on earth is 98 percent ice and 2 percent barren rock. Its temperatures average a bone-chilling -56° Fahrenheit, and the winds clock in at 80 mph. Antarctica is the driest, coldest, windiest, and most desolate place in the world.

HISTORIC FASCINATION

Some come to see historic Antarctica. They want to walk in the footsteps of Norway's Roald Amundsen, the first person to reach Antarctica's South Pole, or England's Robert F. Scott who died in the attempt and wrote these words in his journal: "Had we lived, I should have had a tale to tell."

UNIQUE BEAUTY

Each year, thousands of tourists travel by plane or ship to a land hailed as tourism's last frontier. Most adventurers hope to see nature at its most unique: penguins nesting with their chicks; a pristine panorama; and giant icebergs that change color to pink, lavender, green, or yellow as the sun sets.

What could be a mission statement of a tourist company marketing tourism in Antarctica?

Marketing in All Environments

Marketing is a process that begins with understanding the needs and wants of consumers. Keeping these needs and wants in mind, products are developed, distributed, and promoted. Businesses stay focused on consumer needs to reach their business goals. The marketing plan is a road map to reach business goals. Understanding the marketing environment helps businesses market products successfully.

Quick Check

RESPOND to what you've read by answering these questions.

1. What is the purpose of having a mission? _____

   _____

2. What are the internal and external factors that influence the marketing environment? _____

   _____

   _____

3. What are goals and objectives? _____

   _____

Name _____ Date _____

Worksheet 8.1

Hospitality and Tourism Marketing

For one week, watch television ads. Use a separate sheet of paper to make a chart of four ads. Include the following information in your chart:

- Name of product or service

- Image of product or service

- Reason for using television as the promotion medium

- Celebrity in the ad and reason for using the celebrity

- Target market

- Product utility

Ad #1:

_____
_____
_____
_____

Ad #2:

_____
_____
_____
_____

Ad #3:

_____
_____
_____
_____

Ad #4:

_____
_____
_____
_____

Worksheet 8.2

Mission Statements

Visit five different lodging businesses or their Web sites. Collect mission statements from the establishments. Paste or write the mission statements below. Then answer the questions.

1. What similarities do you find in the mission statements?

   _____

   _____

2. What differences, if any, do you find in the mission statements?

   _____

   _____

Portfolio Works

YOUR MISSION IS . . .

Write a mission statement for an outdoor tours company that targets high school students. Use this page to jot down ideas before organizing them into a final mission statement.

Ideas for the Mission Statement:

_____
_____
_____
_____
_____
_____
_____
_____
_____
_____
_____
_____
_____
_____
_____
_____
_____

Mission Statement:

_____
_____
_____
_____
_____

Add this page to your career portfolio.

CHAPTER SUMMARY

Section 8.1   The Role of Marketing Basics

marketing (p. 166)
distribution (p. 166)
marketing concept
   (p. 167)
target market (p. 167)
marketing mix (p. 167)
utility (p. 169)

- Marketing is the process of developing, promoting, and distributing products, or goods and services, to satisfy customers' needs and wants. The marketing process begins with understanding what product consumers need or want through market research, making consumers aware of it through promotion, and then making it available through distribution.

- The elements of a marketing mix include product, place, price, and promotion.

- Utility is the concept of conveying the value of products. The components of product utility include place, time, possession, and information.

Section 8.2   Planning Marketing

marketing plan (p. 171)
mission (p. 171)
marketing environment
   (p. 172)
demographics (p. 175)
goals (p. 176)
objectives (p. 176)

- The marketing plan is a written document that provides direction for the marketing activities of a company for a specific period of time. Having a plan allows a business to designate resources to accomplish the marketing strategies.

- A mission is a business's purpose or goal. A good marketing plan begins with defining and sharing the company's mission.

- Internal factors of the marketing environment include operations, such as departments interacting within the business or organization, as well as accounting and public relations. External factors are broad, and include factors such as external suppliers of the resources needed to produce the product, product distribution, competition, size of company, demographics, economics, politics, and technology.

CHECKING CONCEPTS

1. **Describe** the marketing process.
2. **Explain** the significance of the marketing concept.
3. **Identify** the four Ps of marketing.
4. **Define** the term *utility*.
5. **Explain** the goal of a marketing plan.
6. **Identify** the purpose of a mission.
7. **Describe** the factors affecting the marketing environment.

Critical Thinking

8. **Explain** how demographics affect a marketing plan.

CROSS-CURRICULUM SKILLS

Work-Based Learning

Thinking Skills—Creative Thinking

9. Write a paragraph that describes the marketing utility strategy for a restaurant during the December holidays.

Personal Qualities—Self-Management

10. Think of a career in hospitality and tourism. Write down your plan to get that job. List several steps to that goal.

School-Based Learning

Computer Technology

11. Create a spreadsheet of the demographics of your class. Include characteristics such as age, gender, income if any, occupation, ethnicity, and education. Write a description of the typical student.

History

12. Use the Internet or the library to research your favorite restaurant chain. Create a time line to illustrate the company's growth.

Role Play: Resort Manager

SITUATION You are to assume the role of manager of a new hotel/ranch resort located in the high desert of New Mexico—an isolated area 85 miles from the nearest city and airport. The resort has positioned itself as a destination for rest and relaxation. Guests are met at the airport by a limousine and transported to a destination free of televisions, alarm clocks, and newspapers. Meals are served family style. Resort features include horseback riding, swimming, a spa, and nature walks.

(ACTIVITY) Initial guest acceptance of the resort has been positive. The resort's owner (judge) has asked you to present ideas to market the resort to international guests.

EVALUATION You will be evaluated on how well you meet the following performance indicators:

- Explain the nature of travel and tourism marketing.
- Explain marketing and its importance in a global economy.
- Describe the impact of international considerations on the travel and tourism industry.
- Differentiate between service marketing and product marketing.
- Make oral presentations.

Use the Internet to access the Web site of the American Marketing Association.

- Click AMA resources.
- Under site search, type "hospitality and tourism."
- List the titles of three different articles.

➡️ For a link to the American Marketing Association Web site to do this activity, go to **marketingseries.glencoe.com**.

Chapter 9

Market Information and Research

Section **9.1**
Target Markets

Section **9.2**
Market Research

Chapter Objectives

- Explain the purpose of market segmentation.
- Identify the methods used to segment markets.
- Explain product positioning.
- Describe the process of market research.
- Explain primary and secondary research.
- Identify methods for gathering primary data.

COWBOY UP

According to African-American historian Paul Stewart, when he played "cowboys and Indians" as a child, he always took the Native-American role because "there was no such thing as a black cowboy." As an adult, his impressions changed when he met an African-American cowboy who led cattle drives at the turn of the 20th century.

Stewart went on to conduct research and collect artifacts from the Old West. He discovered that nearly one-third of all cowboys in the American West were black and that African-American families had traveled west in covered wagons and settled in self-sufficient communities. He collected boots, saddles, and newspapers as well as rare photos of Clara Brown, Bill Pickett, "Black Mary" Fields, and other black personalities. Stewart also taped oral histories from survivors of that era.

In 1971, Paul Stewart organized his collection and created the Black America West Museum and Heritage Center in Denver, Colorado. How would the new museum attract visitors and get established?

ANALYZE AND WRITE

1. List who might be included in the Black America West Museum's potential market?
2. Describe research you would conduct if you were opening a museum.

Case Study Part 2 on page 197

POWER READ

Be an active reader and use these reading strategies:

PREDICT what the section will be about.

CONNECT what you read with your own life.

QUESTION as you read to make sure you understand the content.

RESPOND to what you've read.

Target Markets

AS YOU READ ...

YOU WILL LEARN

- To explain the purpose of market segmentation.
- To identify the methods used to segment markets.
- To explain product positioning.

WHY IT'S IMPORTANT

Understanding how to segment markets and position products in the minds of consumers is critical for successful marketing.

KEY TERMS

- market segmentation
- psychographics
- geographics
- behavioristics
- positioning
- competitive advantage

PREDICT

Describe why it might be important to segment markets.

market segmentation a way of analyzing a market by specific characteristics to create a target market

The Importance of Market Segmentation

Market segmentation is a way of analyzing a market by specific characteristics to create a target market. As you learned in Chapter 1, market segments are groups of consumers categorized by those characteristics because a group may have similar needs and wants. Researchers can use different characteristics, such as age, income, ethnic background, gender, education, and marital status, to segment a target market of consumers. The goal of any segmentation strategy is to understand the different markets and the unique needs and wants within each market. No particular strategy works better than another strategy. In fact, by using a number of market-segmentation strategies, marketers can get a more precise picture of the buying behavior of each group.

Some of the typical market segments are based on demographics, psychographics, geographics, behavioristics, and frequency of product use.

Demographic Segmentation

As discussed in Chapter 8, demographics are statistics that describe a population in terms of personal characteristics, such as age, gender, income, ethnicity, or education. Using demographics is one of the most common ways of segmenting customer groups because demographic characteristics are objective and easy to measure. Most local, state, and national governments take routine census surveys that reveal the size and makeup of its residents. The survey results are available to anyone, including marketers.

AGE GROUPS Knowing the size of a particular age group within a society can be useful for product planning because the needs and wants of customers are often age specific. For example, think about what is important to teenagers. The needs and wants of teens are not the same as those for senior citizens. Marketing campaigns by McDonald's for teens differ from campaigns designed for senior citizens.

INCOME People with similar income levels sometimes have similar needs and wants. For example, a company offering vacation homes and pleasure boats would not market to a target market with low income.

GENDER Another demographic factor is gender. Besides differences in preferences for clothing and toiletries, men and women have distinctly different buying behaviors. In recent years, hotel operators have noticed an increase in the number of female business travelers. They responded to this demographic shift by focusing on women's needs when planning new properties or remodeling old facilities.

Psychographic Segmentation

Psychographics are studies of consumers based on social and psychological characteristics, such as attitudes, interests, and opinions. In Chapter 2, you learned about Plog's theory of psychographics as it related to people's choices in travel destinations. In marketing, psychographics refer to how people spend their leisure time, the way they live, and their personal preferences—all of which define their lifestyles. Lifestyle preferences are determined by activities people pursue, what is important to them, and how they feel about themselves and the world. For example, psychographic segmentation can be used to identify people interested in theme cruises, murder-mystery parties, or family reunions.

CLASSIFYING AMERICANS The VALS Segmentation System, developed by SRI International, classifies people into eight American lifestyle segments. (See **Figure 9.1**.) These segments are based on psychological characteristics. The VALS survey receives answers such as "I like to try new things" or "I like to make things with my hands." Based on these responses, participants are segmented into one of eight groups: innovators, thinkers, achievers, experiencers, believers, strivers, makers, and survivors. For example, *makers* are practical and self-sufficient. They value things with a functional purpose. *Thinkers* are mature, reflective, well educated, and informed. They value knowledge and seek professional occupations. Thinkers are open to new ideas but want durability and functionality in products. Psychographic segments, such as those identified by the VALS survey, represent consumer groups that marketers may target for hospitality or tourism.

psychographics studies of consumers based on social and psychological characteristics such as attitudes, interests, and opinions

Figure 9.1

VALS Segments

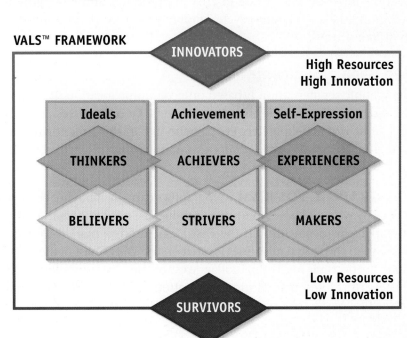

VALS™ FRAMEWORK

INNOVATORS

High Resources
High Innovation

Ideals Achievement Self-Expression

THINKERS ACHIEVERS EXPERIENCERS

BELIEVERS STRIVERS MAKERS

Low Resources
Low Innovation

SURVIVORS

PSYCHOGRAPHIC SEGMENTATION The VALS Framework places American adult consumers in one of eight segments, based on their responses to the VALS questionnaire. *What VALS segment might be categorized as venturers?*

Hot Property

Incentives and More

Maritz RESEARCH

Your hotel has just opened. People are booking rooms. They seem to be satisfied, but you do not know for sure. To find out, you need to do market research. Maritz Research helps companies do just that. In 1894, Edward Maritz opened Maritz, Inc., to sell and manufacture jewelry. Over time, his company created products for sales incentives. In 1973, Maritz, Inc., branched out as Maritz Research to research new products. The research business was so successful that it grew into one of the largest privately held companies in the United States today.

RESEARCH THAT WORKS

Maritz Research specializes in several different industries and customizes its offerings. In addition, they publish results of polls and research reports for anyone in any industry. The Maritz Research Hospitality Group focuses on interactions between guests and employees at various hospitality companies. The group reveals gaps between what companies promise, such as fast service and clean rooms, and what customers really get.

When developing studies, Maritz Research focuses on three core components: choice, experience, and loyalty. In the "choice" area, Maritz helps businesses identify products, messages, and brand images that appeal to potential customers. For "experience," researchers evaluate the quality and flow of customer interactions. For the "loyalty" component, analysts study previous customers' feelings and experiences and possible future reactions. Equipped with this knowledge, businesses can better meet the needs of customers and increase profits.

1. What does the Maritz Research Hospitality Group do for companies?
2. What customer research focus is more important: choice, experience, or loyalty?

PATTERNS Market researchers look for patterns of behavior, lifestyle similarities, and shared attitudes among groups to find relationships between products and possible customers. Understanding these relationships can play a role in creating products and packaging for certain markets. Different psychographic groups respond to products in different ways.

Geographic Segmentation

Geographic segmentation is based on geographic location. It is one of the oldest methods for segmenting markets. **Geographics** are statistics about where people live. People who live in the same town, state, or region do not necessarily share similar wants and needs, but they do share a common geographic location.

geographics statistics about where people live

GEOGRAPHIC TOURISM Geographics can affect buying behavior, especially when it comes to tourism products. Cruise lines with ports of embarkation (departure) on the East Coast tend to market to people who live in the East. Cruise lines located on the West Coast of the United States spend their marketing dollars west of the Mississippi River. Walt Disney World Resort in Florida more often markets to the East Coast versus the West Coast, where Disneyland is located.

CONNECT

Would your choice of a vacation destination be influenced by where you live? Why?

GEOGRAPHIC HOSPITALITY Determining how far your customers will travel to buy or use your product is important information for making marketing decisions. Urban restaurants market their properties differently than restaurants located in suburban shopping malls. A restaurant's menu may also be determined by its clients and where they live. For example, biscuits and grits are typical menu items in the southern United States, but they are not usually on menus in New England restaurants.

Behavioral Segmentation

Behavioristics are statistics about consumers based on their knowledge, attitudes, use, or response to a product. In behavioral segmentation, consumers are divided into groups based on those characteristics. In this type of segmentation, marketers sometimes look for occasions that influence buying behavior. For example, Valentine's Day is an occasion that inspires people to purchase cards, flowers, or candy for loved ones. New Year's Eve creates a demand for special celebrations. Honeymoons and business trips are other occasions that result in product use.

Product Use

Marketers also look at the rate of product use by consumers. For example, business travelers are among the primary sources of customers for airlines and hotels. These service providers are interested in maintaining loyal customers, so they create products that encourage the customer's repeat business. Rewards programs, used by most major airlines and hotel chains, encourage frequent product use by loyal customers.

Determining Markets

When various markets have been segmented, businesses select one or more market segments to target. Evaluating market segments is critical to the process of target marketing. Companies look for the size of the potential market and whether it is a growing market. They also review which of the potential markets is the most desirable to target, given the company's goals and resources.

Target Market Considerations

If a potential target market is the right size, a business will look at competitors already serving that market. If there are several strong competitors already in place, the business may look at another target market—perhaps a smaller one if it is free of competition. However, if marketing to the size of the potential market will cost too much, the target market becomes less attractive.

In addition, if a target market compromises the company's goals or objectives ethically, politically, or socially, it becomes less attractive. For example, despite the growth and profit potential of gaming in many areas, the Disney organization chooses not to pursue it. Gambling would be in conflict with the company's family-value policies.

THE Electronic CHANNEL

Electronic Explorers

Expedia, the online travel service, and Harris Poll Online recently launched an online quiz to help participants determine their travel profiles. More than 85,000 people responded to the survey. Results found that 25 percent of American adults have never left the United States. The survey also found that only 42 percent have passports. These results helped analysts determine that 56 percent of the participants are "intrepid explorers," or people who have a desire to travel out of the country—but never actually have done so.

➥Find out your travel personality online through **marketingseries.glencoe.com.**

behavioristics statistics about consumers based on their knowledge, attitudes, use, or response to a product

MARKETING SERIES *Online*

Remember to check out this book's Web site for market-research information and more great resources at **marketingseries.glencoe.com.**

Product Positioning

positioning the creation of an image for a product in the minds of customers, specifically in relation to competitive products, including services

Positioning, or branding, is the creation of an image for a product in the minds of customers, specifically in relation to competitive products, including services. To do this, marketers look at the qualities of a product that distinguish it from similar products offered by competitors. They examine characteristics of the product that may be important to the consumer, such as price, convenience, quality, security, speed, or value. For example, McDonald's® products have a specific image in customers' minds. Customers who buy a McDonald's hamburger may have a specific image of that product in comparison to a hamburger offered by Jack in the Box®. Advertisements and commercials help create images for positioning, or branding.

QUESTION

What characteristics do marketers examine when positioning a product?

Positioning by Competitors

Marketers examine the product positioning of existing competitors. For example, the makers of 7-Up position 7-Up as the "Un-Cola" to compete against Coca-Cola in the soft-drink market. Avis, an automobile rental company, positions itself by using the motto "We try harder." In the hospitality and tourism markets, you might also find one type of product positioned against another type. For example, cruise ships may be positioned against destination resorts.

World Market

Classic Castles

Would you enjoy a stroll through heather-covered moors? Maybe you have a taste for a plate of buttery scones and a pot o' tea. Do you believe in the Loch Ness monster? Famous for ancient legends, green valleys, and deep blue lakes, or *lochs,* Scotland is also known for its castles.

EVENTFUL SETTINGS

Steeped in history with fairytale-like allure, Scottish castles have become the centerpieces for special events. Castle keeps, or main towers, provide a magical environment for weddings, birthdays, romantic getaways, or even corporate events. Whether luxurious, romantic, or haunted, each castle offers something special. Glenapp Castle near the city of Glasgow features acres of stunning gardens and woodlands. A Viking named Magnus Barelegs built Rothesay Castle on the remote Isle of Bute. Tayside's Glamis Castle has historical ties to the past and present. The five-tower structure is the birthplace of England's "Queen Mum." It is also the setting for Shakespeare's *Macbeth*—and the home of a ghost or two.

If you were developing a marketing campaign to introduce the special attraction of Scottish castles to prospective guests, would you rely on demographics or psychographics to help plan your marketing strategies? Explain.

ENJOYING THE ADVANTAGES Hospitality and tourism businesses offer amenities and special services to attract customers in a competitive market. *List examples of competitive advantages that a small hotel might offer to compete with a large, upscale hotel.*

Competitive Advantages

To differentiate one product from another, a business must understand the competitive advantages of its product. Those advantages must be communicated to the consumer. A **competitive advantage** is an advantage over competitors due to greater value to consumers through lower prices or more benefits. Bed-and-breakfast lodging facilities compete by offering more perceived value for the guest. Value can include individualized service, complimentary beverages, cooked-to-order breakfasts, turn-down service, concierge service, unique décor, or upscale amenities.

competitive advantage an advantage over competitors due to greater value to consumers through lower prices or more benefits

Understanding Markets

Identifying specific markets, understanding buying behavior, and positioning products to fit various consumer segments are part of managing marketing information. Travel and tourism products and services can significantly benefit from target marketing and market research.

Quick Check ✓

RESPOND to what you've read by answering these questions.

1. What is the purpose of market segmentation? _____

   _____

   _____

2. What are common methods for segmenting markets? _____

   _____

3. What is competitive advantage? _____

   _____

   _____

Market Research

AS YOU READ ...

YOU WILL LEARN

- To describe the process of market research.
- To explain primary and secondary research.
- To identify methods for gathering primary data.

WHY IT'S IMPORTANT

Understanding the importance of market research and the methods for gathering information is vital for designing successful products.

KEY TERMS

- market research
- secondary research
- primary research
- observation method
- experimental method
- survey method
- sample

PREDICT

What is primary research?

market research the systematic gathering, recording, analyzing, and presentation of information related to marketing goods and services

Market Research Defined

Market research is the systematic gathering, recording, analyzing, and presentation of information related to marketing goods and services. Collecting information can be as simple as talking with customers. For example, the servers in restaurants routinely ask diners how they are enjoying their meals. Hotels and motels frequently place customer comment cards in guest rooms to gather information about each guest's stay. Larger organizations may also use more formal or structured methods of collecting data, such as surveys or focus groups. Customer surveys can determine levels of customer satisfaction. Cruise lines may use guest surveys at the end of a cruise to measure the effectiveness of onboard services. Focus groups include a cross section of people and are used to evaluate new or improved products. Regardless of the method, the purpose is always the same—to understand customers' needs and wants.

The Importance of Market Research

Why is it important to do market research? A company can be better equipped to address the needs of customers with more information about its customers, its competitors, the changes in the marketing environment, emerging market trends, and external factors influencing the market. We live in an information-rich society that has access to news from around the world, 24 hours a day. Technology allows businesses to collect, process, and distribute that information quickly. With so much data available, it is necessary to sort through what is important and relevant. Market research allows business to focus on relevant information from specific consumers.

Managing the Future

Market research enables a business to process, make use of, and file away information. By collecting information, sorting through the data that relate to the current marketing situation, and identifying possible solutions, organizations can more easily manage the future.

Before beginning a market research project, a business must answer several questions:

- What information does it need to know?

- Who might have that information?

- What is the best method of gathering that information?

Market Research Process

The first step in the market research process is to identify the problem. For research to be most effective, market researchers present the problem in the form of a question. For example, a restaurant may want to attract an upscale market by expanding its menu and enhancing its services. The research question might be: "What changes can we make to our menu and service to attract more affluent diners with sophisticated tastes?" To discover the answer to this question, researchers gather primary and secondary research information.

Secondary Research

When the problem is defined, a marketing department can develop a research plan to determine what information needs to be collected and the best way to collect it. The necessary information can be acquired through **secondary research**, which is published data that have been collected for some other purpose. For example, in the restaurant example, the manager might analyze recent sales, looking for the most expensive item on the menu. Research would reveal how frequently customers order the expensive item and the price other restaurants are charging for similar items. Secondary research may also be available through external sources. Reports published by industry associations such as the National Restaurant Association or articles published in *Food and Wine* or *Gourmet* magazines are examples of external sources. The research question may be answered through secondary research alone. It is the most time- and cost-effective method of gathering information. However, secondary research may provide only part of the answer. To get a bigger picture, researchers use primary research methods.

TECH
NOTES

Online Restaurant Surveys

The marketing research firm of Sandelman & Associates created an Internet-based research division for 85 restaurant chains. Through RestaurantPoll, researchers gather consumer information for clients. After entering demographic information on this Web site, respondents rate restaurants through surveys. For each survey completed, the respondent is entered into a monthly drawing for prizes.

➡ How do restaurants use the information collected by Sandelman & Associates? Answer this question after reading information through **marketingseries.glencoe.com**.

secondary research published data that have been collected for some other purpose

USING ALL SOURCES Market researchers must use all available sources, primary and secondary, to get the best and most accurate picture of a target market. *What type of research data is found in magazines and trade association publications?*

Profiles in Hospitality

HIGHER RATINGS

Cheryl Thompson Griggs
Consultant and President
Optimum Rating, LLC

What does your job entail?

As one of the founders of Optimum Rating, Cheryl Griggs works with hotels to help them earn the highest ratings possible with AAA and Mobil. "I consult with hotel, resort, and restaurant properties to upgrade, enhance, and create physical facilities that appeal to their guests. We also assist properties with development of the appropriate image through intangibles such as service, employee conduct, and appearance. It is not just about making pretty rooms, it's about setting tone and mood."

What kind of training did you have?

"I have a bachelor of science degree in housing, interior design, and resource management (HIDM) from Virginia Tech. However, my education did not end with graduation. I began my career as an in-house designer for a hotel company that owned two-, three-, four- and five-star properties. My supervisor taught me how to apply my formal training."

What advice would you give students?

"Get the most out of your educational opportunities and develop contacts within the hospitality world. Many hospitality designers, architects, resort developers and hotel operators are eager to share their experience and expertise with students. Keep abreast of the latest trends in the hospitality design industry, as well as the hotel, food, and beverage industries. Get familiar with all levels of hotel and restaurant properties."

What is your key to success?

"Constant global research of new properties and design trends. Networking with leaders in the industry is very important."

Why is networking in your chosen field important?

Career Data: Ratings Consultant

Education and Training
Bachelor's or master's degrees in design, hospitality management, or general business

Skills and Abilities
Communication, creativity, and interpersonal skills

Career Outlook Faster than average through 2012

Career Path Entry-level hotel and restaurant jobs to in-house design positions

Primary Research

primary research original research conducted for a specific marketing situation

Primary research is original research conducted for a specific marketing situation. Marketers determine the information needed and the best method for collecting it by the objectives of the research itself. For example, a restaurant owner may need to identify the menu items that appeal to upscale diners and how much they are willing to pay for them. To discover this information, researchers would survey people who eat at upscale restaurants.

Primary Research Methods

There are three types of research methods for collecting primary data:

- Observation
- Experimental
- Survey

OBSERVATION METHOD The **observation method** is a research method that involves watching people and recording their actions by audio, visuals, or writing. For example, the restaurant manager might send a researcher to a competing restaurant to record what people order, menu prices, the quality of service, ambiance, and décor. Such information might not be available if the manager asked the competitor down the street what items sell best and at what price. Observations need interpretation because they do not incorporate feelings, beliefs, and attitudes of the diners. For example, the lobster dish may sell because diners are tourists from a landlocked region with limited access to fresh seafood. On the other hand, many customers might order the dish because the waiter describes it so well.

EXPERIMENTAL METHOD The **experimental method** is a research method whereby a researcher observes the results of changing one or more marketing variables. This method involves selecting two similar groups of subjects and providing them with two different situations. For example, if a restaurant wants to test price sensitivity to premium beef entrées, the restaurant may offer diners in different parts of the restaurant the same menu item with different prices. By experimenting with pricing, the restaurant could determine if the cost of the item is related to how frequently it is ordered. Effective experiments use one uncontrolled factor (number of premium beef entrées sold) and one controlled factor (price) to determine if there is a cause-and-effect relationship between the two factors. The restaurant can use this information to set the best prices for its menu items.

SURVEY METHOD Market researchers use surveys to collect descriptive information. The **survey method** is a research method that involves gathering information from people through the use of surveys, or questionnaires. Surveys may be written questionnaires or a series of verbal questions. (See **Figure 9.2** on page 196 for a sample questionnaire.) Individuals and/or groups take part in surveys. Questionnaires might be completed in person, over the phone, via the Internet, or through the mail.

The gathered information is quantified, or measured. Answers are sorted, counted, and analyzed statistically. Results are tallied in percentages, and then patterns of responses are studied according to demographics of customers. Though survey data is collected quickly and at minimal cost, the information does have some limitations. Some questions could be misinterpreted by the responder or go unanswered. Survey design affects the collection of useful data. For the questionnaire to be effective, market researchers should develop and test it carefully before the survey takes place.

observation method a research method that involves watching people and recording their actions by audio, visuals, or writing

experimental method a research method whereby a researcher observes the results of changing one or more marketing variables

survey method a research method that involves gathering information from people through the use of surveys or questionnaires

CONNECT

Could you gather more information about a restaurant by observation or survey? Why?

Figure 9.2

Resort Hotel Survey

TO BETTER SERVE CUSTOMERS Questionnaires for hotels and restaurants help marketers discover what guests and customers really think of their businesses. *Would you be more honest when responding to a survey if you did not have to identify yourself?*

Please take a moment to rate our services. Thank you for giving us the opportunity to serve you.

	Excellent	Good	Average	Below Average	Poor	N/A
Menu variety	☐	☐	☐	☐	☐	☐
Value for price paid	☐	☐	☐	☐	☐	☐
Promptness of service	☐	☐	☐	☐	☐	☐
Quality of service	☐	☐	☐	☐	☐	☐
Quality of food	☐	☐	☐	☐	☐	☐
Quality of beverage	☐	☐	☐	☐	☐	☐

Overall, how would you rate our staff's hospitality?
(friendliness, courtesy, responsiveness)

☐ ☐ ☐ ☐ ☐ ☐

Overall, how would you rate our resort's public areas?

☐ ☐ ☐ ☐ ☐ ☐

Overall, how would you rate the value for the price paid?

☐ ☐ ☐ ☐ ☐ ☐

Overall, how would you rate the resort's ability to provide a relaxing atmosphere?

☐ ☐ ☐ ☐ ☐ ☐

Please rate the following:

Décor	☐	☐	☐	☐	☐	☐
Cleanliness	☐	☐	☐	☐	☐	☐
Condition of rooms	☐	☐	☐	☐	☐	☐
Housekeeping services	☐	☐	☐	☐	☐	☐
Heating/cooling in room	☐	☐	☐	☐	☐	☐

Comments:

_____

_____

_____

_____

Developing Consumer Questionnaires

To obtain information needed to answer a research question, a questionnaire should be designed, implemented, analyzed, and interpreted. Most researchers start with a *sample* to help develop a good questionnaire. A **sample** is a number of people who are representative of a study's population. To select a good sample, you must ask four questions:

1. Who should be surveyed?
2. How many people should be surveyed?
3. How should the sample be chosen?
4. When will the survey be given?

Survey Questions

The research designer decides what survey questions to ask and the form of those questions. Each question must be related to the research objective.

OPEN-ENDED QUESTIONS Open-ended questions allow the respondent to provide the answer. A question such as "Why do you eat at Joe's Bar & Grill?" is an example of an open-ended question. People completing the survey are not restricted in their answers and can use their own words. Researchers use open-ended questions to understand how people think.

CLOSED-ENDED QUESTIONS Closed-ended questions provide a predetermined choice of answers. The respondent must select his or her most appropriate response. Multiple-choice questions and questions that ask people to rate or rank their answers are examples of these types of closed-ended questions. Researchers can quantify the responses to closed-ended questions.

IMPORTANCE OF PHRASING Phrasing a good question is important for getting useful answers. Careless phrasing of questions can lead to inaccurate and useless data. Questions should be clear and direct. Language must be easily understood. Unless specifically required, avoid using slang, colloquialisms, or jargon. Questions should follow a logical order and not be offensive or too personal.

- **All Possible Answers**—Phrasing of choices should allow for all possible responses. For example, if the restaurant manager asks, "How often do you order filet mignon in a restaurant?" the possible answers should include: always, frequently, once in a while, and never.

Case Study — PART 2

COWBOY UP
Continued from Part 1 on page 185

Paul Stewart recognized that many visitors would come to the Black America West Museum of Denver from schools, libraries, community centers, and other groups. He marketed his museum to them and arranged for group tours and events. He also gained support from community volunteers and corporations.

Stewart then moved the museum to the Dr. Justina Ford House. Dr. Ford was the first black female physician in Colorado. She practiced in her Victorian home for 50 years until her death in 1952. The residence was relocated from its neighborhood, where it was about to be destroyed by developers, to the museum's current location near Denver's downtown. Restoration came with help from a Denver Community Development Agency Block Grant of $197,000. With a new location and listings in Denver guides that are targeted to visitors, Stewart's museum has become an established tourist attraction.

ANALYZE AND WRITE

1. Why would Stewart market the Black America West Museum to groups?
2. List some reasons why Stewart might choose the Ford House as a home for the museum.

sample a number of people who are representative of a study's population

QUESTION
What is a closed-ended question?

Math Check

MARKET-RESEARCH COSTS

A market-research package costs $130 per segment. There is a $27 materials fee. How much does a four-segment package cost?

➡️For tips on finding the solution, go to **marketingseries.glencoe.com**.

- **Range of Answers**—For the question, "How much are you willing to pay for an entrée of filet mignon?" answers allow for a range of responses:

  - Less than $10

  - $11 to $20

  - $21 to $30

  - More than $31

Overall Strategy

Market segmentation is used to identify target markets. It is the first step in creating an effective market-research strategy. Businesses must look at all potential markets and select those that are most economically desirable as well as those that match with the company's goals and objectives. To collect data that will be useful in defining target markets, market researchers must first identify a problem. By using both primary and secondary research methods, researchers can collect information about the wants and needs of the target market to develop products consumers will use.

Quick Check

RESPOND to what you've read by answering these questions.

1. Why is market research important? _____

   _____

   _____

   _____

   _____

2. What is secondary research? _____

   _____

   _____

   _____

   _____

3. What are some methods used for gathering primary research? _____

   _____

   _____

   _____

   _____

Worksheet 9.1

Market Report

Choose a restaurant in your community. Spend time in the restaurant to observe the customers who frequent the establishment. Write a market-research report for the restaurant that includes demographics, psychographics, geographic segmentation, and behavioral segmentation of customers.

_____

_____

_____

_____

_____

_____

_____

_____

_____

_____

_____

_____

_____

_____

_____

_____

_____

_____

_____

_____

_____

_____

_____

_____

_____

_____

_____

Worksheet 9.2

Market Research Elements

Add facts about each segmentation method in the chart below. Then answer the questions that follow.

Demographics

_____

_____

_____

_____

Geographics

_____

_____

_____

_____

Psychographics

_____

_____

_____

Behavioristics

_____

_____

_____

1. How have the demographic changes in the gender of business travelers affected hotel operators?

_____

_____

_____

_____

_____

2. Under which of the VALS categories would you place yourself? Explain your choice.

_____

_____

_____

_____

_____

Portfolio Works

WRITE A SURVEY

You own a market-research company. You have been hired by the World Tourist Association to design a survey that asks people about their favorite vacation destinations. Include a name of a destination, why this destination was chosen, how often the person visits, and other information that would be of interest to people who market travel and tourism.

Survey:

_____

_____

_____

_____

_____

_____

_____

_____

_____

_____

_____

_____

_____

_____

_____

_____

_____

_____

_____

_____

Add this page to your career portfolio.

CHAPTER SUMMARY

Section 9.1 Target Markets

market segmentation
   (p. 186)
psychographics (p. 187)
geographics (p. 188)
behavioristics (p. 189)
positioning (p. 190)
competitive advantage
   (p. 191)

- Market segmentation is a way of analyzing a market by specific characteristics to create a target market. The goal of any segmentation strategy is to understand the different markets and the unique needs and wants within each market.

- Markets can be segmented by demographics, psychographics, geographics, and behavioristics as well as frequency of product use.

- Product positioning is the creation of an image for a product in the minds of customers, specifically in relation to competitive products.

Section 9.2 Market Research

market research (p. 192)
secondary research
   (p. 193)
primary research (p. 194)
observation method
   (p. 195)
experimental method
   (p. 195)
survey method (p. 195)
sample (p. 197)

- Market research is the systematic gathering, recording, analyzing, and presentation of information related to marketing goods and services. The purpose of market research is to understand customers' wants and needs.

- Primary research is original research conducted for a specific marketing situation. Secondary research is published data that have been collected for some other purpose.

- Primary research can be gathered through observation, experimental, and survey methods.

CHECKING CONCEPTS

1. **Explain** the purpose of market segmentation.
2. **Define** geographic segmentation.
3. **Explain** the advantage of product positioning.
4. **Describe** competitive advantage.
5. **Explain** the purpose of market research.
6. **Identify** two main sources of research information.
7. **Explain** the observation method of market research.

Critical Thinking
8. **Compare and contrast** primary and secondary research data.

CROSS-CURRICULUM SKILLS

Work-Based Learning

Information—Acquiring and Evaluating Information

9. Choose three competing restaurants in your community. After doing research, decide which one has the competitive edge.

Interpersonal Skills—Teaching Others

10. Form a three-student group. Have each member choose one-third of the chapter. Write down the key points and discuss them.

School-Based Learning

Language Arts

11. Write a two-page journal entry about the theory of psychographics in relationship to your life.

Math

12. Your market research company has been hired to advise Snoopy's Ski Slope Lodge about a potential market. There are 200,000 skiers who might visit the mountain this winter. Hotels, lodges, and private condominiums offer 150,000 rooms to skiers. What are you going to advise your client? Why?

CONNECTION

Role Play: Marketing Manager

SITUATION You are to assume the role of marketing manager for the convention and visitors' bureau of a popular beach resort. You want to target your marketing efforts to different types of customers who visit your city. The city's primary markets are families and convention attendees. The president of the convention and visitors' bureau (judge) has asked you to develop ideas for market research to help reach this goal.

ACTIVITY You are to discuss your market research ideas with the CVB president (judge) in 30 minutes.

EVALUATION You will be evaluated on how well you meet the following performance indicators:

- Assess marketing information needs.
- Identify information monitored for marketing decisions.
- Develop profile of visitors.
- Design a group convention profile.
- Complete a property analysis.

INTERNET ACTIVITY

Use the Internet to access McDonald's Web site.

- Select USA.
- Click Go.
- Identify a current ad campaign.
- Identify the target market for the campaign.
- Share your findings with the class.

➡ For a link to McDonald's Web site to do this activity, go to **marketingseries.glencoe.com**.

Chapter 10

Designing Products

Section 10.1

Hospitality & Tourism Products

Section 10.2

Product Planning

Chapter Objectives

- Explain the difference between goods and services.
- Identify the levels of hospitality and tourism products.
- Describe the product mix.
- Explain the product life cycle.
- Differentiate between customer satisfaction and customer loyalty.
- Identify the factors that contribute to customer loyalty.
- Explain the importance of relationship marketing.

HOTELS: THE NEXT GENERATION

In the mid-1970s, Ian Schrager and Steve Rubell opened Studio 54, a New York dance club that attracted celebrities such as Andy Warhol, Calvin Klein, and Cher. The college classmates and business partners became as famous as their clientele and opened a series of high-profile restaurants.

However, when the dance-club fad faded, the partners decided to look for a new direction. They chose to renovate a hotel. Schrager realized that the operation of nightclubs and hotels was somewhat similar. "They are both hospitality businesses," he said. "They have the same goal: to take care of guests."

With its emphasis on high style and economy, the first hotel, the Morgans Hotel, was a hit. It set a trend toward boutique hotels that served as a place to meet business associates and friends—and a place to be seen. It was not just a facility that provided a shower and a bed. With one success, how would the hotel chain grow and maintain its unique character?

ANALYZE AND WRITE

1. What might be some similarities between running clubs and hotels?
2. What services could a smaller hotel offer to attract guests?

Case Study Part 2 on page 215

POWER READ

Be an active reader and use these reading strategies:

PREDICT what the section will be about.

CONNECT what you read with your own life.

QUESTION as you read to make sure you understand the content.

RESPOND to what you've read.

Hospitality & Tourism Products

AS YOU READ ...

YOU WILL LEARN

- To explain the difference between goods and services.
- To identify the levels of hospitality and tourism products.
- To describe the product mix.

WHY IT'S IMPORTANT

Understanding the difference between core products and facilitating or supporting products is important for developing a good product mix for your business.

KEY TERMS

- products
- core product
- facilitating products
- supporting products
- product mix

PREDICT

Describe in your own words the difference between goods and services.

products goods and services that have monetary value

Defining Products

Hospitality and tourism **products**, like products in other industries, are both goods and services that have monetary value. Goods are tangible items that you can touch, smell, see, or taste, such as a hotel room, a hamburger, or a rental car. Services are intangible things that people do for each other.

Goods and Services

In hospitality and tourism, goods and services are often intertwined. For example, most state and national tourism offices provide service in the form of information. This information includes details on immunizations or documents required when visiting another country. They may also provide tangible goods such as informational brochures and maps. Travel agents sell travel products, such as air transportation and accommodations, but they also sell services. These services may include finding the least expensive airfare or the most luxurious hotel suite.

Goods and Services Continuum

It is helpful to consider the hospitality and tourism mix of goods and services on a continuum, or spectrum. (See **Figure 10.1**.) At one end of the horizontal spectrum is pure service; at the other end are tangible goods. Tourism offices would be near the service end of the continuum. Fast-food restaurants, which provide mostly goods with minimal service, would be near the goods end of the continuum. Destination resorts would be in the middle because they provide goods and services equally.

Nature of Services

Services are difficult to sample before buying and involve experience, emotion, and memory. In general, services are actions performed by one or more people for the benefit of others. For example, a spa treatment is a good example of a hospitality service. The process and environment for a spa treatment are as important as the creams, lotions, and loofas used in the treatment itself. The goals of a spa treatment are to relax and rejuvenate. Treatment rooms are decorated in muted colors and textures. Background music is soft and soothing. The air is scented and the temperature controlled. It is hard to describe a spa service without referring to its experience. The customer has no tangible evidence of his or her purchase, except for a healthful appearance. However, he or she has benefited from and has a memory of the experience.

Figure 10.1

Continuum of Goods and Services

Hospitality & Tourism Products

SERVICES

Travel information
Serving food
Transportation
Booking reservations
Tours
Entertainment

GOODS

Brochures/maps
Food
Car for rent
Room

MIXING GOODS AND SERVICES Many businesses in the hospitality and tourism industries focus on services, but goods are also part of the mix. *Do travel agents offer more goods or services? Give examples.*

Variety of Products

Within the hospitality and tourism industries, there are hundreds of goods and services. These goods and services can be sold as stand-alone products or combined with other goods and services to create a package.

Hospitality Products

Hospitality products include both lodging and food-service establishments. Lodging properties can include hotels, motels, cottages, bed-and-breakfast inns, resorts, and casinos. Food service can include fast-food restaurants, fine-dining establishments, bistros, snack bars, food courts, concession stands, and catering firms.

Tourism and Transportation Products

Tourism industries include transportation vendors for airlines, cruise lines, rail, auto, and motor-coach travel. Transportation is a critical element of a tour package. Cruise lines, for example, provide transportation, accommodations, food service, entertainment, and recreation. Car rentals can be combined with air travel and hotel rooms for a fly-drive package to any destination.

Product Levels

There are several levels of products. At the heart of any good or service is the **core product**, or the main product that the customer is buying. For example, a customer who books a night at a bed-and-breakfast inn is buying a core product—a bed in which to sleep and breakfast to eat in the morning. Additional goods and services may accompany the core product, such as facilitating products and supporting products.

Facilitating Products

Facilitating products are goods or services that aid the use of the core product. At a lodging property, facilitating products include parking facilities, public telephones, and check-cashing services.

Key Point

TRANSPORTATION DOLLARS
Travelers spend billions of dollars each year on public transportation and auto transportation—almost $164 billion annually.

core product the main product that the customer is buying

facilitating products goods or services that aid the use of the core product

CONNECT
What one facilitating product would you want when booking a hotel?

Supporting Products

Other products besides the core product and facilitating products are called *supporting products*. **Supporting products** are extra goods or services that accompany the core product to add value or to differentiate it from the competition. For example, at a bed-and-breakfast inn, supporting products may include afternoon tea, a hosted social hour, turn-down service, and luxurious towels and linens. In some cases, guests will stay at or return to a hospitality or tourism establishment due to special supporting products.

Identifying Products

Sometimes it is difficult to distinguish between facilitating and supporting products. For example, consider high-speed Internet or wireless Internet access as a service. In a hotel that caters to business travelers, this service may be considered a facilitating product because it allows guests to do business while traveling. However, for a bed-and-breakfast establishment, the service might be considered a supporting product because the service helps differentiate the facility from competing bed-and-breakfast inns that do not offer Internet access to their guests.

Hot Property

The Complete Package

 COLLETTE VACATIONS

In 1918, Jack Collette began to offer tours to Florida from a Greyhound terminal in Boston. By 1927, his business expanded beyond Greyhound to partnerships with other motorcoach businesses. Dan Sullivan, a bus-line manager and Collette's friend, bought into the company in 1962 and brought his family on board. Under their leadership, Collette Vacations grew during the 1960s, expanded to Europe in the 1970s, and went global by the 1990s.

INSPIRED TOURS

Leaving the bus terminal behind, the tour company found many ways to provide travelers with unique experiences. The company formed multiple strategic partnerships to create unique vacations for people with special interests. In one partnership, Collette worked with the Smithsonian Institution to develop special learning vacations. Collette also joined with A&E television networks to offer vacations that matched programming on A&E, Biography, and The History Channel. For example, *The D-Day Battle of the Bulge: Normandy to Berlin* tour took visitors to famous battle sites in Europe, mirroring the content of D-Day documentaries on The History Channel.

It takes more than fascinating scenery and exotic locations to make a great tour. Top tour agencies such as Collette Vacations apply expert planning, experience, and imagination.

1. Classify the products offered by Collette Vacations.
2. Describe how Collette designed its hospitality and tourism products.

CLOSE-UP ON FOOD

Brian Preston-Campbell
Food Stylist

What do you do?

"I am a food stylist."

What does your job entail?

"A food stylist works with photographers and arranges raw ingredients for visual marketing materials such as brochures or Web sites. When not shooting, I am either preparing for a job or making new contacts with photographers, art directors, or production companies. Preparation entails buying all the necessary food and related products for the recipes or concepts. Making contacts involves cold calling, sending out promotional cards by mail, and e-mailing potential business prospects."

What kind of training did you have?

"My formal education is in the culinary arts, and I also have eleven years of cooking experience. But I know of other stylists who have backgrounds in art and film production. Training can be home economics on a post-secondary level, but most home economists work for large food companies."

What advice would you give students?

"Learn to cook in a formal setting, such as a restaurant or hotel with high volume and high standards. Work under top chefs. Learn how to bake. Assist a food stylist for six months or a year."

What is your key to success?

"If you enjoy what you do, you are sure to be successful. I am fortunate that I chose what I think is the ideal job for me so I can express my creativity on a daily basis."

What type of product is a gourmet meal?

Career Data: Food Stylist

Education and Training Bachelor's degree in culinary arts, visual arts, or home economics

Skills and Abilities Artistic, problem-solving, and communication skills

Career Outlook As-fast-as-average growth through 2012

Career Path Entry-level restaurant jobs to diverse opportunities within the culinary arts

Product Mix Sample

A company's **product mix** is the total assortment of products that a company makes or sells. For example, Marriott offers a complete line of hotel products to suit the needs of diverse travelers, from luxurious full-service hotels and resorts to all-suite hotels and extended-stay facilities. Marriott also offers facilitating and supporting products, such as bell staff to assist with luggage, valet parking, concierge service, business services, health clubs, restaurants, express checkout, conference services, and frequent-guest programs.

supporting products extra goods or services that accompany the core product to add value or to differentiate it from the competition

product mix the total assortment of products that a company makes or sells

SERVICES AS PRODUCTS
Bell staff provides the
product of service. *What
other services are offered
in hotels?*

No Limits

The depth and breadth of travel products are vast and limited only by imagination. Travel agents can book air reservations and hotel rooms, arrange for transfers between airport and hotel, and even purchase theater tickets and spa services. They can hire tour guides, arrange fishing charters, make restaurant reservations, and request personal valets. Bed-and-breakfast inns can offer special-interest programs such as cooking lessons. These products appeal to their target markets. Inn owners may also offer concierge services or add supporting goods and services to their product mixes, such as specialized tours or spa services.

Product extras add value to guests' experiences and generate customer satisfaction, loyalty, and retention. These topics are discussed in Section 10.2.

QUESTION

What might be included in a bed-and-breakfast product mix?

Quick Check ✓

RESPOND to what you've read by answering these questions.

1. What are the differences between goods and services. _____

_____

_____

2. What is a core product? _____

_____

3. What might be a sample product mix of a hotel company? _____

_____

_____

Product Planning

Life Cycle of Products

In Chapter 2, you learned about the cyclical nature of travel and the life cycle of destinations. The life cycle applies to all hospitality and tourism products. Businesses consider the product life cycle when planning products for consumers. The **product life cycle** is the various stages that a product goes through during its existence, from development, introduction, growth, and maturity to decline. **Figure 10.2** on page 212 illustrates the stages of the product life cycle.

Product Development

The life cycle begins with the development of a new idea for a product or service. During this stage, the marketing team plans a strategy to introduce the product to the market. They also test various target markets and gather market research to make projections about initial sales and potential market share.

Introduction Stage

Once a product is launched into the marketplace, it has entered the introduction phase. Sales during this phase are slow as customers become aware of the product. Companies spend millions of dollars in advertising and promotion in an effort to educate the consumer about the product's features and benefits. The objective is to get the consumer to recognize the existence of the new product and then try it.

Growth Stage

If the introduction stage is successful, the product will enter a period of growth. Gradually, more retailers carry the product and consumer demand increases. During this stage profits rise and competitors take notice.

Maturity Stage

When growth levels off, the product enters the maturity stage. Sales slow down, and the product does not attract new customers. Repeat customers may switch to a competitor's product or stop buying the product altogether. At this stage, the market is saturated with the product. To revive sales, the company may add new features, redesign packaging, or improve the product to retain customer loyalty. The marketing team searches for new markets for the product and reevaluates its marketing strategy.

Figure 10.2

Product Life Cycle

PLANNING FOR LIFE **Every product moves through stages, from development to final decline. Marketers can make the most of the growth and maturity stages with proper planning.** *What fast-food item might be in the decline stage? Why?*

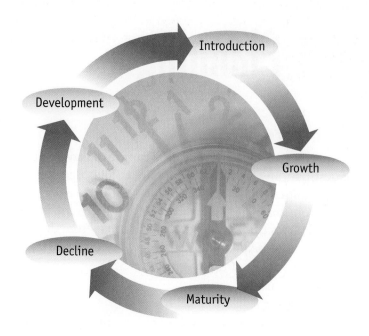

ETHICS & ISSUES

Risky Destinations

In the 1960s and 1970s, Afghanistan was a popular tourist destination for backpackers traveling to enjoy the country's scenery and ancient artifacts. Then in 2001, when the United States and Afghanistan were on the verge of war, Kabul, the capital of Afghanistan, was off-limits to tourists. One year later, the tourism department of Afghanistan registered only 75 tourists from Turkey, Japan, England, Switzerland, Iran, and Pakistan. Today, as the country slowly rebuilds, and government agencies and utilities are reorganizing, it is an unpredictable destination. *Is it appropriate to promote tourism to a destination in decline that could be dangerous?*

Decline Stage

When sales begin to fall off, the product enters a period of decline. Many things can lead to decline: a lag in technology, competitive products, political or financial factors, or a shift in consumer trends. When this happens, businesses may drop a product entirely or keep it only to satisfy loyal customers. The product usually gets very little marketing support as company priorities shift to new or improved products.

Dealing With Life Cycles

To respond to product decline, managers and marketers have several choices. They can examine the product and look for ways to improve it, add value to it, or change its appearance. The goal is to reintroduce the new and improved product and increase sales. New target markets can be found, and new marketing messages can be directed at this new audience. Other responses include examining the marketing mix and making changes. Such changes might include lowering the price or changing the method of product distribution.

Defining Customer Satisfaction

A product must satisfy customers, or the product will go into the decline stage. A satisfied customer is the most valuable asset a business can have. But what does customer satisfaction mean and how can a business create satisfied customers? **Customer satisfaction** is a positive feeling or reaction customers have when a business or product meets their needs. Satisfaction is a matter of perception. What satisfies one person may dissatisfy another person. Customer satisfaction is based largely on expectation.

Expectations and Satisfaction

Where do expectations come from? A customer might have firsthand experience with the product. Friends or family members may describe the product. The product may be advertised in magazines or newspapers with words and pictures. In other words, consumers develop expectations through preconceived ideas.

For example, when you order a pizza in a restaurant you have an idea of what will be delivered to your table. You picture a round "pie" with a tasty crust, sauce, melted cheese, and toppings that you might order. The pizza might be cut into six or more equal slices and served hot after a minimal wait. In your mind, you might see, smell, and taste what you have ordered. However, what if the pizza you are served falls short of your expectations? You will be disappointed and dissatisfied.

Marketers must also be careful to create realistic expectations for products, or they may fail to satisfy customers' expectations. For example, a resort in the Caribbean might promise sun-filled days and moonlit nights as well as a suite with an ocean view on a faraway island. However, the guest may arrive during the annual monsoon rain season with hurricane-force winds. It is likely the guest will not be satisfied.

Achieving Satisfaction

Customer satisfaction comes from delivering what is expected—and more. If customers receive what they expect, they are satisfied. If they receive more than what they expect, they are extremely satisfied.

MARKETING SERIES *Online*

Remember to check out this book's Web site for information on products, product planning, and customer loyalty as well as more great resources at **marketingseries.glencoe.com**.

customer satisfaction a positive feeling or reaction customers have when a business or product meets their needs

CONNECT

What situation would dissatisfy you most as a restaurant customer?

World Market

A Dream in Dubai

"We all have dreams, but only a leader can change those dreams into reality," says the Crown Prince of Dubai. Dubai, the second largest state of the United Arab Emirates, is building a dream—the world's largest mixed-use real estate complex. Dubai Festival City will stretch 2.5 miles along Dubai Creek, a natural inlet of the Persian Gulf. This "city within a city" will blend 1,600 acres of waterfront land into a huge complex of shops, restaurants, and businesses. Other highlights include an 8,000-seat amphitheater, a championship golf course, and luxury hotels. A Global Village features family fun. Water is the project's signature attraction. Giant waterfalls, crystal-clear pools, fountains, and a water promenade create stunning backdrops in this city of dreams. A central canal with water taxis disguised as ancient Arabian fishing vessels will create a sense of place.

How is Dubai creating expectations?

UNITED ARAB EMIRATES

customer loyalty the customer's faithfulness to a business and its product, demonstrated by the customer purchasing the product again

Customer Loyalty

Loyal customers are usually satisfied customers, but not all satisfied customers are loyal. **Customer loyalty** is the customer's faithfulness to a business and its product, demonstrated by the customer purchasing the product again. Customer satisfaction is one piece of the loyalty puzzle, but there are other things to consider. Satisfied customers may still seek variety. For example, if a traveler has a good experience while visiting Ireland, he or she may still want to visit other countries as well. That traveler may not return to Ireland for some time, if ever. Guests who enjoy their stay at one bed-and-breakfast inn may want to have a new experience at another in the same area. Other factors may influence repeat business. Some customers are price sensitive and will seek out the best deal—even if they absolutely love one particular place or thing that is priced high. Loyalty stems not just from being satisfied, but from being extremely satisfied.

Value of Loyal Customers

A loyal customer is more valuable than a satisfied customer. Not only do loyal customers return to do business, but they share information with friends and family members. A loyal customer becomes an ambassador of goodwill for the business or product.

COMPLETE SATISFACTION By partially satisfying a customer, the door is left open for a competitor to get that customer's business. If a customer is not completely satisfied, he or she may look elsewhere. A customer must be completely satisfied.

What Builds Customer Loyalty?

Many factors contribute to customer loyalty. Quality is one factor. Service is also important. Businesses must provide better products that customers need and want. Other factors that build loyalty include employee relations and price and value.

Employee Relations

Employees play an important role in building customer loyalty. They must be knowledgeable about the products. Individual customers should be attracted to the business because of the quality of the employees. For example, Disney was one of the first companies to refer to its customers as "guests," which implies their customers are unique and appreciated by the staff. Instead of being simply a paying customer using the Disney product, each customer is treated as an invited visitor to the amusement parks and resorts.

Price and Value

Another factor that contributes to customer loyalty is the price/value equation. Price should reflect the value of the product as perceived by the customer. For example, guests of luxury hotels are willing to pay more because of the perceived value of luxury accommodations and services.

Relationship Marketing

Relationship marketing is building relationships with customers by adding value to the interaction that will lead to long-term customer satisfaction and retention. One of the key roles of a product manager is to identify customers who are most likely to become loyal to a product. In addition, a product manager must create links to these customers by building strong relationships. Businesses are moving away from the traditional sales approach to marketing, which focuses on individual sales. Instead, they are building relationships with customers. In relationship marketing, the focus is less on a product's features and more on service, meeting customer expectations, and adding long-term value for the customer. The goal is to create a customer for life. Methods to achieve this include applying financial benefits, personalization, and special services.

Financial Benefits

To create relationships, managers must look for opportunities that benefit a customer's experience. *Financial benefits* are always attractive and can lead to increased customer satisfaction and loyalty. For example, reward programs add financial value to long-term customer relationships. By rewarding loyalty, the business creates an incentive for customers to continue using goods or services. In many instances, frequency-reward programs are tiered: Reward is based on the amount of usage. Examples of these programs include frequent-flyer programs and hotel-reward programs.

Personalization

Relationship marketing also means *personalization* as well as creating social ties to customers. Greeting guests by name, remembering birthdays and anniversaries, or writing a special note on direct-mail pieces are all ways to personalize the interaction with customers. Hotels and restaurants keep VIP (very important people) lists. They train personnel to provide special services to guests to make them want to return.

Special Services

Another useful way to build strong relationships with customers is to create *special services* for preferred customers. Hotels have special concierge-level floors that offer complimentary services such as continental breakfast and afternoon beverages. Cruise lines offer special discounts to repeat travelers and host special events for them onboard. Car-rental companies have express check-in and white-glove delivery service for preferred customers.

Case Study PART 2

HOTELS: THE NEXT GENERATION
Continued from Part 1 on page 205

Ian Schrager continued to open boutique hotels with unique atmospheres with help from notable designers such as Philippe Starck. He opened hotels in the cities of New York, Los Angeles, Miami, and London. Many of these establishments offer conference facilities, event resources, and day spas.

To complement the unique chain, Schrager launched a Web site that offers customers an online reservation service with special rates. The Web site also includes an e-tail store that carries terrycloth towels, cashmere blankets, and other merchandise related to the hotels. To provide added incentive for customers to book rooms, the Web site displays images of movie premieres, concert after-parties, celebrity birthdays, and other events held at the trendy Schrager hotels.

ANALYZE AND WRITE
1. What goods and services are offered on the hotel chain's Web site?
2. In what ways has Schrager applied relationship marketing?

relationship marketing
building relationships with customers by adding value to the interaction that will lead to long-term customer satisfaction and retention

QUESTION
What are three ways to promote relationship marketing?

FRIENDLY SERVICE A local independent restaurant can prosper through relationship marketing. Building good relationships with customers encourages repeat business. *What type of "personalization" could a restaurant offer its customers?*

Benefits of Customer Retention

By building strong relationships with customers, loyalty develops. Loyal customers are less price sensitive. They are less likely to switch brands to pay a lower price. They may also refer friends and family. By acquiring loyal customers, businesses can reduce marketing costs and lost revenue.

Products for Customers

Designing products that meet the expectations of customers is the first step in achieving customer satisfaction. Monitoring the product's life cycle enables product managers to make adjustments to prolong the life cycle. Customer satisfaction is one of many elements of customer loyalty. Building relationships adds value to the customer's experience. When businesses meet and exceed customers' expectations, they gain customers for life.

Quick Check

RESPOND to what you've read by answering these questions.

1. What are the stages in a product life cycle? _____
   _____
   _____

2. What contributes to customer loyalty? _____
   _____

3. What are the benefits of customer retention? _____
   _____
   _____

Worksheet 10.1

Product Levels

Visit two of your favorite restaurants and determine what they offer at the different product levels. Fill in the chart below with your answers.

Restaurant 1:

CORE PRODUCT	FACILITATING PRODUCTS	SUPPORTING PRODUCTS

Restaurant 2:

CORE PRODUCT	FACILITATING PRODUCTS	SUPPORTING PRODUCTS

Worksheet 10.2

Customer Satisfaction and Loyalty

Visit two of your favorite restaurants. Then write a paragraph about why you are satisfied with each restaurant and why you return.

Restaurant 1:

_____

_____

_____

_____

_____

_____

_____

_____

_____

_____

_____

_____

Restaurant 2:

_____

_____

_____

_____

_____

_____

_____

_____

_____

_____

_____

_____

Portfolio Works

PLANNING A PRODUCT

Create a hospitality and tourism product that you would like to operate, such as a hotel, restaurant, tourist attraction, or amusement park. Then complete the statements.

1. I would like to operate a _____

_____

_____

2. The product mix in my _____ includes _____

_____

_____

_____

_____

3. I define customer satisfaction by _____

_____

_____

_____

_____

4. I intend to create customer loyalty by _____

_____

_____

_____

_____

5. Customer retention is good for my business because _____

_____

_____

_____

_____

Add this page to your career portfolio.

CHAPTER SUMMARY

Section 10.1 Hospitality & Tourism Products

products (p. 206)
core product (p. 207)
facilitating products
(p. 207)
supporting products
(p. 208)
product mix (p. 209)

- Goods are tangible items that you can touch, smell, see, or taste, such as a hotel room, a hamburger, or a rental car. Services are intangible things that people do for each other. They are difficult to sample before buying and involve experience, emotion, and memory.

- There are several levels of products. At the heart of any good or service is the core product, which is the main product that the customer is buying. Facilitating products and supporting products may accompany the core product.

- The product mix is the total assortment of products that a company makes or sells.

Section 10.2 Product Planning

product life cycle
(p. 211)
customer satisfaction
(p. 212)
customer loyalty (p. 214)
relationship marketing
(p. 215)

- The product life cycle is the various stages that a product goes through during its existence, from development, introduction, growth, and maturity to decline.

- Customer satisfaction is the positive feeling or reaction customers have when a business or product meets their needs. Loyal customers are usually satisfied customers, but not all satisfied customers are loyal. Customer loyalty is the customer's faithfulness to a business and its product demonstrated by the customer purchasing products again.

- Customer loyalty can be developed through providing quality, service, good employees, and price and value.

- Relationship marketing is building relationships with customers by adding value to the interaction that will lead to long-term customer satisfaction and retention.

CHECKING CONCEPTS

1. **Define** the terms *goods* and *services*.
2. **Differentiate** between facilitating and supporting products.
3. **Explain** the product mix.
4. **Define** the term *product life cycle*.
5. **Differentiate** between customer satisfaction and customer loyalty.
6. **Identify** methods to build customer relationships.
7. **Describe** examples of personalization.

Critical Thinking

8. **Explain** the value of customer retention.

CROSS-CURRICULUM SKILLS

Work-Based Learning

Thinking Skills—Problem Solving

9. Choose a partner for your travel agency business. Your product is luxury cruises. With your partner, expand and describe your product mix.

Basic Skills—Writing

10. Write an article on relationship marketing for the opinion section of the newspaper. Use a local restaurant as an example of a business that applies or does not apply relationship marketing.

School-Based Learning

Computer Technology

11. Use the computer to create a graphic representation of the stages of the product life cycle.

Social Studies

12. Use graph paper to create the floor plan of the main floor of a luxury, family-oriented hotel. Use different colored cutouts to represent different types of amenities, such as a swimming pool, spa, or game room.

 CONNECTION

Role Play: Management Team Member

SITUATION You are to assume the role of a management team member for a riverboat that your company has purchased. The riverboat will cruise up and down a major river. Your company plans to offer theme cruises with tours as package offerings. The theme cruises will appeal to a wide variety of customers. Some of the themes under consideration are garden cruises, food and cooking cruises, music cruises, and historical cruises. The cruises will vary from five to 21 days.

ACTIVITY You are to recommend activities for guests between tours and while on the riverboat.

EVALUATION You will be evaluated on how well you meet the following performance indicators:

- Plan a variety of guest/client activities.
- Select tourist destinations.
- Develop tours.
- Explain the concept of product in the travel and tourism industry.
- Explain the concept of product mix.

 INTERNET ACTIVITY

Use the Internet to access the Marriott hotel chain's Web site.

- Click Corporate Information.
- Click About Brands.
- Check the list of Marriott brands against the list in the textbook.
- Tell a school friend if any brands have been added or deleted.

➡️ For a link to Marriott's Web site to do this activity, go to **marketingseries.glencoe.com**.

Chapter 11

Pricing Products

Section 11.1
Pricing Strategies

Section 11.2
Factors Affecting Price

Chapter Objectives

- Explain the concept of price.
- Identify typical pricing strategies.
- Describe how hospitality and tourism businesses use discounting.
- Describe the concept of supply and demand.
- Explain elasticity of demand.
- Explain how the product life cycle affects price.

TRUE BLUE

With travel agent June Morris, David Neeleman launched his first airline company in 1984, Morris Air. They used Southwest Airlines as a business model and succeeded by outdoing Southwest's legendary cost-cutting and customer-friendly strategies.

Morris Air was eventually bought by Southwest Air, which hired Neeleman as part of its management. However, being part of an established company stifled Neeleman's entrepreneurial spirit. So he left the company to help a Canadian airline called WestJet find success. But he was planning another airline—JetBlue.

Neeleman recognized that New Yorkers were paying high prices to travel from Manhattan to cities in upstate New York and Florida. So he solicited funds from past investors, and he renovated a neglected, run-down terminal at John F. Kennedy Airport for JetBlue. He then assembled a fleet of fuel-efficient Airbus A320s. But how would he draw customers to make his vision of cheap-and-chic travel a reality?

ANALYZE AND WRITE

1. Describe one of the reasons for creating JetBlue.
2. Is price, convenience, or comfort most important to passengers? Write one paragraph explaining your answer.

Case Study Part 2 on page 231

POWER READ

Be an active reader and use these reading strategies:

PREDICT what the section will be about.

CONNECT what you read with your own life.

QUESTION as you read to make sure you understand the content.

RESPOND to what you've read.

Pricing Strategies

AS YOU READ ...

YOU WILL LEARN

- To explain the concept of price.
- To identify typical pricing strategies.
- To describe how hospitality and tourism businesses use discounting.

WHY IT'S IMPORTANT

Understanding the various methods used to price goods and services is the first step in assigning prices to products that will increase sales.

KEY TERMS

- price
- prestige pricing
- markup
- cost-plus pricing

PREDICT

Describe in your own words the importance of accurate pricing.

price the value placed on goods or services being exchanged

What Is Price?

For any product, **price** is the value placed on goods or services being exchanged. There are several terms for prices in hospitality and tourism industries: airfare, cruise passage, rack rate, toll, tariff, tuition, tip, commission, and tax. All prices are associated with goods and services. Understanding price is important for marketers and managers. High prices can drive customers away, but low prices may not be enough to cover costs and increase sales.

The Value of Price

How much are you willing to pay for tickets to see your favorite band in concert? Are you willing to pay as much for tickets to a neighbor's ballet recital? You probably are not because you may value seeing your favorite band more than watching your neighbor dance. Value is in the eye of the beholder—or in this case, the consumer. The consumer determines if exchanging money (the price of the ticket) is worth the benefit or value (seeing the concert or ballet). Price is more than just the cost of an item. It is also the value that the item holds for the consumer.

Pricing Hospitality & Tourism

A number of techniques are used to assign prices to hospitality and tourism products. Airlines use a class system to categorize the costs of airfare—first class, business class, and coach. Cruise lines assign cabin prices based on size and location. Hotels offer room categories such as standard and deluxe. Car rental companies determine price by automobile type, such as compact, economy, or luxury. In addition, special prices, or rates, are offered to travel agents, tour operators, other intermediaries, and to customers who book through the Internet.

Restaurant Pricing

Restaurants have several pricing options. Prices might be set *à la carte* for single menu items, such as appetizers, entrées, or dessert. A restaurant might provide a *prix fix* menu, which offers several courses for one set price.

Pricing Strategies

Some typical pricing strategies include promotional pricing, psychological pricing, market-penetration pricing, breakeven pricing, cost-based pricing, discounting, and other special pricing strategies.

Promotional Pricing

Hospitality and tourism businesses use promotional pricing strategies to generate sales during traditionally slow periods. Early-bird specials at restaurants and happy-hour specials at clubs are good examples of promotional pricing. Knowing that business may be sparse between 4 P.M. and 6 P.M., restaurants use special promotions to attract customers. The concept usually works because customers coming in for the special will order additional food or beverage items apart from the promotion. Losses incurred from lower-priced promotional items will be made up by purchases of other items.

Lodging Packages

Lodging properties also use promotional pricing. They create special packages that include more than just overnight accommodations. Instead of simply discounting the price of a hotel room, hotel managers create special events that give guests a reason to book rooms. Events might include New Year's Eve parties, dinner and movie deals, or weekend getaways that include in-room treats. Packaging several products together for one price adds value for the customer and creates a positive image for the business.

Psychological Pricing

The price of a product has a psychological impact on customers. Many people believe that an expensive item is high quality, or that an inexpensive item may be poor quality. Price and quality perception are very closely linked in the minds of many consumers. Hotels and restaurants that focus on establishing a luxury image use **prestige pricing**, which is pricing based on consumer perception. A high price may be linked to a product in order to communicate quality to consumers.

TECH *NOTES*

Wi-Fi Hotspots

Wireless fidelity, or "wi-fi," is high-speed wireless Internet access. Many hotels and restaurants provide wi-fi access points known as "hotspots" so that customers with laptops or handheld computers can connect to the Internet. Some businesses charge a fee for this service, while others offer wi-fi access at no cost. According to the deli/restaurant chain Schlotzsky's, offering free wi-fi service has been good for business, which now extends beyond the lunch hour.

➡ List the pros and cons of offering free wireless Internet access after reading information through **marketingseries.glencoe.com.**

prestige pricing pricing based on consumer perception

SPECIAL PRICES Hotels offer special promotional prices for special-occasion events. *What might be included in the price of a New Year's Eve party at a hotel?*

markup the difference between the retail or wholesale price and the cost of an item

CONNECT

Would you pay more for a meal in a restaurant that has luxurious decor?

cost-plus pricing pricing products by calculating all costs and expenses and adding desired profit

Market-Penetration Pricing

Some companies will price their products at or below cost just to enter the market and gain a market share quickly from competitors. This pricing is called *market-penetration pricing*. Using this pricing method, a business can gain entry into the market by attracting high numbers of price-sensitive buyers.

Breakeven Pricing

For breakeven pricing, a business determines the price of a product or service at which it will break even. To break even, the price must generate enough revenue to cover the costs and expenses of the product. Consider the costs and expenses of a small, ten-room bed-and-breakfast inn. To break even on providing a room for one night, the owner must charge enough money to cover all costs of operating the facility. These costs may include:

- Mortgage
- Utilities
- Insurance
- Employee salaries
- Food and beverages
- Office supplies
- Marketing expenses

By knowing the breakeven point, the owner has a benchmark, or standard level, for determining room prices throughout the year. If the costs and expenses (breakeven point) total $75, then the price of that room should not go below that amount, or the inn will lose money.

Cost-Based Pricing

One of the easiest methods used to set price is markup. **Markup** is the difference between the retail or wholesale price and the cost of an item. A retailer buys goods from the wholesaler or manufacturer and then marks them up for resale to customers. The markup is the difference between what the wholesaler charges, including shipping and labor costs, and the retail price to the customer. Each retailer wants to cover the cost of the item and make a profit.

Cost-Plus Pricing

When using cost-plus pricing, the goal is the same—to make a profit. **Cost-plus pricing** is pricing products by calculating all costs and expenses and adding desired profit.

Discounting

Discounting is a strategy used to reward consumer behavior, such as booking early, buying off-season, or buying in volume. Prices are adjusted by a certain percentage, or special rates are assigned to specific periods. For example, in the lodging industry, there are seasons—the high season, the low season, and the seasons in between. The high season commands the highest rates. The in-between season is referred to as the *shoulder season*. Low-season and shoulder-season rates are adjusted to attract customers during these slower periods.

Cruise Discounts

The cruise industry also uses discounting. Cruise passengers who book early, typically 6 to 12 months prior to sailing, are offered reduced prices. This is to encourage them to commit to a specific sailing date.

Airline Adjustments

Airlines adjust their rates by the time of day, day of the week, or month of the year. The lowest rates are usually for early-morning, or red-eye, flights and weekend departures. Rates for routes to seasonal destinations are also adjusted according to the time of year.

Key Point !

ONLINE ON TARGET
The travel Web site Orbitz discovered that 91 percent of Americans with Internet access prefer comparison shopping hotels online. The 2003 Orbitz survey, fielded by Harris Interactive®, also revealed that travelers believe they will get the lowest rates on hospitality and tourism Web sites.

Hot Property

The World on a Click

Expedia.com®

Many travelers want the best deal, but they may not know how to find it. Enter Expedia.com®. When the world was just beginning to discover the Internet, the idea of booking flights and hotel reservations online was unfamiliar. Despite the risks, Microsoft® launched Expedia in 1996 and provided an online resource for trip planning. Expedia allows consumers to compare many hotels, cars, air tickets and cruises—and book online.

By the 21st century, Expedia had a winner with the #1-rated travel Web site for do-it-yourself business or leisure travelers. The innovative travel service is also the fourth largest travel agency in the United States. Expedia and its network of partners work together to secure great prices, availability, and choices for consumers.

Partners include more than 20,000 merchant hotels through North America, Canada and Asia, plus a wide variety of travel-service providers.

PRICING EXPERTS

Technology has made Expedia possible with its award-winning Expert Searching and Pricing (ESP) technology, providing travel and lodging options online. With many newcomers to the travel Web-site business, which is expected to outpace traditional travel agencies, Expedia.com continues to expand and help people explore the world.

1. How has Expedia applied technology to reduce travel prices?
2. What pricing strategies has Expedia employed?

Special Pricing Strategies

Special pricing techniques are practiced in the hospitality and tourism industries. These methods include price lining, bundle pricing, loss-leader pricing, and yield management. (See **Figure 11.1**.)

Price Lining

Price lining is selling all the products in a product line at specific price points. For example, a car rental business may offer three levels of cars for rent: economy, midsize, or luxury.

Bundle Pricing

Bundle pricing involves selling several items as a package for a set price. Purchased separately, the items would cost more than the price of the package. This strategy is used frequently in the tourism industry because it benefits both consumers and businesses.

Loss-Leader Pricing

Loss-leader pricing is pricing an item at cost or below cost to draw customers or capture the attention of customers. Restaurants often employ this strategy by offering two-for-one deals on entrées, hoping that customers will spend more on alcohol, appetizers, and dessert.

Yield Management

Yield-management pricing is pricing items at different prices to maximize revenue when limited capacity is involved. Hotels use this pricing strategy to fill rooms during slow periods. To be effective, a property must be able to estimate occupancy for a specified period.

Figure 11.1

Pricing Strategies

GOOD DEALS Many businesses offer products using bundle pricing. In hospitality and tourism, bundle pricing gives travelers and businesses many options for good deals. *What would be the pros and cons of bundle pricing when choosing a vacation package?*

Price Lining	Bundle Pricing	Loss-Leader Pricing	Yield-Management Pricing
$15/day Compact	$109/night 1 room	$15 for two meals (regularly $15 for one meal)	$99 January 25 (advance booking)
$22/day Midsize	$129/night 1 room + breakfast + spa treatment		$199 March 25
$30/day Luxury			

The Ultimate Hostel

Nestled in the Blue Mountains region of New South Wales, Australia, the town of Katoomba is famous for scenic surroundings. As a World Heritage site, Katoomba also lays claim to one of the world's best youth hostels. Like other hostels, the YHA (Youth Hostels Association) Backpackers Hostel provides many young tourists with cheap accommodations if they share rooms with other travelers. Adults may pay as little as $20 a night; guests under 18 pay less. Formerly a cabaret club, Katoomba's hostel combines artsy surroundings with modern facilities, such as computer service, game and reading rooms, videos, laundry, and a full kitchen. A giant refrigerator provides a "free shelf" for food that is left behind.

When not socializing at the hostel, guests can explore the mountains. The more ambitious travelers can "bushwalk," rock climb, or ride horses. Others might prefer to take a tour of the nearby national park or local museums. It is a "gorgeous, magical place," comments one happy customer. "I'll definitely be back!"

Why do you think youth hostels can charge so little and still stay in business?

Value, Price, and Strategy

Like most commercial businesses, travel and tourism businesses use a variety of pricing strategies to attract customers. It is important to know the value of a product or service before pricing it. Value differs from one consumer to another.

QUESTION
Why do businesses use loss-leader pricing?

Quick Check

RESPOND to what you've read by answering these questions.

1. What is cost-plus pricing? _____

_____

_____

2. How do hospitality and tourism businesses use discounting? _____

_____

_____

3. Describe the concept of yield management. _____

_____

_____

Factors Affecting Price

AS YOU READ ...

YOU WILL LEARN

- To describe the concept of supply and demand.
- To explain elasticity of demand.
- To explain how the product life cycle affects price.

WHY IT'S IMPORTANT

Understanding the internal and external factors that affect price can help businesses determine successful pricing strategies.

KEY TERMS

- supply
- demand
- elasticity of demand

PREDICT

What might be some external factors affecting price?

supply the amount or quantity of goods and services that producers provide at various prices

demand the amount or quantity of goods and services that consumers are willing to buy at various prices

elasticity of demand the variation of consumer demand due to a change in price

External and Internal Factors

External and internal factors can affect product-pricing decisions. External factors include market-demand issues, competition, the world's economy, and environmental conditions. Some internal factors are a company's marketing objectives and marketing mix.

External Factors and Market Demand

If the supply of an item is limited, the price is usually higher. If supplies increase, the price may sometimes decrease. This illustrates the law of supply and demand. **Supply** is the amount or quantity of goods and services that producers provide at various prices. How much product a company will sell is directly related to how much consumers will buy. This is **demand**, or the amount or quantity of goods and services that consumers are willing to buy at various prices.

FLUCTUATING DEMAND Demand can be influenced by seasons. For example, the demand for turkey increases near Thanksgiving in the United States. Turkey prices are highest during that time. After the holiday, turkey prices fall as consumer demand decreases. Manufacturers can manipulate demand by limiting the amount of available product.

ELASTICITY OF DEMAND High-priced items, such as luxury goods, may have less demand because fewer people can afford to buy them. If prices were lowered, and more people could afford to buy luxury items, the demand might increase. When demand for a product increases because the price decreases, or vice versa, there is **elasticity of demand**, which is the variation of consumer demand due to a change in price. Under certain circumstances, demand is *inelastic,* which means that the price has no bearing on the demand for the product.

Competition

Businesses do research to find out what their competitors are charging for the same or similar products. This should be the starting point for determining price. To be competitive, a business must price its products lower than its competitors' products to draw customers.

PERCEIVED VALUE If a company wants to charge higher prices, it can increase the perceived value of a product by adding extra services or quality. For example, Hotel A has a rate of $99 per night for two persons, but Hotel B has a rate of $129 per night for two persons—including breakfast and free stay for children. Hotel B has a greater perceived value for families.

The Economy

A business must look beyond what its competitors are doing and examine the current market demand when setting prices. It must also look at the economic environment. During periods of recession, consumer spending decreases. Businesses may lower prices to keep customers. If a state or local government increases business taxes or imposes new regulations that increase overhead expenses, consumer prices may rise. This is because the cost of doing business has gone up. Inflation, rising interest rates, or other economic changes require businesses to reassess their pricing strategies and either increase or lower prices.

Environmental Conditions

War or the threat of war, terrorist acts, bad weather, and other environmental conditions can negatively affect a travel/tourism company's pricing. Travel-related businesses suffer. People become unwilling to travel, especially by air. Airline companies, cruise lines, and hotels experience cancellations. In a ripple effect, the businesses that supply goods and services to these tourism industries also suffer losses. Without guests, hotels do not need laundry services, food items, or paper goods. Employees are laid off, and people stop eating out. Thus, the economy slows down, and businesses may close. Under these circumstances, prices for hospitality and tourism products require serious adjustments.

ADJUSTING PRICES AND POLICIES The events and effects of September 11, 2001, on the travel and tourism industries forced change. Many cruise lines implemented no-penalty cancellation policies, allowing travelers to cancel up to a day before travel without losing deposits. (See **Figure 11.2** on page 232.) Lodging properties offered value-added, all-inclusive packages to address price sensitivity. Restaurants redesigned menus to offer lower-cost items that could be sold at lower prices to customers.

Costs and Expenses

A business must first look at the cost of doing business to determine price. To make a profit, a business must cover expenses involved in developing and delivering a product. The amount a company charges for goods or services is a direct result of external and internal production costs and the value they have to the consumer. A company does not want to charge a price that is too low or too high. A low price might reduce profits for the company; but a high price might discourage demand for the product.

Case Study PART 2

TRUE BLUE
Continued from Part 1 on page 223

Since launching JetBlue in 2000, Neeleman has distinguished the airline from its competitors through a combination of cost cutting, customer service, and image promotion. To save money, JetBlue does not serve meals and emphasizes online sales. Operators sell tickets via telephone from their homes. In an effort to decrease prep time between flights, everyone (including the pilot and board members) is expected to help clean up. JetBlue also promotes a chic image by providing leather seats and a satellite television for every passenger. In addition, catchy advertising is aimed at different markets. For example, northern California residents traveling to southern California take the "Fog to Smog" route. Under Neeleman's leadership, JetBlue has flourished in an era when other airlines have suffered.

ANALYZE AND WRITE

1. List some ways JetBlue has cut costs.
2. Why is it important for JetBlue to be marketed as chic—and not just cheap? Write a few sentences explaining your answer.

CONNECT

What is one environmental condition that may have affected hospitality and tourism in the last year?

Figure 11.2

No Strings Travel

PRICE ADJUSTMENTS In an effort to address travel concerns following 9/11, the SeaDream Yacht Club issued a "No Stress, No Strings" cancellation policy to accommodate shifts in the travel and tourism industries. *What other pricing adjustments could be made for a boating business to draw uncertain customers?*

No Stress, No Strings

"In unsettling times such as the world is experiencing at present, travelers can change or postpone their SeaDream travel plans for any reason up to the day before departure and receive 100 percent travel credit of the yacht tariff, including government fees and handling and service charges. This money is applied toward a future sailing on SeaDream I or II within two years of the original booking. This innovative program is offered at no cost to our guests."

Math Check

CALCULATING COSTS
Revenue and expenses for The Whistle Stop Restaurant are as follows: cash sales, $9,600; charge sales, $11,300; other, $250; salaries, $7,890; rent, $1,500; supplies, $1,800; and advertising, $500. What is the restaurant's net income?

➡For tips on finding the solution, go to **marketingseries.glencoe.com.**

Internal Factors

Depending on the size of the company, pricing decisions are made by senior management staff, the marketing or sales department, or by company policy. Factors such as the company's marketing objectives and marketing mix must be considered for pricing to be effective.

Marketing Objectives

To effectively set prices, a company must be clear about its marketing objectives. What is the company attempting to do with the launch of the product? Is it trying to generate cash flow? Is the company trying to increase profits? Objectives have specific goals in mind, based on the target market and the position a company seeks within that market.

Marketing Mix

Using price is one way to achieve marketing objectives, but it is not the only way. To effectively reach the target market, a company must consider all four Ps of the marketing mix—product, price, place, and promotion. Packaging design and promotion affect pricing decisions.

The Product Life Cycle and Pricing

As you learned in Chapter 10, all products go through a life cycle: introduction, growth, maturity, and decline.

Product Introduction and Growth

In the introduction stage, prices are generally high because a company must cover the costs of production, distribution, and promotion. During the growth stage, prices tend to remain the same. A company may also lower prices to attract new customers.

 marketingseries.glencoe.com

VINEYARD MANAGEMENT

Sue Conca
Business Manager
Lost Mountain Vineyard

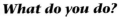

What do you do?

"I am the business manager of a vineyard and winery." Located in Sequim, Washington, Lost Mountain began as a family business in 1982.

What do you do in your job?

"I must wear all the hats in my job. I handle all the paperwork, pricing, and financial management and create the marketing materials. I also assist in the manufacturing of our product and run our tasting room."

What kind of training did you have?

"Some of my college classes were English, math, business administration, accounting, computers, marketing, and economics. I spent seven years as a real estate agent and learned to listen to customers. I also learned the importance of having schedules and paperwork trails. I took a lot of classes in marketing and learned to write effective advertising."

What advice would you give students?

"The people on the front line of the tourism industry have to want to be there. You must go out of your way when dealing with customers. You have to enjoy talking to a lot of people every day and remain cheerful."

What is your key to success?

"The number-one key is to be professional. Think like the tourists and try to anticipate what they need or want to do. Tourists are looking for an experience and fond memories."

Why is it important to keep good financial records in the hospitality and tourism businesses?

Career Data: Tourism Business Manager

Education and Training
Bachelor's degree or master's degree in marketing, economics, accounting, or general business

Skills and Abilities
Interpersonal, organizational, creative, and multitasking skills

Career Outlook Faster than average through 2012

Career Path Entry-level positions to management positions

A Mature Product

When growth becomes stable and products enter the maturity stage, product managers face some marketing challenges. If supply exceeds demand, prices may need to be lowered to keep customers. Promotional efforts may increase at this point, thus increasing overhead costs. Overcoming competition may lead to a price war. Airlines sometimes have price wars, which cause airfares to decrease. Eventually, weaker competitors fall off. If not, the product may enter decline.

QUESTION

During the mature stage of a product, how are prices affected if supply exceeds demand?

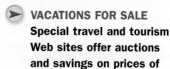

VACATIONS FOR SALE
Special travel and tourism Web sites offer auctions and savings on prices of luxury accommodations and vacation packages. *Identify the life-cycle stages represented by products offered at discount prices.*

MARKETING SERIES *Online*

Remember to check out this book's Web site for information on pricing products and more great resources at **marketingseries.glencoe.com.**

A Declining Product

During the decline stage, a company that continues to market a declining product will lose money. Prices may be lowered, but costs can increase. If a marketing department directs efforts to promoting a weak product, stronger products may suffer. Managers need to identify products in decline, whether a menu item or a destination resort. Then they must keep them—or drop them and find replacements.

Prices Subject to Change

Customers want the best value for their money, and businesses want to sell as much product as possible. Assigning accurate prices requires examining different factors that can affect price. Smart businesses study competitors, the environment, and their organizations. These factors help determine a company's marketing objectives before setting prices. When a product's price is set, it should be reviewed regularly to determine if adjustments are necessary.

Quick Check

RESPOND to what you've read by answering these questions.

1. What is meant by elasticity of demand? _____

_____

2. What are some of the internal and external factors affecting price? _____

_____

3. What is the effect of the growth stage on price? _____

_____

Worksheet 11.1

Pricing Strategies

Interview a person who works in the hospitality and tourism industries to learn about his or her pricing strategies. Write a short report about the interview and explain what pricing strategies are used to attract business.

Here are sample questions for someone who owns or manages a lodging property with an attached restaurant:

1. What special packages do you offer at the lodge to entice people to stay with you? Do you offer special weekend packages, family packages, or business travelers' packages?

2. What special packages do you offer at the restaurant to entice people who are staying in the lodge to also eat in the restaurant?

3. What special packages do you offer at the restaurant to entice people who are not staying at the lodge to eat in the restaurant? Do you have a happy hour or an early-bird dinner special?

4. Do you offer seasonal discounts? If so, what are they?

5. Do you offer special rates for special-interest groups, such as government employees or members of AAA or AARP?

Report:

_____

_____

_____

_____

_____

_____

_____

_____

_____

_____

_____

_____

_____

_____

_____

_____

Name ______________________________ Date ______________

Worksheet 11.2

Pricing Competition

Use the Internet to find three car rental agencies. Determine the prices that the three competitors are charging for the same or similar vehicles. Use the chart below to record information about three different vehicles from each of the agencies. Answer the questions that follow.

Car Agency 1:

Type of Vehicle	Cost Per Day	Special Promotions/Services Included

Car Agency 2:

Type of Vehicle	Cost Per Day	Special Promotions/Services Included

Car Agency 3:

Type of Vehicle	Cost Per Day	Special Promotions/Services Included

Questions:

1. From which car agency would you rent a vehicle? ______________________________

____

2. Why would you choose this agency? ______________________________

____

Portfolio Works

PRICING STRATEGIES EXPLAINED

In your own words, write a brief definition of each of the following pricing strategies:

1. **Promotional Pricing** _____

_____

2. **Psychological Pricing** _____

_____

3. **Market-Penetration Pricing** _____

_____

4. **Breakeven Pricing** _____

_____

5. **Cost-Plus Pricing** _____

_____

6. **Discounting** _____

_____

7. **Price Lining** _____

_____

8. **Bundle Pricing** _____

_____

9. **Loss-Leader Pricing** _____

_____

10. **Yield Management** _____

_____

Add this page to your career portfolio.

CHAPTER SUMMARY

Section 11.1 Pricing Strategies

price (p. 224)
prestige pricing (p. 225)
markup (p. 226)
cost-plus pricing (p. 226)

• For any product, price is the value placed on goods or services being exchanged. There are several terms for prices: airfare, cruise passage, rack rate, toll, tariff, tuition, tip, commission, and tax. High prices can drive customers away, yet low prices may not cover costs.

• Some pricing strategies include promotional pricing, psychological pricing, market-penetration pricing, breakeven pricing, cost-based pricing, discounting, and other special pricing strategies.

• Discounting is used to reward certain consumer behavior, such as booking early, buying off-season, or buying in volume. Prices are adjusted by a certain percentage, or special rates are assigned to specific periods.

Section 11.2 Factors Affecting Price

supply (p. 230)
demand (p. 230)
elasticity of demand (p. 230)

• Supply is the amount or quantity of goods and services that producers will provide at various prices. Demand is the amount or quantity of goods and services that consumers are willing to buy at various prices.

• Elasticity of demand is the variation of consumer demand due to a change in price. If prices are lowered so more people can afford to buy luxury items, the demand increases.

• A product's life cycle affects pricing. During the growth stage, prices tend to remain the same or may dip slightly. During the growth stage, a company may lower prices to attract new customers. During the decline stage, prices may drop.

CHECKING CONCEPTS

1. **Define** the term *price*.
2. **Identify** who decides if exchanging money for a product is worth the benefit.
3. **List** the typical pricing strategies.
4. **Give** two examples of discounting in hospitality and tourism.
5. **Explain** consumer demand.
6. **Describe** how the economy may affect prices.
7. **Explain** how prices are affected during a product's decline stage.

Critical Thinking

8. **Discuss** adjusting prices according to environmental conditions.

CROSS-CURRICULUM SKILLS

Work-Based Learning

Basic Skills—Speaking

9. You work for a private spa. In a two-minute speech, use prestige pricing to sell the spa to your classmates.

Interpersonal Skills—Negotiating to Arrive at a Decision

10. Work with a classmate. One student is a traveler, and the other student is the manager of a motor inn. The traveler wants to negotiate a better price for a room. Negotiate a price.

School-Based Learning

Math

11. The breakeven point for room prices at an inn is $60. Explain to a classmate what will happen if the inn always charges $50 per room.

Language Arts

12. As a class, write five questions to ask a hotel manager about how the market demand affects the cost of hotel rooms. Invite a hotel manager to class. Ask the manager your questions and discuss the answers.

Role Play: Hotel Front-Desk Manager

SITUATION You are to assume the role of front-desk manager in a big-city luxury hotel. The hotel charges prices that reflect the luxurious appointments of the guest rooms and extra services offered to guests. Services include nightly shoe cleaning/polishing, in-room breakfast served on silver trays, and afternoon tea. During periods of low occupancy, the hotel offers some lower-priced rooms through its Web site. The rates are good on specific dates. A customer (judge) has asked why her friend, who booked at the last minute, has a lower room rate.

ACTIVITY You are to explain to the customer (judge) the reason for the price difference.

EVALUATION You will be evaluated on how well you meet the following performance indicators:

- Explain the concept of price in the hospitality industry.
- Explain the principles of supply and demand.
- Explain factors affecting pricing decisions.
- Interpret business policies to customer/client.
- Handle customer inquiries.

Use the Internet to access the Automobile Association of America's (AAA's) Web site.
- Do a search for Hot Deals.
- Make a list of five Hot Deals offered through AAA membership.

For a link to AAA's Web site to do this activity, go to **marketingseries.glencoe.com**.

Chapter 12

Distribution

Section 12.1

Selling Hospitality & Tourism

Section 12.2

Channels of Distribution

Chapter Objectives

- Explain the types of selling.
- List the steps of selling.
- Differentiate between features and benefits.
- Define channels of distribution.
- Identify indirect channels of distribution.
- Discuss the Internet channel of distribution.

SUPERFUTURE GUIDE

Every time a friend or relative would visit Wayne Berkowitz in Japan, Berkowitz had to use poorly drawn tourist maps to describe the dense and clustered geography of Tokyo. So he created his own online guide—Superfuture City. He highlighted hotspots of design, fashion, art, and street culture on accurate maps. The online guide provided an invaluable resource for adventurous and creative travelers.

Since launching the original Superfuture City Web site in 1999, the former art director's city-guide project has evolved into a series of maps of more than 70 urban landscapes around the world. The Web site includes descriptions and reviews of everything, from upscale couture boutiques, exclusive sneaker shops, and designer hotels to low-budget noodle joints.

The Superfuture City site earned a loyal following, including travelers planning trips, creative adventurers in search of inspiration, and Web surfers looking for something different. However, with this niche of Web "browsers," could the super-cool, online travel guide earn a profit?

ANALYZE AND WRITE

1. List ways that Berkowitz's guide might affect tourism businesses in Japan.
2. Write a sentence explaining why the Web is a good place for distributing Berkowitz's product.

Case Study Part 2 on page 247

POWER READ

Be an active reader and use these reading strategies:

PREDICT what the section will be about.
CONNECT what you read with your own life.
QUESTION as you read to make sure you understand the content.
RESPOND to what you've read.

Selling Hospitality & Tourism

AS YOU READ ...

YOU WILL LEARN

- To explain the types of selling.
- To list the steps of selling.
- To differentiate between features and benefits.

WHY IT'S IMPORTANT

Selling is a process. It is important to understand the steps in the process to be effective at selling and servicing your customers.

KEY TERMS

- personal selling
- business-to-business selling
- buying signals
- cross-selling
- selling up
- feature
- benefit

PREDICT

Describe a recent purchase you made. How did the sales associate approach you?

personal selling the type of selling that involves direct interaction between sales associates and customers

business-to-business selling the type of selling whereby one business sells goods or services to another business

Types of Selling

Selling involves identifying the needs of customers and being able to meet those needs through providing products, or goods and services. Selling is also part of promotion, one of the four Ps of the marketing mix. Two types of selling are personal selling and nonpersonal selling. Nonpersonal selling does not involve interaction between people. Sales promotion, publicity, and advertising are types of nonpersonal selling. To be successful with any type of sales, a seller must know how to get information from customers to identify their needs. It is also important to be able to provide customers with information about a product and to convince them to make a buying decision. Personal selling is a process that involves a series of steps to exchange information.

Personal Selling

Most of us are familiar with **personal selling**, or selling that involves direct interaction between sales associates and customers. Personal selling can occur in a retail store, in your own home, over the telephone, or in an office. For example, personal selling is one aspect of telemarketing. A direct-marketing strategy, telemarketing involves more than just selling. Careful research, good timing, and a well-trained sales staff are necessary for effective telemarketing. Sellers must be able to convince and overcome customers' objections over the telephone. When properly applied, telemarketing can be a useful personal-selling method.

DO-NOT-CALL LISTS An increase in telemarketing calls caused the enactment of recent legislation to limit these calls. Consumers who do not want to hear from telemarketers register their telephone numbers on do-not-call lists nationwide. This prevents telemarketers from calling numbers on the lists.

Business-to-Business Selling

Business-to-business selling is the type of selling whereby one business sells goods or services to another business. For example, a hotel needs linens, towels, food, beverages, and many other products to operate its business and to provide its product, which is overnight accommodations.

Products can be sold over the telephone, through a catalog, in a retail store, or over the Internet. Regardless of where the selling occurs and to whom, the process that leads to a sale involves a series of activities called the *steps of selling*.

The Sales Process

All sales of products—from overnight accommodations and romantic cruises to fine dining and escorted tours—involve a series of steps, or a process, which lead to the desired outcome, or the sale. (See **Figure 12.1** on page 245.)

Seven Steps of Selling

The sales process usually involves the following seven steps:

1. **Approach**—Identify customers.
2. **Determine needs**—Find out what the customers want or need.
3. **Present the product**—Select a product to fit the need or want and make a recommendation.
4. **Overcome objections**—Answer questions or eliminate doubts about a product or service.
5. **Close the sale**—Motivate the customer to action.
6. **Perform suggestion selling**—Present ideas for additional product sales.
7. **Follow up**—Stay in touch with the customer after the sale.

Every sales situation is different. Some situations may require repeating steps, taking the steps out of sequence, or skipping a step. For example, if your first recommendation for a tour package is rejected, you might go back to step three and get more information. The following segments focus on the specific steps of selling and provide examples of how a travel agent might apply the steps.

STEP 1: APPROACH Identifying customers means more than just finding new or potential customers. It also means qualifying them. When you qualify a customer, you try to determine if he or she is ready to buy or is just browsing. You also need to know if the customer is able to pay for the product, and if he or she has the ability to make a buying decision if presented with one. Once you are satisfied that you are dealing with a qualified buyer, you start building a rapport to find out what he or she needs or wants.

STEP 2: DETERMINE NEEDS In step two, find out what the customer needs or wants. To fully understand this, ask open-ended questions. This allows a customer to provide personal information and to communicate what he or she seeks from the product. Open-ended questions cannot be answered with a simple "yes" or "no." They require more detailed answers. By asking questions, such as who, what, where, when, and why, you can get useful information to determine a customer's needs to offer the right product.

For example, you are a travel agent, and one of your customers wants to book a trip. You will need to know who is traveling and what type of travel experience he or she wants. Find out the destination, the travel dates, and the reason for the trip.

Hot Property

Selling the New JetBlue

jetBlue AIRWAYS

How do you stir up the airline industry? If you're David Neeleman, you create a discount airline that makes new rules and turns a profit. After years of experience in the airline industry, Neeleman started JetBlue. In the 1980s, he ran Morris Air Corporation, a discount carrier that pioneered the use of electronic ticketing. Over the next decade, he worked at different airlines and technology companies. These experiences led up to his dream of creating his own airline. This airline would right the wrongs of current industry leaders. He would improve customer experience, eliminate inefficiencies, and pass the value on to customers.

BREAKING THE MOLD

Unlike other start-up companies, Neeleman raised a record amount of investor cash before the business opened. The funds allowed JetBlue to acquire a fleet of new Airbus A320 airplanes instead of old cast-offs. While the new planes were more expensive, they required less maintenance. The aircrafts also featured an all-coach-class design with leather seats and individual DirecTV screens. These amenities surpassed those of other coach and discount competitors.

In addition, JetBlue used technology to streamline operations and cut costs. Sales agents worked from home, which saved on office expenses and improved employee morale. Pilots used laptops instead of bulky paper flight manuals. Tickets were electronic instead of paper. Passengers could receive a $5 discount when they purchased tickets through the JetBlue Web site instead of through travel agents. These strategies resulted in smoother operations and big profits. Legacy airlines such as United and Delta took notice and began creating their own discount carriers to duplicate the success of JetBlue.

1. How did JetBlue use technology to assist in selling?
2. Describe JetBlue's sales approach to customers.

CONNECT

What are some signals that you might give to show you are ready to buy?

buying signals verbal or nonverbal signs of a customer's readiness to buy

STEP 3: PRESENT THE PRODUCT After you have listened to the customer, you should select a product to meet his or her needs or wants. During this stage of the sales process, restate what the customer told you and ask for confirmation. For example, you might say, "Paul, you told me you are looking for a romantic getaway near the ocean to celebrate your wife's 50th birthday. You would like to schedule spa treatments for you and your wife. If possible, you would like a tee time at the golf course on Saturday afternoon. Later you want to surprise your wife with red roses in the room before dinner. Does that sound right?" Asking for feedback allows the customer to confirm your understanding of what product he or she wants and can provide more details that will help you make the best recommendation. Then you make your product recommendations to the customer. Look for **buying signals**, which are verbal or nonverbal signs of a customer's readiness to buy. Buying signals can be verbal, such as "that sounds good to me," or nonverbal, such as nodding in agreement or touching a brochure. Depending upon the customer's buying signal, you, the sales associate, may take step four or five.

STEP 4: OVERCOME OBJECTIONS A customer may object to making a buying decision for many reasons. He or she may not be convinced that your recommendation is right. The customer may doubt what you have said is true or accurate. Step back and demonstrate how your recommendation addresses his or her needs. Offer more information, such as a brochure or photograph. A customer's objections can be due to your lack of information. For example, the answers to questions in step two did not give you information about the customer's budget—and so you recommended a product that was out of the customer's price range. Go back to step two and get more information to make another, more suitable recommendation.

STEP 5: CLOSE THE SALE If you have been successful with the earlier steps, you will probably be successful at motivating your customer to buy. Closing the sale means getting a commitment from the customer to purchase the product. Before this step, you might seek commitment from your customer by asking indirectly for the sale. You can do this throughout the sales process by asking "Does that sound good to you?" or "Can you picture yourself on that beach?"

STEP 6: PERFORM SUGGESTION SELLING This step involves presenting ideas for additional product sales. The suggested products might be related to the original purchase. For example, you can offer a car rental with a travel package. You may also have the opportunity to cross-sell or sell up. **Cross-selling** is the method of selling the customer additional related products tied to one name. **Selling up** is offering a more expensive or upgraded version of the original recommendation.

Math Check

CALCULATING NET REVENUE
Vin sells a vacation package for $1,200. His costs include 37 percent for hotels, 15 percent for bus rentals, and 25 percent for advertising. What is his net income?

➡ For tips on finding the solution, go to **marketingseries.glencoe.com**.

QUESTION
What is closing the sale?

cross-selling the method of selling the customer additional related products tied to one name

selling up offering a more expensive or upgraded version of the original recommendation

---

Figure 12.1

The Sales Process

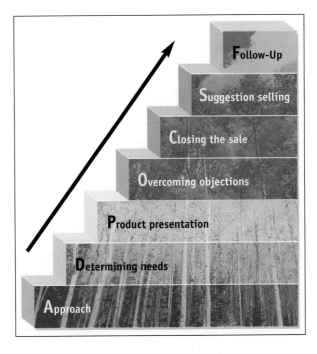

PERSONAL SALES STEPS
This selling process is used in all industries. The principles also apply to sales of hospitality and tourism products. *During which step does the sales associate or agent eliminate customers' doubts about the product?*

QUALITY SERVICE In hospitality and tourism businesses, service can make a big difference to customers who may become lifetime clients. *Why would service be especially important for keeping a small agency in business?*

STEP 7: FOLLOW UP Your goal is to gain a customer for life. As we learned in Chapter 10, the sales process continues with repeat customers or new customers who have been referred by existing customers. To establish a long-term relationship with a customer, you need to ensure his or her satisfaction. Following up after the sale might include a phone call the next week to check on the customer's satisfaction with the purchase. You might send a postcard to wish the client a "bon voyage" or a note thanking the client for his or her business. Keep files on clients with information about anniversaries and birthdays. You can send additional notes or cards that remind the customer about your business. Follow-up is an important part of providing excellent service, and excellent service helps market hospitality and tourism products.

Sales-and-Service Link

You have learned that hospitality and tourism products have an intangible quality because they are difficult to sample in advance. Only menus, brochures, tickets, and maps are tangible goods that are available to see prior to experiencing the product. Photos and memories are all that remain of intangible experiences, such as vacations or a meal at a special restaurant. Service is what distinguishes hospitality and tourism products from other products.

The Importance of Service

Selling without service is a disappointment. The waiter who ignores you or is rude can ruin even the most exquisite meal. A coffee-stained carpet or an unmade bed can ruin your impression of a five-star hotel. Providing quality service means more than just meeting the needs of a client. Customers expect their needs to be met. They also expect respect, prompt and efficient service, and a knowledgeable sales staff with a professional attitude. In today's society, customers demand more and expect good service.

Selling Features and Benefits

Because most hospitality and tourism products are intangible, it is helpful to make those products more real to customers. One of the best ways to make a product more tangible is to emphasize its features and benefits.

Product Features

A **feature** is a basic, physical, or extended attribute of a product or purchase. For example, in addition to an engine and tires, a car may have antilock brakes and all-wheel drive. It may also offer a number of other features, such as a sunroof, air bags, automatic windows, and a CD player. These features describe the functions.

Product Benefits

A **benefit** is a feature advantage of a product. For example, air bags allow maximum safety in a head-on collision. A CD player allows the driver and passenger to listen to music while riding in the car. Customers buy a product based on what it does for them. In other words, features tell, and benefits sell.

USING BENEFITS TO SELL How will an all-inclusive cruise in a balcony cabin benefit customers? An all-inclusive cruise means there are no hidden charges and no need to carry money for meals and entertainment. A balcony cabin means that guests can enjoy a sunset on a private deck.

Selling to the Customer

Product benefits can be described in a variety of ways. They can be adjusted to appeal to the different needs and wants of your clients. It is important to apply the information learned from the customer during the sales process to sell the benefits that will satisfy those needs.

Case Study PART 2

SUPERFUTURE GUIDE
Continued from Part 1 on page 241

As the Superfuture City online guide grows, the Web site continues to provide free information for curious Internet users. However, special services have been added to generate income from the site. Specialized tour itineraries can be created for users. Advertising and promotional opportunities are available. In addition, users can book hotel reservations online, with discounts for Superfuture customers. Over 120,000 loyal users have been attracted without the costs of advertising. Berkowitz created partnerships with companies such as Diesel, Prada, Tokyo Designers Block, and other groups. With more cities, shops, and services being added, the site's future looks super.

ANALYZE AND WRITE

1. Write two sentences about how Superfuture reviews might sell travel.
2. Is the Superfuture Web site a good channel of distribution for travel products? Write a paragraph explaining your answer.

feature a basic, physical, or extended attribute of a product or purchase

benefit a feature advantage of a product

Quick Check

RESPOND to what you've read by answering these questions.

1. What are the steps of selling? _____

_____

2. How are sales and service linked? _____

_____

3. What is feature-benefit selling? _____

Channels of Distribution

AS YOU READ ...

YOU WILL LEARN

- To define channels of distribution.
- To identify indirect channels of distribution.
- To discuss the Internet channel of distribution.

WHY IT'S IMPORTANT

To make goods and services available, producers must get them to the marketplace. Choosing the right distribution channels for a product is critical for successful marketing.

KEY TERMS

- direct channel
- indirect channel
- consolidator
- tour operator
- e-tail

PREDICT

Think of a recent purchase you made. How did that product get to the store?

direct channel the path a product takes without the help of any intermediaries between the producer and consumer

indirect channel the path a product takes using intermediaries between the producer and consumer

Channels of Distribution

After goods and services are produced or created, they must reach the consumer. As you learned in Chapter 6, a channel of distribution is the path a product takes from the producer to the consumer. Distribution channels can be direct or indirect.

Direct Channels

Direct channels are the simplest forms of distribution. A **direct channel** is the path a product takes without the help of any intermediaries between the producer and consumer. A direct channel provides direct access to the product for the consumer. For example, when you personally call an airline, hotel, or restaurant to make a reservation, you are using a direct channel of distribution.

Indirect Channels of Distribution

An indirect channel of distribution requires an intermediary or third party. An **indirect channel** is the path a product takes using intermediaries between the producer and consumer. For example, travel suppliers, such as airlines and cruise lines, use wholesalers and tour operators to distribute their products to consumers. The products are distributed to consumers by using more than one step. The product moves from an airline to a tour operator, and then from that tour operator to a consumer. The wholesaler, or tour operator, may serve as an intermediary who purchases a number of different products, such as hotel rooms, airline seats, and cruise-ship cabins, to resell to the travelers, or consumers.

Travel Agents as Intermediaries

Travel agents serve as the most familiar indirect channels of distribution for the tourism industry. Travel agents do not own or provide the goods and services they sell. Instead, they act as brokers, or intermediaries, between suppliers and travelers for a fee or commission. A commission is a fee, or percentage of the price of an item that is paid to an agent. Most travel agencies are full-service agencies, offering a wide range of travel products, including airline tickets, cruise-ship reservations, rail service, car rentals, hotels, resorts, tour operators, theater tickets, travel insurance, and more. Travel agents provide more than travel information and itinerary planning—they also serve as an important link in the indirect channel of distribution.

RANCH-STYLE GETAWAY

Lari Shea
Owner
Ricochet Ridge Ranch

What is your job?
"I am the owner and manager of a horse ranch." (Located in Fort Bragg, California, Ricochet Ridge Ranch offers horse riding vacations, daily trail rides, and "weekend getaway" rides.)

What do you do in your job?
"I oversee a dozen employees and create training programs for humans—and horses. I monitor the veterinary condition of 66 horses and provide routine and first-aid veterinary care. I work on advertising and promotion with print and Internet ads and speaking engagements, and answer about 75 e-mails per day."

What kind of training did you have?
"I was an animal health technician and taught the horse husbandry program at the College of the Redwoods for 12 years. I've taken over 1,000 riding lessons and train with dressage trainers to improve my own riding and teaching skills."

What advice would you give students?
"Take business courses and learn all you can before starting your own business. Also, you might apprentice with a successful business."

What is your key to success?
"I never purchase anything, such as real estate or a new truck, unless I can pay cash for it. I also accept responsibility for the safety, health, and enjoyment of my clients, staff, and horses—and accept no compromises."

Would this type of business benefit from a direct or indirect channel of distribution? Why or why not?

Career Data: Tourism Manager

Education and Training
Bachelor's degree or master's degree in business or management

Skills and Abilities
Interpersonal, planning, and organizational skills

Career Outlook As fast as average growth through 2012

Career Path Entry-level positions at a tourism facility to management positions with established tour companies, or work as a freelance tour provider

COMMISSIONS Airlines have altered the commission structure, and the amount of commission paid to travel agents has decreased. There is a cap on some fees. Many travelers now use the Internet instead of agents to do research and book travel arrangements. To make up for lost revenue in airline commissions, many agents charge fees for their services. Some agents specialize in specific target markets, such as business travelers or cruise-only travelers. Others specialize in travel to specific regions.

CONNECT
Do you think a travel agent should get a commission or a flat fee?

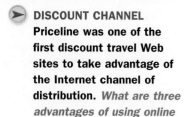

DISCOUNT CHANNEL
Priceline was one of the first discount travel Web sites to take advantage of the Internet channel of distribution. *What are three advantages of using online hospitality and tourism services?*

QUESTION
What do consolidators buy?

consolidator an agent who buys unsold products in bulk from suppliers and resells the products at a discount to intermediaries or to consumers

tour operator an intermediary who negotiates special rates and blocks space with transportation services, cruise lines, and hotels, and packages multiple components of a vacation for resale to the public or to another intermediary

e-tail the sale of goods or services to the customer by means of the Internet

Other Types of Intermediaries

In addition to travel agents, there are several other types of intermediaries, such as consolidators and tour operators, who also serve as indirect channels of distribution.

CONSOLIDATOR A **consolidator** is an agent who buys unsold products in bulk from suppliers, and then resells the products at a discount to intermediaries or to consumers. Travel clubs use this strategy and offer discount travel to their members.

TOUR OPERATORS A **tour operator**, also known as a wholesaler, is an intermediary who negotiates special rates and blocks space with transportation services, cruise lines, and hotels, and packages components of a vacation for resale to the public or to another intermediary. Working with all segments of the tourism industry, tour operators can offer travelers multiple pieces of a vacation in one unique package at a discounted rate.

Internet Channels

E-mail is the media of choice for direct-mail marketers. E-mail promotion and advertisements are quick and inexpensive, and e-mail reaches a large market. **E-tail** is the sale of goods or services to the customer by means of the Internet. It is fast, economical, and offers another distribution channel for goods and services—one that can be accessed from anywhere in the world via computer. Products can be e-tailed from business to consumer and from consumer to consumer on Internet auction sites, such as eBay.

Internet Travel Companies

Online travel companies have contributed to the growth of electronic distribution. The Internet has allowed for numerous nontraditional travel intermediaries to have reservations capabilities. (See **Figure 12.2** for examples.) Internet channels include four main categories:

- Company Web sites
- Affinity sites
- Discount sites
- Portal sites

The Cost-Effective Web

Using the Internet to distribute products is a cost-effective strategy for most businesses. However, success depends on understanding and following the sales process. To succeed, online travel Web sites must be easy to use, provide good service, offer what the customer wants, and add value to the experience. The goal is to develop loyal customers. Electronic distribution may continue to evolve in the coming years. According to the research company, Forrester Research, online travel sales are expected to grow to $28.9 billion in 2004—and reach 29.2 million households.

Figure 12.2

Internet Distribution Channels

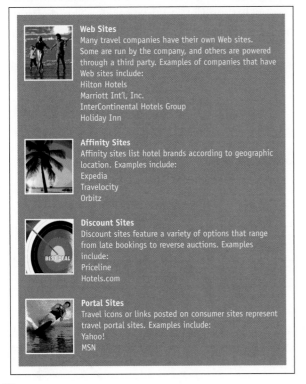

Web Sites
Many travel companies have their own Web sites. Some are run by the company, and others are powered through a third party. Examples of companies that have Web sites include:
Hilton Hotels
Marriott Int'l, Inc.
InterContinental Hotels Group
Holiday Inn

Affinity Sites
Affinity sites list hotel brands according to geographic location. Examples include:
Expedia
Travelocity
Orbitz

Discount Sites
Discount sites feature a variety of options that range from late bookings to reverse auctions. Examples include:
Priceline
Hotels.com

Portal Sites
Travel icons or links posted on consumer sites represent travel portal sites. Examples include:
Yahoo!
MSN

WEB-WIDE TRAVELERS There are a variety of Internet channels that feature travel and tourism products. *Name at least three Web sites you might use to compare hotel room prices.*

World Market

New Year's in Tibet

Imagine celebrating the New Year in the shadows of Mount Everest. Tibet is famous for its views of the world's highest mountain and for its colorful festivals. Tibet's most important holiday is *Losar*, or New Year's. Originating 2,500 years ago, Losar takes place over several days (usually in February). Tibetans make new clothes, spruce up their homes, and leave offerings of fruit and other items on family shrines. New Year's Eve brings everyone together for fun and food, including dumplings stuffed with "surprise" ingredients—chilies, wool, rice, white stones, or coal. Traditional ancient rites, folk songs, dances, and games are also part of the festivities. On New Year's Day, Tibetans enjoy a special breakfast, pray at monasteries, and visit neighbors. The phrase *Tashi Delek*, meaning "good fortune," is heard across Tibet's "roof of the world."

What type of distribution channel would be suitable for a trip to Tibet?

Key Elements of Selling

Getting products to the marketplace through distribution channels is the first step before sales can occur. Selling is a process that requires a series of steps to achieve the desired result. It involves identifying the customer's needs, selecting a product to fit those needs, and then motivating the customer to buy the product. Because hospitality and tourism products are intangible, quality service can distinguish one product from another. Adding value to an experience and demonstrating the benefits of the product's features will help gain customers for life.

Quick Check

RESPOND to what you've read by answering these questions.

1. What is a channel of distribution? _____

_____

2. What is the role of an intermediary? _____

_____

3. What are some indirect channels of distribution? _____

_____

Worksheet 12.1

The Sales Process

You have been appointed to be the lead sales associate to sell a package to your coworkers for a trip aboard a cruise ship. Gather information from the Internet, a travel agent, or a cruise line about available cruises. Go through the seven steps of selling.

1. **Approach**—Identify tour customers. (Who are your customers?)

   _____

   _____

2. **Determine needs**—Find out what the customers want or need. (Ask your peers what they want on a cruise.)

   _____

   _____

3. **Present the product**—Select a product to fit the need or want and make a recommendation. (Create a cruise that will appeal to your peers. What are you going to say to your peers to convince them to go on this cruise?)

   _____

   _____

4. **Overcome objections**—Answer questions or eliminate doubts about a product or service. (Ask your peers why they would not come on the cruise, and then write down their objections and a way to overcome each one.)

   _____

   _____

5. **Close the sale**—Motivate the customer to action. (Write down a way to motivate your peers to agree to the cruise.)

   _____

   _____

6. **Perform suggestion selling**—Present ideas for additional product sales.

   _____

   _____

7. **Follow up**—Stay in touch with the customer after the sale. (What are you going to do to follow up after your peers agree to take the cruise?)

   _____

   _____

Worksheet 12.2

Research Travel Agencies

The Internet has changed the way many travel agencies conduct business. Interview someone (in person, over the phone, or over the Internet) from a school that specializes in training travel agents. Ask the following questions:

1. How has the Internet changed the travel-agency business?

_____

_____

_____

_____

_____

_____

2. What changes have you made in the curriculum to address the Internet-related changes in the business?

_____

_____

_____

_____

_____

_____

_____

3. What advice do you have for people entering the travel-agency business in today's marketplace?

_____

_____

_____

_____

_____

4. What do you predict for the future of the industry?

_____

_____

_____

_____

_____

Portfolio Works

BUILDING THE SALES PROCESS

Make a visual representation of the sales process. Use art supplies, computer graphics, or magazine cutouts. Your visual representation of the sales process can be one-, two-, or three-dimensional.

Add this page to your career portfolio.

CHAPTER SUMMARY

Section 12.1 Selling Hospitality & Tourism

personal selling (p. 242)
business-to-business
   selling (p. 242)
buying signals (p. 244)
cross-selling (p. 245)
selling up (p. 245)
feature (p. 247)
benefit (p. 247)

- Types of selling include personal selling, or selling that involves direct interaction between sales associates and customers, and non-personal selling, which is selling that does not involve interaction between people.

- The steps of selling include approach, determine needs, present the product, overcome objections, close the sale, perform suggestion selling, and follow up.

- A feature is a basic, physical, or extended attribute of a product or purchase, and a benefit is a feature advantage of a product or service.

Section 12.2 Channels of Distribution

direct channel (p. 248)
indirect channel (p. 248)
consolidator (p. 250)
tour operator (p. 250)
e-tail (p. 250)

- A channel of distribution is the path a product takes from the producer to the consumer. Channels can be direct or indirect.

- An indirect channel of distribution is the path a product takes using intermediaries between the producer and consumer.

- Internet channels of distribution include company Web sites, affinity sites, discount sites, and portal sites, and provide a channel of distribution for online travel services.

CHECKING CONCEPTS

1. **Explain** personal selling.
2. **Identify** the steps of selling.
3. **Identify** the key to providing quality service.
4. **Discuss** the role of using product benefits in the selling process.
5. **Define** a direct channel of distribution.
6. **Identify** at least two indirect channels of distribution in tourism.
7. **Name** four types of Internet channels of distribution.

Critical Thinking

8. **Explain** the characteristics of successful online travel services.

CROSS-CURRICULUM SKILLS

Work-Based Learning

Basic Skills—Speaking

9. You are the operator of Tour for Teens. Give a short sales presentation to new teenage sales associates about how to sell one of your tours.

Thinking Skills—Knowing How to Learn

10. Work with another student to make a list of ten questions and answers about Chapter 12 content. Join with another team of two students. Quiz each other.

School-Based Learning

Science

11. You are a sales associate for a salt wholesaler. Restaurant owners want to know about FDA restrictions on salt. Use the Internet or library to research the FDA regulations, and then write a short report.

Social Studies

12. Choose a country. Use the Internet or library to research foods served at restaurants in this country. Write a one-page proposal to your local chamber of commerce selling the idea of opening a restaurant from that country in your community.

Role Play: Sales Manager of Beach Resort

SITUATION You are to assume the role of sales manager for a beach resort located on an isolated part of the Mexican Gulf Coast. Your resort is in a quiet area and offers rest and relaxation in a private setting. Some of the activities available to guests are boat excursions along the scenic coastline, horseback riding, and trips to ancient ruins. You are making a sales call to a representative (judge) of a large travel agency.

ACTIVITY You are to answer the travel agent's (judge's) questions about how your resort will provide activities.

EVALUATION You will be evaluated on how well you meet the following performance indicators:

- Explain land transportation services.
- Explain water transportation services.
- Guide client in making travel decisions.
- Recommend specific destinations and travel services to travelers.
- Sell goods/services/ideas to individuals.

INTERNET ACTIVITY

Use the Internet to access the Web site of the Hospitality Sales and Marketing Association International, also known as HSMAI.

- Click one of the scheduled events about sales in the hospitality and tourism industries.
- After reading about the event, write a short summary.
- E-mail your summary to a classmate.

➡For a link to Hospitality Sales and Marketing Association International to do this activity, go to **marketingseries.glencoe.com**.

Chapter 13

Promoting Hospitality & Tourism

Section 13.1

Promotion and Advertising

Section 13.2

Public Relations and Sales Promotion

Chapter Objectives

- Explain the promotional mix.
- Identify the types of advertising media.
- Discuss how to create an advertising message.
- Identify methods used to determine an advertising budget.
- Explain the concept of public relations.
- Identify strategies used in sales promotion.

Case Study PART 1

MARKETING NEW MEXICO

One of the first statewide efforts to promote tourism in the United States occurred in 1935 in New Mexico. Hoping to increase tax revenue, state officials established the New Mexico Tourist Bureau. Its first project benefited the State Highway Department, which used gasoline taxes to create new roads.

Since then, the bureau has altered its name, offices, and responsibilities several times. Tourism became a division in the New Mexico Department of Development in 1959. In 1991, tourism was designated as a separate department with a magazine division, a travel and marketing division, and an anti-litter campaign.

Currently, by providing visitor centers, vacation guides, and a Web site, the Tourism Department focuses on present and future tourists. The New Mexico Tourism Department's official goal is "to create, promote, and develop economic benefit to the state." What steps could this department take to accomplish these goals?

ANALYZE AND WRITE

1. During the first half of the 20th century, how did the state of New Mexico promote tourism?
2. How might tourism affect New Mexico in terms of environment and culture?

Case Study Part 2 on page 271

POWER READ

Be an active reader and use these reading strategies:

PREDICT what the section will be about.

CONNECT what you read with your own life.

QUESTION as you read to make sure you understand the content.

RESPOND to what you've read.

Promotion and Advertising

YOU WILL LEARN

- To explain the promotional mix.
- To identify the types of advertising media.
- To discuss how to create an advertising message.
- To identify methods used to determine an advertising budget.

WHY IT'S IMPORTANT

Understanding the various media available to advertise and promote products helps marketers determine promotional strategies.

KEY TERMS

- promotion
- promotional mix
- advertising
- promotional advertising
- institutional advertising
- direct mail
- AIDA model

PREDICT

Describe a typical restaurant advertisement.

promotion any form of communication used to persuade people to buy products

promotional mix any combination of advertising, sales promotion, public relations and publicity, and personal selling

What Is Promotion?

Promotion is any form of communication used to persuade people to buy products. Promotion can be used to inform the public about a company's goods and services or to enhance the image of a business. The purpose of promotion is to increase sales, generate interest among a target market or markets, and create a positive image. Communicating with the public is a continuous process. It is an integral part of marketing. Hospitality and tourism marketers use the **promotional mix**, which is any combination of advertising, sales promotion, public relations and publicity, and personal selling. Some companies rely heavily on advertising, while others prefer sales promotions and public relations activities to promote products. Each strategy serves a different purpose.

What Is Advertising?

Businesses use advertising to promote their products. **Advertising** is any paid promotion of an idea, good, or service by an identified sponsor. Advertisements can introduce a new product, keep customers aware of existing products, and create an image for the product and/or business. Different media are used for advertising, which can be an expensive but effective method of communicating with the public. There are two basic categories of advertising: promotional advertising and institutional advertising.

Promotional Advertising

Promotional advertising is advertising with a goal of selling an item being promoted. Businesses use promotional advertising to introduce new products, make people aware of a special deal or sale, or encourage customers to visit a retail outlet. For example, airlines use promotional advertising to announce airfare sales or to introduce new routes and/or destinations.

Institutional Advertising

Institutional advertising is advertising with a goal of developing goodwill or a positive image. Rather than focusing on an individual product, a business may use institutional advertising to sell itself. A business may sponsor a charitable event or another type of promotion and use advertising to thank people who made donations. For example, a restaurant may advertise a customer appreciation day to thank customers for their patronage at the close of a successful season.

Types of Advertising Media

The choice of media outlets to use for advertising is an important decision. Advertising media include all of the different methods used to bring an advertising message to the public. There are several types of media, each with its own set of advantages and disadvantages. Types of advertising media include:

- Print
- Broadcast
- Online
- Specialty

Print Media

Print media include newspapers, magazines, direct mail, and outdoor advertising. These types of media use printed material to convey a message. Each medium offers benefits to advertisers, but prices vary.

NEWSPAPERS Newspapers carry messages targeted to a specific geographic location. Advertising rates are determined by the particular newspaper's circulation. Circulation refers to how many copies of each edition are printed and distributed, thus indicating the number of people who read it. Newspapers are published daily or weekly, so advertisements reach many people quickly. Newspaper advertisements are relatively inexpensive. However, a disadvantage of this print medium is that the shelf life of a newspaper is short; most people read the paper and throw it away. Thus, ads can be overlooked and discarded.

MAGAZINES Many magazines are published monthly. Their reach is greater than most newspapers—going beyond local areas to whole regions or the entire country. A major advantage of advertising in a magazine is that individual magazines appeal to specific target markets, or people with specific interests. For example, people who like to travel are likely to read *National Geographic Traveler* or *Travel and Leisure*. Many of *Travel and Leisure*'s advertisers sell travel-related products. Magazines also have a longer shelf life than newspapers. Most readers will keep an issue until the next issue is published or may pass old issues on to other readers. Advertising rates for magazines are higher than those for newspapers, due to the large circulation and readership of magazines.

DIRECT MAIL Another effective print media outlet is **direct mail**, which is any advertising message sent directly to customers via the mail. The message can be personalized per customer or target group. Postcards, letters, newsletters, catalogs, flyers, and coupons are all considered direct-mail pieces. Direct-mail advertising uses mailing lists of existing customers or lists that have been purchased from other sources. A business can target qualified buyers with an interest in or previous experience with its products. For example, lodging facilities mail special discounts on packages to previous guests.

advertising any paid promotion of an idea, good, or service by an identified sponsor

promotional advertising advertising with a goal of selling an item being promoted

institutional advertising advertising with a goal of developing goodwill or a positive image

direct mail any advertising message sent directly to customers via the mail

WIDE AUDIENCE Monthly travel magazines include print advertisements that reach specific target markets across the country or in other countries. *Describe the target market for this print advertisement for the Queen Mary 2.*

OUTDOOR ADVERTISING The variety of outdoor advertising is broad, including signs, billboards, and posters found on major highways, in sports arenas, and in transportation centers. This type of advertising is effective because it targets a specific geographic market or demographic. The message must be short and concise enough to understand and remember in the time it takes to drive or walk past it.

Broadcast Media

Television and radio are broadcast media. Advertising rates for running commercials can be expensive. Rates vary according to a number of factors, including an advertisement's length and the time of day it is aired. Broadcast-media advertising allows a business to reach a targeted demographic group based on audience profiles and geographic location. Radio advertising is less expensive than television advertising. This is because it relies on an audio message with no visuals to accompany it.

CONNECT

Do you pay more attention to television commercials or billboard ads?

TELEVISION ADVERTISING By using television as a medium, advertisers can show a product and describe its features and benefits through pictures and words. Although it is an expensive medium to use, television commercials reach a large audience. Another advantage is that advertisers can choose the programs during which their ads run. This allows them to target specific markets according to type of TV program.

INFOMERCIALS The infomercial is a longer type of television advertisement, usually 30 minutes in length. Infomercials air during non-prime time and mostly on cable networks. Each segment is designed like a TV show and educates viewers about a specific product. Infomercials are produced and purchased by advertisers.

Online Media

The Internet has become a valuable tool for selling. Many businesses have their own Web sites for promoting goods and services directly to the consumer. In addition to their own Web sites, businesses may advertise on other Web sites. To do this, a business purchases a product listing on another site and links it back to its own Web site.

BANNER ADS Banner ads and tile ads are also other methods of online advertising. Advertisers purchase space at or near the top of a Web page. The space may promote a special offer or simply call the viewer's attention to a certain business.

SEARCH ENGINES Internet search engines, such as Yahoo! and Google, provide opportunities for another form of advertising. Known as pay-for-click listings, advertisers pay a set fee each time a viewer clicks through to their site.

COUNTING HITS Using the Internet as an advertising medium is fast and cost effective. Results can be measured by tracking visits or "hits" to a specific Web site. However, there are still a significant number of people who do not have access to computers. To rely on electronic media alone may overlook a good portion of a target market.

E-MAIL Electronic newsletters are e-mail communications sent to subscribers. These newsletters provide information and updates about a business, service, or subject. An example of an e-mail newsletter is the Mount Washington Valley Chamber of Commerce's *E-Traveler*.

Specialty Media

Have you ever received a calendar, a pen, a coffee mug, or a key chain imprinted with a company's name and logo? Some businesses use this giveaway strategy when promoting a new or improved product. Other companies regularly distribute small items printed with their logos. Lodging properties and cruise ships may place postcards, notepads, and pens in guest rooms. Restaurants give out matchbooks, while taxi services and pizza delivery services give away refrigerator magnets. The concept behind specialty-media giveaways is simple: Consumers who use the item or carry it to another location are always reminded of the company or product.

TECH *NOTES*

Travel Niche on Cable TV

With digital cable systems making hundreds of channels available, television is narrowing its focus. Rather than providing a wide variety of programs that may or may not appeal to a large audience, cable channels seek niche audiences. These audiences include viewers with specific interests. Available to more than 70 million homes throughout the United States, the Travel Channel is the only television network devoted entirely to travel and tourism.

➡How do advertisers benefit from the narrow focus of niche cable channels? Answer this question after reading information through **marketingseries.glencoe.com**.

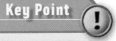

Key Point

ONLINE ADVERTISING
The travel industry spends heavily on advertising, but travel companies put less than 15 percent of their advertising budgets online.

The End of the Earth

Enter the keyword "Patagonia" on the computer search engine Google, and over 1,920,000 entries pop up. This figure indicates that tourism is booming in this region. The region known as Patagonia is located in southern Argentina.

The Andes mountains form Patagonia's western border. The blue waters of the Atlantic Ocean edge its eastern coast. In between these boundaries, travelers discover a land of contrasts. Features include snowfields, ice sheets with enormous glaciers, grassy plains, and wildlife habitats that are home to animals found only in Patagonia. The Central Steppes region features a petrified forest. Patagonia is ideal for naturalists as well as adventurers. "Come to the end of the earth," the travel ads say, "and see planet Earth, the way it used to be."

Create an imaginative motto for a unique place.

PATAGONIA

Creating Advertising Messages

Regardless of the medium chosen to convey a product's message, the message itself is the most important aspect of an advertisement. To create an effective message, marketers can apply the **AIDA model**, which is a framework for creating an advertising message that gets **A**ttention, holds **I**nterest, stimulates **D**esire, and achieves **A**ction. The model focuses on content, structure, and format.

AIDA model a framework for creating an advertising message that gets **A**ttention, holds **I**nterest, stimulates **D**esire, and achieves **A**ction

Content of the Message

The content of a message can appeal to consumers in a number of different ways—rationally, emotionally, and morally. Rational appeal focuses on how the product can benefit the user, or how it is in his or her self-interest to buy it. Emotional appeal uses feelings to motivate customers to buy. A moral appeal is directed at a person's sense of ethics.

Structure and Format

The impact of an advertising message can be determined by the style and tone of the message. Each word is important. Even more important is the placement of the words in context with the overall format. This is referred to as *message execution*. Some message executions include:

QUESTION

What is the most important aspect of an advertisement?

- Testimonial evidence
- Scientific evidence
- Technical expertise
- Personality symbol

- Slice of life
- Lifestyle
- Fantasy
- Mood or image

Budgeting for Advertising

Budgeting for advertising is a critical element of marketing. A large budget is not required to create an effective communication strategy. However, the travel industry spends billions of dollars each year to advertise travel. **Figure 13.1** lists typical advertising spending in the United States by travel businesses. Businesses usually employ one of four methods to determine a budget:

- Affordable method
- Percentage-of-sales method
- Competitive-parity method
- Objective-and-task method

Affordable Method

A simple but unscientific strategy to determine an advertising budget is to figure out what the business can afford. The business does not consider the impact that advertising might have on the amount of product sold. Thus, this strategy can be shortsighted.

Figure 13.1

Travel Advertising

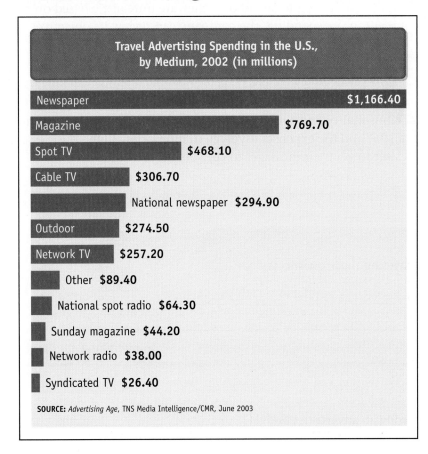

Travel Advertising Spending in the U.S., by Medium, 2002 (in millions)

Medium	Spending
Newspaper	$1,166.40
Magazine	$769.70
Spot TV	$468.10
Cable TV	$306.70
National newspaper	$294.90
Outdoor	$274.50
Network TV	$257.20
Other	$89.40
National spot radio	$64.30
Sunday magazine	$44.20
Network radio	$38.00
Syndicated TV	$26.40

SOURCE: *Advertising Age*, TNS Media Intelligence/CMR, June 2003

BIG BUDGETS Travel businesses spend millions of dollars on a variety of media to get their messages to the public. *Which medium accounts for the biggest advertising expenditure?*

Percentage-of-Sales Method

This method is easy to calculate. Based on past or predicted sales volume, the percentage-of-sales method assigns a certain percentage of sales for advertising and promoting the product. The flaw in this method is that if sales volume is down, so is the budget. It does not address the relationship between advertising and sales—or the need to spend more funds to revive sales of a product that is in a late stage of its life cycle. This method makes it difficult to do any long-range planning for marketing, because the budget depends on performance.

Competitive-Parity Method

It makes sense to look at what other businesses are spending to advertise similar products. This is the basis for competitive parity. The word *parity* means similarity or likeness. Businesses will look for trends in competitors' spending, and then evaluate whether they need to spend more or less to gain a competitive advantage. The disadvantage of this method is that it does not take into consideration the marketing objectives. Two companies with similar products may have two different marketing objectives.

Objective-and-Task Method

This method of determining an advertising budget is perhaps the most logical. Based on the company's marketing objectives, tasks are determined to achieve those objectives. Costs are assigned to each task. The sum of those costs determines the budget. If the costs exceed what the company can afford to spend or if they are unrealistic based on what competitors are spending, the company can review its objectives.

Effective Advertising

Advertising is one of the most important strategies for promoting hospitality and tourism. Understanding the methods and media available and the expenses involved in promotion allows businesses of all sizes to get their messages to consumers.

Quick Check ✔

RESPOND to what you've read by answering these questions.

1. What is the promotional mix? _____

_____

2. What is advertising? _____

_____

3. What are four methods of determining an advertising budget? _____

_____

Public Relations and Sales Promotion

Public Relations and Publicity

As a component of the promotional mix, businesses use **public relations**, which is any activity designed to create a favorable image of a business, its products, or its policies. It is an integral part of any promotional strategy and is extremely cost effective. A business needs to create a positive image with customers, among staff members, in the community, and in the media. A public relations (PR) department in large organizations is responsible for dealing with the press, communicating with employees, publicizing products, and sometimes lobbying the government.

Publicity

One function of a PR department is **publicity**, which is a type of public relations that involves the free mention of a product or company in the media. Publicity can come in the form of news and feature articles, television coverage, award recognition, or critical reviews. It can reflect a positive or negative image. This is because any newsworthy event, be it good or bad, attracts the attention of the media. It is the responsibility of a PR department to create a good relationship with the news media.

Good Press Relations

Good press relations are important to attract attention to a business and its products. If a restaurant is reviewed in the local paper or a hotel is mentioned on the Travel Channel, people tend to pay attention. A customer or critic praising a business or product lends more credibility than an advertisement designed and written by the business itself. Coverage of a product by the news media can be very influential.

Press Releases

Public relations departments work hard to attract the attention of the news media. One of the most useful tools for capturing the attention of the media is a **press release**, which is a newsworthy article that provides the basic information to answer questions such as who, what, where, when, and why. Press releases are written by PR departments and sent to various media outlets. When published or broadcast, a press release informs the public about an event involving the business or products it represents.

Figure 13.2

Sample Press Release

BREAKING NEWS A press release is designed as a news article and made available by a company or organization for use by various media outlets at no charge. *Do you think consumers can tell when a press release is a form of advertisement?*

TravelDailyNews
.com
International

INTERNATIONAL TRAVEL TRADE MARKET SINCE 1999

Her Majesty The Queen to Name Queen Mary 2

Cunard is delighted to confirm that **Her Majesty The Queen** will name the company's new flagship **Queen Mary 2** at a ceremony to take place in Southampton, England, on Thursday, January 8, 2004. Her Majesty will be accompanied by His Royal Highness The Duke of Edinburgh. The launch will be a milestone in British maritime history and will be a major event of worldwide interest.

According to **Pamela Conover**, President of Cunard Line, *"This will be an historic occasion in the true sense of the word."*

The British-registered **Queen Mary 2**—the largest, longest, tallest, widest and—at $780 million—the most expensive passenger liner ever built, will enter service on January 12, 2004, with a maiden voyage from Southampton to Fort Lauderdale, Florida.

Theodore Koumelis (theodore@traveldailynews.com)—Thursday, October 16, 2003

CASE STUDY: QM2 PRESS RELEASE Sometimes news reporters use press releases as sources of public-interest stories. For example, when Cunard launched the *Queen Mary 2* in early 2004, hundreds of press releases were sent to newspapers, online publications, and travel magazines around the world. (See **Figure 13.2**.) Each release provided interesting information about the ship, such as how long it took to build it, the size and decor, and the history of the cruise line. Additional details included human-interest stories about the people who worked on building the ship. Newspapers, magazines, and news reporters used the press releases to write their own stories and to produce reports prior to and after the launch. This type of "news" also served as publicity for the cruise ship and for Cunard.

The Spin Zone

In addition to creating a positive image about a business and its products, the PR department is often called upon to put a positive *spin*, or slant, on a negative situation. For example, a serious accident may occur on a boat trip on the Amazon River. Perhaps tourists are injured. Afterward the tour operator's PR department would work to keep reporters informed about what happened and what the company was doing to assist the families affected by the accident.

CONNECT

Do you think a news report based on a business's press release should be considered a legitimate news story?

Crisis Management

Businesses do everything possible to avoid crisis and prevent risk, but accidents do happen. Airplanes crash; hotels have fires; outbreaks of illness or food poisoning can occur on cruise ships and in restaurants. To effectively manage these negative events, a PR staff must be ready with crisis-management plans. These plans must address the need for good communication with the media. Ignoring, hiding from, or misleading the public during a crisis invites bad press. Honest, forthright efforts to manage a negative event can minimize the damage to a company's image.

Creating Goodwill

Many companies want to create a positive image within the community or improve relationships with other businesses in the same location. They do this by contributing time, money, and resources to local projects or charities. Donating to community-supported activities creates goodwill in the minds of the public and leads to a positive image of the business within that community. This is a strategy used by many cruise lines and hotel chains. Creating goodwill in the travel industry also helps to maintain strong relationships with cultures in foreign destinations. At home, goodwill can generate public support for business expansion. Restaurants and other hospitality businesses may develop goodwill by sponsoring community events, such as running or bike races, that raise funds for cancer research or other worthy causes.

ETHICS & ISSUES

Tainted Travel?

In 2003, a television station in Hawaii, KITV, returned $4,100 to the Hawaii Visitors Bureau. The bureau had given the money to the station to pay for a reporter to travel to Japan to cover the governor of Hawaii's visit there. KITV came under fire for breaching journalistic ethics. The Society of Professional Journalists' code of ethics states that journalists should, "refuse gifts, favors, fees, free travel, and special treatment." Critics of KITV felt that the station and reporter might have provided publicity in favor of the governor. *Do you agree? Why or why not?*

COMMUNITY SUPPORT Sponsorship of events, such as charity bike races, can create goodwill within the community and generate a positive image for any business. *What types of events might a hospitality or tourism business sponsor to create goodwill?*

PROMOTING THROUGH PRODUCT

David Hepburn, Jr.
Owner
Ace Marketing and Promotions

What is your job?

"I am owner of Ace Marketing and Promotions."

What do you do in your job?

"My company works with hotels, resorts, and tourist destinations. We provide everything from water bottles and monogrammed robes to T-shirts, writing pads, and pens. The most time is spent in finding the right promotion and putting the right product together."

What kind of training did you have?

"I have a master's degree in English and degrees in psychology, history, and education. However, when it comes to promotional products and marketing, I graduated from 'SoHK'—the School of Hard Knocks. The business was not as widespread when I started. It requires a lot of cold calls and networking."

What advice would you give students?

"Remember that you are not selling a product, you are selling a marketing program. You get back what you put into the job. Many smart people fail at this job because they are unwilling to put in time and effort."

What is your key to success?

"Persistence, belief in yourself, and personal attention to detail. Only 3 percent of potential customers are ready to buy any product at any time. This means that 97 percent of the people are saying 'No' or 'Not now.' The key is to realize this and to keep contacting them until they move from the 97 percent group to the 3 percent group."

What promotional strategies does Ace Marketing offer?

Career Data: Product Promotion Sales Representative

Education and Training
Bachelor's degree or master's degree in business, communication, or psychology

Skills and Abilities
Interpersonal, initiative, and creative skills

Career Outlook Faster-than-average growth through 2012

Career Path Self-employed or entry-level sales associate to sales manager to owner of company

Sales Promotions

As part of the promotional mix, sales promotions encourage consumers to buy products. These promotions can generate new interest in existing products or create demand for new products. Sales promotional strategies may include contests and sweepstakes, special offers and sales events, coupons, premiums, and rewards programs. Designed as incentives for consumers to buy, sales promotions are one part of the complete promotional strategy.

Contests and Sweepstakes

Contests and sweepstakes offer consumers the opportunity to win prizes in return for a specific activity. There is a wide range of contests, such as naming a new product or answering a question about a product or service. Another type of sales contest is used in-house. Businesses inspire their sales staff to generate more sales by rewarding top sellers with special prizes. Sweepstakes may require nothing more than submitting an entry form with winners chosen by random drawing.

Special Offers and Sales Events

Special offers and special sales events are used to increase overall sales of a particular product. These might include a buy-one-get-one-free offer, a one-day sale, or an end-of-the season sale. Restaurants offer early-bird specials to attract the senior market during an otherwise quiet time. To increase occupancy, hotels promote discounted prices for extended stays or during the shoulder season.

Coupons

Other useful promotional tools are coupons. Coupons offer special savings to customers or, in some cases, free products or services in return for redeeming a certificate. Coupons are easily distributed via direct mail, in a print advertisement, packaged with the product, or given away at special promotional events. Used to revive sales of a mature product or as part of a new product launch, coupons may have expiration dates.

Premiums

Small items or free samples given to customers free of charge or with the purchase of another product are called *premiums*. For example, cruise ships may give a souvenir glass to passengers who purchase a drink special. Restaurants, hotels, and cruise lines also sell promotional items adorned with the company's name and logo. Sales of items such as T-shirts and bathrobes can provide additional income for gift shops.

Rewards Programs

Many businesses offer rewards programs to consumers who frequently purchase their products. One of the most common programs is the frequent-flyer mileage program offered by many airlines. Travelers earn free travel awards, such as tickets and upgrades, based on the accumulation of miles flown with that airline. Many hotels, restaurants, and cruise lines have also developed frequent-guest programs to reward repeat customers.

Case Study | PART 2

MARKETING NEW MEXICO
Continued from Part 1 on page 259

Through broadcast and print advertising, New Mexico attempts to create and maintain a tourist-friendly image within the state, out of state, and internationally. Visitor information centers distribute maps, brochures, and other literature promoting tourist attractions. Highlights include historic locations, sightseeing opportunities, national parks, and Native-American-related destinations. The state also sends a 27-foot recreational vehicle (RV) to events in Texas and throughout New Mexico to publicize travel opportunities.

To evaluate its effectiveness, the New Mexico Tourism Department measures traffic at its visitor information centers, tracks related broadcast and press appearances, and counts its Web-site hits. It also conducts surveys at visitor information centers and sends follow-up e-mails to Web-site visitors. By taking vacationers seriously, the state has succeeded in raising tax revenues from tourism in the Land of Enchantment.

ANALYZE AND WRITE

1. List ways that the New Mexico Tourism Department measures its effectiveness in promoting tourism.
2. Write a paragraph describing the type of image New Mexico might promote to potential tourists.

QUESTION

What are strategies used for sales promotions?

Resort Promotions

Since its debut in 1981, Sandals has used innovative programs to advertise and promote its all-inclusive resorts. Gordon "Butch" Stewart, the chairman, began the resort chain with the purchase of a hotel in his birthplace, Jamaica. As a successful businessman, Stewart developed the chain into a thriving Caribbean-centered business with eleven resorts catering exclusively to couples. He worked to distinguish his resorts through the "couples-only" focus and the quality of the resorts themselves. Each resort offers gourmet restaurants, sports facilities, and concierge services at no additional charge. Following in the successful footsteps of Sandals, Stewart then opened another chain of resorts called *Beaches* in 1997. Beaches Resorts are all-inclusive resorts that cater to families.

INNOVATIVE PROMOTIONS

To attract customers, Sandals promotes its products in various ways. Sandals recognizes the importance of the wedding industry in promoting its couples resorts. The company advertises in bridal magazines, marketing itself as an ideal destination for honeymoons and "weddingmoons," which combine weddings with honeymoons. Sandals Resorts partners with the WeddingChannel.com. Special promotions offer couples a free wedding ceremony when they book a six-night honeymoon. Sandals also works with Waterford and Wedgwood to provide free crystal and china. These kinds of promotions last a lifetime.

1. How does Sandals advertise its resorts?

2. Do you think giveaways make Sandals more attractive to honeymooners? Why?

Successful Promotion

The key to any successful product promotion is selecting the right promotional mix. Advertising is just one element. Selecting the right media for an advertising campaign is determined by budget and marketing objectives. The message is also critical. Public relations are another key ingredient. Developing positive relations with the media and creating goodwill build a positive image for the business and its products.

Quick Check

RESPOND to what you've read by answering these questions.

1. What is the definition of public relations? _____

_____

2. What is a press release? _____

_____

3. What are three sales promotional strategies? _____

_____

Worksheet 13.1

Institutional Advertising at Work

Look through several newspapers and magazines for examples of institutional advertising. Cut out three stories about three different businesses in the hospitality and tourism industries. Summarize the stories below. Then staple the stories to this page.

(**Note:** Many hotel chains have in-house publications with stories about their facilities. Trade publications and travel magazines are also good sources.)

Story 1:

_____

_____

_____

_____

_____

_____

_____

Story 2:

_____

_____

_____

_____

_____

_____

_____

Story 3:

_____

_____

_____

_____

_____

_____

_____

Worksheet 13.2

Charting Sales Promotions

1. Use direct mailers, newspapers, and magazines. Collect several sales promotional pieces from businesses in the hospitality and tourism industries. Use this chart to count the different types of sales promotions.

Number of Promotions

	Restaurants	Hotels	Amusement Parks	Other
Sales Events				
Coupons				
Premiums				
Free Samples				
Sweepstakes				
Contests				
Games				
E-Mail Offers				
Rebates				

2. Write a paragraph about the conclusions you draw from the sales promotional pieces you found. For example, do restaurants offer more coupons than other types of hospitality and tourism businesses? Do water parks offer more premiums than amusement parks? What types of businesses offer contests?

_____

_____

_____

_____

_____

_____

_____

Portfolio Works

CREATE A BROCHURE

Select a hospitality and tourism good or service that you would like to promote. Use the space below to plan a brochure that promotes the product. Using a computer or art supplies, create the brochure. Present the brochure to your class.

Add this page to your career portfolio.

CHAPTER SUMMARY

Section 13.1 Promotion and Advertising

promotion (p. 260)
promotional mix (p. 260)
advertising (p. 260)
promotional advertising
  (p. 261)
institutional advertising
  (p. 261)
direct mail (p. 261)
AIDA model (p. 264)

- The promotional mix is any combination of advertising, sales promotion, public relations and publicity, and personal selling.

- Different types of advertising media include print, broadcast, online, and specialty media.

- To create an effective message, marketers can apply the AIDA model, which is a framework for creating an advertising message that gets attention, holds interest, stimulates desire, and achieves action. The model focuses on content, structure, and format.

- There are four methods used to determine advertising budgets: affordable method, percentage-of-sales method, competitive-parity method, and objective-and-task method.

Section 13.2 Public Relations and Sales Promotion

public relations (p. 267)
publicity (p. 267)
press release (p. 267)

- Businesses use public relations, which is any activity designed to create a favorable image of a business, its products, or its policies. It is an integral part of any promotional strategy and is extremely cost effective.

- Various sales promotional strategies include contests, sweepstakes, special offers, sales events, coupons, premiums, and rewards programs.

CHECKING CONCEPTS

1. **Explain** the purpose of promotion and the promotional mix.
2. **Identify** various types of print advertising media.
3. **Describe** the use of online advertising media.
4. **Explain** the focus of the AIDA model for creating an advertising message.
5. **Identify** the method for determining an advertising budget that may be shortsighted.
6. **Define** public relations.
7. **Explain** the various forms of publicity.

Critical Thinking

8. **Describe** a possible sales promotion campaign for a new restaurant opening in a downtown business district.

CROSS-CURRICULUM SKILLS

Work-Based Learning

Personal Qualities—Integrity/Honesty

9. You would like to be an ad copywriter, but you have an entry-level clerical job at an advertising agency that promotes a restaurant chain. You see an ad for a freelance copywriting job with a competing restaurant. Write a paragraph about what you would do.

Basic Skills—Writing

10. Peter's Pizza sponsors your high school soccer team. Write a press release on the restaurant's behalf about an event the team is hosting with Peter's Pizza.

School-Based Learning

Arts

11. Design a display ad for a newspaper that advertises a beachfront hotel. Ads may be black and white or in color.

Computer Technology

12. Use the Internet to find three ads for hotels. Print the ads and display them in class. Compare and contrast the ads in a class discussion.

Role Play: Promotions Manager

SITUATION You are to assume the role of promotions manager for a mountain lodge located in a western state. The lodge was designed as an executive retreat. It features 20 suites, a conference room, a dining room, and a lounge. Recreational opportunities include hiking, horseback riding, and swimming. Also on site are natural hot springs, four tennis courts, and a nine-hole golf course. The management wants to promote the lodge to businesses across the nation.

(ACTIVITY) You are to discuss your promotional ideas with the lodge's general manager (judge).

EVALUATION You will be evaluated on how well you meet the following performance indicators:

- Explain the nature of a promotional plan.
- Explain the types of advertising media.
- Develop a promotional plan for a business.
- Obtain publicity.
- Select advertising media.

INTERNET ACTIVITY

Use the Internet to access the Web site for the Queen Mary 2.

- Click News at the bottom of the page.
- Read two press releases.
- Write summaries of the releases.
- Exchange the summaries with a classmate.
- Edit each other's summaries and return them.

➡ For a link to the Queen Mary 2 Web site to do this activity, go to **marketingseries.glencoe.com**.

BusinessWeek News

HOME SWEET HOTEL

We turned to the smartest business folks we know—our readers—and asked them to name the best places for the business traveler to stay. Nearly 1,200 subscribers participated in this, our first hotel survey. The results were revealing.

It was virtually impossible to find the single best hotel. We asked readers to name their favorite property and got almost 1,200 different answers. But they did center on what really counts (after price and location): 39 percent said the quality of the guest rooms was paramount. The hotel staff and health-club were also high on the list, but the real surprise was high-speed Internet access, which placed a strong second.

Marriott International, with 24 percent, was the winner by a wide margin. True, Marriott is the largest hotelier in the world, but respondents almost universally lauded the company for its consistency. "In every Marriott throughout the world, the staff is always caring."

Consistency and number of locations were also reasons 12 percent of the respondents picked Hilton Hotels—the No. 2 finisher. They singled out the company's loyalty program, which allows members to earn points for each stay in both an airline frequent-flyer program and the Hilton plan. The number of brands under the Hilton umbrella was also a plus.

No. 3 on the best-chain list was Westin. With just 120 hotels worldwide, it's much smaller than many of its rivals. Readers cited Westin's exclusive Heavenly Bed—a custom-designed mattress with 250-thread-count linens and a down comforter and pillows—and its Heavenly Shower, which features a double-headed, massaging showerhead. Close behind was Four Seasons. The 49-unit tries to make it easier on guests by letting them store luggage between visits.

Freebie Fest

Indeed, many of our survey respondents indicated they like getting something for nothing, even if they are traveling on an expense account. Readers picked Embassy Suites as the No. 7 chain overall, mentioning the free hot breakfasts, after-work drinks, and hors d'oeuvres. Marriott is rolling out free in-room Internet access.

When they look for the best rates, most travelers troll for bargains on independent Internet sites, a practice the hotel chains say they are trying to discourage. Earlier this year, for example, Hilton began requiring its franchisees to offer the same rates on Hilton.com as they do through a third-party site.

By Christopher Palmeri

CREATIVE JOURNAL

In your journal, write your responses.

CRITICAL THINKING
1. Why do the top three hotels in the survey rank high?

APPLICATION
2. Describe the ideal hotel offering, including room rates and free goods and services, to business guests based on the results of the survey.

 Go to **businessweek.com** for current *BusinessWeek* Online articles.

UNIT LAB

The Inn Place

Y ou've just entered the real world of hospitality and travel and tourism. The Inn Place owns and operates a number of hospitality and tourism businesses, offering the finest accommodations and most desirable destinations in the world. Acting as the owner, manager, or employee of this diverse company, you will have the opportunity to work on different projects to promote the business.

Positive Press—Create a Resort's Promotional Plan

SITUATION You have been sent to assist the advertising and promotions department of a desert resort in the American West. Activities for guests include live entertainment, three pools, tennis courts, a full-service spa, several shopping outlets, and an 18-hole golf course. However, the resort experienced negative publicity because a theft ring was operating at the resort. The thieves were caught, but the negative publicity has caused the resort's security team to appear incompetent. As a result, reservations have been cancelled and bookings have fallen off. Your assignment is to create a promotional plan that will attract new guests and assure the public that the resort is a safe and secure place to stay.

ASSIGNMENT Complete these tasks:
- Determine the media to use in your promotional plan.
- Estimate the approximate cost of your promotional plan.
- Make a report to your supervisor.

TOOLS AND RESOURCES To complete the assignment, you will need to:
- Conduct research at the library, on the Internet, or by talking to local hotel/resort owners.
- Ask an advertising executive about the reality of your proposed promotional plan budget.
- Have word-processing, spreadsheet, and presentation software.

RESEARCH Do your research:
- Research the demographics and psychographics of the target market.
- Determine costs of the types of media.
- Determine a method of evaluating the success of your promotional plan.

REPORT Prepare a written report using the following tools:
- *Word-processing program:* Prepare a written report listing the demographic and psychographic characteristics of the target market.
- *Spreadsheet program:* Prepare a chart comparing the costs of the types of media you are proposing. Prepare a chart to illustrate the percentage each of the types of media will cost of your total budget.
- *Presentation program:* Prepare a ten-slide visual presentation with key points, mock-ups of each component of the plan, and key descriptive text.

PRESENTATION AND EVALUATION You will present your report to the head of the advertising and promotions department. You will be evaluated on the basis of:
- Your knowledge of promotional plans
- Continuity of presentation
- Voice quality
- Eye contact

PORTFOLIO
Add this report to your career portfolio.

UNIT 4

EXPLORING CAREERS IN HOSPITALITY & TOURISM

In This Unit ...

Chapter 14
Customer and Employee Relations

Chapter 15
Finding a Job

Chapter 16
Careers in Hospitality & Tourism

> " Choose a job you love, and you will never have to work a day in your life. "
>
> —Confucious
> Chinese philosopher

Unit 4 of *Hospitality & Tourism* explores a variety of careers in these industries and how to train for and find jobs. Chapter 14 highlights the importance of customer and employee relations for all hospitality and tourism businesses. In Chapter 15, you will learn about general employment skills, such as communication, as well as skills that are unique to jobs in these industries. Also covered in the chapter are the springboard activities for a job search: research, preparation, and follow-up. To conclude the unit and the text, Chapter 16 examines and describes the career opportunities available in the four segments of the hospitality and tourism industries. In addition, the chapter also provides educational resources for gaining the background and tools needed for working in the exciting and global fields of hospitality and tourism.

■ UNIT LAB Preview

The Inn Place

Have you ever thought about how many different jobs are available in hospitality and tourism businesses? How would you explore specific careers?

These functions are highlighted in this unit:
- Marketing-Information Management
- Products/Service Management
- Promotion
- Distribution

Chapter 14

Customer and Employee Relations

Section 14.1
Customer Relations

Section 14.2
Employee Relations

Chapter Objectives

- Explain the importance of good customer relations.
- Identify methods of service in the hospitality industry.
- Describe the steps to resolve guest complaints to retain customers.
- Identify external and internal factors that motivate employees.
- Define the term *leadership*.
- Describe ethical issues in the hospitality industry.

Case Study   PART 1

SEA CRUISE

Princess Cruises was founded in 1964 when entrepreneur Stanley McDonald purchased a steamship and operated it as a luxury liner between the Mexican Riviera and Alaska. The company's immediate success resulted in the addition of more luxury liners. In 1974, the Peninsular and Oriental Steam Navigation Company purchased Princess Cruises and added its own ships to the fleet.

A year later, in 1975, Princess Cruises as well as the cruise industry benefited when its ships were used as the setting for a hit television show—*The Love Boat.* The show aired across America and introduced the cruise ship concept to a new generation of vacationers.

Today Princess Cruises operates lines to all seven continents. To maintain its leadership role in the industry, the company has designed ships with more private balconies and also developed innovative environmental and waste-management systems. What else could Princess Cruises offer to stay competitive?

ANALYZE AND WRITE

1. Write two sentences about how Princess Cruises has promoted good customer relations through its offerings.
2. How can media exposure help develop good customer relations? Write a paragraph explaining your answer.

Case Study Part 2 on page 295

POWER READ

Be an active reader and use these reading strategies:

PREDICT what the section will be about.

CONNECT what you read with your own life.

QUESTION as you read to make sure you understand the content.

RESPOND to what you've read.

Customer Relations

AS YOU READ ...

YOU WILL LEARN

- To explain the importance of good customer relations.
- To identify methods of service in the hospitality industry.
- To describe the steps to resolve guest complaints to retain customers.

WHY IT'S IMPORTANT

The success of any business is based on its ability to anticipate and satisfy the needs of its customers. In the hospitality industry, these customers are guests who support hotels, restaurants, sports facilities, and travel destinations worldwide.

KEY TERMS

- exemplary guest service
- guest satisfaction
- loyal customer
- empowerment

PREDICT

Write your own definition of the term *empowerment*.

exemplary guest service
consistent hospitality service that exceeds guest expectations

Customer Relations and Service

In today's highly competitive hospitality industry, successful hotels, restaurants, tourist attractions, sporting events, and entertainment and event providers have one thing in common: They must offer exemplary service to their guests. In turn, guests recognize this attention and reward establishments by returning to their facilities. In this way, positive guest relations are created.

What Is Service?

Exemplary guest service is consistent hospitality service that exceeds guest expectations. Every guest is unique. To satisfy a guest, it is important to find out exactly what he or she values. A corporate client may value the speed of service or being recognized as a frequent user of services. Senior citizens on a motor-coach tour may want to have buffet-style meal service. Most families on vacation appreciate access to recreational activities geared toward children. By identifying and knowing selected areas of importance, a hospitality service provider can exceed each guest's expectations and build a strong service relationship that will result in repeat business.

Service Qualities

Hospitality service providers need to understand which specific service qualities guests value in order to better serve customers. These service qualities include:

- Product quality
- Cost
- Convenience
- Reputation
- Staff service
- Service after a sale
- Communication
- Efficiency

Service Relationship

Merely satisfying a guest does not guarantee that he or she will return. Many factors come into play when a guest purchases a hospitality product. The guest and the hospitality provider are linked to the overall service experience. A guest will evaluate the entire experience to determine the level of satisfaction. This experience includes the physical or tangible product, such as a hotel room or a restaurant's food. It also includes the intangible service received before, during, and after the purchase. For example, was the sales representative helpful when making an airline reservation? Were flight attendants efficient during the flight? Were the baggage-claim employees conscientious after landing?

Methods of Service

Hospitality providers can serve customers or guests in three ways. Methods of service include in-person service, indirect service by telephone or other reservation systems, and electronic service via e-mail or other automated systems.

In-Person Service

The most effective method of service is face-to-face personal service. A guest can evaluate a property or facility by its appearance as well as by the attitude, appearance, and overall professionalism of the service provider.

Indirect Service

Guests use indirect transactions to make reservations, inquiries, or complaints. The service employee must communicate a consistent message of good service involving any type of transaction in a professional manner.

INDIRECT SERVICE **Many hospitality and tourism businesses, such as airlines and lodging facilities, provide customer service by telephone.** *What are the other methods of serving customers or guests?*

CONNECT
If you were staying at a hotel, what would be the most important factor for your satisfaction?

Electronic Service

With the growth of technology, businesses need trained personnel and easy-to-use systems. Most guests appreciate the speed and efficiency provided by electronic service through automated systems. However, some guests will always prefer personal attention. Whatever type of technical service is offered, it must suit the customer's unique need at any given time.

Guest Satisfaction and Guest Loyalty

Guests expect quality hospitality products without defects. Delivering quality assures **guest satisfaction**, or the fulfillment of guests' needs and wants regarding receiving quality hospitality products. Rooms must be clean; food must be safe to eat; and transportation must be reliable. With consistent quality, customers will return.

guest satisfaction the fulfillment of guests' needs and wants regarding receiving quality hospitality products

loyal customer a returning customer or guest who refers friends, family, and colleagues to an establishment

Guest Loyalty

Loyal customers are even more valuable than return customers. A **loyal customer** is a returning customer or guest who refers friends, family, and colleagues to an establishment. A returning client tends to spend more than a first-time guest spends and may use more services. Hospitality businesses recognize loyal guests by offering lower rates, extra nights, complimentary meals, or upgrades.

Hot Property

Lettuce Makes History

The humorous name, Lettuce Entertain You Enterprises (LEYE), belongs to a serious company that is a force in the restaurant business. LEYE was created when aspiring restaurateur Richard Melman teamed with real estate agent Jerry Orzoff in 1970. Together they dreamed up R.J. Grunts, a Chicago eatery that catered to young singles with diverse tastes. The success of the restaurant led to a number of new high-concept restaurants. Concepts ranged from Chinese takeout to Spanish tapas. Orzoff passed away in 1981, but Melman pressed ahead. By 2004, LEYE had a stake in more than 50 restaurants in the United States and Japan.

LOYAL TO CUSTOMERS
The company's special loyalty program made it a leader in the field. Originally, LEYE modeled its loyalty plan on frequent-flyer programs. Over time, however, LEYE refined the program to better fit the hospitality business. Loyalty programs serve dual purposes of gathering customer information and offering special benefits. LEYE's frequent-dining program focused on educating customers and bringing in business. The loyalty program costs members $25, which customers can recoup with three LEYE visits. Members receive points that can be used toward food, gift certificates, and vacations. In 2003, LEYE estimated that their 60,000 frequent-dining members generated about 20 percent of the company's sales.

1. What is the purpose of LEYE's loyalty program?
2. Which loyalty rewards would appeal to you—free food or gift certificates? Why?

Figure 14.1

The Value of One Guest

Satisfied Guest

	Room	Meals	Airline	Special Event
	$75 per night	$50	$300	$25
	× 3 nights	× 4 people	× 1 flight	× 200 people
	$225	$200	$300	$5,000

Revenue

Dissatisfied Guest

	Room	Meals	Airline	Special Event
	$225	$200	$300	$5,000
	× 12	× 12	× 12	× 12
	$2,700	$2,400	$3,600	$60,000

Loss

RIPPLE EFFECT This chart illustrates how much revenue could be lost if one dissatisfied guest told 12 people not to purchase a travel package. *Why do you think dissatisfied customers tend to be more outspoken than satisfied customers?*

Customer Retention

Hospitality service providers work very hard to satisfy every guest every time. In an ideal world, this would mean perfection—no errors, no mistakes, no defects, and no miscommunication. However, because the hospitality service experience depends on both guest and provider involvement, this is not always the case. Situations may occur that cause a guest to become dissatisfied, perhaps through no fault of the service provider. It is very important to remedy a problem as soon as it occurs. A dissatisfied guest will not return and will tell others about the experience. In fact, statistics indicate that a dissatisfied guest will tell 12 people about the experience. On an annual basis, the effects of word-of-mouth dissatisfaction can add up to thousands of dollars in lost revenue. Over several years, that amount could total millions of dollars. (See **Figure 14.1**.)

Guest Feedback

Dissatisfied guests often complain to friends, family, and colleagues. They may not inform or complain to the service provider. Without this information, it is difficult for the vendor to know that a problem exists and act on it. This is why hospitality providers need to continually ask for feedback from guests. Businesses can gather feedback in a variety of ways.

Key Point

SLEEP SELLS

According to J.D. Power and Associates, a good night's sleep is key to customer satisfaction and retention. A 2004 survey of hotel guests found a strong correlation between satisfaction with the comfort of the bed and the likelihood a guest will return to a hotel. "A growing number of hotel chains are heavily marketing a good night's sleep through enhanced beds, such as pillow-top beds," says Linda Hirneise of J.D. Power.

Spa Central

If you have aching joints or "the blues," one of Hungary's best assets—the spa—may have a cure for what ails you. It is all in the water. The word *spa* is the Latin acronym for *sanus per aquam*, meaning "health by water." Legend says that wherever you drive a stick into Hungarian soil, thermal water with healing minerals will bubble up.

Spa-goers have flocked to Hungary ever since the Romans first built baths there nearly 2,000 years ago. Hungarians bathe in the water for health reasons. Vacationers from other countries appreciate a relaxing soak. Clients have their pick of bathhouses, ranging from exotic to no-frills—mud spas; thermal "curing" caves; luxurious resorts that include exercise, beauty, and diet programs; and the world's largest thermal lake.

Hungary plans on spending $510 million to refurbish old spas. How might these plans affect customer relations?

QUESTION

What are three forms of guest feedback?

ETHICS & ISSUES

Travel Alerts

The travel industry faced a decline in tourism in the years following 2001. The events of September 11, 2001, resulted in less air travel. The SARS health crisis in 2003 caused travelers to postpone travel plans. Does media coverage of events contribute to a decline in tourism? According to the Secretary General of the WTO, "Research has shown that the media is more influential in the selection of holiday spots than travel agents and friends." *Is the media obligated to be balanced and accurate when reporting tourism issues?*

Sources of Guest Feedback

To receive valuable guest feedback, hospitality and tourism businesses use questionnaires or surveys following a guest's experience. For example, a hotel may include a short questionnaire with other paperwork upon check-out. Comment cards are another source of feedback. Hospitality providers also train personnel to listen to guests' comments. Businesses value the opinions of loyal and repeat guests.

Handling a Complaint

A manager must deal with guest complaints. Special management training is extremely helpful in several areas, such as the service encounter, stress management, and dealing with difficult guests. A friendly attitude and interpersonal communication skills go a long way to soothe disgruntled guests.

Steps for handling complaints include:

1. Listen to the guest.

2. Ask questions to clarify.

3. Take notes.

4. Address the guest's feelings.

5. Suggest alternatives.

6. Thank the guest for bringing the problem to your attention.

7. Begin working on a solution immediately.

8. Follow up.

Staff Empowerment

Many of the steps for handling complaints can be bypassed if the staff is allowed or empowered to make decisions that immediately resolve complaints. **Empowerment** is the granting of authority or power to front-line personnel for handling and solving guests' problems. A guest's needs are always the top priority. After a problem has been resolved, the employee informs the manager of the incident and suggests a follow-up conversation if necessary.

The empowerment system requires that all employees share in a service culture—from top management to front-line service personnel. This system differs from the traditional hierarchical structure and bureaucratic system found in many corporations. Both guests *and* employees are important.

Critical Elements of Service

The service element is important in every guest interaction. Successful companies recognize the importance of satisfying not only guests but also employees. Customer relations and employee relations go hand in hand.

Math Check

MORALE-BUILDING BURGERS

Flameburgers provides employee meals to 33 restaurants with 16 employees each. What is the total cost of meals if each one costs $3?

➡ For tips on finding the solution, go to **marketingseries.glencoe.com**.

empowerment the granting of authority or power to front-line personnel for handling and solving guests' problems

Quick Check ✓

RESPOND to what you've read by answering these questions.

1. What are any three service qualities that motivate guests? _____

_____

_____

_____

_____

2. What are the three ways guests are serviced by hospitality providers? _____

_____

_____

_____

_____

3. What is the first step in handling a guest complaint? _____

_____

_____

_____

_____

Employee Relations

YOU WILL LEARN

- To identify external and internal factors that motivate employees.
- To define the term *leadership*.
- To describe ethical issues in the hospitality industry.

WHY IT'S IMPORTANT

Companies depend on internal and external customers. By satisfying both of these groups, businesses succeed with good reputations. Leaders in the industry understand this principal and run operate in an ethical manner.

KEY TERMS

- compensation
- incentive
- motivation
- leadership
- ethics

PREDICT

What do you think motivates employees to do a good job?

The Importance of Employees

The hospitality industry services four interrelated and interdependent groups: guests, employees, owners, and operators. Employees can be the most important resource for any company. This is particularly true in hospitality because the industry is so labor intensive. Management profits by recognizing employees as valued assets. It is important for managers to create a supportive environment that fosters personal and professional employee growth. If management responds to the needs of internal customers, or employees, the employees will in turn respond to the needs of external customers, or the guests. Satisfied guests will continue to purchase products from the operators, which satisfies the owners. The results are positive employee relations and favorable profits.

Retaining Employees

Effort goes into choosing the right employee for a job. Companies spend a great deal of time and money forecasting job openings, projecting staffing requirements, recruiting candidates, and screening them before selecting employees. All of this effort is wasted if a newly hired employee is trained and then leaves quickly. It is important to develop ways to attract, develop, and keep loyal employees.

Job Satisfaction

Customers are more likely to return if their needs are satisfied. Similarly, employees are more likely to stay with a company if they feel their needs are satisfied. Job satisfaction refers to how an employee likes his or her job. Satisfaction is affected by elements such as the job itself, the manager or supervisor, fellow workers, and salary and benefits. It also includes intangible elements, such as overall working conditions.

Employee Expectations

An employee's attitude is influenced by the qualitative, or subjective, aspects of the job, such as how an employee believes he or she is being treated. For example, managers who are viewed as fair, competent, and considerate contribute to creating employee satisfaction. Amount of pay affects employee satisfaction. An employee's expectations and values also influence satisfaction on the job. For example, receiving a promotion should lead to satisfaction. However, if an employee expects a 10 percent raise with that promotion and receives a 5 percent raise, the employee may be dissatisfied.

External Factors

There are three external factors in the workplace that may increase employee satisfaction. These are compensation, company reputation, and professional development opportunities.

Compensation

Compensation is a form of payment that may include wages, benefits, and/or incentives in return for work. Companies offer an attractive combination of these three forms of compensation to attract and retain employees. Job candidates evaluate the pay portion of a proposed compensation package to see if it is adequate, motivating, and similar to other packages in the particular industry. Supplemental benefits include insurance programs, holiday and vacation plans, and pension assistance. An **incentive** is a reward that is usually in the form of money but may also be stock options, profit-sharing privileges, a company vehicle, and/or a bonus program. Incentives are usually offered to qualified upper-level executives or long-term employees.

Company Reputation

The reputation of a company also contributes to employee satisfaction because it can indicate financial security. Most workers want to know that a company has a solid reputation within its industry. They also look at the company's recent growth or expansion. Growth implies stability and may point to future opportunities. In addition, financial health may indicate the company will stay in business.

Professional Development

Professional development includes formal and informal training opportunities as well as advancement potential. Offering employees a chance to learn new skills or acquire knowledge can benefit both the employee and the company. Typical training opportunities in the hospitality industry revolve around orientation training, skill development, safety training, professional and technical education, and supervisory or management training.

THE Electronic CHANNEL

On Schedule

To stay competitive, Ethiopian Airlines overhauled their scheduling system. It signed a three-year agreement with Sabre Airline Solutions to computerize and streamline its scheduling process, using a program called *Scheduling Manager*. This program automates tasks previously done manually, and it allows managers to view, edit, and report schedule information using a computer system.

➡ Find out more about how airline automation can improve efficiency online through **marketingseries.glencoe.com**.

compensation a form of payment consisting of wages, benefits, and/or incentives in return for work

incentive a reward that is usually in the form of money but may also be stock options, profit-sharing privileges, a company vehicle, and/or a bonus program

 GOOD RELATIONS Job satisfaction and rewards are incentives for good employees to stay on the job. *What are some other forms of compensation besides salaries?*

 marketingseries.glencoe.com

IN THE KITCHEN

Ellen Cirillo
Owner
By Word of Mouth Restaurant

What is your job?
"I am owner and manager of a restaurant." By Word of Mouth is located in Ft. Lauderdale, Florida, and offers American gourmet cuisine to dine-in customers and provides catering.

What do you do in your job?
"I am involved in menu concept, cooking, purchasing, and organizing daily production responsibilities for the bakery and kitchen. I oversee wait staff and managers, and I have a physical presence in the dining room to greet customers and to make sure all patrons are served. I make insurance decisions, help employees with problems, and schedule their hours. As an owner, you have to be involved in the entire operation."

What kind of training did you have?
"I received training in school and also from practical hands-on experience. You cannot start at the top in the hospitality industry, unless you understand how it works from the bottom up. You learn through observation."

What advice would you give students?
"Take part-time or full-time jobs at entry-level positions and prove yourself. Be reliable and willing to help where needed, even if it is not something you usually do. You cannot tell somebody how to do a job if you have never done it."

What is your key to success?
"Sticking to it and being a responsible and reliable person."

Why should a manager be involved in every aspect of the business in terms of customer and employee satisfaction?

Career Data: Restaurant Owner

Education and Training
Associate degree or bachelor's degree in management or business

Skills and Abilities
Interpersonal and organizational skills and resourcefulness

Career Outlook Average growth through 2012

Career Path Entry-level jobs to manager to owner of a restaurant

Internal Factors

Managers need to understand their employees' needs and motivations to increase employee satisfaction and to predict performance. Not all employees are motivated by external rewards, such as bonuses, salaries, or new automobiles. Internal, or intrinsic, factors, such as pride in a job well done or a supportive working environment, can lead to greater employee satisfaction.

Motivation

Motivation is the force that moves a person to action. Although most employees work to earn a living, many employees are motivated to go to work by several other factors. Some work to receive personal satisfaction from their jobs. Their jobs may provide them with social rewards, such as working with friends. Others may enjoy the independence and/or recognition that certain jobs provide in the form of responsibility, authority, or advancement. In addition, a supportive workplace environment that fosters praise, recognition, and encouragement will also motivate employees to stay at their jobs.

Money is often thought of as a primary motivator. However, while pay is important and necessary, it is a secondary reward for most employees. Money can represent security and social recognition. However, by itself, money will not make someone happy at his or her job. The reason most employees leave a job is not always related to pay. Given the choice, most employees would choose a job in a comfortable, supportive workplace environment instead of a high-paying job in a stressful workplace environment.

motivation the force that moves a person to action

CONNECT
What type of reward would motivate you as an employee?

Figure 14.2

Leadership Styles

Leadership Styles

1. Power-oriented style
Managers who use a power-oriented style try to maintain total control over an entire operation. This style is effective in large organizations and in situations where employees are untrained, inexperienced, or involved in a crisis.

2. Routine-oriented style
Routine-oriented managers are concerned with keeping the business running smoothly rather than with accomplishing other goals. This style is most appropriate for middle managers in a large corporation.

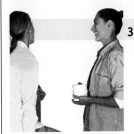

3. Achievement-oriented style
Managers who are achievement oriented are open to new ideas and seek employee suggestions. Achievement-oriented leadership is most effective when a manager is dealing directly with employees who are producing work.

WHAT'S YOUR STYLE?
There are three styles of management leadership, depending on personality and the business situation. *What leadership style would be best for a large restaurant that has many new, untrained employees?*

Leadership

The responsibility for motivating employees falls on the shoulders of their supervisors. In the hospitality industry, managers and supervisors must also be leaders or managers. **Leadership** is the ability to influence others to work toward the goals of an organization or group. (See **Figure 14.2** on page 293 for a chart listing three leadership styles.) Management is a formal approach to achieving a company's objectives. Leadership, however, is a more participatory function relating to people rather than to objectives.

leadership the ability to influence others to work toward the goals of an organization or group

Characteristics of Leaders

Many characteristics differentiate leaders from managers. Communication is a key skill for successful leadership, because leaders must provide instruction, direction, and training to employees. They also need to ensure that employees understand and are motivated to complete a task. Also, leaders must take corrective action when necessary—or provide praise and encouragement.

EFFECTIVE LEADERS An effective leader keeps employees informed about matters that affect work and involves them in discussions. This helps workers feel like active participants. A leader also listens well and tries to put him- or herself in the employee's shoes. This is very important when an employee has complaints or personal issues. The supervisor should listen, show empathy, and document the information. Then the supervisor should address the situation immediately and follow up. Each situation is unique. Employees often assess a leader's authority based on how well he or she handles all types of situations and gets results.

LEADING THE WAY Effective leaders are able to communicate and motivate a group, large or small. *Why is communication a key skill for leadership success?*

Ethics and Leadership

In today's rapidly changing world, one element that separates a company from other companies as an industry leader is its practice of good business ethics. **Ethics** are an expression of the standards of right and wrong based on conduct and morals in a particular society or a system or theory of moral values or principles.

Business Policies

Many laws exist to deal with unethical business practices. For example, laws regarding affirmative action were designed to increase the number of opportunities for minorities and females in the workplace. Similarly, the goal of the Equal Employment Opportunity Act (EEOA) is fairness in hiring procedures. This law requires that companies implement and adhere to a nondiscrimination policy on the basis of race, religion, age, sex, color, national origin, or disability.

Ethics in the Workplace

Typical daily activities in the hospitality and tourism industries can involve ethical issues that are not specifically covered by laws. Most companies have policies to deal with issues such as harassment in the workplace, conflicts of interest, and abuse of expense accounts.

HARASSMENT Sexual harassment in the workplace is a complex issue for both employers and employees. The EEOA defines sexual harrassment as "unwelcome sexual advances, requests for sexual favors, and other verbal or physical conduct of a sexual nature." Awareness of this issue has heightened as a result of publicity surrounding various incidents. Policies exist and are enforced in many companies to ensure that all employees have a comfortable and safe working environment.

CONFLICTS OF INTEREST Companies have rules and regulations relating to situations that may result in conflicts of interest. Vendors or suppliers often want to give valued customers gifts to thank them for their business. This practice may challenge fair business procedures. Many experts in the hospitality field are asked to share their time and knowledge outside the workplace. This activity could be considered a conflict of interest, especially if the expert's information about his or her employer's company is leaked to a competitor and causes loss of customers and revenue.

Case Study PART 2

SEA CRUISE
Continued from Part 1 on page 283

To remain competitive in the growing cruise-ship industry, Princess Cruises maintains the quality of its ships and also maintains services on shore. At more than 250 ports around the world, the cruise company offers excursions, tours, and activities as diverse as snorkeling, shopping, and cultural celebrations.

Special attention is given to one of Princess Cruises' original destinations—Alaska. In the Land of the Midnight Sun, the company operates five wilderness lodges, railcars with domed ceilings, and luxurious buses that allow visitors to appreciate the state's inland beauty.

Because Princess Cruises serves a global market, the company developed different lines to address the needs of different cultures. The *Aida* and *Arkona* ships, for example, are designed for German guests. Such attention to detail allows the company to keep growing.

ANALYZE AND WRITE

1. List some ways an ocean liner might be designed for a particular customer group.
2. What possible employee satisfaction issues might exist on a cruise ship? Write a paragraph explaining your answer.

ethics an expression of the standards of right and wrong based on conduct and morals in a particular society or a system or theory of moral values or principles

QUESTION

What are three ethical issues in the workplace?

EXECUTIVE PERKS On a daily basis, executives use company expense accounts or company cars. Use of items such as computers or purchases of food and beverages might come into question. Abusing these expense-account privileges can result in disciplinary action by the company.

Valuing Employees

Different factors motivate different people. A company should recognize employees' needs and find various ways to satisfy them. Understanding the unique nature of each employee and rewarding him or her accordingly demonstrates a company's ability to value diversity. In the end, the businesses as well as the individuals are responsible for their actions. How both groups handle a given situation, based on personal or prescribed codes of behavior, will contribute to everyone's success.

Quick Check ✓

RESPOND to what you've read by answering these questions.

1. What are three external factors that help create employee satisfaction? _____

_____

_____

_____

_____

_____

2. What are the three elements in compensation? _____

_____

_____

_____

_____

_____

_____

3. What are three types of typical hospitality training opportunities? _____

_____

_____

_____

_____

_____

Worksheet 14.1

Guest-Service Survey

Survey ten people of various ages. Ask the questions below and tally the answers in the appropriate columns.

1. When choosing a hospitality product, such as an airline ticket, a hotel room, or a meal in a restaurant, how important is service?

Very Important	Somewhat Important	Not Important
1.		
2.		
3.		
4.		
5.		
6.		
7.		
8.		
9.		
10.		

2. What do you do when you are dissatisfied with a service?

Tell someone in charge	Write a letter or phone	Do nothing
1.		
2.		
3.		
4.		
5.		
6.		
7.		
8.		
9.		
10.		

3. What conclusions can you draw from your survey?

_____

_____

_____

_____

_____

Worksheet 14.2

Plan for Employee Retention

Think about a hospitality or tourism business you might like to operate and how you would retain employees. Then answer the following questions.

1. What type of business would you choose?

_____

2. How many employees would you hire for your business?

_____

3. What external factors would you offer your employees? Give details.

_____

_____

_____

_____

_____

_____

4. What internal factors would you use to motivate your employees? Give details.

_____

_____

_____

_____

_____

_____

5. What leadership style would you use? Why do you think this would be the best leadership style for you and your employees?

_____

_____

_____

_____

_____

Portfolio Works

RESTAURANT QUESTIONNAIRE

Use the space below to design a questionnaire for your favorite restaurant. It will be used to survey customers after they dine. Be sure the questions focus on both customer satisfaction and complaints.

Name of Restaurant: _____

Type of Restaurant: _____

_____

_____

_____

_____

_____

_____

_____

_____

_____

_____

_____

_____

_____

_____

_____

_____

_____

_____

_____

_____

_____

Add this page to your career portfolio.

Chapter 14 | Review and Activities

CHAPTER SUMMARY

Section 14.1 Customer Relations

exemplary guest service
(p. 284)
guest satisfaction
(p. 286)
loyal customer (p. 286)
empowerment (p. 289)

- When businesses offer exemplary service to guests, the guests recognize the attention, and they reward businesses by returning to their facilities.

- Guests are serviced by hospitality providers in person, indirectly by telephone or reservation systems, and electronically via e-mail or other automated systems.

- Steps for handling guest complaints are: 1) Listen to the guest; 2) ask questions to clarify; 3) take notes; 4) address the guest's feelings; 5) suggest alternatives; 6) thank the guest for bringing the problem to your attention; 7) begin working on a solution immediately; and 8) follow up.

Section 14.2 Employee Relations

compensation (p. 291)
incentive (p. 291)
motivation (p. 293)
leadership (p. 294)
ethics (p. 295)

- External factors that motivate employees include compensation packages, company reputation, and professional development opportunities. Internal factors include pride in a job well done and a supportive working environment.

- Leadership is the ability to influence others to work toward the goals of an organization or group.

- Some ethical issues in the hospitality industry may involve issues of sexual harassment, conflicts of interest, and abuse of expense accounts.

CHECKING CONCEPTS

1. **Explain** the meaning of exemplary guest service.
2. **Identify** different methods of delivering guest service.
3. **Explain** the importance of guest satisfaction.
4. **Describe** some rewards for loyal customers offered by hospitality and tourism businesses.
5. **Name** some forms of guest feedback.
6. **List** internal and external factors that motivate employees.
7. **Differentiate** between management and leadership.

Critical Thinking
8. **Discuss** conflicts of interest in the hospitality industry.

CROSS-CURRICULUM SKILLS

Work-Based Learning

Information—Acquiring and Evaluating Information

9. Survey 15 people and ask them which local restaurants they think have the best service. Write down the names of the people you surveyed. Beside each name, write the person's response. Compare your list with other students' lists by writing results on the board.

Basic Skills—Writing

10. Write a letter of appreciation to your favorite restaurant. In the letter, explain why you return to the restaurant.

School-Based Learning

Math

11. Rooms in the ski lodge rent for $75 per night. Meals average $25 per guest. If a family of four rents a room for three nights and eats two meals a day in the restaurant, what is the revenue from this family?

Arts

12. Use computer graphics or art supplies to create a poster about steps for handling customer complaints.

Role Play: Hotel Personnel Manager

SITUATION You are to assume the role of personnel manager of a privately owned hotel that is about to be purchased by a major hotel chain. The staff members are uncertain about their employment, and rumors circulate daily. Employee morale is low. The hotel's current owner (judge) has asked you to help reassure the staff that the hotel chain plans to keep all the current employees and that there will be no drastic changes. The hotel owner (judge) plans to hold a staff meeting to accomplish this.

ACTIVITY You are to draft some ideas for the staff meeting and present them to the hotel's owner (judge) for approval.

EVALUATION You will be evaluated on how well you meet the following performance indicators:

- Explain the nature of staff communication.
- Demonstrate problem-solving skills.
- Treat others fairly at work.
- Foster positive working relationships.
- Conduct staff meetings.

INTERNET ACTIVITY

Use the Internet to access an online bookstore such as Amazon.
- Search books.
- Type "hospitality and tourism employee empowerment."
- Click Go.
- Click any of the books listed.
- Scroll down to Editorial Review.
- Read the editorial of any book listed.
- Write a summary of the book from the review.
- Post your summary.

➤For a link to Amazon to do this activity, go to **marketingseries.glencoe.com.**

 marketingseries.glencoe.com

Chapter 15

Finding a Job

Section 15.1

Employment Skills

Section 15.2

The Employment Process

Chapter Objectives

- Identify the skills required for workplace employment.
- Identify different communication skills.
- Describe the skills specific to the hospitality and tourism industries.
- Identify the steps of the employment process.
- Discuss the elements of a résumé.
- Describe a traditional job interview.

FOODS FOR "DUDES"

How did three brothers, who were avid surfers from Brazil with parents from China, start a fish-taco craze? When Mingo Lee, Eduardo Lee, and Wing Lam moved to Southern California, they brought experience gained from working at their family's restaurant in Brazil. However, their culinary experiences while on surfing trips to Mexico inspired the trio to open the first Wahoo's Fish Taco restaurant in 1988.

The first Wahoo's was located in Costa Mesa, California. The brothers struggled to pay operating expenses as the business began to build a customer base. However, other California restaurants noticed a trend and started offering fish tacos on their menus. Santa Barbara's La Salsa Fresh Mexican Grill and Carlsbad's Rubio's Baja Grill became direct competitors with Wahoo's. Meanwhile, larger chain restaurants, such as El Torito, Chevy's, and Islands, also added the dish to their menus. The local eatery Wahoo's faced stiff competition from established corporate restaurants as the fish-taco wave grew.

ANALYZE AND WRITE

1. Write a paragraph about the background knowledge that enabled the brothers to open Wahoo's.
2. List marketing advantages Wahoo's might have over larger restaurant businesses.

Case Study Part 2 on page 313

Be an active reader and use these reading strategies:

PREDICT what the section will be about.

CONNECT what you read with your own life.

QUESTION as you read to make sure you understand the content.

RESPOND to what you've read.

Employment Skills

AS YOU READ...

YOU WILL LEARN

- To identify the skills required for workplace employment.
- To identify different communication skills.
- To describe the skills specific to the hospitality and tourism industries.

WHY IT'S IMPORTANT

In today's competitive job market, applicants must acquire the skills needed to succeed. The hospitality industry also requires industry-specific skills.

KEY TERMS

- nonverbal communication
- hospitality-specific traits
- work ethic
- time management

PREDICT

What might be the definition of the term *work ethic*?

Working in Hospitality & Tourism

World events have a major impact on how businesses operate, particularly in the hospitality and tourism industries. Students preparing to enter the workplace need to constantly evaluate the changes taking place globally and locally. Successful candidates for hospitality or tourism jobs and any other jobs are people who develop practical skills and have a desire for learning. They must also be able to adjust to the many challenges and opportunities developing in the real worlds of hospitality and tourism.

Required Skills

The U.S. Department of Labor has identified three critical skill areas for job seekers entering the workforce. Designed to measure work readiness, these skills can help people prepare for the job market. Colleges, universities, and employee-training programs focus on these three skill areas:

- Basic skills
- Thinking skills
- Personal qualities

Basic Skills

Basic skills include abilities in reading, writing, mathematics, speaking, and listening. Most of these skills are the foundation of elementary and secondary education in the United States. Many states require that students demonstrate proficiency in these basic skills prior to high school graduation through coursework and qualifying examinations. Federal and state legislation may also require that students achieve specific standards before a high school diploma is awarded. These basic skills also provide a solid foundation for a lifetime.

Thinking Skills

Thinking skills are difficult to measure. Some of these skills include creativity, decision making, problem solving, and the abilities to reason and learn. Upper-division high school and college courses focus a great deal of time and effort on these areas. Younger students can also develop these skills by joining clubs and organizations, such as Boys and Girls Clubs of America, YMCA, and YWCA.

Personal Qualities

Of the three skill areas, personal qualities are the most difficult to teach and measure in a formal classroom. These skills are developed through social settings, in a family environment, or through mentoring relationships. Personal qualities can include responsibility, self-esteem, self-management, sociability, and integrity.

The Importance of Basic Skills

Employers seek applicants with mastery in the three skill areas. The more qualified a candidate is, the less time and money a company will need to spend on initial training to prepare him or her for a job. A job candidate with a good balance of basic skills, thinking skills, and personal qualities will succeed in the job marketplace.

Hospitality & Tourism Skills

The basic skill areas are important for every job. However, the hospitality and tourism industries are unique and require individuals to demonstrate additional skills to achieve success. These skills focus on guest service and communication.

Guest-Service Skills

Employees are the basic link between the guest and the service provider. A service staff member's interpersonal skills and treatment of a guest will help determine if that guest returns to become a repeat guest and loyal customer.

Communication Skills

Every hospitality and tourism employee uses communication skills throughout the day. Critical to success in these businesses, the skills include listening, speaking, reading, and writing.

LISTENING The skill of listening is perhaps the most important of all communication skills. Many people believe they listen, but in reality, they may not hear the true message. Good listening requires patience and practice. To be successful in the world of hospitality and tourism, you need to become an active listener rather than a passive listener.

An active listener must pay attention to the spoken word as well as to nonverbal signals. Eye contact, hand gestures, and body posture are examples of nonverbal signs. A good listener does not interrupt or react immediately and avoids distractions, such as music, telephones, and televisions. In addition, taking notes is helpful while listening, and notes can be used for later reference. Listening will make you a more effective communicator and a valued employee.

SPEAKING As we learned earlier, how something is said is just as important as what is said. Guests and employers constantly evaluate how rapidly an employee speaks as well as the tone and volume of his or her voice. It is always best to think before speaking and check for understanding after speaking. The goal is clarity and concern in guest interactions. Care, concern, and interest emphasize any message expressed to a guest.

TECH NOTES

Wanted: Techies
Hotel guests who use laptops or handheld computers do not want to experience technical difficulties. Ritz-Carlton's "technology butlers" are trained to help hotel guests with all sorts of technology-related issues, such as connecting to the Internet and installing compatible software. The Fairmont hotel chain has a similar "virtual assistant" program, featuring a toll-free technical support hotline.

➡ List three job skills a technology butler or a virtual assistant should have after viewing reference material at **marketingseries.glencoe.com.**

PUBLIC SPEAKING

In most jobs, you may need to give presentations or present other information to the public, coworkers, or employees. Keep these factors in mind: rehearsal, eye contact, appropriate tone and volume, correct language, relaxed nonverbal signs, appropriate attire, and good timing.

SPEAKING VIA TELEPHONE In today's world of voice mail and e-mail, telephone skills remain an important part of communication in the hospitality industry. PBX (private branch exchange) operators, who communicate with guests over a private telephone network, as well as telemarketing sales representatives need telephone skills in their work, as do many hospitality employees. A guest's first contact with a lodging facility is often over the telephone. The communication should create a positive impression or the guest will look elsewhere for accommodations. See **Figure 15.1** for a variety of tips to use when serving guests via the telephone.

READING AND WRITING The need for producing well-written materials does not end after high school or college. In your job search, a well-written résumé and cover letter will speak volumes about you. Most jobs require employees to create written documents. Content, style, and format are three criteria for judging good writing.

Content is the message of a document. Style and format represent *how* something is written. Writing style may reflect the author's personality, but it should also be appropriate for the purpose of the written material. For example, a research report should be more formal and factual than a personalized note.

Reading and writing skills are essential communication skills needed to perform any hospitality or tourism job.

Figure 15.1

Telephone Tips

SERVICE SELLS These tips for hospitality staff will help promote excellent service to customers over the telephone. *Why is speaking on the telephone so important to a hospitality business?*

Telephone Tips

- Answer the phone in a timely manner (within 3 rings).
- Smile when you answer the phone.
- Use your name or company name as well as a greeting.
- Return all calls within 24 hours or one business day.
- Never leave guests on hold longer than one minute.
- When taking a message, be sure to get the caller's correctly spelled name and title, complete telephone number, company name, time and date of call, an indicator of urgency, and the message itself.
- When transferring a call, provide the correct individual information (name, title, and phone number) to the caller before forwarding the call.

◄ NONVERBAL SERVICE
Communication through nonverbal hand gestures is sometimes the only way to understand the needs of guests in order to provide excellent service. *What are some other forms of nonverbal communication?*

NONVERBAL COMMUNICATION Nonverbal signals often provide more information than we realize. **Nonverbal communication** is the process of giving and receiving messages without words, via eye contact, hand gestures, and body posture. Facial expressions and body language reveal moods, feelings, and levels of interest. While at work, it is important to maintain a professional appearance at all times. This includes being poised, confident, and positive during interactions with guests. It also means avoiding distracting habits that might detract from a lasting impression. Nonverbal cues are important in face-to-face interactions, particularly when resolving complaints or solving problems. Smiling, nodding, and maintaining eye contact all demonstrate empathy for a guest.

nonverbal communication the process of giving and receiving messages without words, via eye contact, hand gestures, and body posture

CONNECT
What might be your strongest communication skill?

Sales Skills

Guests must be convinced that a hospitality product will satisfy their wants and needs. Hospitality and tourism employers need individuals who can communicate effectively to guests. In the sales process, an exchange is taking place. It can be an exchange of money, information, time, skill, or effort. If the buyer is convinced of a good deal or correct match, then a sale is made.

hospitality-specific traits professional characteristics needed in the hospitality industry, including a positive personal attitude, good work ethics, maturity, and good personal appearance as well as leadership and time-management skills

work ethic a belief in work as a moral good, demonstrated by a willingness to perform to the best of one's abilities

Technical Skills

Technology is constantly changing, and it is difficult for anyone to be proficient in current computerized systems. Most hospitality employers require basic knowledge of word processing, spreadsheets, and reservations software systems from entry-level employees. Internet savvy and Web-site design skills may be useful, but they will not guarantee employment or success. Most companies evaluate each employee to determine what training is needed for their particular system.

Hospitality-Specific Traits

Hospitality-specific traits are professional characteristics needed in the hospitality industry, including a positive personal attitude, good work ethics, maturity, and good personal appearance as well as leadership and time-management skills. Many traits desired by employers can be classified under the heading of professionalism. This includes, but is not limited to, hospitality-specific traits.

Personal Attitude

A positive mental attitude goes a long way to project self-confidence, poise, and decisiveness. These are important attributes to an employer or to a guest. Enthusiasm indicates interest and improves performance.

Work Ethic

The hospitality industry does not function during a traditional work week. Hours are not always 9 A.M. to 5 P.M., five days a week. Many positions require employees to work night shifts and during holiday and weekend periods. Employees with strong work ethics will be successful. A **work ethic** is a belief in work as a moral good, demonstrated by a willingness to perform to the best of one's abilities.

Maturity

Maturity can be measured in several ways. This quality represents the ability to focus on tasks and set goals. Other signs of maturity include having self-discipline to complete tasks, to avoid distractions, and to deal with conflicts in a professional manner. All of these signs demonstrate self-sufficiency and independence.

Personal Appearance

Personal appearance refers to personal hygiene, grooming, wellness, and attire. Hygiene is particularly important for jobs involving sanitation and health codes, such as those in the restaurant business. Good grooming contributes to your total image. A healthy diet and exercise help you feel better, so you look better. Professional attire should be appropriate for the company culture.

Leadership

The ability to motivate others to achieve a common objective is a valued quality in the hospitality industry. Leadership skills are vital for many career opportunities.

CARIBBEAN FLAVORS

Charmaine and Louis James
Owners
Taste of Jamaica

What is your job?
"We own and operate our restaurant, Taste of Jamaica, which serves authentic Caribbean-style cuisine."

What do you do in your job?
"When we first opened the restaurant, we had to get many permits, remodel the space, budget our expenses, purchase equipment, and plan menus. Menu planning is still our favorite task. We include the most authentic foods from our home in Jamaica—jerk chicken, a very spicy dish; Irish moss, a kind of seaweed; several curried dishes; our homemade fruit punch; callaloo soup—and fried plantains, which are like bananas and are very popular. We work long hours, six days a week, but we enjoy it. Louis bakes bread every morning, and I prepare some traditional dishes. We started by waiting the tables ourselves, but now we have a staff of four."

What kind of training did you have?
"We both have worked in restaurants as servers and managers. But when we decided to open our own business, we took business and hospitality courses at our community college."

What advice would you give students?
"You must love the restaurant business and people—because you spend so much time with both of them! We have a day off each week, but we spend that day planning our next week's specials and purchasing food."

What is your key to success?
"We had some difficulty attracting a blend of customers. So we expanded our menu to include some other dishes that would appeal to a broad range of tastes."

What hospitality-specific traits does this couple have?

Career Data: Restaurant Owner/Manager

Education and Training
Associate degree or bachelor's degree in ethnic studies, business, hospitality, or management

Skills and Abilities
Interpersonal, personal appearance, leadership, and time-management skills as well as good work ethics and maturity

Career Outlook As-fast-as-average growth through 2012

Career Path Server/host, assistant manager, manager to owner of own restaurant

Time Management

Time management is the ability to plan, track, and accomplish tasks efficiently within a designated period of time. Managing time requires balancing effectiveness with efficiency. This means being able to analyze a situation, apply information, and take appropriate actions. *Effectiveness* is completing a task in a quality manner. *Efficiency* means prioritizing important tasks and completing them in a timely manner.

time management the ability to plan, track, and accomplish tasks efficiently within a designated period of time

Fascinating Planet

Lonely Planet

Lonely Planet began as an adventurous hobby in the early 1970s. At a time when many people traveled in groups with escorts, Tony and Maureen Wheeler loved to travel on their own. The young couple set off on an ambitious trek from London to Asia, and then to Australia. After the trip, like-minded trekkers asked them for travel tips. The couple decided to create a guidebook from their experiences. *Across Asia on the Cheap* became the first Lonely Planet guidebook.

The mission to provide independent travelers with accurate, impartial guidance struck a chord with readers. Today Lonely Planet publishes more than 650 guidebooks and employs a diverse staff of more than 400. Lonely Planet authors and photographers live in every corner of the world.

LONELY NO MORE

What started out as a solo journey for Tony and Maureen Wheeler now touches many lives around the world today. Lonely Planet has branched out from guidebooks to create television shows, mobile-phone contests, and a bustling online community. The Web site features forums where travelers can directly exchange information. In the Postcards section, visitors can read inside scoops from other travelers. Together, independent travelers are finding that the planet is not so lonely after all.

1. What qualities would someone need to start a company such as Lonely Planet?
2. What qualities would someone need to work for a company such as Lonely Planet?

QUESTION

What is the meaning of *efficiency* in relation to time management?

Other Attributes

Most service providers believe in giving back to the community. For example, they make donations to charities or give away free meals to the homeless. They may also recognize and reward community-service activity by their employees. This personal commitment is mutually beneficial.

Finding Employment

Finding a job requires a variety of skills and attributes specific to the hospitality industry. Successful candidates use these skills and their knowledge to take the next step in the employment process.

Quick Check

RESPOND to what you've read by answering these questions.

1. What are three types of required skills for applicants entering the workforce? _____

_____

2. What are three types of communication skills? _____

_____

3. What are three hospitality-specific traits? _____

_____

The Employment Process

Finding and Getting a Job

Career success requires careful planning. Job seekers must possess a combination of skills and specific traits to get a first or entry-level job. Personal goals and individual style will affect a job search. Available opportunities in the current job market will also affect a job search.

The Steps to Employment

There are six steps to finding a job: Research; compile a portfolio; draft a résumé; apply for jobs; interview; and follow up.

Research the Job Market

The choice of an occupation is not an overnight decision. A person's background, community, interests, and skills all influence a career choice. Factors such as geographic location, pay, benefits, hours, responsibilities, and independence also determine which type of job to seek. With the right research, it is possible to find a job that matches a person's talents.

RESEARCH SOURCES Some common places to begin your search include:

- **Newspaper ads**—Newspapers post job listings for all types of positions. Jobs may be grouped in categories or alphabetized.

- **Trade publications**—Every segment of the industry has associations that publish trade journals and magazines. These publications list job ads geared to the particular industry segment.

- **The Internet**—Internet job-search sites provide job listings and tips on how to find a job. In addition, many companies post open positions on their own Web sites.

- **Referral services**—Referral services include placement agencies that screen applicants for specific jobs. Other referral services are employment agencies, college placement offices, and job hotlines.

- **Face-to-face contact**—Employers organize job fairs, trade shows, or open houses. They provide company information and interview candidates on the spot.

- **Networking**—Networking involves discussing job opportunities with teachers and a current part-time employer or speaking with friends, relatives, neighbors, and community members.

THE
Electronic
CHANNEL

Optimizing Opportunities

The Internet is a tremendous resource for job seekers. It is important to search for industry-specific jobs on the right Web sites while maintaining a professional online presence. For example, having a dedicated e-mail address to use for corresponding with employers is a good idea. Posting a neat and organized résumé on dedicated job-search sites is also an option for attracting potential employers. Most importantly, searching online company job boards as well as dedicated hospitality and tourism sites can keep you on top of the job market.

➡️Find out more about searching for hospitality and tourism jobs through **marketingseries.glencoe.com.**

portfolio a collection of samples of best work, designed to highlight strengths, skills, and competencies

Compiling a Portfolio

A **portfolio** is a collection of samples of best work, designed to high-light strengths, skills, and competencies. It contains employment tools such as a résumé and letters of reference. It may also include evidence of work experience and academic skills. You can begin to collect these items during high school and continue throughout your career.

Portfolio Contents

Besides a résumé, here are some possible items for your portfolio:

- **CDs or videotapes**—records demonstrating your skills during projects or speech

- **Photos**—illustrations of meals you have created or field experiences in which you have participated

- **Certificates**—memberships to organizations such as DECA or other student or professional associations

- **Awards**—copies of all honors related to your career interest

- **Articles**—pertinent notices from local newspapers in which your name appears

- **Projects**—sample written works demonstrating writing skills

- **Letters**—references from teachers, community leaders, past employers, or others who can assess your abilities

- **Evaluations**—performance reviews from current employers

- **Attendance records**—records demonstrating responsibility

- **Grades**—transcripts of your grades in high school and college

HOSPITALITY PORTFOLIO Some hospitality-specific items to add to your portfolio might include a sample menu you have developed, a certification, or a license.

> **SHOWING OFF YOUR BEST**
> Save special items you have created or earned and place them in your career portfolio. *Name at least three other items for a portfolio related to hospitality and tourism.*

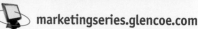

Building a Résumé

A résumé is a brief summary of a job seeker's personal information, skills, work experience, education, activities, and interests. It introduces the job seeker to a potential employer. A résumé may be the first impression an employer has of an applicant. Because of this, résumés must be error-free and professional in appearance. Résumés vary in terms of format. Some formats can highlight work experience or skills, for those with less experience. A résumé should include the following items:

- **Contact information**—name, address, telephone numbers, and e-mail address

- **Objective**—a clear description of the career opportunity you seek

- **Skills summary**—a list of relevant work-based and personal skills

- **Work experience**—a list of part-time and full-time positions, employers, and dates

- **Educational summary**—a list of diplomas, degrees, and training, and the names of educational institutions

- **Other relevant information**—extracurricular activities, clubs, hobbies, community service, honors or awards received, international experience, and/or language fluency

Résumé Transmittal

Formats for transmitting résumés can vary. Some companies prefer a hard copy résumé sent through the mail or faxed. Others may accept an electronic résumé over the Internet.

Job Applications

A job application is a document that job seekers fill out to help employers screen applicants. Complete each section of the application carefully, legibly, and neatly. At this point in the hiring process, you might also be asked to submit other items with your application. These might include copies of legal documents, such as a birth certificate, proof of age or citizenship, or copies of educational records.

Interviews

Many companies require a series of interviews. Each interview serves as a screening tool so that companies can choose the most suitable candidate. There are several types of interviews—informational, mock, telephone, group, panel, and traditional.

Case Study — PART 2

FOOD FOR "DUDES"

Continued from Part 1 on page 303

To keep Wahoo's alive, the founding brothers went back to their roots—surfing and the action-sports industry. They canvassed local surf and skateboard businesses and sponsored events and contests. To reach potential customers, they also advertised at the beach and at local high schools. The strategy worked, and a second Wahoo's opened in Laguna Beach, California, in 1990. As the business continued to grow, the surfing brothers decided to become more professional and hired restaurant expert Steve Karfaridis to implement inventory-control systems. But Wahoo's did not change its image: surf, skateboard, and snowboard stickers, posters, videos, and artifacts still decorate the casual interiors of the 24 Southern California locations and seven Colorado restaurants. As they ride the "big one," the brothers have plans for more restaurants.

ANALYZE AND WRITE

1. List some possible reasons that the brothers chose to hire a restaurant veteran.
2. List some items for a portfolio to be used for getting a marketing job at Wahoo's.

résumé a brief summary of a job seeker's personal information, skills, work experience, education, activities, and interests

job application a document that job seekers fill out to help employers screen applicants

CONNECT

What would you emphasize on your résumé—your skills or your work experience?

Volunteers for Turtles

Turtles have been movie heroes, beloved storybook characters, and tiny pets. Unfortunately, turtles in the wild are disappearing globally. Earth's largest turtle is the leatherback turtle, at up to eight feet long and between 1,200 and 1,500 pounds. In Mexico the number of leatherbacks continues to decrease. Conservation efforts to save these turtles include sea-turtle sanctuaries, protective laws, and volunteer vacations.

Mexico invites people to be volunteers and enjoy its beautiful coasts while helping to preserve the newest generation of leatherback turtles. Volunteers look for turtle nests, relocate turtle eggs to the safety of hatcheries, and collect data. Releasing hatchlings, or just-born turtles, to the sea highlights the experience.

Volunteer vacations in Mexico and other countries offer work experience in many fields: environment, construction, child care, community service—and hospitality.

List ways volunteer experience might benefit your life or career.

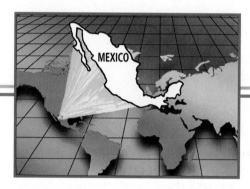

---

informational interview
a formal or informal interview with a professional to help the job seeker learn more about a specific career field or company

Informational Interview

This type of interview can help an applicant explore a particular company or position within the industry. An **informational interview** is a formal or informal interview with a professional to help the job seeker learn more about a particular career field or company.

Mock Interview

A mock, or practice, interview gives you the opportunity to polish your interview skills. Practicing can help you to prepare for a formal interview. Preparation can also increase self-confidence.

Telephone Interview

Unlike face-to-face encounters, telephone interviews are more direct and focused. This type of interview may take place when a job candidate is far away or when an interview must take place immediately.

Group Interview

A potential employer may conduct a group interview when a company wants to collect information from several applicants simultaneously. Group interviews are used to assess leadership potential, communication skills, problem-solving ability, and teamwork skills. By design, group interviews are competitive.

Panel Interview

Panel interviews are usually reserved for upper-level management candidates on second or third interviews. A team of individuals from a company may conduct a panel interview. This procedure saves time because all of the decision makers are gathered together.

Traditional Interview

One applicant, or interviewee, and one company representative, or interviewer, participate in a traditional interview. This type of interview is most common. The interviewer wants to find out what the candidate can offer the company. Some companies conduct highly structured interviews. Questions are designed in advance to receive a series of possible responses. Other companies use unstructured interviews during which a few general questions are posed, and then discussion flows from those questions. However, most companies use a semi-structured format with questions designed to guide the interview.

Parts of the Interview

Most interviews have three general parts: the introduction, the body, and the conclusion. During the introduction, an interviewer welcomes the job applicant and sets the tone for the discussion. During the body of the interview, the interviewer asks questions to obtain additional information about qualifications and background. During the conclusion segment, the interviewer offers the opportunity for the applicant to ask questions, and then thank the interviewer for the time spent. (See **Figure 15.2** for interview tips.)

QUESTION
What are the different types of job interviews?

Figure 15.2

Interview Checklist

Prior to the interview, ask yourself:
- How much do you know about the hospitality industry?
- How much do you know about this particular company?
- How much do you know about this specific job? (e.g., salary, benefits, growth opportunities, policies, and programs)

On the day of the interview, consider:
- Do you have a plan for the day of the interview? (parking location, outfit you will wear, time to commute, location of the office, and interviewer's name and title)
- Are you mentally prepared? (enough sleep, knowing your future goals, a list of questions, confidence, and a professional image)

BE PREPARED Preparation is the key to the success. Preparing for an interview will make you feel at ease so you can present yourself well. *Why would it be important to have a plan for the day of the interview?*

Math Check

GETTING A PROMOTION
A job promotion at the hotel will earn you an additional $5,000 each year. You now earn $32,000. What is the percentage of increase in salary?

➡️For tips on finding the solution, go to **marketingseries.glencoe.com.**

follow-up a phone call or thank-you note from the interviewee to the interviewer after the interview takes place

After the Interview

Most employers complete evaluation forms for each job applicant at the conclusion of an interview. You should also conduct a post-interview evaluation, or assessment. Ask yourself what you did well and what you could do to improve. It is important to follow up immediately after an interview even if the job is not right for you. **Follow-up** is a phone call or thank-you note from the interviewee to the interviewer after the interview takes place.

Workplace Expectations

When you begin a new job, your success depends on your ability to make the transition from school to work. Making a good initial impression is important. Equally important is establishing a record of achievement. Some practical tips for on-the-job success include:

- Study the employee handbook or manual.

- Take advantage of training opportunities offered by the company.

- Choose a mentor or role model to guide you.

- Work to be part of the team, not just an individual contributor.

- Demonstrate willingness to learn and take initiative.

- Admit mistakes, but do not dwell on them.

- Ask for feedback, and then listen.

- Show respect.

- Be a professional.

Many Opportunities

A career in hospitality and tourism offers many fascinating employment opportunities. Getting started requires research, preparation, and follow-up. Maintaining a strong work ethic and demonstrating excellence will help you advance in your career.

Quick Check

RESPOND to what you've read by answering these questions.

1. What is the first step of the employment process? _____

_____

2. Where is one place to begin your job search? _____

_____

3. What are two items that are part of a portfolio? _____

_____

Worksheet 15.1

Potential Employee Self-Assessment

Think about how you rate as a potential employee in the hospitality and tourism industries. For each type of skill, circle the rating that best describes you.

Basic Skills

1. Proficiency level in reading skills:

    Excellent   Average   Poor

2. Proficiency level in writing skills:

    Excellent   Average   Poor

3. Proficiency level in mathematic skills:

    Excellent   Average   Poor

4. Proficiency level in speaking skills:

    Excellent   Average   Poor

5. Proficiency level in listening skills:

    Excellent   Average   Poor

Thinking Skills

1. Proficiency level in creativity skills:

    Excellent   Average   Poor

2. Proficiency level in decision-making skills:

    Excellent   Average   Poor

3. Proficiency level in problem-solving skills:

    Excellent   Average   Poor

4. Proficiency level in abilities to reason and learn:

    Excellent   Average   Poor

Personal Qualities

Write a brief paragraph about your personal qualities that will make you a good employee in the hospitality and tourism industries.

_____

_____

_____

_____

_____

_____

_____

Worksheet 15.2

Job Interview

1. Make a list of the positive traits and negative traits that you might display during a job interview.

Job Interview

Positive Traits	Negative Traits

2. Study the negative traits. What could you do to change them into positive traits?

_____

_____

_____

_____

_____

_____

_____

_____

_____

_____

_____

Portfolio Works

CLASSIFIED AD SEARCH

Study the classified sections of newspapers, magazines, and the Internet to find jobs in the hospitality and tourism industries. Clip four job ads that interest you and paste them onto this page. Beneath each ad, write the reasons you find the particular job interesting.

1. Paste an ad here:

I find this job interesting because:

_____

_____

2. Paste an ad here:

I find this job interesting because:

_____

_____

3. Paste an ad here:

I find this job interesting because:

_____

_____

4. Paste an ad here:

I find this job interesting because:

_____

_____

Add this page to your career portfolio.

CHAPTER SUMMARY

Section 15.1 Employment Skills

nonverbal
  communication
  (p. 307)
hospitality-specific traits
  (p. 308)
work ethic (p. 308)
time management
  (p. 309)

- The workplace skills include: basic skills, such as reading, writing, mathematics, speaking, and listening; thinking skills such as creativity, decision making, problem solving, and the abilities to reason and learn; and personal qualities, such as responsibility, self-esteem, self-management, and integrity.

- Communication skills include listening, speaking, reading, and writing.

- Skills that relate specifically to hospitality and tourism careers include guest-service skills, which require interpersonal skills, and communication skills.

Section 15.2 The Employment Process

portfolio (p. 312)
résumé (p. 313)
job application (p. 313)
informational interview
  (p. 314)
follow-up (p. 316)

- Six steps of the employment process include: 1) Research; 2) compile a portfolio; 3) draft a résumé; 4) apply for a job; 5) interview; and 6) follow up.

- The elements of a résumé may emphasize work experience or skills but should include contact information, an objective, a skills summary, work experience, an educational summary, and other relevant information such as honors and membership in clubs or associations.

- In a traditional job interview, one applicant, or interviewee, and one company representative, or interviewer, participate. The interviewer wants to find out what the candidate can offer the company. Most companies use a semi-structured format with questions designed to guide the interview.

CHECKING CONCEPTS

1. **List** the basic skills for job success.
2. **Identify** the personal skills for job success.
3. **Identify** the thinking skills for job success.
4. **Discuss** communication skills.
5. **Name** hospitality-specific traits.
6. **List** the steps of the employment process.
7. **Explain** the importance of workplace expectations.

Critical Thinking

8. **Discuss** preparation for a job interview.

CROSS-CURRICULUM SKILLS

Work-Based Learning

Basic Skills—Listening

9. Choose a travel book and select a partner. One person reads two or three pages to the other partner. The listening partner writes down the main ideas. Switch roles. Check your listening accuracy.

Personal Qualities—Self-Esteem

10. Personal appearance is an important trait in the hospitality and tourism industries. Write a two-page journal entry that describes your personal appearance and your self-esteem.

School-Based Learning

Writing

11. Write a newspaper ad for the perfect job in the hospitality and tourism industries. Post your ad in class.

Computer Technology

12. Use the computer to write your résumé. Exchange résumés with another student. Edit each other's résumés, and then return them.

Role Play: Motel Employee

SITUATION You are to assume the role of part-time employee of a family-owned motel. You will be graduating from high school and have decided to pursue a career in the hospitality industry. You have explored many career options and decided this industry suits your interests. A fellow part-time employee (judge) has asked you how you conducted your career research and about some of the career options you have explored.

ACTIVITY You are to explain to the part-time employee (judge) your career findings and your research methods.

EVALUATION You will be evaluated on how well you meet the following performance indicators:

- Explain employment opportunities in the hospitality industry.
- Describe traits important to the success of employees in the hospitality industry.
- Analyze employer expectations in the business environment.
- Identify sources of career information.
- Utilize job-search strategies.

Use the Internet to access an online job-listing Web site such as Monster.
- Click Search Jobs.
- Under Choose Location, choose your state.
- Under Choose Job Category, choose Hospitality/Tourism.
- Click Get Results.
- Click different jobs to learn about them.
- Choose one job.
- Write a summary of the job description.

➡For a link to a Web site to do this activity, go to **marketingseries.glencoe.com**.

Chapter 16

Careers in Hospitality & Tourism

Section 16.1
Career Choices

Section 16.2
Educational Resources

Chapter Objectives

- Identify the advantages of working in the hospitality and tourism industries.
- Describe career segments in the hospitality and tourism industries.
- Identify possible career paths in the hospitality and tourism industries.
- Explain the advantages and disadvantages of owning a hospitality business.
- Identify the main types of educational resources.

ISLAND RIDING

Josh Brewer worked his way up the corporate ladder in Chicago, Illinois, before moving to South Carolina to work in a brewery. Alexia Chianis was a police officer in Baltimore, Maryland, before she went to South Carolina where she became a personal trainer—and met Brewer. In 2004, they decided to change their lives. They moved to Hawaii and purchased Kona Coast Cycling Tours.

The big island of Hawaii offers open landscapes flattened by lava, dense forests, and mountain paths—a spectacular setting for cycling. However, treacherous paths, private land, and high altitudes make local guides from Kona Coast Cycling Tours essential for visiting bike riders.

With a fleet of bicycles ranging from hardcore mountain bikes to easier hybrid styles and a growing selection of paths, the "pedal pushers" were ready for business. But how would they attract customers in a market with many tourist services already available?

ANALYZE AND WRITE

1. List some advantages and disadvantages of buying an established tourism business.
2. How did their prior jobs prepare Brewer and Chianis? Write a paragraph explaining your answer.

Case Study Part 2 on page 327

POWER READ

Be an active reader and use these reading strategies:

PREDICT what the section will be about.

CONNECT what you read with your own life.

QUESTION as you read to make sure you understand the content.

RESPOND to what you've read.

Career Choices

AS YOU READ ...

YOU WILL LEARN

- To identify the advantages of working in the hospitality and tourism industries.
- To describe career segments in the hospitality and tourism industries.
- To identify possible career paths in the hospitality and tourism industries.
- To explain the advantages and disadvantages of owning a hospitality business.

WHY IT'S IMPORTANT

It is important to be informed about all of your career options because the choices you make early in your career will affect your ultimate career goal.

KEY TERMS

- entry-level
- operations
- entrepreneur
- career plan

PREDICT

How might a career plan help you?

entry-level the position of an employee at the beginning level of a particular career

Choosing a Career

You make choices on a daily basis. These choices range from the personal-care products you buy to the food you eat to the car you drive. However, your selection of a career is one of the most important choices you will make and requires thought and research. That decision affects how you will spend eight hours a day, each workweek, for most of your life. It may also determine where you live, your family arrangements, and your continuing or graduate educational options. Your career choice affects your professional and personal experiences.

Variety of Opportunities

As the largest employers in the world, the hospitality and tourism industries offer a variety of exciting career options. Opportunities exist at all levels, including **entry-level**, which is the position of an employee at the beginning level of a particular career. These opportunities range from front-line, entry-level service positions to upper-level managers and owners. See **Figure 16.1** on pages 328–329 for examples of career paths.

Hospitality & Tourism Career Segments

You can expand your horizons in any of the four segments of the hospitality and tourism industries: food and beverage; lodging; travel/tourism; and sports, events and entertainment.

Food and Beverage

As discussed in Chapter 3, the food-and-beverage industry offers various career choices. You might begin your career as an entry-level server at a quick-service restaurant, and then someday retire as the owner of a chain of assisted-living care centers or several independent restaurants. The possibilities are endless.

In general, careers in food and beverage are divided into three basic areas: operations, production, and service. All of these areas provide management opportunities. A manager must meet the operational and cost objectives of a company. Most managers also oversee personnel decisions. All food-service management positions require strong skills in leadership, time management, strategic planning, and multitasking as well as knowledge of safety standards.

Operations

Operations are functions of a business that focus on the daily procedures necessary to maintain a business or establishment. Managers ensure that each work shift is properly staffed and that operations run efficiently. They are also responsible for implementing company standards and ensuring guests' satisfaction. Food-service managers, unlike other workers in the hospitality and tourism industries, must focus on compliance with all federal, state, and local safety standards and legislation. Some examples of operations positions include restaurant manager, contract food-service manager, or food-and-beverage director.

Production

In hospitality businesses, production involves the daily planning, organization, and production of high-quality, consistently prepared food. Performance standards and teamwork are essential to the success of the production staff. Production managers are responsible for staffing, scheduling, training, and development of their staff. Although not as visible as other functions in the industry, production is critical to the success of any food-service establishment. Some typical production positions include purchasing director, receiving manager, and chef.

Service

Service is critical to every segment of the hospitality and tourism industries. In the food-and-beverage segment, it is vital to provide timely delivery of quality food in a prompt and efficient manner. That is the sign of a true service professional. Service positions are the most visible to external customers, or the guests. Therefore, service managers focus on satisfying guest needs. Some typical service positions include beverage-service manager, catering manager, banquet manager, and convention-service manager.

Lodging

The lodging industry is extremely diverse. It includes everything from youth hostels and budget properties to glamorous five-star resorts. Careers in this segment are equally diverse. Career paths in lodging divide into five basic areas: finance and accounting, human resources, operations, rooms, and sales and marketing. In addition, food-and-beverage outlets inside lodging facilities provide job opportunities.

Finance and Accounting

A finance and accounting department employs managers who are organized and aware of the latest accounting trends. Financial managers maintain daily, weekly, monthly, and yearly reports. They are also responsible for the overall financial success and profitability of the property. Managers must be proficient in math and other accounting procedures. Some positions include night auditor, accounts receivable manager, and controller.

operations the functions of a business that focus on the daily procedures necessary to maintain a business or establishment

Human Resources

The human resource department is responsible for recruiting, staffing, and training hotel personnel. Skills in planning and organizing are critical to the success of this job. Human resource managers must be up-to-date on all legal issues regarding the workplace. Some positions in this field include training manager, human resource director, and diversity manager.

Operations

Similar to the food-and-beverage segment, the day-to-day operations of a lodging facility are the responsibility of the operations division. Operations managers interact with other divisions within a facility, such as sales, marketing, rooms, finance, and human resources. The need for guest safety and security has created many new operations positions. Some typical operations positions include revenue manager, engineer, and security manager.

Rooms

The rooms division requires the largest percentage of staff positions in any lodging facility. It is also the largest revenue generator for a property. Jobs include front-desk positions as well as housekeeping and uniformed services. Staff members who work with telephones and retail services report to the rooms division. Employees in the rooms division are the first staff members to meet guests. Thus, creating a good first impression and having a strong focus on service are important. Typical positions are rooms division manager, concierge, and bell captain.

Sales and Marketing

The sales and marketing team is responsible for providing revenue for a property by selling sleeping rooms and meeting space. The sales staff generates leads and sells all services relating to special events. The marketing staff is the strategic planning unit that determines target markets and future customer base. Both groups closely monitor the competitive environment. Some typical positions include director of sales, marketing director, and catering manager.

Travel/Tourism

Many businesses serve travelers domestically and internationally. As people travel more frequently, due to increased leisure time, rising incomes, and changing demographics, job opportunities in the travel/tourism segment continue to expand. Careers in travel/tourism divide into three areas: destinations, distribution channels, and transportation.

Destinations

Promotion of an area's scenic beauty, cultural attractions, and special events is critical to the success of a destination. Cruise ships offer on-shore and onboard positions. Some typical positions are destination marketing operator, reservations manager, and purser.

Distribution Channels

Intermediaries, or agents, who help promote goods and services to guests are distribution channels. Though many retailers deal directly with the public, travel suppliers also use distribution channels to connect with travel consumers. Agents in this category are responsible for recognizing guest needs and matching them to specific travel providers. Service and sales are critical skills for these agents. Positions in this area include tour operator, tour director, corporate travel manager, and incentive travel specialist.

Transportation

Passenger transportation includes air, ground, and water transportation systems. Customer-service skills and attention to detail are vital in this area of travel/tourism. An understanding of scheduling and intermodal transportation issues is also critical. Some typical positions include dispatcher, reservation manager, and flight attendant.

Sports, Events, and Entertainment

As noted in Chapter 7, the sports, events, and entertainment industries focus on leisure activities. From country clubs to large arenas, sports facilities offer a wide variety of career options. For example, a venue manager might arrange for a rock concert one evening and a major soccer game the next day.

Sports

Managing sporting events involves the operation of an actual facility as well as supervision of other areas, such as concessions, parking, security, spectators/fans, and talent. The world of sports management also features a variety of jobs. Typical sports-related positions are facility manager, fitness instructor, and sports agent.

Events

Events can enhance a tourist's experience, help attract guests to hotels, and generate revenue for restaurants. Typical positions include event planner, meeting planner, and special-event coordinator.

Entertainment

The entertainment side of the industry generates huge revenue. Jobs in this area can include promoting and booking acts as well as negotiating contracts. Some positions are box-office manager, cruise director, and activity director.

Case Study PART 2

ISLAND RIDING
Continued from Part 1 on page 323

To compete with local tour businesses, Brewer and Chianis assemble an inventory of bikes and find established bike paths for vacationing cyclists. The partners also assess the needs of their customers. For example, if approached by a group of expert and beginning cyclists, the Kona Coast Cycling Tours create a tour in which the less advanced riders take breaks to enjoy scenery or take photos. They also arrange for a van to accompany the group. This allows cyclists to rest and nonathletes to enjoy the trail. Brewer and Chianis also have a tandem bike for visitors with visual impairments to pedal their way through the lava fields and jungles of the big island of Hawaii.

ANALYZE AND WRITE

1. What businesses might compete with Kona Coast Cycling Tours? Write a sentence(s) in response.
2. What are some unique risks Brewer and Chianis might face? List some ways they can prepare for them.

Figure 16.1

Hospitality & Tourism Career Paths

UNLIMITED OPPORTUNITIES **The hospitality and tourism businesses offers a vast number of career options to suit many people's interests.** *Choose a place to seek employment and identify the career path. What would be the entry-level and top-level positions for the career path?*

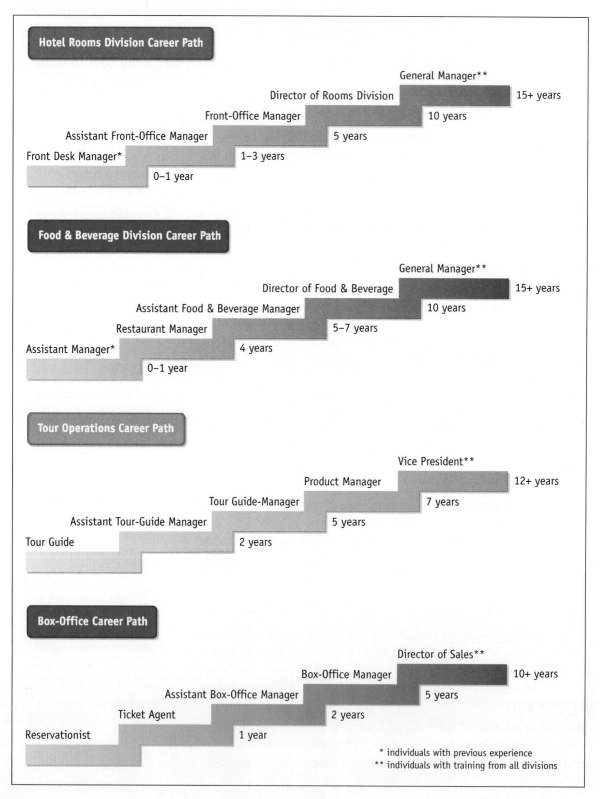

Hotel Rooms Division Career Path

General Manager**
Director of Rooms Division 15+ years
Front-Office Manager 10 years
Assistant Front-Office Manager 5 years
Front Desk Manager* 1–3 years
0–1 year

Food & Beverage Division Career Path

General Manager**
Director of Food & Beverage 15+ years
Assistant Food & Beverage Manager 10 years
Restaurant Manager 5–7 years
Assistant Manager* 4 years
0–1 year

Tour Operations Career Path

Vice President**
Product Manager 12+ years
Tour Guide-Manager 7 years
Assistant Tour-Guide Manager 5 years
Tour Guide 2 years

Box-Office Career Path

Director of Sales**
Box-Office Manager 10+ years
Assistant Box-Office Manager 5 years
Ticket Agent 2 years
Reservationist 1 year

* individuals with previous experience
** individuals with training from all divisions

Places to Seek Employment	Educational Career Path
Airline	TT
Amusement Park	SEE
Assisted Living Facility	F&B – HOTEL – SEE
Auditorium	SEE
Bed & Breakfast	F&B – HOTEL
Car Rental Agency	TT
Casino	F&B – HOTEL – SEE
Civic Center	SEE
Conference Center	F&B – HOTEL
Contract Catering Company	F&B – HOTEL
Convention Center	F&B – HOTEL – SEE – TT
Convention & Visitors Center	TT
Country Club	F&B – SEE
Cruise Ship: shipboard	F&B – HOTEL – SEE – TT
Cruise Ship: shore side	F&B – HOTEL – SEE – TT
Entertainment Complex	SEE
Extended-Stay Property	F&B – HOTEL
Ground Transportation Carrier	TT
Health/Fitness Club	SEE
Hotel	F&B – HOTEL – TT
Institutional Food-Service Operations	F&B – HOTEL
International Property	F&B – HOTEL – TT
Limited-Service Property	F&B – HOTEL
Museum	F&B – SEE – TT
Park	SEE – TT
Private Club	F&B – SEE
Railway	F&B – TT
Resort	F&B – HOTEL – TT
Restaurant	F&B
Spa	SEE
Specialty Resort	F&B – HOTEL – SEE
Sports Venue	SEE
Theater	SEE
Tourism Board	TT
Tour Operator/Wholesaler	TT
Transient Property	F&B – HOTEL
Travel Agency	TT
Zoo	F&B – SEE – TT

HOTEL = Lodging
F&B = Food and Beverage
TT = Travel and Tourism
SEE = Sports, Events, and Entertainment

Owning Your Own Hospitality Business

People who dream of owning their own businesses become entrepreneurs. An **entrepreneur** is a person who organizes, manages, and takes the risk of owning and operating a business. They trade a typical "nine-to-five" schedule for more control of personal time, decision-making freedom, and hopefully, a better quality of life. A business owner must follow his or her heart and also make smart choices along the way. Good financial models and practical marketing decisions can determine the success of any start-up or home-based business.

entrepreneur a person who organizes, manages, and takes the risk of owning and operating a business

Working Hours

Hard work is also necessary when starting a business. Instead of the standard eight-hour workday, business owners often work around the clock, performing different tasks, almost every day throughout the year. For example, restaurant owners and operators wear many hats and may do the jobs of several staff members—host, manager, server, and accountant.

Pros and Cons

Independent business ownership offers many advantages—and many potential pitfalls as well.

China: Touring the Past

Ever since Italian explorer Marco Polo returned to Italy from China in the 13th century, the world has been curious about this ancient land that gave us many firsts, including paper and noodles. Today's China welcomes millions of travelers.

To navigate this vast country's countless attractions, many tourists book tours. The first stop is usually the capital city of Beijing, home of the Forbidden City and the Temple of Heaven. Both of these sites recall China's imperial past. Another site to visit is Tianamen Square, where an infamous protest took place in 1989. At Dunhuang's Mogao Caves, 492 chambers are filled with ancient Buddhist art. At Xian, 7,500 clay warriors still stand, guarding the tomb of China's first emperor. China's most famous landmark is the Great Wall of China. This massive military structure snakes about 4,000 miles across the northern region of China. The late Mao Tse-Tung told followers, "You cannot be a great man (or woman) if you have not climbed the Great Wall of China." These days, greatness is only a cable-car lift away for visitors touring the Great Wall.

What could be some pros and cons of a tour-guide job in the travel industry today?

CHINA

◀ **YOUR OWN TERMS** Most entrepreneurs in hospitality and tourism are willing to trade long hours and effort for the satisfaction of owning and operating their own small businesses. *Besides time and effort, what else must entrepreneurs be willing to risk?*

ADVANTAGES Independent entrepreneurs can provide something unique and different in the marketplace. They can also be more flexible in rules and decision making. An entrepreneur's motivation and enthusiasm will probably attract business that larger more impersonal companies might not attract. Local community connections and involvement can promote additional revenue and marketing leads. Having good relationships with employees who stay for a length of time can save money through reduced turnover costs.

DISADVANTAGES On the other hand, owning a business is not always easy. Most owners work long hours. Unlike larger chains, independent businesses usually have no brand recognition. Independents do not have large-scale marketing and purchasing strength. Unless money is not an issue, access to initial funding can be challenging. In the area of technology, chains or franchises can afford to use centralized systems, which have a wealth of marketing, reservations, and security software that is difficult to duplicate.

Belief in Yourself

For those who prefer to earn money for themselves rather than for a corporate giant, owning a business may be the best decision. Many successful restaurant or bed-and-breakfast owners would never trade the private business lifestyle. If you believe in your ideas, yourself, and your ability to succeed, then owning your own business may be the best career choice for you.

QUESTION
What are some advantages of owning your own hospitality or tourism business?

Profiles in Hospitality

EXECUTIVE SEARCH

Harry R. Kellett
Executive Search Consultant
Hospitality Careers, U.S.A.

What is your job?
"I am an executive search consultant. I help hospitality companies find executives. Some call my job *headhunting*."

What do you do in your job?
"I find experienced people at the department-head level and in the corporate ranks. At the same time, I assist people with their careers and career paths. We make sure we are helping an individual find the best job for him or her to ensure the success of that individual's career."

What kind of training did you have?
"The basic concept of how to do the job correctly came from years of experience in the hotel industry managing staffs, getting training advice, and receiving company training."

What advice would you give students?
"If you want to be a recruiter, you must have patience, understanding, and compassion for human beings. Handling a search is more than just recruiting people into jobs. It is also about understanding the industry or industries you serve. Establishing credibility with employers and potential employees is critical. If an employer does not think you know something about his or her business, he or she will not have confidence that you can find the best candidate. The individual seeking employment needs to believe you have his or her best interests at heart."

What is your key to success?
"If you are standing still, you are actually falling behind. That is a watch phrase of mine that I keep in mind every day. Information doubles every 18 months. Do not stand still, or you will fall behind."

Why should a recruiter be knowledgeable about the specific industry for which he or she is recruiting?

Career Data: Executive Recruiter

Education and Training
Bachelor's degree or master's degree in marketing or business

Skills and Abilities
Interpersonal, creative, and organizational skills

Career Outlook Faster-than-average growth through 2012

Career Path Freelance for small agencies or internship at large firm to full-time recruiter to owner of recruiting agency

Endless Opportunities

career plan a written statement of career goals and the necessary steps to achieve them

There are numerous career opportunities in the hospitality and tourism industries. It is important to have a **career plan**, which is a written statement of career goals and the necessary steps to achieve them. A career plan maps out your goals and aspirations.

Proven Success in Hospitality

The names Marriott and Disney are known worldwide. However, the people who started these brands had humble beginnings. Here are a few examples of hospitality industry successes:

- J. Willard Marriott opened an A&W Root Beer stand in 1927. Today Marriott International is a $20 billion global corporation.

- Following a trip with his family in 1951, Kemmons Wilson opened a small, family-style hotel. Today Holiday Inns welcome traveling families all across the country.

- In 1923, Walter E. Disney and his brother invested $3,200 in a cartoon business. Today The Walt Disney Company is a multibillion dollar, diversified global business.

The hospitality industry is more than a mint on the pillow and nightly turn-down service. As an employer, it accounts for 200 million jobs in a broad range of fields, including sports management, casino management, and marketing.

Quick Check ✓

RESPOND to what you've read by answering these questions.

1. Why is your career choice one of the most important decisions you can make? _____

_____

_____

_____

_____

2. What are the duties of a food-and-beverage manager? _____

_____

_____

_____

_____

3. What are three possible food-and-beverage production positions? _____

_____

_____

_____

_____

_____

_____

Educational Resources

AS YOU READ ...

YOU WILL LEARN

- To identify the main types of educational resources.

WHY IT'S IMPORTANT

Researching additional educational offerings can assist you in finding training and education to suit your interests and advance your career in hospitality and tourism.

KEY TERMS

- certification
- professional/trade organization
- apprenticeship

PREDICT

What might be some sources of education for careers in hospitality and tourism?

Resources for Education and Training

Education and training can provide the foundation for success in any career area of hospitality and tourism. The main types of educational resources include colleges and universities, community colleges, specialty schools, certificate programs, apprenticeships, professional trade organizations, and cooperative education and internships.

Four-Year Degree Options

In the last 30 years, hospitality and tourism educational programs have developed and advanced, providing comprehensive and practical knowledge about these industries.

The following ranking of four-year bachelor's degree programs was developed by Stacy L. Gould and David C. Bojanic of the University of Massachusetts. This top-ten list was published in the *Journal of Hospitality & Tourism Education* in 2003.

1. **Purdue University**
   West Lafayette, Indiana
   Hotel and Lodging Management
   Restaurant and Foodservice Management
   Travel and Tourism Management

2. **University of Nevada**
   Las Vegas, Nevada
   Hotel and Lodging Management
   Leisure/Sports Management

3. **Cornell University**
   Ithaca, New York
   Hotel and Lodging Management

4. **Michigan State University**
   East Lansing, Michigan
   Hotel and Lodging Management
   Restaurant and Foodservice Management

5. **Pennsylvania State University**
   University Park, Pennsylvania
   Hotel and Lodging Management
   Restaurant and Foodservice Management

6. **Delaware University**
   Dover, Delaware
   Hotel and Lodging Management
   Travel and Tourism Management

7. **Johnson and Wales University**
   Providence, Rhode Island
   Hotel and Lodging Management
   Leisure/Sports Management
   Restaurant and Foodservice Management
   Travel and Tourism Management

8. **Florida International University**
   North Miami, Florida
   Hospitality Management
   Travel and Tourism Management

9. **University of Houston**
   Houston, Texas
   Hotel and Restaurant Management

10. **Washington State University**
    Pullman, Washington
    Hotel and Lodging Management
    Restaurant and Foodservice Management

Community College Options

Community colleges provide convenient and low-cost options for beginning your educational career. In addition, many community college two-year programs are affiliated with four-year colleges and universities and offer transfer programs. Some community college programs include:

- Hotel and Restaurant Management

- Travel and Tourism

- Culinary Technology Program

- Hospitality Systems Management Program

- Hospitality and Tourism Management

- Hotel, Restaurant, and Resort Management

- Travel Systems Operations

- Hospitality Management

- Chef Apprenticeship

- Dietetic Technician

- Food Service/Restaurant Management

TECH
NOTES

Long-Distance Learning
Imagine earning a college degree or certificate of specialization without setting foot on campus. Getting an education no longer requires you to always be in a classroom. Many colleges and universities offer distance-learning degree programs and online courses. Students take classes through the Internet, completing assignments as their schedules allow. They can also interact with instructors and students through e-mail, online chat rooms, or virtual bulletin boards.

➡️ Is distance learning right for you? Answer this question and explore distance-learning opportunities in hospitality and tourism through **marketingseries.glencoe.com**.

Math Check

TUITION COSTS
Tuition for chef school costs $25 per unit. The registration fee is $35 per quarter. How much does an eight-unit course cost?

➡️ For tips on finding the solution, go to **marketingseries.glencoe.com**.

Specialty School Options

certification an authorization
stating that one has fulfilled
the requirements for practicing
in a field or career

In addition to two- and four-year programs, there are many certification programs that require less time for completion. A **certification** is an authorization stating that one has fulfilled the requirements for practicing in a field or career. The following list includes some of the recognized hospitality and tourism industries designations and programs.

- **The American Hotel & Lodging Educational Institute**
  Certified Hotel Administrator (CHA)
  Certified Lodging Manager (CLM)
  Certified Lodging Security Director (CLSD)
  Certified Rooms Division Executive (CRDE)
  Certified Food and Beverage Executive (CFBE)
  Certified Hospitality Housekeeping Executive (CHHE)
  Certified Human Resources Executive (CHRE)
  Certified Engineering Operations Executive (CEOE)
  Certified Hospitality Sales Professional (CHSP)
  Certified Hospitality Department Trainer (CHDT)
  Certified Hospitality Supervisor (CHS)
  Certified Lodging Security Supervisor (CLSS)
  Certified Lodging Security Officer (CLSO)
  Master Hotel Supplier (MHS)
  Certified Hospitality Educator (CHE)

GETTING A GOOD START
Certification programs as well as degree programs can open the door to a satisfying and lucrative career in hospitality and tourism. *Do you think on-the-job training is more valuable than classroom education? Why?*

A Gourmet Education

While many college students study math, literature, and science, students at The Culinary Institute of America (CIA) concentrate on cuisines, restaurant management, and baking and pastry arts. The decades-old college has more than 2,300 students in its programs. The school also offers continuing education classes to professionals in the hospitality industry each year.

The CIA began as a storefront cooking school in 1946. Frances Roth and Katharine Angell ran the small New Haven Restaurant Institute as a vocational training institution for veterans of World War II. Over the years, the school grew and offered continuing education for professionals. As the school expanded, it needed more space—and a new name. In 1970, the CIA settled into a large complex in Hyde Park, New York. The new campus allowed for more facilities. Then in 1995,

the CIA opened a West Coast outpost in Napa, California.

DELICIOUS DEGREES

Because it is an accredited four-year college, students can graduate from the CIA with a bachelor's degree in culinary arts management or baking and pastry arts. Programs teach students hands-on cooking techniques, as well as business-management and marketing skills. Associate degree programs focus on food preparation techniques with an emphasis on nutrition, food safety, and menu design. Sampling the cooking is also part of the coursework—a good education never tasted so good!

1. What types of educational programs does The Culinary Institute of America offer students?
2. Would you rather study culinary arts, baking and pastry arts, or restaurant management? Why?

- **The National Restaurant Association Educational Institute**
  The ServSafe® Program

- **Meeting Professionals International**
  Certification in Meeting Management (CMM)
  Certified Meeting Professional (CMP)

- **American Society of Travel Agents**
  USA Travel Expert Program
  Family Travel Specialist
  Niche Travel Specialist
  Mature Adult Travel Specialist
  Travel Marketing Specialist
  North American Rail Travel Specialist

- **The Travel Institute**
  Certified Travel Associate (CTA)
  Certified Travel Counselor (CTC)

- **International Association of Assembly Managers**
  Certified Facilities Executive (CFE)

- **Cruise Lines International Association**
  Cruise Counselor Certification

CONNECT

Would you prefer to pursue a shorter-term certificate program instead of a bachelor's degree program if you could start work immediately? Why or why not?

Professional and Trade Organizations

professional/trade organization a group or association dedicated to a specific trade or profession

Each division in the hospitality and tourism industries has its own **professional/trade organization**, which is a group or association dedicated to a specific trade or profession. Most of these organizations or associations provide valuable resources to the particular industry and its members. Here is a partial listing of some organizations:

- American Camping Association (ACA)

- American Bed-and-Breakfast Association (ABBA)

- American Hotel and Motel Association

- American Resort Development Association (ARDA)

- American Society of Association Executives (ASAE)

- American Society of Travel Agents (ASTA)

- American Tour Association

- Association of Destination Management Executives (ADME)

- Club Managers Association of America (CMAA)

- Cruise Lines International Association (CLIA)

- CrossSphere—The Global Association for Packaged Travel

- Foodservice Consulting Society International

- Hotel and Catering International Management Association (HCIMA)

- International Association of Culinary Professionals

- International Association of Leisure and Entertainment Industry

- International Association of Assembly Managers

QUESTION

What are three trade organizations that specialize in hospitality?

Figure 16.2

Hospitality Myths and Facts

REALITY CHECK There are many myths regarding the hospitality and tourism job marketplace. Knowing the facts will give you a solid foundation for making your career choices. *Which myth did you believe was a fact before studying hospitality and tourism?*

 The hospitality industry is a dead-end career choice.

 It is the world's largest employer accounting for more than 200 million jobs. The projected annual job growth is 5.5 million jobs.

 There is no money to be made in the industry.

 The median salary as of 2003 for a general manager is $97,300; directors of sales and marketing earn $70,100; directors of revenue management earn $71,250.

 The industry is shrinking and businesses are consolidating.

 The industry is thriving and more dynamic due to this consolidation. Travel expenditures add up to $1,000,000 per minute.

On-the-Job Training

The hospitality and tourism industries rely on workers with practical hands-on experience and education. Many employers offer on-the-job training and apprenticeships. An **apprenticeship** is an educational, hands-on experience working in an established business under the guidance of a skilled worker. These programs may also be internships or cooperative educational experiences (co-ops). As with any job, there are pros and cons as well as myths and facts. (See **Figure 16.2**.) The following list identifies some companies that offer on-the-job learning experiences:

apprenticeship an educational, hands-on experience working in an established business under the guidance of a skilled worker

- **ARAMARK**
  Type of company: Food service
  Internship opportunities and management training programs are offered in all food-related businesses.

- **Association for International Practical Training**
  Type of company: Convention and meeting services
  AIPT programs are offered for individuals seeking work experience outside of the United States. The Americans Abroad Program is available for Americans participating in international training programs.

- **Hyatt Hotels Corporation**
  Type of company: Lodging
  Co-op and internship programs exist within the company. Corporate Management Training Programs are available for employees interested in a career within the Hyatt Corporation.

- **Marriott Corporation**
  Type of company: Lodging
  The company offers co-op/work experience and internship programs as well as a management training program.

- **Red Lobster**
  Type of company: Restaurant
  A ten-week paid internship program focuses on hands-on training. The Red Lobster Manager in Training Program is a 13-week comprehensive in-restaurant program. The program ends with a one-week classroom session at the company's Restaurant Support Center in Orlando, Florida. This program is recognized as one of the top-ten hospitality management programs in the United States.

- **Sodexho**
  Type of company: Food service
  The company offers internships and co-op programs for students. Management programs are also available.

- **U.S. Navy Morale, Welfare, and Recreation**
  Type of company: Recreation services
  MWR has a year-round international internship. The 12-week program consists of both domestic and international experience.

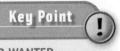

Key Point

HELP WANTED
With U.S. residents taking over one billion vacation and business trips per year, the travel/tourism industry is the nation's second-largest employer in the United States.

Job-Search Resources

Web sites for job-search information are good sources of information and job listings. Some sites include Adventures in Hospitality Careers, Cruise Ship, Hospitality Career Net, Hospitality Jobs Online, Resort Jobs, and many others. For a more complete list with links to Web sites for job searching as well as schools, associations, and on-the-job training programs, go to the student Web site at **marketingseries.glencoe.com**.

Not Just a Job

Whether you choose to pursue educational or job-training programs to start your own business or work your way up the corporate ladder, the world of hospitality and tourism offers many satisfying career choices in a variety of businesses. In these growing and exciting industries, hospitality and tourism professionals have flexibility, the opportunity for advancement, unlimited personal growth potential, and the chance to work with people locally, nationally, and internationally.

Quick Check ✓

RESPOND to what you've read by answering these questions.

1. What is ASTA? _____

_____

_____

_____

_____

2. What are two hotel corporations that offer management-training programs? _____

_____

_____

_____

_____

3. What organization would you contact for information on international cruise lines? _____

_____

_____

_____

_____

Worksheet 16.1

Entrepreneurial News

Choose an entrepreneur in the hospitality or tourism industry and write a news story about him or her. Your story should describe why the entrepreneur chose self-employment, the career path the person followed, and what the person sees as the pros and cons of owning a business in the hospitality or tourism business. Use the Internet for research or conduct an in-person interview with someone in your community. Title your story and, if possible, include a photo.

_____

_____

_____

_____

_____   (Photo)

_____

_____

_____

_____

_____

_____

_____

_____

_____

_____

_____

Name _____ Date _____

Worksheet 16.2

Researching Hospitality & Tourism Education

Contact three educational institutions that offer degrees or certificates in an area of hospitality or tourism. Then fill in the information for each institution.

Area of Specialization: _____

_____

_____

School #1:

1. Name of school: _____

2. Observations: _____

_____

_____

_____

3. This is/is not a good choice for me because: _____

_____

School #2:

1. Name of school: _____

2. Observations: _____

_____

_____

_____

3. This is/is not a good choice for me because: _____

_____

School #3:

1. Name of school: _____

2. Observations: _____

_____

_____

_____

3. This is/is not a good choice for me because: _____

_____

Portfolio Works

ORGANIZE A CAREER PATH

Choose one of the sample career paths in this chapter. Think about how this career path might work in your life. Use the space below to make a graphic organizer of each step. Include details about the requirements of the job with each step, the attributes you would bring to each of the steps, and the areas in which you will need more training or improvement.

Add this page to your career portfolio.

CHAPTER SUMMARY

Section 16.1 Career Choices

entry-level (p. 324)
operations (p. 325)
entrepreneur (p. 330)
career plan (p. 332)

- The hospitality and tourism industries are the largest employers in the world. A variety of exciting career opportunities exist at all levels, including entry-level. Opportunities range from front-line, entry-level service positions to upper-level managers and owners.

- Career segments include: food and beverage; lodging; travel/tourism; and sports, entertainment, and events.

- Some possible career paths include those for hotel rooms division, food-and-beverage division, tour operations, and box-office careers.

- Advantages of owning a hospitality business include: providing something unique and different in the marketplace, having more flexibility in rules and decision making, and attracting business that larger more impersonal companies might not attract. Independent owners may retain employees through good relationships. Disadvantages include long hours, no brand recognition, no large-scale marketing and purchasing strength, funding challenges, and no centralized technology systems.

Section 16.2 Educational Resources

certification (p. 336)
professional/trade
   organization (p. 338)
apprenticeship (p. 339)

- The main types of education resources for learning about hospitality and tourism are colleges and universities, community colleges, specialty schools, certificate programs, apprenticeships, professional trade organizations, and cooperative education and internships.

CHECKING CONCEPTS

1. **List** two advantages of working in hospitality and tourism.
2. **Identify** the career segments in the hospitality and tourism industries.
3. **Name** the career segments in the lodging industry.
4. **Describe** a career path for the rooms division.
5. **Describe** a career path for tour operations.
6. **Define** the term *entrepreneur*.
7. **Identify** three disadvantages of owning a small hospitality business.

Critical Thinking

8. **Explain** why someone might pursue a four-year degree instead of other education options for hospitality and tourism.

CROSS-CURRICULUM SKILLS

Work-Based Learning

Interpersonal Skills—Participating as a Team Member

9. Form four groups—food and beverage; lodging; travel/tourism; or sports, events, and entertainment. Each group is to present a multimedia presentation that describes its segment.

Personal Qualities—Self-Management

10. Think about the job that you might want to pursue. Make a list of the steps you will need to take to obtain the position.

School-Based Learning

Writing

11. Use the Internet to research corporate management training programs for employees interested in a career within the Hyatt Corporation. Write a letter to explain why you are a good candidate.

Computer Technology

12. Access online one of the schools listed in the text. Write a fact sheet of the courses and requirements for admission.

Role Play: Cruise-Line Recruiter

SITUATION You are to assume the role of recruiter for a cruise-ship line. The human resource manager (judge) has been asked to make a presentation to a community group about the cruise industry and careers in the cruise industry. The human resource manager (judge) is your boss and has asked you to outline some ideas for the presentation.

ACTIVITY You are to review your ideas for the presentation with the human resource manager (judge) in 30 minutes.

EVALUATION You will be evaluated on how well you meet the following performance indicators:

- Explain employment opportunities in the travel and tourism industries.
- Describe traits important to the success of employees in the travel and tourism industries.
- Identify skills needed to enhance career progression.
- Describe techniques for obtaining work experience, such as volunteer activities and internships.
- Identify sources of career information.

INTERNET ACTIVITY

Use the Internet to access *Hospitality Upgrade* magazine.

- Click one of the news stories.
- Write a summary of the story.
- Send the summary in an e-mail attachment to your teacher.

➡ For a link to *Hospitality Upgrade* to do this activity, go to **marketingseries.glencoe.com**.

START YOUR ROCKETS

Hoping to promote transatlantic tourism, French-born New York hotelier Raymond Orteig in 1919 pledged a prize of $25,000—worth about $750,000 today—for the first nonstop flight between New York and France. In the 1920s, nine teams scrambled to try to win that prize. Then Charles A. Lindbergh piloted the Spirit of St. Louis across the Atlantic in May 1927, and commercial airlines followed.

About ten years ago, entrepreneur Peter H. Diamandis figured a prize might have the same effect on manned space travel. So he set up the X Prize Foundation and coaxed wealthy contributors to offer a purse of $10 million to the first privately funded, three-person spacecraft to fly into suborbital space twice within a two-week period. On June 21, the world witnessed the lead contender, SpaceShipOne, designed by aeronautics engineer Elbert L. "Burt" Rutan with backing from billionaire Paul G. Allen, soar up 62 miles to the edge of the earth's atmosphere.

Stiff Competition

Two other X Prize contenders suffered minor setbacks with tests of unmanned rockets. On August 8, the Rubicon, built by Space Transport Corp. in Forks, Washington, dove into the Pacific Ocean. A day earlier the Black Armadillo rocket, developed by Armadillo Aerospace, climbed to only 600 feet before crashing back to earth.

Space Tourists

Now that Rutan and Allen have shown that suborbital hops are possible, the roadblock to space tourism isn't technology. It's politics. Contender Carmack notes, "There is no commercial spaceport in the U.S. licensed for vertical rocket launches from ground level." Until Congress enacts legislation for launches, his only alternative would be to pay nearly $200,000 per launch. That would drastically hike ticket prices.

Before Rutan's feat, says Sheerin of Canadian Arrow, "If you suggested building a space-tourist vehicle, you couldn't find the capital." But since June 21, there has been a sea of change:

"The business community is now starting to look hard at suborbital tourism."

That is just the result that Diamandis envisioned. Hooked on space since he watched Apollo 11 land on the moon in 1969 at age 9, he earned an M.D. in hopes that the credential would help get him on missions as an astronaut. He gave up when he realized "the government wasn't going to get us into space routinely," he recalls. For that, he says, "We need a mass market."

By Otis Port in New York

CREATIVE JOURNAL

In your journal, write your responses.

CRITICAL THINKING

1. Why did Diamandis set up the contest for private space flights?

APPLICATION

2. If you were starting up one of the first space-travel airlines, what staff would you need and what would be the destinations, special features offered, and promotional plan?

 Go to **businessweek.com** for current *BusinessWeek* Online articles.

UNIT LAB

The Inn Place

Y ou've just entered the real world of hospitality and travel and tourism. The Inn Place owns and operates a number of hospitality and tourism businesses, offering the finest accommodations and most desirable destinations in the world. Acting as the owner, manager, or employee of this diverse company, you will have the opportunity to work on different projects to promote the business.

Publishing Tourism—Advertise Jobs

SITUATION You are an employee for the *Travel and Tourism Weekly*. It is a weekly newsletter for travel and tourism professionals prepared by The Inn Place in association with a tourism trade association. The newsletter is published as a membership service of the association. You work in the "help wanted" department. You help subscribers who want to place ads to find new employees. Part of your job is to list the qualifications and the work experience required for each job that you list in your newsletter. Most employers who list have only general ideas of the qualifications and experience requirements a candidate should have for a particular job opening.

ASSIGNMENT Complete these tasks:
- Determine the qualifications and work experience necessary for at least three jobs in the travel and tourism industry.
- Determine the average starting salary for each job you select.
- Make a report to the editor of the newsletter.

TOOLS AND RESOURCES To complete the assignment, you will need to:
- Conduct research at the library, on the Internet, or by talking to local travel and tourism professionals.
- Ask a travel and tourism professional about current job availability and salary ranges.
- Have word-processing, spreadsheet, and presentation software.

RESEARCH Do your research:
- Research the availability of the jobs you are studying in your local area. Also research the availability of those jobs in the nearest large city and nationally.
- Determine local salaries for the jobs you select.
- Determine how salaries in your local area compare to the national average for the same position.

REPORT Prepare a written report using the following tools:
- *Word-processing program:* Prepare a written report about the availability of the jobs that you are studying in your local area, in the nearest large city, and nationally.
- *Spreadsheet program:* Prepare a chart comparing the availability of the positions and their salaries locally and nationally.
- *Presentation program:* Prepare a ten-slide visual presentation with key points, photos of work settings, and descriptive text.

PRESENTATION AND EVALUATION You will present your report to the newsletter editor. You will be evaluated on the basis of:
- Your knowledge of the jobs you selected
- Continuity of presentation
- Voice quality
- Eye contact

PORTFOLIO
Add this report to your career portfolio.

Glossary

advertising any paid promotion of an idea, good, or service by an identified sponsor (p. 260)

aesthetic pollution the spoiling or contamination of the natural beauty and features of an environment, due to poor planning and design of tourism projects (p. 31)

AIDA model a framework for creating an advertising message that gets **A**ttention, holds **I**nterest, stimulates **D**esire, and achieves **A**ction (p. 264)

amateur sports athletic activities and competitions for athletes who do not get paid (p. 139)

Amtrak a company that operates a railroad system with combined passenger and rail service throughout the continental United States (p. 106)

apprenticeship an educational, hands-on experience working in an established business under the guidance of a skilled worker (p. 339)

average daily rate (ADR) a rate based on total sales for the day divided by the total number of sold rooms (p. 76)

back of the house the area in a hospitality establishment that guests usually do not view, including all areas responsible for food quality and production, such as the kitchen and receiving, office, and storage areas (p. 59)

back of the house (lodging) the area in a lodging facility where support services take place, which guests usually do not view (p. 81)

bed-and-breakfasts (B&Bs) small unique inns that offer a full breakfast with a night's stay (p. 6)

behavioristics statistics about consumers based on their knowledge, attitudes, use, or response to a product (p. 189)

benefit a feature advantage of a product (p. 247)

business travel travel for the sole purpose of conducting an individual's or company's business (p. 34)

business-to-business selling the type of selling whereby one business sells goods or services to another business (p. 242)

buying signals verbal or nonverbal signs of a customer's readiness to buy (p. 244)

career plan a written statement of career goals and the necessary steps to achieve them (p. 332)

certification an authorization stating that one has fulfilled the requirements for practicing in a field or career (p. 336)

chain a type of business that has more than one location with the same name under the same ownership (p. 54)

changeability a condition of being subject to change or alteration (p. 9)

channel of distribution the path a travel product takes from the producer to the consumer, or traveler (p. 128)

charter tour a tour in which a tour operator buys all the seats on an airplane, train, or bus and resells them to travelers (p. 99)

commercial recreation any recreational activity for which a guest pays a fee (p. 145)

commercial site an establishment, such as a restaurant, where a food-and-beverage business competes for customers (p. 50)

commission a fee or payment for services based on a percentage of products sold (p. 127)

compensation a form of payment that may include wages, benefits, and/or incentives in return for work (p. 291)

competitive advantage an advantage over competitors due to greater value to consumers through lower prices or more benefits (p. 191)

concierge a hotel staff member who helps guests make arrangements for transportation, restaurant reservations, event reservations, and entertainment tickets, and advises guests about activities in the area (p. 85)

consolidator an agent who buys unsold products in bulk from suppliers and then resells the products at a discount to intermediaries or to consumers (p. 250)

consumer show a single- or multi-day exhibition held at a convention or civic center arena (p. 149)

convention and visitors bureau (CVB) an organization that works with meeting planners to provide tourist information services to business and leisure travelers (p. 129)

core product the main product that the customer is buying (p. 207)

cost-plus pricing pricing products by calculating all costs and expenses and adding desired profit (p. 226)

cross-selling the method of selling the customer additional related products tied to one name (p. 245)

customer loyalty the customer's faithfulness to a business and its product, demonstrated by the customer purchasing the product again (p. 214)

customer satisfaction a positive feeling or reaction customers have when a business or product meets their needs (p. 212)

customized tour a tour that is more expensive than a package tour and is designed specifically for an individual tourist (p. 99)

demand the amount or quantity of goods and services that consumers are willing to buy at various prices (p. 230)

demographics statistics that describe a population in terms of personal characteristics, such as age, gender, income, ethnicity, or education (p. 175)

dependables travelers who prefer familiarity and creature comforts and seldom try anything new or different (p. 32)

destination marketing the process of developing, promoting, and distributing specific locations to satisfy travelers and maintain appeal as long as possible (p. 118)

destination resort a resort property in a specific location with a concentration of resources or facilities (p. 120)

destination the final stop of a journey, or the goal for travelers (p. 118)

direct channel the path a product takes without the help of any intermediaries between the producer and consumer (p. 248)

direct mail any advertising message sent directly to customers via the mail (p. 261)

disposable income the money left from a person's gross income after taking out taxes (p. 96)

distribution the process of getting the product to the consumer (p. 166)

Glossary

diversity ethnic variety as well as socioeconomic and gender variety in a group or society (p. 15)

economic multiplier the process of how money filters through a local economy and is spent and re-spent, creating income for other businesses (p. 26)

ecotourism a branch of tourism encompassing adventure tourism and sustainable development of regions for future generations (p. 15)

elasticity of demand the variation of consumer demand due to a change in price (p. 230)

empowerment the granting of authority or power to front-line personnel for handling and solving guests' problems (p. 289)

entrepreneur a person who organizes, manages, and takes the risk of owning and operating a business (p. 330)

entry-level the position of an employee at the beginning level of a particular career (p. 324)

e-tail the sale of goods or services to the customer by means of the Internet (p. 250)

ethics an expression of the standards of right and wrong based on conduct and morals in a particular society or a system or theory of moral values and principles (p. 295)

exemplary guest service consistent hospitality service that exceeds guest expectations (p. 284)

experimental method a research method whereby a researcher observes the results of changing one or more marketing variables (p. 195)

facilitating products goods or services that aid the use of the core product (p. 207)

feature a basic, physical, or extended attribute of a product or purchase (p. 247)

follow-up a phone call or thank-you note from the interviewee to the interviewer after the interview takes place (p. 316)

franchise a type of business that is set up through a franchise agreement, which is a contract between a franchisor and franchisee to sell a company's goods or services at a designated location (p. 54)

frequent-flyer program a program in which an airline offers free travel, upgrades, and discounts to program members (p. 103)

front of the house the area in a hospitality establishment that guests view, such as the entrance and the dining room (p. 59)

front of the house (lodging) the area in a lodging facility that guests view, such as the lobby (p. 81)

full-service restaurant a restaurant where a customer sits at a table, gives an order to a server, and is served food at the table (p. 51)

geographics statistics about where people live (p. 188)

globalization the increasing integration of the world economy (p. 28)

goal the eventual desired outcome (p. 176)

guest or uniformed services staff members in uniforms, including the bell staff, valets, security officers, concierge, and door or garage attendants (p. 84)

Glossary

guest satisfaction the fulfillment of guests' needs and wants regarding receiving quality hospitality products (p. 286)

guest service agent (GSA) a hotel staff member who performs all of the functions of a desk clerk/agent, concierge, and valet (p. 82)

hallmark event a local or regional event with national or possible international appeal that occurs once or annually (p. 147)

hospitality industry a group of businesses composed of establishments related to lodging and food-service management (p. 6)

hospitality-specific traits professional characteristics needed in the hospitality industry, including a positive personal attitude, good work ethics, maturity, and good personal appearance, as well as leadership and time-management skills (p. 308)

hub-and-spoke system an effective network for an airline formed by a hub, or a large airport, connected to other smaller airports called spokes (p. 103)

incentive a reward that is usually in the form of money but may be stock options, profit-sharing privileges, a company vehicle, and/or a bonus program (p. 291)

indirect channel the path a product takes using intermediaries between the producer and consumer (p. 248)

informational interview a formal or informal interview with a professional to help the job seeker learn more about a specific career field or company (p. 314)

infrastructure the physical components of a destination, such as hotels, restaurants, roadways, and transportation, that support tourism (p. 26)

institutional advertising advertising with a goal of developing goodwill or a positive image (p. 261)

intangibility a state of being abstract, as are things that cannot be touched (p. 8)

intermediary an agent who does not work directly for a travel provider but sells his or her products for a fee (p. 127)

job application a document that job seekers fill out to help employers screen applicants (p. 313)

leadership the ability to influence others to work toward the goals of an organization or group (p. 294)

leakage tourist dollars spent on imported goods so that revenue ends up in foreign economies (p. 26)

leisure travel travel for the sole purpose of enjoyment (p. 36)

loyal customer a returning customer or guest who refers friends, family, and colleagues to an establishment (p. 286)

market research the systematic gathering, recording, analyzing, and presentation of information related to marketing goods and services (p. 192)

market segmentation a way of analyzing a market by specific characteristics to create a target market (p. 186)

market segments groups of consumers categorized by specific characteristics to create a target market (p. 15)

marketing concept the idea that an organization needs to satisfy its customers while also trying to reach its organization's goals (p. 167)

Glossary

marketing environment the internal and external factors that influence marketing decisions and the ability of the marketing plan to reach its goal (p. 172)

marketing mix a combination of four basic marketing strategies, known as the four Ps—product, price, place, and promotion (p. 167)

marketing plan a written document that provides direction for the marketing activities of a company for a specific period of time (p. 171)

marketing the process of developing, promoting, and distributing products, or goods and services, to satisfy customers' needs and wants (p. 166)

markup the difference between the retail or wholesale price and the cost of an item (p. 226)

Maslow's hierarchy of needs a theory that explains what motivates people to act in certain ways or make certain decisions (p. 37)

meal plan a room rate that includes meals; some choices of meal plans are European Plan, Continental Plan, Bermuda Plan, Modified American Plan, and American Plan (p. 76)

meeting and incentive travel business travel by employees to attend a business meeting or as a reward for having met or exceeded company goals (p. 35)

meeting planner a person who organizes and plans a meeting (p. 35)

mega-event the largest type of event, which is a unique, "must-see" happening that has international appeal (p. 147)

mission a business's purpose or goal (p. 171)

motivation the force that moves a person to action (p. 293)

niche market a new market in tourism that bases travel on specific interests, such as ecotourism (p. 97)

night auditor the hotel staff member who does the night audit and balances the guests' accounts each evening (p. 82)

nonverbal communication the process of giving and receiving messages without words, via eye contact, hand gestures, and body posture (p. 307)

objectives the steps that lead to the goal (p. 176)

observation method a research method that involves watching people and recording their actions by audio, visuals, or writing (p. 195)

occupancy percentage (OCC%) a percentage calculated daily and based on the number of rooms sold as a percentage of the total number of available rooms (p. 76)

on-site facility an institutional or noncommercial establishment, such as a hospital or corporation, that provides meals for people involved with the property (p. 50)

operations the functions of a business that focus on the daily procedures necessary to maintain a business or establishment (p. 325)

package tour a prearranged tour that offers value, guaranteed sightseeing, and a quality product (p. 99)

Paralympics competitions in which the world's best athletes with physical disabilities showcase their talents (p. 140)

Glossary

performing arts a segment of the entertainment industry that includes the exhibition of live presentations by artists, such as actors in theaters or performance artists in other venues (p. 154)

perishability the probability of a product ceasing to exist or becoming unusable within a limited amount of time (p. 8)

personal selling the type of selling that involves direct interaction between sales associates and customers (p. 242)

portfolio a collection of work samples designed to highlight strengths, skills, and competencies (p. 312)

positioning the creation of an image for a product in the minds of customers, specifically in relation to competitive products, including services (p. 190)

press release a newsworthy article that provides the basic information to answer questions such as who, what, where, when, and why (p. 267)

prestige pricing pricing based on consumer perception (p. 225)

price the value placed on goods or services being exchanged (p. 224)

primary research original research conducted for a specific marketing situation (p. 194)

product life cycle the various stages that a product goes through during its existence, from development, introduction, growth, and maturity to decline (p. 211)

product mix the total assortment of products that a company makes or sells (p. 209)

production an assembly-line process by which food is prepared, plated, and expedited by teams at various food stations, such as salad, cooking line, prep, and dessert (p. 61)

products goods and services that have monetary value (p. 206)

professional/trade organization a group or association dedicated to a specific trade or profession (p. 338)

promotion any form of communication used to persuade people to buy products (p. 260)

promotional advertising advertising with a goal of selling an item being promoted (p. 261)

promotional mix any combination of advertising, sales promotion, public relations and publicity, and personal selling (p. 260)

psychographics studies of consumers based on social and psychological characteristics, such as attitudes, interests, and opinions (p. 187)

public recreation free or paid recreation that takes place on state and federal lands and in city, state, or national parks (p. 145)

public relations any activity designed to create a favorable image of a business, its products, or its policies (p. 267)

publicity a type of public relations that involves the free mention of a product or company in the media (p. 267)

quick-service restaurant (QSR) a restaurant offering speedy basic services, convenience, and consistent quality at low prices (p. 52)

relationship marketing building relationships with customers by adding value to the interaction that will lead to long-term customer satisfaction and retention (p. 215)

Glossary

resort a destination that provides entertainment, recreation, leisure activities, accommodations, and food for guests (p. 120)

résumé a brief summary of a job seeker's personal information, skills, work experience, education, activities, and interests (p. 313)

return on investment (ROI) a calculation used to determine the ability of a product to generate profits (p. 64)

revenue per available room (revPAR) a rate that reflects a hotel's revenue per available room (p. 76)

sample a number of people who are representative of a study's population (p. 197)

seasonality the concept that certain destinations appeal to travelers at certain times of the year, based on climate and geography (p. 118)

secondary research published data that have been collected for some other purpose (p. 193)

selling up offering a more expensive or upgraded version of the original recommendation (p. 245)

service an intangible thing that is a task performed for customers by a business (p. 7)

supply the amount or quantity of goods and services that producers provide at various prices (p. 230)

supporting products extra goods or services that accompany the core product to add value or to differentiate it from the competition (p. 208)

survey method a research method that involves gathering information from people through the use of surveys or questionnaires (p. 195)

sustainable tourism tourism that allows a destination to support both local residents and tourists without compromising future generations (p. 28)

target market a specific group of consumers that an organization selects as the focus of its marketing plan (p. 167)

therapeutic recreation any recreation that includes activities to help a person's emotional, mental, or physical health (p. 146)

time management the ability to plan, track, and accomplish tasks efficiently within a designated period of time (p. 309)

tour operator an intermediary who negotiates special rates and blocks space with transportation services, cruise lines, and hotels, and packages multiple components of a vacation for resale to the public or another intermediary (p. 250)

tourism industry a group of businesses that encompass travel/transportation vendors for air, rail, auto, cruise, and motor-coach travel, and promote travel, and vacations (p. 6)

transient guest an individual traveler with a reservation, staying in a hospitality property for a maximum of 30 consecutive days (p. 75)

utility the concept of conveying the value of products through appropriate and convenient placement, adequate information, and easy exchange (p. 169)

variables factors that can cause something to change or vary (p. 8)

venturers travelers who tend to be the first to discover a new, unspoiled destination (p. 32)

VFR travel travel for the purpose of visiting friends or relatives (p. 36)

windjammer a sailing ship that offers passengers the opportunity to sail privately and work with a crew (p. 108)

work ethic a belief in work as a moral good, demonstrated by a willingness to perform to the best of one's abilities (p. 308)

yield management a system of maximizing revenue through adjusting room rates according to demand (p. 76)

Index

A

Abercrombie & Kent tours (Africa), 31
Aberdare National Park (Kenya), 80
Accessibility, 97. *See also* Disabilities, people with
Accounting, as hospitality career, 325
Achievement-oriented style of leadership, 293
Across Asia on the Cheap (Wheeler and Wheeler), 310
Adventure travel, 97
Advertising, 260–264
Aesthetic pollution, 31
Affordable method, of advertising budgeting, 265
Afghanistan, 212
Agritourism, 98
AIDA model of promotional messages, 264
Air Carrier Access Act (ACAA) of 1986, 246
Airline Deregulation Act of 1978, 102
Air route traffic control center, 104
Air traffic control, 104
Air travel, 13
    discounts on, 227
    food services for, 58
    history of, 102–105
    hotels and, 77
    low-cost airlines and, 97, 231
    technology and, 18
All-suite hotels, 78
Amenities, 75, 109
American Automobile Association (AAA), 122
American Hotel and Lodging Association (AH&LA), 129
American meal plans, of hotels, 76
American Orient Express trains, 106
Amtrak rail transportation, 106–107
Amundsen, Roald, 178
Amusement Business magazine, 143
Amusement parks, 122–123
Anderson, Lloyd, 95
Anderson, Mary, 95
Angell, Katharine, 337
Anshutz, Philip, 137, 149
Antarctica, 178
Applications, job, 313

Apprenticeship, in hospitality careers, 339
Approach, in selling, 243
Aramark Corp., 143, 339
Argentina, 264
Arison, Micky, 108
Arison, Ted, 108
Assistant manager, of restaurants, 60
Association for International Practical Training, 339
Athletic directors, in college sports, 143
Attendants, in hotels, 87
Australia, 229
Automobile transportation, 106, 207
Avellar, Al, 25
Average daily rate (ADR), of hotels, 76

B

Baby boomers, 96
Background checks, 308
Back-of-the-house operations, 61–63, 81
Baker, in restaurants, 62
Balance sheets, for restaurants, 66
Ballantines movie colony, 87
Ballantines Original Hotel, 73, 87
Banner ads, on Web sites, 263
Banquet facilities, 55
Bartenders, of restaurants, 60
Beaches Resorts, 272
Bed-and-breakfasts (B&Bs), 6, 79
Behavioristics, 189
Behavior on vacation, 195
Bellagio resort, Las Vegas, 122
Bell staff, in hotels, 84
Benchmark, in pricing, 226
Benefits, features and, 247
Berkowitz, Wayne, 241, 247
Bermuda, 18
Bermuda meal plans, of hotels, 76
Better World Club (BWC), 165, 177
Billette, Cynthia, 100
Black America West Museum, 185, 197
Block, Ann, 124
Blue Moon Burgers, 64
Blue Water Excursions, 16
Bora Bora, French Polynesia, 28
Boston Blues Festival, 176
Boutique hotels, 79, 205, 215

Branding, 190
Branson, Richard, 103
Breakeven pricing, 226
Brewer, Josh, 323, 327
Bribery, 140
Broadcast media, 143, 262–263
Brown, Clara, 185
Budget hotels, 75
Budgeting for promotion, 265–266
Bumping, in air travel, 104
Bundle pricing, 228
Business etiquette, 98
Business-to-business selling, 242
Business travel, 34–36, 74
Bussers, of restaurants, 60
Bus transportation, 107
Buying signals, 244

C

Campus recreation, 146
Careers in hospitality, 322–345
    choosing, 324
    community college programs for, 335–336
    examples of, 333
    food-and-beverage segment in, 324–325
    four-year degrees for, 334–335
    lodging segment in, 325–326
    on-the-job training for, 339
    paths in, 328–329
    professional and trade organizations in, 338
    resources for, 340
    self-employment in, 330–332
    specialty school programs for, 337
    sports, entertainment, and events segment in, 327–329
    travel and tourism segment in, 326–327
    See also Jobs in hospitality; Profiles in Hospitality
Carnival Cruise Lines, 108, 120
Car rental agencies, 106, 207
Cashiers, of restaurants, 60
Casual dining restaurants, 51
Catering facilities, 50, 55
Cell phones, 175
Centralized reservation system (CRS), 82
Certification programs in hospitality, 335–336

Chain restaurants, 50, 54
Changeability, 9
Channels of distribution, 128, 166, 248, 327. *See also* Distribution
Charters, 99, 104, 107
Chefs, 62
Chianis, Alexia, 323, 327
China, People's Republic of, 130, 330
Choi, Terri, 49
Cirillo, Ellen, 292
Closed-ended questions, in market research, 197
Closing manager, of restaurants, 60
Closing sales, 243, 245
Code of ethics, Society of Professional Journalists, 269
Colleges, food services for, 56
Collette, Jack, 208
Collette Vacations, 208
Columbia Crossroads tour agency, 100
Commercial recreation, 145
Commercial sites, restaurant, 50–53
Commission payments, 127, 249
Communication services, in hotels, 85. *See also* Internet
Communication skills, 305–307
Community college programs, in hospitality, 335–336
Compensation, of employees, 291
Competition
    airline, 102
    destination, 32, 119
    as external marketing factor, 174
    positioning and, 190
    pricing and, 230
    restaurant, 303
Competitive advantage, 191
Competitive-parity method, of advertising budgeting, 266
Complaints, 288
Conca, Sue, 233
Concierge services, 77, 85
Condé Nast Traveler magazine, 73, 122
Conducted tours, 13
Conference centers, 77
Conflicts of interest, 295
Connections, in air travel, 104
Consolidator, as travel intermediary, 250
Consumer confidence, 175

Contests, as sales promotion, 271
Continental meal plans, of hotels, 76
Convenience stores, 58
Convenience trends, 15
Convention and visitors bureaus, 129
Conversion of currency, 214
Cook, Thomas, 12–13
Coral reefs, 30
Core product, 207
Corporate hotel guests, 75
Correctional facilities, food services for, 58
Cost-based pricing, 226
Cost-plus pricing, 226
Costs, in restaurants, 65–66. *See also* Pricing
Counting hits, on Web, 263
Coupons, as sales promotion, 271
Credit checks, 308
Crisis management, 269
Cross-selling, 245
Cruise Line International Association (CLIA), 129
Cruises, 108–110
    Carnival Lines, 108, 120
    description of, 207
    destination marketing of, 120–121
    disabled people and, 97
    discounts on, 215, 227
    Princess Lines, 283, 295
    technology and, 18
Culinary Institute of America, 337
Culture, tourism and, 28–29, 167
Currency conversion, 214
Customers
    employee empowerment and, 289
    feedback from, 287–288
    loyalty of, 213, 286
    relationship marketing and, 215
    retention of, 216, 287
    satisfaction of, 212–213, 286
    service and, 284–286
    See also Selling
Custom tours, 99, 124

D

Dalai Lama (Tibet), 130
Dangerous destinations, 212, 288
Darden, Bill, 54

Demand and supply, 230
Demographics, 175, 186
Denied boarding, in air travel, 104
DeNiro, Robert, 117
Denver Nuggets basketball team, 137
Dependables, travelers as, 32, 37
Designing products, 204–221
    customer loyalty in, 213
    customer satisfaction in, 212–213
    goods *versus* services in, 206
    life cycle in, 211–212
    product levels in, 207–208
    product mix in, 209–210
    product types in, 207
    relationship marketing and, 214–215
Destination marketing, 116–135
    of amusement parks, 122–123
    convention and visitors bureaus and, 129
    of cruises, 120–121
    definition of, 118
    of gaming facilities, 123–124
    of museums and historical sites, 125
    of national parks, 125
    of resorts, 120
    seasonality and, 118–119
    of shopping facilities, 124–125
    of sports, recreation, and entertainment, 121–122
    tour operators and, 128
    trade and government organizations and, 129–130
    travel agencies and, 127
Direct distribution, 243, 248
Direct flights, in air travel, 104
Direct mail, 261
Disabilities, people with, 36, 96–97, 246
Discounts, 75, 227
Discrimination, price, 228
Disney, Walt, 8, 333
Disposable income, 96
Distance learning, in hospitality programs, 335
Distribution, 128, 166, 240–257
    careers in, 327
    channels of, 248
    features and benefits in, 247
    intermediaries in, 248–250

Index

Internet channels of, 250–251
sales-and-service link in, 246
selling in, 242–246, 252
Diversity trends, 15
Dolphin Fleet, 25, 37
Do-not-call lists, 242
Downtown hotels, 77
Dr. Justina Ford House, 197
Dual-family income, 96
Dubai, 213
Dynamic Currency Conversion (DCC), 214

Eames, Charles, 73
Eames, Ray, 73
East of Chicago Pizza, 285
Economic multiplier, process of, 26–27
Economics
business travel and, 34–36
consumer confidence and, 175
employment and, 27
environmental impacts and, 30–32
globalization and, 28
multiplier effect of, 26–27
pleasure travel and, 36
pricing and, 231
social and cultural impacts and, 28–29
tourism impact on, 98
travel cycles and, 32–33
travel motivation and, 37–38
Ecotourism, 15, 98, 174
Effectiveness, 309
Efficiency, 309
Elasticity of demand, 230
El Bulli restaurant (Spain), 51
Electronic Channel feature
business etiquette, 98
Carnival Cruise Lines Web site, 120
fraud, 325
Hotels.com, 82
Hotwire.com, 226
Internet job services, 311
Lastminute.com, 168
online travel magazines, 261
Priceline.com, 226
purchasing travel online, 35
restaurant suppliers online, 65

Scheduling Manager program, 291
sports travel, 139
tracking travel purchases, 251
travel profiles, 189
travel Web sites, 11
wireless Internet access, 208
E-mail, 250, 263
Employees, 290–296
company reputation and, 291
compensation of, 291
customer loyalty and, 214
entry-level, 324
leadership and, 294–296
motivation of, 293
professional development of, 291
retention of, 290
valuing, 296
Employment, in tourism, 27. *See also* Careers in hospitality; Employees; Jobs in hospitality; Profiles in Hospitality
Empowerment of employees, 289
Engineers, in hotels, 87
Entertainment, 6
careers in, 327–330
destinations for, 121–122
movies, 152
musical, 151–152
performing arts, 154
radio, 153
television, 152
See also Cruises
Entrepreneurs, in hospitality, 330–331
Entry-level job opportunities, 324
Environmental analysis, in marketing, 172–175, 231
Environmental impacts of tourism, 30–32
EPCOT, 8
Equal Employment Opportunity Act (EEOA), 295
Escoffier, Auguste, 12–13
Escorted tours, 99, 101
E-tail (electronic retail), 250
Ethics and Issues feature
accessibility, 97
bribery, 140
coral reefs, 30
credit checks, 308
disabilities, 246

ecotourism, 174
fake promotional photos, 18
leadership, 295
overtime work, 326
price discrimination, 228
reality restaurant (NBC-TV), 53
risky destinations, 212
tainted travel, 269
Tibet travel, 130
travel alerts, 288
vacation behavior, 195
Ethiopian Airlines, 291
Etiquette, business, 98
European meal plans, of hotels, 76
Events, 6
careers in, 150, 327–330
destinations for, 121–122
private, 150
public, 147–149, 271
Exchange rates, 214
Executive chefs, 62
Executive perks, 296
Exemplary guest services, 284
Expectations, customer, 212, 213
Expedia.com, 189, 227
Expediter, in restaurants, 63
Experimental method, in market research, 195
Explorations, historical, 12
Extended-stay residences, 57, 78

Face-to-face contact, for job research, 311
Facilitating products, 207
Fairmont Hotels, 305
Fast-food restaurants, 52
Features and benefits, in selling, 247
Federal Aviation Act of 1958, 102
Federal Aviation Administration, 102
Feedback, customer, 287–288
Ferry boats, 107
Fields, "Black Mary," 185
Film entertainment, 152–153
Finance, as hospitality career, 325
Fine-dining restaurants, 51
Florida, 33, 208
FlyNet service, Lufthansa Airlines, 208
Follow-up
to interviews, 316
in selling, 243, 246

Food-and-beverage career segment, 324–325
Food and Wine magazine, 193
Food-cost percentage, in restaurants, 65
Food stylist, 209
Fooks, Dave, 148
Ford, Justina, M.D., 197
Forrester Research, Inc., 251
Fortune magazine, 95, 172
Four-year degrees, in hospitality, 334–335
Franchia teahouse (New York), 63
Franchise restaurants, 50, 54
Freighters, 107
French Polynesia, 28
Frequency-reward programs, 215
Frequent-dining programs, 286
Frequent-flyer programs, 103, 215
Front-office operations, of hotels, 81–85
Front-of-the-house operations, 59–61, 81
Full-service restaurants, 51

Gaming destinations, 15, 123–124, 189
Garde-manger, 62
General manager of restaurants, 59
Geocaching, 146
Geographic segmentation, 188
Geotourism, 98
Germany, 123
Globalization, 28
Global Positioning System (GPS), 146
Goals, of marketing, 176–177
Goods *versus* services, 7, 206
Goodwill, in promotion, 269
Gourmet magazine, 193
Government, tourism and, 129–130
Grand tour, 12
Griggs, Cheryl Thompson, 194
Groundskeepers, in hotels, 87
Ground transportation, 105–107
Group hotel guests, 75
Group interviews, for jobs, 314
Guest service agent (GSA), of hotels, 82
Guest services, 18, 84. *See also* Customers
Guided tours, 99, 101

Hallmark events, 147
Handicaps. *See* Disabilities, people with
Hangawi restaurant (New York), 49, 63
Harassment, sexual, 295
Harnick, Larry, 64
Harris Interactive, 227
Harris Poll Online, 189
Hatkoff, Craig, 117
Hawaii Visitors Bureau, 269
Health and fitness, 144
Health-care facilities, food services for, 57
Heller, Judy, 36
Highways, hotels near, 77
Hilton, Conrad, 11–13
Historical sites, 125
Holiday Inns, 333
Home Depot Center, 149
Honeymoons, 272
Hospitality Careers, U.S.A., 332
Hospitality industry, 6, 10–11, 14–16. *See also* Economics
Hosted tours, 99
Hostels, 229
Hosts, of restaurants, 60
Hotels, 72–93
    all-suite, 78
    careers in, 325–326
    front office operations of, 81–85
    guest type classification of, 74
    location classification of, 77
    price classification of, 75–76
    restaurants in, 55
    style and function classification of, 78–80
    support staff of, 87–88
    system-wide departments of, 85–86
Hotels.com, 82
Hot Property feature
    Abercrombie & Kent Tours, 31
    Bellagio resort, Las Vegas, 122
    Carnival Cruises, 108
    Collette Vacations, 208
    Culinary Institute of America, 337
    Expedia.com, 227
    incentives, 188
    JetBlue Airlines, 244

Lettuce Entertain You Enterprises, 286
Lonely Planet publishers, 310
Madonna Inn (San Luis Obispo, CA), 78
Marriott Hotels, 172
Red Lobster restaurants, 54
Sandals Resorts, 272
SMG, 143
Hotwire.com, 226
Housekeepers, in hotels, 84
Hub-and-spoke system, of air travel, 103–104
Human resources, as hospitality career, 326
Hungary, 288
Hyatt Hotels Corporation, 143, 339

Identity theft, 325
Incentives, 35, 188, 215, 270, 291
Income statements, for restaurants, 66
Independent restaurants, 50, 54
Independent tours, 99
Indirect channels of distribution, 248
Inelastic demand, 230
Infomercials, 263
Informational interview, for a job, 314
Information management, 17
Information utility, 170
Infrastructure, in tourism, 26
In-house restaurants, 50, 57
Institutional advertising, 260
Intangibility, 8
Intermediaries
    distribution, 248–250
    online, 243
    in tourism, 127
International Air Transport Association (IATA), 102
International Olympic Committee, 141
Internet
    advertising on, 263
    airplane passenger access to, 208
    booking reservations on, 97
    channels of distribution in, 250–251
    distance learning by, 335

hotel room access to, 17, 34
hotel "technology butlers" for, 305
identity theft and, 325
job searching on, 311
restaurant buying on, 65
wireless access to, 17, 61, 208, 225
Interstate Commerce Commission (ICC), 107
Interviews, job, 313–316
Inventory control, in restaurants, 63

Jamaica, 272
James, Charmaine, 309
James, Louis, 309
JetBlue Airlines, 231, 244
Jobs in hospitality, 302–321. *See also* Careers in hospitality; Employees; Profiles in Hospitality
applications for, 313
communication skills in, 305–307
entry-level, 324
expectations for, 316
guest-service skills in, 305
hospitality-specific traits in, 308–309
interviews for, 313–316
overtime work in, 326
portfolios for, 312
required skills in, 304–305
researching, 311
résumés for, 313
sales skills in, 307
technical skills in, 308
Journeys Travel agency, 165, 177

Katoomba, New South Wales, Australia, 229
Kellett, Harry R., 332
Keyless electronic locks, 14, 18
Key Points feature
cultural tourism, 167
Internet selling, 243
Orbitz.com, 227
public speaking, 306
railroad speed, 105

ski resorts, 119
sleep in hotels, 287
sports dollars, 142
Kiosks, in hotels, 85
Knott, Walter, 5
Knott's Berry Farm, 5, 15
Kona Coast Cycling Tours, 323, 327
Kutztown Folklife Festival, 148

Lam, Wing, 303
Land resources, 30
Language, in market research, 197
La Salsa Fresh Mexican Grill restaurant, 303
Lastminute.com, 168
Las Vegas, NV, 122
Leadership, employees and, 293–296, 308
Leakage of tourist dollars, 26–27
Lee, Eduardo, 303
Lee, Madeline, 49
Lee, Mingo, 303
Legs, in air travel, 104
Leisure travel, 36, 74, 97
Lettuce Entertain You Enterprises, 286
Life cycle of products, 211–212, 232–234
Limited-service facilities, 52
Limousine-rental agencies, 106
Listening skills, 305
Locks, keyless electronic, 14, 18
Lodging. *See* Hotels
Lonely Planet publishers, 310
Long-distance learning, 335
Los Angeles Galaxy soccer team, 137, 149
Los Angeles Kings hockey team, 137, 149
Loss-leader pricing, 228
Lost Mountain Vineyard, 233
Loyalty, customer, 214, 286
Lufthansa Airlines, 208

Madonna, Alex, 78
Madonna Inn (San Luis Obispo, CA), 78
Magazines, travel, 261. *See also entries for specific magazines*
Mailing lists, 261

Managers of restaurants, 59–60
Maritz, Edward, 188
Maritz Research, 188
Market information, 184–203
market research for, 192–197
product positioning in, 190–191
segmenting markets in, 186–189
targeting markets in, 189
Marketing, 164–183
careers in, 326
concept of, 167
environmental analysis and, 172–175
hotel, 87
marketing mix and, 167–168
mission statement and, 171–172
objectives of, 176–177, 232
plan for, 171
process of, 166
relationship, 214–215
utility concept and, 169–170
See also Destination marketing
Market-penetration pricing, 226
Market segments, 15, 186–189
Markup, in pricing, 226
Marriott, J. Willard, 172, 333
Marriott Corporation, 172, 175, 209, 339
Maslow, Abraham, 37–38
Maslow's hierarchy of needs, 37–38
Mayo, Stormy, 25
McDonald, Stanley, 283
Meal plans, of hotels, 76
Media, advertising, 261–263, 288
Media directors, in college sports, 143
Meeting and incentive travel, 35
Meeting-planning services, 6, 35, 77
Mega-events, 147
Melman, Richard, 286
Melvill, Mike, 103
Messages, advertising, 264
Mexico, 314
Microsoft Corp., 227
Midprice hotels, 75
Military facilities, food services for, 57
Military recreation, 146, 339
Miller, Herman, 73
Mirage Resorts, Las Vegas, NV, 122

Mira Loma hotel, 73
Mission statement, 171–172
Mock interview, for a job, 314
Modified American meal plans, of hotels, 76
Morgans Hotel, 205
Morris, June, 223
Morris Air Corporation, 223, 244
Motels, restaurants in, 55
Motivation, of employees, 293
Motor-coach transportation, 107
Movie entertainment, 152–153
Museums, 125
Music entertainment, 151–152

National Collegiate Athletic Association (NCAA), 139
National Geographic Traveler magazine, 261
National parks, 125
National Restaurant Association (NRA), 50, 129, 193
National Tour Association (NTA), 129
Needs determination, 243
Neeleman, David, 223, 231, 244
Networking, in job searches, 311
New Mexico Tourism Department, 259, 271
New South Wales, Australia, 229
Newspapers, 261, 311
Niche markets, in tourism, 97
Night auditor, of hotels, 82
9/11, 14, 231–232, 288
Noise pollution, 31
Nonpersonal selling, 242
Nonstop flights, in air travel, 104
Nonverbal communication skills, 307
Nursing homes, food services for, 57
Nutrition, 56

Objections, overcoming, in selling, 243, 245
Objectives
    and-task method, 266
    in marketing, 176–177, 232
Observations, in market research, 195

Occupancy percentage (OCC%), of hotels, 76
Ocean liners, 14. *See also* Cruises
Off-premise take-out restaurants, 50
Olympic Games, 12, 138, 140–141
One-way trips, in air travel, 104
Online media, for promotion, 263
Online travel magazines, 261
On-site facilities, for restaurants, 50, 56–58
On-the-job training, 339
Open Door Organization, 97
Open-ended questions, in market research, 197
Opening manager of restaurants, 60
Operations careers in hospitality, 325–326
Optimum Rating, LLC, 194
Orbitz.com, 227
Ordinary (tavern), 10
Orient Express trains, 106
Orlando, Florida, 33
Orzoff, Jerry, 286
Outdoor advertising, 262
Outdoor recreation, 146
Outside magazine, 95
Overtime work, in hospitality jobs, 326

Package tours, 99
Panel interviews, for jobs, 315
Papua New Guinea, 119
Paralympic Games, 140
PAR stock, in restaurants, 63
Passport control, 14
Pastry chef, 62
Patagonia, Argentina, 264
Peninsular and Oriental Steam Navigation Company, 283
People's Republic of China, 130
Percentage-of-sales method, of advertising budgeting, 266
Performing arts entertainment, 154
Perishability, 8, 128
Perks, executive, 296
Personalization, in marketing, 215
Personal selling, 242
Phrasing, in market research, 197
Pickett, Bill, 185
Pilgrimages, 12
Pineapple symbol of hospitality, 10–11

Place utility, 170
Pleasure travel, 36
Plog, Stanley, 37–38
Plog's psychographic analysis, 37–38, 187
Point-of-sale currency conversion, 214
Point-of-sale (POS) systems, 66
Pollution, 30–31
Portfolios for jobs, 312
Positioning, product, 190–191
Possession utility, 170
Post houses, 10
Power-oriented style of leadership, 293
Preferred customers, 215
Premiums, as sales promotion, 271
Prep cooks, 62
Presenting products, in selling, 243–244
Press releases, 267–268
Prestige pricing, 225
Preston-Campbell, Brian, 209
Priceline.com, 226
Price lining, 228
Pricing, 222–239
    breakeven, 226
    changing, 234
    competition and, 230
    cost-based, 226
    of cruises, 109
    customer loyalty and, 214
    definition of, 224
    determining, 168
    discounting and, 227
    discrimination in, 228
    economics and, 231
    environmental conditions and, 231
    of hotel stays, 75–76
    market demand and, 230
    marketing objectives and, 232
    market-penetration, 226
    product life cycle and, 232–234
    promotional, 225
    psychological, 225
    in restaurants, 224
    special strategies for, 228
    value, 229
Primary research, in market research, 194
Princess Cruise Lines, 283, 295
Print media, for promotion, 261
Prisons, food services for, 58

Index

Private clubs, 55
Production careers, 325
Production operations, of restaurants, 61–64
Product positioning, 190–191
Products. *See* Designing products; Selling
Professional development, of employees, 291
Professional organizations, 338
Profiles, travel, 189
Profiles in Hospitality feature
    Business manager, Blue Mountain Vineyard, 233
    Consultant to hospitality industry, 86
    Event planner, Boston Blues Festival, 176
    Executive director, Kutztown Folklife Festival, 148
    Executive search consultant, 332
    Food stylist, 209
    Founder, Take My Mother, Please, custom tours, 124
    Owner, Ace Marketing and Promotions, 270
    Owner, Ricochet Ridge Ranch, 249
    Owner, Word-of-Mouth Restaurant, 292
    Owners, Taste of Jamaica restaurant, 309
    President, Blue Moon Burgers, 64
    President, Blue Water Excursions, 16
    President, Columbia Crossroads travel agency, 100
    President, hospitality consulting business, 194
    Travel agent for travelers with special needs, 36
Profits, 65, 226. *See also* Pricing
Promotion, 166–167, 258–277
    advertising as, 260
    budgeting for, 265–266
    careers in, 326
    effective, 266
    goodwill in, 269
    media for, 261–263
    messages for, 264
    public relations and publicity as, 267–269

sales, 270–271
    successful, 272
Promotional mix, 260
Promotional pricing, 225
Property management systems, of hotels, 81
Provincetown Center for Coastal Studies (MA), 25, 37
Psychographics, 37–38, 187
Psychological pricing, 225
Public recreation, 145
Public relations and publicity, 267–269
Public speaking skills, 306
Purchasing, 35, 63, 65

Quality, price and, 225
Queen Mary 2 ocean liner, 14
Questionnaires, in market research, 195–197
Quick-service restaurants (QSRs), 52

Radio entertainment, 153
Rail transportation, 105–107
Range of answers, in market research, 198
Reading skills, 306
Reality restaurant (NBC-TV), 53
Recreation, 145–146, 339
Recreational Equipment, Inc. (REI), 95, 109
Red Lobster restaurants, 54, 339
Referral services, for jobs, 311
Relationship marketing, 215–216
Renaissance, 12
Research. See Market information
Reservations, hotel, 82, 87, 97
Resorts, 77, 119–120
Restaurant, The (NBC-TV), 53
Restaurants, 48–71
    back-of-the-house operations of, 61–63
    commercial for profit, 50–53
    on cruise ships, 109
    front-of-the-house operations of, 59–61
    history of, 11
    on-site facilities for, 50, 56–58
    in other properties, 55
    pricing in, 224

production operations of, 63–64
    return on investment in, 64–66
    surveys by, 193
    types of, 53–54
Résumés for jobs, 313
Retail establishments, 55
Retail price, 226
Retail sporting goods, 144
Retention
    of customers, 216, 287
    of employees, 290
Retreat centers, 80
Return on investment, 64–66
Revenue per available room (RevPAR), of hotels, 76
Revenues and expenses, 14
Reward programs, 215, 270–271
Ricochet Ridge Ranch, 249
Rigney, John, 16
Risky destinations, 212, 288
Ritz, César, 11, 13
Ritz-Carlton Hotels, 305
Riverboats, 108
Roberts, Sarah, 73, 87
Robertson, Fraser, 73, 87
Rofsky, Mitch, 165, 177
Rosenthal, Jane, 117
Roth, Frances, 337
Round-trips, in air travel, 104
Routine-oriented style of leadership, 293
Rubell, Steve, 205
Rubio's Baja Grill restaurant, 303
Rutan, Burt, 103

Sabre Airline Solutions, 291
Safety, 14
Sales. *See* Selling
Sales-and-service link, 246
Sales promotion, 270–271
Sample, in market research, 197
Sampras, Pete, 149
Sandals Resorts, 272
Sanitation, 14
Sarni, Gail, 176
SARS health crisis, 288
Satisfaction
    customer, 212–213, 286
    employee, 290
Scarlet, Peter, 121
Scheduling Manager program, 291

Schlotzsky's Deli, 225
Schools, food services for, 56
Schrager, Ian, 205, 215
Scotland, 190
Scott, Robert F., 178
Search engines, on Web, 263
Seasons
 cruise, 109, 121
 in destination marketing, 118–119
 discounts and, 227
 hotel, 75
Secondary research, in market research, 193
Security, 14, 85
Segmenting markets, 186–189
Selling
 elements of, 252
 for hotels, 87
 seven steps of, 243–246
 skills in, 307
 types of, 242
Selling up, 245
September 11, 2001, 14, 231–232, 288
Servers, restaurant, 60
Service
 careers in, 325
 factors in, 7–9
 good versus, 206–207
 as job skill, 305
 qualities and methods of, 284–286
 sales link to, 246
Sexual harassment, 295
Shea, Lari, 249
Shopping, as destination, 124–125
Shoulder season, in cruises, 121
Shuttle service, 106
Silberman, Todd, 165, 177
Ski resorts, 119
Sleep, in hotels, 287
SMG, 143
Smithsonian magazine, 167
Social impacts, of tourism, 28–29
Society of Professional Journalists, 269
Sodexho Company, 339
Sous chefs, 62
Southwest Airlines, 223
SpaceShipOne, 103
Space travel, 103
Spas, 15, 79, 288
Speaking skills, 305–306

Specialized tourism, 36
Special Olympic Games, 140
Specialty media, for promotion, 263
Specialty restaurants, 53
Spin zone, in promotion, 268
Sporting goods, 95, 144
Sports, 6, 121–122, 136–146
 amateur, 139
 careers in, 142–143, 327–330
 disabilities and, 140
 extreme, 140
 history of, 138
 hospitality and, 146
 international, 140
 lifestyle and, 144
 Olympic Games, 141
 professional, 139
 recreation and, 145–146
 venues for, 55
Stand-alone restaurants, 50
Staples Center, 137
Starck, Philippe, 215
Stewards, in restaurants, 62
Stewart, Gordon "Butch," 272
Stewart, Paul, 185, 197
Studio 54 (New York), 205
Suggestion selling, 243, 245
Suite hotels, 78
Sullivan, Dan, 208
Superfuture City online guide, 241, 247
Suppliers, to restaurants, 65
Supply and demand, 230
Supporting products, 208
Surveys, 193, 195–197
Sustainable tourism, 28
Sweepstakes, as sales promotion, 271
SWOT analysis, 172–173

(T)

Tainted travel, 269
Target markets, 167. *See also* Market information
Taste of Jamaica restaurant, 309
Taverns, as early hospitality, 10
Technology, 16–18, 175. *See also* Internet
"Technology butlers," 305
Tech Notes feature
 cell phones, 175
 direct distribution, 243
 geocaching, 146

kiosks, 85
 long-distance learning, 335
 Papua New Guinea Web site, 119
 point-of-sale conversion, 214
 restaurant surveys, 193
 space travel, 103
 technology butlers, 305
 virtual customer service, 285
 wireless applications, 61, 225
Telemarketing, 242
Telephone interview, for a job, 314
Telephone skills, 306
Television entertainment, 152, 263
TGV Atlantique train, 105
Theme cruises, 121
Theme parks, 55
Therapeutic recreation, 146
Thinking skills, for jobs, 304
Tibet, 130, 252
Time management, 309
Time-sharing, 15, 79
Time utility, 170
Tourism, 6, 94–115. *See also* Economics
 air transportation and, 102–105
 benefits of, 100
 destination marketing and, 128
 economic impact of, 98
 employment in, 101
 geographic, 188
 ground transportation and, 105–107
 growth of, 96–98
 history of, 11–13
 integrated systems for, 110
 specialized, 36
 sustainable, 28
 trends in, 14–16
 types of, 99–100
 water transportation and, 107–110
Tour operators, 250
Tracking travel purchases, 251
Trade organizations, 129–130, 338
Trade publications, 311
Transient hotel guests, 75
Transportation
 air, 102–105
 careers in, 327
 ground, 105–107
 water, 107–110
Travel
 alerts on, 288

Index

cycles of, 32–33
motivation for, 37–38
profiles of, 189
See also Business travel; Pleasure travel
Travel agencies, 127, 248–249
Travel and Leisure magazine, 122, 261
Traveler's checks, 13
Travel Industry Association of America (TIA), 98, 167
Travel Web sites, 11
Treetops (Kenya), 80
Tribeca Film Festival (New York), 117, 121
Tripadvisor service, 251

U.S. Navy, Morale, Welfare, and Recreation, 339
Uniformed services, in hotels, 84
Uniform System of Accounts (USAR), 66
United Arab Emirates, 213
Universities, food services for, 56
University programs in hospitality, 334–335
Upscale hotels, 75
Utility concept, in marketing, 169–170

Vacation behavior, 195
Vacation ownership (time-sharing), 15, 79
Valet staff, in hotels, 85
VALS Segmentation System, 187

Value
customers and, 214–215
of employees, 296
perceived, 230
pricing and, 229
Van service, 106
Variables, in services, 8–9
Venturers, travelers as, 32, 37
Verret, Carol, 86
VFR (visiting friends and relatives) travel, 36
Virgin Atlantic Airways, 103
Virtual customer service, 285
Visual pollution, 31
Volunteer vacations, 314

Wahoo's Fish Taco restaurant, 303, 313
Waitlisting, in air travel, 104
Walk-in hotel guests, 75
Walt Disney World, 8, 33
Waste disposal, 30
Water resources, 30
Water transportation, 107–110
Web sites
banner ads on, 263
for Carnival Cruise Lines, 120
for Papua New Guinea, 119
reservation booking via, 17
travel, 11, 251
See also Internet
Weddings, 272
Westley, Wes, 143
Whale watching, 25, 37
Wheel, invention of, 11
Wheeler, Maureen, 310
Wheeler, Tony, 310
"White tablecloth" restaurants, 51

Wholesale price, 226
Wilson, Kemmons, 333
Windjammers, 108
Wireless Internet access, 17, 61, 208, 225
"Women only" floors, in hotels, 14
Woo, Peter, 49
Word of Mouth Restaurant, 292
World Ice Golf Championships (Iceland), 141
World Market feature
Antarctica, 178
Bora Bora, French Polynesia, 28
Dubai, 213
El Bulli restaurant (Spain), 51
German holiday markets, 123
ocean liners, 14
Orient Express, 106
Patagonia, Argentina, 264
People's Republic of China, 330
Scotland, 190
spas, 288
Tibet, 252
Treetops (Kenya), 79
volunteer vacations, 314
World Ice Golf Championships, 141
youth hostels, 229
World Trade Organization, 288
Wright, Orville and Wilbur, 13
Writing skills, 306
Wynn, Steve, 122

Yachts, 108
YHA Backpackers Hostel, 229
Yield management, 76, 228
Youth hostels, 229